WRITING THE MIND

> My thought is *me*: that is why I can't stop. I exist by what I think . . . and I can't prevent myself from thinking.
>
> —*Jean-Paul Sartre, Nausea*

Writing the Mind: Representing Consciousness from Proust to the Present explores how writers across the last hundred years have risen to the challenge of putting the workings of the conscious and unconscious mind on the page. Against the backdrop of a century of cultural and scientific development, the study examines the work of seven ground-breaking French and European authors: Marcel Proust, whose writing is the cornerstone of the modern psychological novel; Georges Bernanos and the Catholic novelists; André Breton and Surrealism; Jean-Paul Sartre and the existentialist novel; Samuel Beckett; Nathalie Sarraute; and, finally, bringing us into our own century, Marie Darrieussecq. Simon Kemp examines the influence of science, faith, and philosophy on these writers, and demonstrates how writers learn from or react against their predecessors or quarrel with their peers. Kemp's elegant study also charts the rise and wane of Freudian influence on literature through the twentieth century, and the emergence of cognitive and neo-Darwinian ideas at the dawn of the twenty-first. In the work of these seven writers, we discover radically different understandings of how consciousness and the unconscious mind are constituted, which are the most salient characteristics of mental life, and even what it is that defines a mind at all.

Simon Kemp is Associate Professor of French at Somerville College, Oxford.

WRITING THE MIND

Representing Consciousness from Proust to the Present

Figuring the Mind, Volume One

Simon Kemp

Routledge
Taylor & Francis Group
NEW YORK AND LONDON

First published 2018
by Routledge
711 Third Avenue, New York, NY 10017

and by Routledge
2 Park Square, Milton Park, Abingdon, Oxon OX14 4RN

Routledge is an imprint of the Taylor & Francis Group, an informa business

Library of Congress Cataloging-in-Publication Data
A catalog record for this book has been requested

ISBN: 978-1-138-71026-9 (hbk)
ISBN: 978-1-138-71705-3 (pbk)
ISBN: 978-1-315-19669-5 (ebk)

Typeset in Bembo
by Apex CoVantage, LLC

Printed and bound by CPI Group (UK) Ltd, Croydon, CR0 4YY

For Hannah, Raffy, and Zak

CONTENTS

ACKNOWLEDGEMENTS

This was a foolishly expansive project to embark upon, several years ago, while still a college lecturer on a fixed-term contract, and it is more in spite of it than because of it that I now find myself a Fellow of Somerville College, Oxford, to which institution I owe a huge debt of gratitude, and most particularly to my colleagues there in modern languages, Almut Suerbaum and Manuele Gragnolati. I am equally indebted to my encounters at TORCH, the Oxford research centre for the humanities, and its Unconscious Memory network bringing together scholars from the arts and sciences with a shared interest in the mind, including Larry Squire, Ben Morgan, Terence Cave, and, most particularly Sowon Park, with whom I have honed my ideas over many post-seminar discussions. Above all, thanks to Hannah Thompson, Raffy, and Zak Kemp for getting me through it. This book is the first volume in *Figuring the Mind*, an academic trilogy on the representation of the conscious and unconscious mind. It is followed by *Reading the Mind: Theories of Consciousness and Literary Criticism* and *Seeing the Mind: Representing Consciousness on Film.*

INTRODUCTION

In 1913, as the European century stumbled towards the first of the calamitous wars that would define it, Marcel Proust published *The Way by Swann's* (*Du côté de chez Swann*), the opening part of his seven-volume novel, *In Search of Lost Time* (*À la recherche du temps perdu*). To the bafflement of some of his first readers, he chose to begin his story in bed, with a description of sleep, wakefulness, and the no-man's-land that lies between:

> For a long time, I went to bed early. Sometimes, my candle scarcely out, my eyes would close so quickly that I did not have time to say to myself: 'I'm falling asleep.' And, half an hour later, the thought that it was time to try to sleep would wake me; I wanted to put down the book I thought I still had in my hands and blow out my light; I had not ceased while sleeping to form reflections on what I had just read, but these reflections had taken a rather peculiar turn; it seemed to me that I myself was what the book was talking about: a church, a quartet, the rivalry between François I and Charles V. This belief lived on for a few seconds after my waking; it did not shock my reason but lay heavy like scales on my eyes and kept them from realizing that the candlestick was no longer lit. Then it began to grow unintelligible to me, as after metempsychosis do the thoughts of an earlier existence; the subject of the book detached itself from me, I was free to apply myself to it or not; immediately I recovered my sight and I was amazed to find a darkness around me soft and restful for my eyes, but perhaps even more so for my mind, to which it appeared a thing without cause, incomprehensible, a thing truly dark.[1]

A century later, in the year the Twin Towers fell, Marie Darrieussecq published *A Brief Stay with the Living*, a novel that draws on scientific research into consciousness for its themes, and on a hundred years of literary innovation in writing the mind for its style. It begins with a tranquil morning scene viewed through the eyes of the unnamed mother of the family:

> Summer is drawing to a close. There are fewer roses, fewer buds. On the old white bush, the Madame de Sévigné, there are two little green-helmeted flower heads, pointing stiffly upwards, like tiny soldiers among the thorns. Snips from the secateurs clip away the abandoned blooms. Watch you don't catch tetanus. Momo tells her that summer is drawing to a close and there is no point in hosing down the patio today; they'll be able to read there without suffocating, the summer heat has evaporated. The spoon chinks in the cup. A smell

> of coffee. She cuts a beautiful rose, only two of its petals have uncurled from the bud, it isn't even a proper flower yet, not with just two open petals. She thanks God knows who or what for this morning's reprieve, the flow of breath, happiness so huge and liquid.[2]

The two novels are set apart from each other by more than just historical period, as their opening paragraphs show. Proust's account of his Narrator's habitual bedtime reading explores how the activity of waking consciousness persists into sleep, and how dream-states linger into the first moments of wakefulness. The Narrator discusses his experience of semi-consciousness, in which the faculties of reason and perception remain dormant as the rudderless mind of the newly awoken sleeper continues to be dominated by the confused merging of his bedtime reading with his sense of his own self. Proust's text is analytical in tone. It is written retrospectively by someone who in no way shares or attempts to mimic the state of consciousness he is recalling. Biblical and Classical allusions are employed to elucidate the experience through readers' cultural associations. In the use of the imperfect tense we see that the Narrator is describing a typical example of what was for him a habitual phenomenon, and we infer an appeal for readers to endorse the account from their own experience. Darrieussecq's text, by contrast, plunges us into the immediacy of the experience itself, narrated in the present tense with a free indirect style that aligns so closely with the consciousness we're inhabiting that it almost overwhelms the voice of the impersonal narrator telling the story. Sense-impressions are concisely evoked: the cooler air, the smell of coffee and the sound of the coffee-spoon, the shapes, colours and textures of the roses. The mother hears and inwardly responds to her husband's words. Her thoughts are in linguistic fragments, naming the roses, or slipping into a momentary associative flash between thorns and tetanus. (In the rose variety, incidentally, we may see a veiled allusion by the author to the lineage of psychological studies in which she wishes to situate her novel: Madame de Sévigné features strongly in Proust's *In Search of Lost Time*, in which she is the favourite writer of the Narrator's grandmother, who delights in quoting her to her grandson.) Other thoughts have a more ambiguous status: the style leaves us uncertain whether the words we read transcribe the character's inner monologue, or whether they belong instead to the Narrator, who is transposing into language the mother's non-linguistic thoughts, perceptions and feelings. The 'tiny soldiers' metaphor, for instance, might belong to character or to narrator, or the image may belong to the former and the words to the latter. That Darrieussecq wishes to take her representation of the mind beyond the purely linguistic stream-of-consciousness style made famous by James Joyce seems evident in the final metaphor: 'so huge and liquid', as a description of happiness, ventures into the territory of Nathalie Sarraute's tropisms, which use flowing liquids and other quasi-biological images to evoke mental activity below the threshold of language, and at the furthest fringes of consciousness.

These two novelists are the subjects of the opening and closing chapters of this book, which aims to trace the representation of the mind through the century that separates them. Does 'mind' mean the same thing to all writers across a hundred years of cultural change and scientific progress? Do the fictional characters they invented, inhabiting fictional universes of their authors' creation, all possess identical mental architecture, or can we discern variations between them? If so, how do these various kinds of minds relate to our own minds, and to developments across the decades in the understanding of consciousness and the unconscious from outside the literary sphere? Proust is my starting point in the investigation into these questions, as his monumental introspective study was the landmark of early twentieth-century European literature that would influence everyone who came after him. Darrieussecq is my end point, since, alone in contemporary French literature, she combines a fascination with new theories of the mind arising from cognitive science and evolutionary psychology with a striking literary style that both innovates and draws on the previous century's traditions of writing the mind. Five further writers make up the chapters between Proust and Darrieussecq: Georges Bernanos, André Breton, Jean-Paul Sartre, Samuel Beckett, and Nathalie Sarraute. Each of them has been chosen for their important contribution to European culture, in their own right and as a representative of a broader phenomenon in intellectual history. Bernanos and the other notable Catholic novelists who flourished in the first half of the century, such as Julien Green and François Mauriac, are included for the cultural significance of the Catholic novel, but also for the importance in twentieth-century culture of religious understanding of the mind, the enduring influence of which is not to be underestimated alongside the brash new theories that the century itself brought into being. Breton is a central figure of Surrealism, the movement which swept the literary and visual arts in the inter-war years with its attempts to unlock the creative potential of the unconscious mind. For his explorations of dreams, madness, and the uncanny, and his role in introducing psychoanalytic theory into the cultural sphere, Breton demands a prominent role in our investigations. Sartre represents the only serious rival to Freud in the influence of his thought on twentieth-century representations of the mind. His existentialist philosophy had a wide cultural impact in the post-war decades in France and beyond, and his own fiction is a paragon of the philosophical novel, vividly bringing to life his vision of consciousness and its relationship to the world. Beckett, who accepted the honour Sartre declined of a Nobel prize, is without question one of the most important twentieth-century writers in any language, including the two he made his own. His prose fiction presents us with questioning minds, marshalling fragments of religion and philosophy in the attempt to understand their own consciousness from within. Sarraute is the first and most psychologically oriented of the New Novelists who revolutionized literary fiction in the mid-century. Her life-long exploration of the 'tropisms' which, she believed, are the simple beginnings of more complex conscious experience, make her work an essential inclusion here, as does her positioning of her work in opposition to behaviourist theories of the mind and what she saw as their deleterious influence on literature. With overlapping lives and writing careers, the seven novelists span the twentieth century, as well as reaching forwards into our own century in their cultural impact and backwards for very much longer in the sources of influence they draw on.[3]

All our writers share a common subject, which is perhaps inevitable, if we subscribe to the view that *every* novel is a novel about the mind, at least to some extent. For the critic and theorist Jean-Louis Chrétien, the aim of the novel from its very inception has been 'transparent vision of the consciousnesses of the characters'. He dubs such representation *cardiognosia*, borrowing from Biblical Greek a term for the divine attribute of knowing the secrets of human hearts.[4] David Lodge echoes this view in his description of the novel as 'man's most successful attempt to describe the experience of individual human beings moving through space and time'.[5] Unlike theatre and film, the novel specializes in representing human nature *from the inside*, as it were. First-person narrators engage in introspection and testify to the reader on their inner lives. Impersonal narrators of third-person texts focalize their narrative through the minds and eyes of their protagonists, or blend their own voices with the protagonist's thoughts through a free indirect style. A novel can explore and label its characters' mental activity through detached analysis, or it can thrust its readers into the whirl of thoughts and perceptions via stream-of-consciousness. The seven œuvres we are examining here distinguish themselves from other literature only in degree, not in kind. They simply offer a more sustained focus on their protagonists' inner self than is usual in fiction, tracing deeper the motivations behind actions, dissecting emotional states at greater length, or speculating on the physical or philosophical underpinning of conscious experience, while at the same time experimenting with new literary techniques to evoke the working mind. They differentiate themselves from other discourses, such as the philosophical essay, through their particularity: they offer us the portrait of one specific mind in action, be it real, invented, or somewhere between the two.

*

Before we can begin the business of analyzing the kinds of minds presented by our writers, there are two pieces of groundwork to be laid. The first is to establish what we're talking about when we use the word 'mind', how it is to be distinguished from 'consciousness', and how other terms such as 'unconscious' and 'preconscious' are related to it. The second is to lay out a brief sketch of major theories of the mind and their cultural impact as they stood at the dawn of the twentieth century and to trace the development of the understanding of the mind through the course of that century to the time of our most recent text. So what is a mind? We might venture to define it as the private sphere of perception, cognition, sensation and emotion, and the language and images of conscious thought, memory, and imagination, plus the mental activity of which we're not conscious. Consciousness and the unconscious will thus be the two sub-categories of which our primary concept is composed, although the relationship, and the dividing line, between the pair will be open to debate. The mind has often been associated primarily with intellect and cognition, set in Cartesian opposition to the body, which is viewed as the seat of the emotions (as in the phrase, 'hearts and minds'). The seductive metaphor of the computer, presenting the brain as a biological information-processor, has maintained this bias to some extent in the resurgence of scientific interest in the workings of the mind which has taken place since the mid-1990s. Recent years have restored both emotion and embodiment to the study of the mind, for instance through the work of the neuroscientist Antonio Damasio, who argues that minds and, ultimately, consciousness develop out of basic processes by which an organism maintains the integrity and functionality of its body in response to the changing internal and external environment. From self-regulation comes self-awareness, while from self-protective impulses come emotion.[6] Religious division between soul and body similarly dissociated the emotional and the sexual from other mental functions, while in the course of the twentieth century, psychoanalysis and more latterly evolutionary psychology have sought to restore these elements of human nature to the centre of mental life. Unsurprisingly, the novels on which we focus here include major life events in their stories, due to which the protagonists experience a full range of emotions, from love and sexual desire to grief and despair. The depictions of the mind that they offer are correspondingly rich in these non-intellectual aspects, and we shall naturally be treating such aspects as being every bit as intrinsic a part of mental activity as are purely cognitive processes.

Consciousness itself is surprisingly difficult to define, given our intuitive understanding of what it means to be conscious. It has two distinct meanings in common usage, as V.S. Ramachandran points out, referring to the sensations and thoughts that we experience, and to the self which has these experiences.[7] An awareness of the self seems to be an essential element of consciousness: if I am a conscious being I must know not only that there is a feeling of pain, say, but that *I* am in pain. This self-image has a unifying function, linking the sensory inputs and mental processes together in the conscious awareness that I am the one who is seeing and thinking, and extending this unity via memory into the stable persona which has been labelled 'the autobiographical self'.[8] For some philosophers, this unity is illusory: Daniel Dennett suggests that theorists of consciousness have long been misled by their presupposition 'that somewhere, conveniently hidden in the obscure "centre" of the mind/brain, there is a Cartesian Theatre, a place where "it all comes together and consciousness happens"'.[9] Dennett proposes in its place his 'multiple drafts' model, in which thoughts and sense-impressions are constantly revised and updated in various parts of the brain, but no 'final version' is presented to a single seat of awareness as a result, however much our introspection may give us such an impression. Steven Pinker, following Ned Block and the linguist Ray Jackendoff, teases out three aspects to his own definition of consciousness: it is characterized by *self-knowledge*, *access to information*, and *sentience*.[10] For Pinker, the importance of self-knowledge is overstated by theorists of consciousness, who mistake its tractability, compared with the problematic concept of sentience, for centrality. Where information is concerned, the mind has access to the contents of short-term memory and perceptual input, plus less reliable access to the contents of long-term memory, which may be recalled easily, with time and effort, or not at all. Much information about the self is inaccessible to consciousness, either contingently, as with a half-remembered name that lurks beyond reach, or necessarily, as with the many elements of our physiological and mental existence that are beyond our knowledge, from the muscle movements required to ride a bicycle to the processing in our visual system. Lastly, sentience, the experience of thoughts and impressions by the self, is the aspect of consciousness which is at once most essential and most mysterious, in that it is accessible for study only by private intuition, not objective measurement. It has long been the subject of philosophical speculation, and it seems that it will remain so, untouched by the incursions into other aspects of consciousness made by cognitive science and related fields. A minority of philosophers of mind, Michael A. Arbib among them, would include the faculty of language as a prerequisite for full human consciousness, and a link between language and selfhood also forms the cornerstone of Jacques Lacan's psychoanalysis. Beckett, Sarraute, and Darrieussecq all take a lively interest in this particular question, and we'll discuss the connection between language and consciousness in detail in the chapters on their work.

One characteristic of consciousness that has received much philosophical attention, in particular from phenomenology and existentialism, is its *intentionality*: to be conscious is necessarily to be conscious *of something*, either externally through perception or internally through memory or imagination.[11] As Edmund Husserl asserts in his *Logical Investigations*: 'In perception, something is perceived, in imagination, something is imagined, in a statement, something is stated, in love something loved, in hate hated, in desire desired etc.'[12] In writing inspired by phenomenology, intentionality may become consciousness's defining trait: consciousness is in itself a nothingness, simply a direction of attention, a spotlight to shine where we will. There is a parallel here with other theories which attempt to strip consciousness down to the purest essence: Henri Bergson distinguishes the 'immediate' consciousness of sense-impressions from the 'reflective' consciousness of rational thought; Damasio differentiates between the 'core' consciousness of basic wakefulness and 'extended' consciousness of the alert and fully functional human mind.[13] My own approach will follow Jackendoff, Block, and Pinker in accepting the broader definition of consciousness, including the sense of self and the perceptual or introspective information at its disposal, and, where necessary, using 'sentience' to designate the point of awareness at the centre of the phenomenon.

If the expanded definition of consciousness seems more natural to the modern reader, this may well be due to the influence of Freudian psychoanalysis, for which consciousness is not a point, but a realm. Freud describes his system of consciousness, preconscious, and Unconscious as a 'psychical topography', leaving open the question of whether this is spatial metaphor or a literal topography of yet-to-be-discovered sites in the physical brain.[14] Here is Freud's description of the divisions he posits between mental systems:

> We may say that in general a psychical act goes through two phases as regards its state, between which is interposed a kind of testing (censorship). In the first phase the psychical act is unconscious and belongs to the system *Ucs.* [the Unconscious]; if, on testing, it is rejected by the censorship, it is not allowed to pass into the second phase; it is then said to be 'repressed' and must remain unconscious. If, however, it passes this testing, it enters the second phase and thenceforth belongs to the second system, which we will call the system *Cs.* [consciousness]. But the fact that it belongs to that system does not yet unequivocally determine its relation to consciousness. It is not yet conscious, but it is certainly capable of becoming conscious (to use Breuer's expression)—that is, it can now, given certain

> conditions, become an object of consciousness without any special resistance. In consideration of this capacity for becoming conscious we also call the system *Cs.* the 'preconscious'. If it should turn out that a certain censorship also plays a part in determining whether the preconscious becomes conscious, we shall discriminate more sharply between the systems *Pcs.* and *Cs.* For the present let it suffice us to bear in mind that the system *Pcs.* shares the characteristics of the system *Cs.* and that the rigorous censorship exercises its office at the point of transition from the *Ucs.* to the *Pcs.* (or *Cs.*).[15]

Freud later overlays on this model the further division into id, ego, and superego, which respectively represent primitive instincts, autobiographical self, and inhibiting factors internalized from parental authority. The existence of mental activity of which we're not aware is an uncontroversial fact of psychology, as is the existence of stored memories which are not immediately present to consciousness. Where Freud's Unconscious stands apart from much of modern psychology is in the immovable barrier and censoring gatekeeper he sets around it, dividing it from other matter in the preconscious realm that is not conscious, yet available to consciousness if required. Within this inaccessible domain, the Freudian Unconscious is viewed almost as an independent entity, in which 'wishful impulses' are born, develop, combine with one another, and manifest themselves through encoded dreams or neurotic symptoms, all without the participation or knowledge of the conscious mind.[16] The contents of the Unconscious are, for Freud, dominated by shameful desires and traumatic memories which have been repressed by a consciousness that is unable to countenance them. The Freudian model thus posits far more specific characteristics to its Unconscious than simply an absence of consciousness, many of which are regarded with scepticism by psychologists, who sometimes employ the word 'nonconscious' to avoid Freud's term.[17] In the coming chapters, the Freudian Unconscious is designated by its capital letter, and the term 'unconscious' refers to any contents or activity of the mind which are not present to consciousness, including those Freud would term 'preconscious'.

Finally, the most quintessentially literary element in the representation of the mind is the depiction of what philosophers call 'qualia', defined by Block as 'experiential properties of sensations, feelings, perceptions, and, more controversially, thoughts and desires as well'.[18] Qualia are *what it is like* to have an experience, to feel a pain or see a colour, or to experience a purely internal mental state such as dizziness or rage. The primary characteristic of qualia is that they are private: my personal experience of, say, looking at a clear blue sky cannot be objectively measured, and, famously, if you are beside me looking at the same sky, you can't be sure that the quale of sky-blue inside my head is the same as the one inside yours.[19] Expressing hidden inner life is one of literature's fundamental tasks. Metaphors and other devices of poetic language are deployed in the attempt to open up an individual subjectivity to be shared by an outsider: the reader is invited in to experience vicariously how drowsiness feels, how a rosebud looks, what happiness is like from the perspective of another person. This may even be literature's *raison d'être.* If we are prisoners of our own subjectivity, surrounded by others with whom we must make our way in the social world, but whose inner lives we can never truly know, then an invitation to enter another mind and to experience another life through different eyes must be a powerful draw. All seven of our novelists call on readers to measure the mind in the text against our own subjective experience, to endorse shared characteristics, to hypothesize about our own response in the protagonist's circumstances, and to increase our knowledge of psychological diversity from the differences we encounter. These novels are not simply inert records of consciousness set down by their authors. They are meeting places for minds.

These are not the only terms which will be of importance in our discussion of the literary representation of mind, but others, from 'tropism' to 'being-for-itself' can safely be left for the chapters in which they feature. For now, let us move on to the remaining task of this Introduction, which is to set our understanding of the mind in some historical context. The nature of the mind is a problem that has been debated by philosophers and theologians from earliest times: Plato raised the question of whether the soul is an immaterial entity that forms a temporary alliance with a body, or whether it is a property of that body, analogous to the tuning of a lyre.[20] These two possibilities resolve into 'substance dualism', whereby the mind is made of a different substance from the physical body, as most famously advocated by René Descartes, and 'property dualism', in which the mind may not be reducible to the brain, but is nonetheless created by the latter's activity. Descartes argued that the soul or mind (he declares that he will use the two terms interchangeably) must necessarily be immaterial in nature, since it can neither be divided like the material body, nor can the mind doubt its existence as it can doubt the material world.[21] He posited that the immaterial mind could nevertheless interact with the material body—notoriously, he named the brain's pineal gland as the point of transference—in a two-way process by which the body modified the mind as well as vice versa. The *Méditations* (1647) lay out the procedure of systematic doubt by which the immaterial nature of the mind is inferred:

> Now, I am a true thing, and truly existing, but what kind of a thing? I have already said it: a thinking thing. And what beyond this? I shall put my imagination to work again, to see if I am not something more. I am not this assembly of limbs that is called the human body; I am not an agile, penetrating air, spread through all these limbs; I am not a wind, a breath, a vapour, nor anything I can feign and pretend, since I have supposed that all these things are nothing, and that, without changing this supposition, I find that I do not leave off being certain that I am something.[22]

Descartes's scepticism set the mind apart from the doubtable physical body and material universe, and in doing so set the terms of philosophical debates on consciousness for the next few centuries. In Christian Europe through much of the last millennium, dualism was particularly associated with the religious doctrine of the immortal soul, from which dissent was often dangerous. Blaise Pascal offers an example of Cartesian thought transposed into religious terms in his *Pensées* (1669):

> We are made up of two opposing natures of different kinds, soul and body. For it is impossible that the part of us that reasons be anything but spiritual; and should it be claimed that we are simply corporeal, that would exclude us very much more from understanding things, there being nothing so inconceivable as to say that matter knows itself.[23]

The intuitive appeal of substance dualism has led to it being dubbed the 'common sense' view of consciousness, and it's still a widely held conviction.[24] Among philosophers, though, serious consideration of it is now largely limited to religious thinkers, since the problem of an immaterial soul's means of interaction with a material body, plus the Darwinian challenge of accommodating a dualist mind within the evolutionary spectrum of neural complexity, raise difficulties for the model. Secular philosophy of mind now finds itself debating variants on property dualism, in which mental properties *supervene* on the physical state of the brain, meaning that a given state of my brain will give rise to a corresponding state of my mind, but not necessarily vice versa. Influential offshoots of property dualism notably include *functionalism*, which views the mind as analogous to software run on the hardware of the brain. The approach emphasizes the flexibility of the link between mind and brain, in line with neurological evidence that mental functions impaired by brain damage can sometimes be restored by the substitute activity of other parts of the brain: thus, one particular mental state may be able to supervene on more than one state of the brain.

Questions of nature and nurture dominated much of the Enlightenment philosophy of the mind. John Locke argued that the mind at birth is a *tabula rasa*, and that everything later found within it, from our emotional responses to our basic structures of thought, has developed from data that was once perceived through our senses. Immanuel Kant, a half-century later in the *Critique of Pure Reason* (1781), would posit that certain aspects of our mental architecture are innate. He attempted to synthesize the opposed epistemological doctrines of rationalism and empiricism, the former of which seeks *a priori* knowledge independent of the senses, while the latter posits that all that can be known about the world by the mind must be perceived through the senses. For Kant, our knowledge comes from the senses, but the mind receives and orders this knowledge through prior concepts, such as 'substance' and 'causality', which are fundamental to existence. Rousseau and Hobbes debated a variant of this question in relation to the social sphere: for Rousseau, an innate moral nature is corrupted by society, while for Hobbes, society controls and civilizes humanity's innate violence and selfishness. Rousseau's *Discours sur l'origine et les fondements de l'inégalité parmi les hommes* (*Discourse on the Origin and Basis of Inequality Among Men*, 1755) speculated on what human nature would be like in a primitive, solitary state, without the influence of society and civilization, and concluded that an innately good nature is corrupted by socio-cultural influence. His argument found little favour with the Church, which saw in it a conflict with the doctrine of Original Sin, nor with Voltaire, who declared to Rousseau that 'never has such wit been employed to render us as dumb as animals; reading your work gives one a desire to walk on all fours'.[25]

A second strand of thought on mind and world also begins with Kant, whose ideas would inspire G.W.F. Hegel and become a crucial element in French phenomenology and existentialism in our period. Of particular importance to phenomenology is Kant's distinction between the appearances of things in the world, which are all we have access to through our senses, and the things themselves, which are beyond our reach. Phenomenology proceeds by 'bracketing off' the ontological questions of the true nature of reality in order to explore the world as it appears, and the process of perception that connects the mind to the world. We will explore the connections with the phenomenology of Edmund Husserl and Maurice Merleau-Ponty in detail in the chapter on Sartre, while Hegel's legacy will be discussed both for Sartre and for Breton, who was a keen follower of his thought. Other thinkers will influence French culture in the later years of the century, blurring the boundaries between philosophy of mind and other disciplines of the humanities, including Michel Foucault's historicizing and relativistic explorations of sexuality or madness, or Jacques Derrida's linguistic investigations into the elusiveness of meaning. Outside France, philosophy of mind is dominated by the analytic tradition, which will come to play a role in the cognitive theories of consciousness at the century's end, as we shall see later.

While the philosophy of mind continued to flourish through the twentieth century, including the birth of French existentialism, the principal developments in understanding consciousness of the last hundred years came from outside philosophy, in psychoanalysis and scientific psychology. Freud's impact on twentieth-century ideas about the self can hardly be over-estimated. Even his harshest critics acknowledge that psychoanalysis 'has every claim to be regarded as richer and more original than any other single intellectual tradition in the twentieth century'.[26] Psychoanalysis has engaged closely with literature from the very beginning. Freud took inspiration from literary texts, such as E.T.A. Hoffmann's *The Sand Man* (1816) for his theory of the uncanny as the return of the repressed: the demonic figure who haunts Hoffmann's protagonist seems to be conjured from a childhood memory of a traumatic incident involving his father. Freud was the first psychoanalytic literary critic, analyzing fictional characters to uncover their neuroses: The psychoanalyst diagnosed repression in the protagonist of Wilhelm Jensen's *Gradiva* (1902), and interpreted Hamlet's inertia as being a consequence of Claudius having fulfilled the prince's own Œdipal wish for him by killing his father. Freud was also the first practitioner of the psychoanalytic narrative in his gripping case studies, which, it has often been remarked, bear some resemblance in their structure to the detective fiction of which their author was fond. Once psychoanalysis was adopted by the French, it became more literary still. Lacan, the most prominent French psychoanalytic theorist of the twentieth century, used art and literature in his writings to illustrate his case more frequently than he employed actual case studies. His discussion of Edgar Allan Poe's 'The Purloined Letter' (1844) remains one of his best-known pieces of writing: in it, he argues that the story's re-enacted drama around the compromising letter, with power relations between the protagonists shifting in each iteration, stages a repetition automatism in which the same actions are neurotically repeated in hope of a different outcome.[27] For Lacan, language is central to the understanding of the mind: drawing on the poststructuralist vogue for Saussurean linguistics, he imported the concepts of signifier and signified, metaphor and metonymy, into his discipline, and divided the mind into the pre-linguistic Imaginary and the post-linguistic Symbolic. The emphasis on linguistic and semiotic analysis allows Lacanian psychoanalysis to interpret texts in much the same manner as it diagnoses people, and indeed it is in faculties of the humanities, more than in practical psychotherapy, that Lacan's often wilfully gnomic teachings have flourished. Elsewhere in French psychoanalytic theory, Félix Guattari, the founder of the radical 'schizoanalysis' in the 1960s, reached his widest audience in collaboration with Gilles Deleuze. The pair's reinvention of psychoanalytic theory via revolutionary Marxism proposes that our acculturation to capitalist society causes us to perceive our desires as a lack, and that the Œdipus complex itself is a consequence of capitalism. The most notable contemporary psychoanalytic theorist, Julia Kristeva, is at the same time both a literary critic and a novelist, and combines these roles at will. The twentieth century saw psychoanalytic concepts become part of Western public discourse, aided by cultural diffusion from interested practitioners of high culture, such as Surrealist writers, painters, and film-makers, as well as in mainstream culture, such as Alfred Hitchcock's 1945 Freudian thriller, *Spellbound*. By the century's final decades, repression, the Unconscious and the Œdipus complex were an integral part of how many people understood their own minds, while the methodology of psychoanalysis, particularly its interest in disinterring childhood memories and decoding hidden meanings in slips of language and symbolic dreams, moved beyond the consulting room into everyday life. In the same period, psychoanalysis would come to hold a dominant position in critical theory, becoming a major paradigm for the interpretation of human nature and its cultural representations in many areas of the humanities.

Psychoanalytic criticism in the arts remains widespread in the early years of the twenty-first century, but its dominance is now challenged by the rise of cognitivist and evolutionary approaches to understanding the mind. The heritage of these disciplines in neurology and clinical psychology is at least as old as that of psychoanalysis; indeed, psychoanalysis arguably develops out of neurology, which, as a nascent discipline, was studied by Freud under Jean-Martin Charcot in Paris during his formative years. Psychology in the late nineteenth century was an emerging discipline that was in many ways more closely related to Cartesian and empiricist philosophy than medical science. When Wilhelm Wundt set up the first laboratory for 'experimental psychology' at the University of Leipzig in 1879—the event which has best claim of founding psychology as a distinct field of study—his introspective methodology had far more in common with the methods of Bergsonian or phenomenological philosophy, not to mention Proustian novel-writing, than with the third-person observations of modern-day clinical and experimental psychology. And this blurring of the scientific and philosophical is equally to be found in Franz Brentano and William James, whose work would lay foundation stones for twentieth-century phenomenological and analytic philosophy of mind respectively. Brentano's revival of the scholastic concept of intentionality was the inspiration for the development of phenomenology by his sometime student,

Husserl. Brentano, however, considered himself a psychologist: his most famous work is entitled *Psychology from an Empirical Standpoint* (1874), and his methods stress the importance of scientific precision and rigour in observation, while, like Wundt, including the unverifiable first-person findings of introspection among the evidence. James, meanwhile, was a trained physician who saw no contradiction in combining practical studies of mind and behaviour with speculative philosophy on free will, truth, and religious belief.

At the point in history where our investigation begins, then, scientific study of the mind has yet to distinguish itself from other modes of investigation. James cites Brentano, meets Charcot, Freud, Wundt, and Bergson, and is read by Husserl. Charcot's teachings lead Freud to psychoanalytic theory, and inspire another of his students, Pierre Janet, into the development of medical methodology in psychological research, a path that will take him from being a fellow-traveller of Freud's to one of his fiercest critics. In an assessment of psychoanalysis delivered at the 18th International Congress of Medicine in 1913, Janet accused the discipline of abandoning the precepts of evidence-based medicine:

> Psychology can only be accepted into medical science if it abandons immoderate ambitions and limits itself to summing up the behaviour and attitudes of illnesses in precise and well-defined terms while connecting all the facts in as rigorously deterministic a fashion as possible. This task is clearly very difficult, it can only be accomplished slowly, and we are tempted to outrun our incomplete observations and slow inductions by bold generalizations and simplistic symbolic interpretations.[28]

Phenomenology too took its distance from science in the twentieth century, with attitudes between phenomenological and analytic philosophical approaches ranging 'from complete disregard to outright hostility' according to Shaun Gallagher and Dan Zahavi.[29] It was a situation that would leave phenomenology lagging behind when cognitive science entered the scene with early computational theories of mind, with which the logical investigations of analytic philosophy are more immediately compatible. The birth of cognitive science—an amalgam of neuroscience, psychology, psycholinguistics, artificial intelligence, and related disciplines—was itself the first step in a rapprochement, however, from a state of affairs in which the very concept of mind looked to have been ruled unscientific. During the mid-century zenith of behaviourism as a movement in psychology, the discipline found itself redefined as the study of behaviour, explicable in terms of the external stimuli from the subject's environment without reference to internal mental processes. The blank slate was for a time replaced by the black box, as we shall explore in the penultimate chapter of this book.

The change came with Francis Crick's declaration in 1994 that 'now is the time to think scientifically about consciousness (and its relationship, if any, to the hypothetical immortal soul) and, most important of all, the time to start the *experimental* study of consciousness in a serious and deliberate way', which heralded an immense growth over the following decades in scientific research into consciousness.[30] Crick brought up the notion of the immortal soul the better to emphasize his radically opposed view of mind as 'nothing but a pack of neurons', and the materialist model is the foundational assumption of most cognitive scientists and those influenced by them.[31] The implications of the discipline are thus in several respects opposed to traditional religious understanding of the self, although this does not exclude religious believers such as John C. Eccles from playing a central role in neuroscientific research, nor does it prevent authors who draw on cognitive science from dabbling in ghosts, telepathy, and other matters outlawed by the materialist view of mind, as we shall see.[32] The incursion of Darwinian theory into depth psychology at around the same time offered a more scientifically grounded alternative to psychoanalysis in the interpretation of formative influences and unconscious motivations. A move away from computational models of mind among cognitive scientists in our own century to explore phenomenal consciousness, coupled with the rise of fMRI as an experimental tool, allowing neural images to be correlated with reported conscious experience, have brought phenomenological approaches back into contact with scientific research for the first time in many decades. This rapprochement of phenomenology and cognitive neuroscience can be most clearly seen in the latter's embrace of the so-called 4EA model: a mind that is *embodied*, *embedded* within a physical and socio-cultural environment, *enacted* through dynamic interaction with this environment, *extended* through our external aids to thought and memory, from notebooks to laptops, and *affective* through the pervasive role of emotion. French philosophy has also moved to meet the scientists half-way, as, for example, in the work of Catherine Malabou, who explores the implications of neuroplasticity for the mind and self, asking whether the continuing development of the brain through the course of life implies a malleability of the self to environmental conditioning, or a freedom to self-sculpt.[33]

The advent of new research into the mind has caused a resurgence of Enlightenment philosophical debates around the roles of nature and nurture in the development of the self, especially where questions of gender are concerned. In the twentieth century, Simone de Beauvoir's *Le Deuxième Sexe* (*The Second Sex*, 1949) was the polemical essay against which all subsequent debate on gender in France measured itself. Beauvoir's contention that gender differences arise through a process of cultural indoctrination from a starting point reminiscent of Locke's and Hume's blank slate set out the social constructivist theory which would dominate the humanities for the latter half of the century. Our own century has seen the debate intensify over the extent and causes of psychological difference between the sexes. There is some evidence, for example, that men are more likely to compete violently or lethally than are women, that they are more interested in anonymous sex than women, that they are better at mental manipulation of objects in space, but worse on verbal memory and on interpreting facial expressions and body language.[34] There is also evidence that many of these differences may not be entirely cultural in origin. To take attitudes to sex as just one example: differences in sexual behaviour between men and women are universal across all human cultures; mitochondrial evidence shows that for millennia men have had much greater variation in their reproductive success than women, providing the conditions for sexual selection and male competition; influences of oestrogen and testosterone cause male and female brains to develop differently during puberty, and adult male brains have visibly larger versions of brain areas associated with sexual behaviour and aggression. Live case studies also support the physiological basis of some degree of psychological gender difference: female-to-male transsexuals perform progressively worse on tests of verbal fluency and better on mental rotation as their regime of androgens proceeds.

Facts like these have sometimes been unwelcome in the humanities, where the social constructivist model is associated with progressive gender politics, and its opponents allied to the patriarchal status quo. Adèle King suggests that theories of human nature which have recourse to evolutionary theory have 'covert aims' of demonstrating 'natural' male dominance by comparing human behaviour with that of other primates; more recently, Cordelia Fine and Angela Saini have demonstrated methodological flaws and bias in several scientific studies of gender difference.[35] While the discovery of innate psychological characteristics may inform us about our species in general, it tells us little about the psychology of any given individual, of course. Such traits vary widely within the population, overlapping substantially between the genders, and the expression of a latent tendency to, say, aggression or promiscuity, will be hugely influenced by the particular cultural influences to which the individual is subject in development and adulthood. While current scientific thinking may oppose the 'all-nurture' hypothesis of extreme social constructivism, it in no way attempts to replace it with an 'all-nature' alternative. Rather, it deconstructs the nature/nurture binary itself, as we discover more about how environment affects the expression of genetic predispositions, and how innate characteristics shape the cultural environment in a complex process of reciprocation.

Gender is not the only area in which new theories of the mind arouse controversy for the humanities. Darwinian ideas, which have been part of European literary culture since the time of Hippolyte Taine and Émile Zola, continue to provoke hostility for their implication that unpleasant or unjust aspects of human behaviour may have a genetic component, and that this 'naturalness' might be used to justify them or declare them inevitable.[36] Current enthusiasm in the arts over scientific theories of the mind has been denounced as 'Darwinitis' and 'neuromania'.[37] There is some validity to such criticism, both of the science itself, which may claim to 'locate' complex aspects of human nature in a particular part of the brain, or explain aspects of modern culture through evolutionary adaptation, and of its application to literary studies, where 'neuroaesthetics' are arguably too blunt a tool to describe individual minds in particular situations.[38] Raymond Tallis, chief among the sceptics of cognitive literary studies, criticizes A. S. Byatt's evocation of neurophysiology to describe her reaction to the poems of John Donne with the suggestion that the same neural activity she describes might equally well result from a reaction to a lack of milk in the refrigerator.[39] Cognitive approaches yield insights into the interpretive processes of reading narrative or the understanding of metaphor, but, at our present level of knowledge, would have little of interest to say on, say, how Swann's love for Odette distinguishes itself from anyone's love for anyone else.[40] Approaches drawing on evolutionary psychology, while often speculative in their attribution of adaptive origins to modern psychological traits, provide a much-needed alternative to psychoanalytic explanations of behaviour. Martin Daly's and Margo Wilson's evolutionary substitute for the Œdipus complex as an explanation for parent-offspring conflict, for instance, proposes that Freud's theory conflates two separate rivalries, a non-sexual rivalry beginning in infancy as the child competes with the father to monopolize the limited resources of attention and care available from the mother, and a sexual rivalry developing later as the child grows towards sexual maturity while the parent ages and declines.[41] Only one of these rivalries has the mother as its object, and neither involves incestuous sexual desire, in accordance with growing evidence that incest avoidance mechanisms may be innate to human sexuality.[42] Michelle Scalise Sugiyama demonstrates the usefulness of the evolutionary alternative in literary criticism by applying it to the story of Œdipus himself, where it provides a noticeably better fit than the Freudian version.[43] Like cognitive approaches, evolutionary psychology also deals in human universals, however, making it similarly suited to broad generalizations and typical examples rather than the individual or extraordinary.

Despite these misgivings in some quarters of academia, it's undeniable that evolutionary and cognitive science have profoundly affected how we understand our own minds. When, only two decades ago, Crick offered his hypothesis that '"You", your joys and your sorrows, your memories and your ambitions, your sense of personal identity and free will, are in fact no more than the behaviour of a vast assembly of nerve cells and their associated molecules', he considered it 'so alien to the ideas of most people alive today that it can truly be called astonishing'.[44] While it may still be some way from received wisdom, there are few people familiar with contemporary Western culture who would now be astonished by such a proposition.

It is not my intention to champion cognitive or evolutionary theories, or indeed any of the aforementioned theories of the mind in my analysis of the seven authors that follows. It is common for critics with an interest in the mind to produce, say, committed psychoanalytic, existentialist or cognitivist readings of literature, but my aim here is different. Rather than interpreting the literary text through the filter of a preconceived theory, the analyses in this book start with the literary text itself, in order to examine the particular model of the conscious and unconscious mind it presents to us. We can then reflect this literary model back onto the dominant theories of mind in the period, as well as on to the other literary models created by our other authors. Instead of producing, say, a Bergsonian reading of Proust or a Freudian reading of Bernanos, I'm aiming to unravel Proust's and Bernanos's own understanding of how the mind works, to situate this understanding with reference to Freud and Bergson, to other views of the mind, and to each other, and in this way to build up a picture of changing visions of the mind through the century.[45] In the course of our explorations we will come across some very different, sometimes incompatible, models of what the mind is and how it works. Although I shall note parallels with currently accepted ideas on the mind, it is not my goal to judge who is the most 'correct' among the seven authors explored. A work of literature creates its own universe, within which the writer has a certain licence to set the rules. In real life, it remains an open question whether, say, male and female minds are indistinguishable at a preconscious level, or whether the mind's unspoken thoughts may be perceived by an omniscient deity. In the worlds of the texts, Sarraute's tropisms may exist in a realm untouched by sexual difference and Bernanos's priest may have his prayers heard by God, and we should respect the writer's prerogative to assert that, in their universe at least, these things are so. My purpose is to trace these changing literary universes through the course of the last hundred years, and in doing so, to venture towards a cultural history of consciousness.

We'll be exploring each of these writers' œuvres in general, and, where appropriate, we'll venture beyond them to examine related work by other writers who travel with them or rail against them. In order not to lose focus among the dozens of texts involved, however, one text from each writer will be reserved for particular attention. For Proust and Darrieussecq these will be *In Search of Lost Time* and *A Brief Stay with the Living*, as quoted earlier; for Bernanos, we will pick out *Diary of a Country Priest* (*Journal d'un curé de campagne*, 1936); for Breton, *Mad Love* (*L'Amour fou*, 1937); for Sartre *Nausea* (*La Nausée*, 1938); for Beckett, the trilogy of *Molloy*, *Malone Dies*, and *The Unnamable* (*Molloy*, *Malone meurt*, *L'Innommable*, 1951–53); and for Sarraute, *Childhood* (*Enfance*, 1980). For Proust, Sartre, and Darrieussecq, this choice is inevitable, since the text in question is either the only or the most notable foray into the representation of the mind in their prose fiction. For Bernanos, Breton, Beckett, and Sarraute, other choices out of their extensive psychological œuvres might have served equally well, but none better than the texts selected. One reason for dwelling on *Mad Love* and *Diary of a Country Priest* alongside *Nausea* is to highlight a meeting point in the careers of Breton, Bernanos, and Sartre in the 1930s. Each is at a very different stage in his life, with Bernanos in his penultimate decade, Breton at the height of his fame, and Sartre an unknown young writer publishing his first novel, and each offers a strikingly different conception of the mind from the others, drawing on medieval theology, nineteenth-century psychoanalysis, or philosophy still in its early development. We witness a moment when models of mind from different ages find a point of contact, which forces cross-evaluation and even sparks into open conflict. While this book is primarily conceived as a comparative analysis of writers across the century, each of the seven chapters also functions as a self-contained study of the writer in question, and readers whose interest is solely in one particular author are invited to head directly for the relevant chapter. With those who remain, let us begin at the beginning, with Marcel Proust.

Notes

1. Marcel Proust, 'Du côté de chez Swann (The Way by Swann's)', in *A la recherche du temps perdu* (*In Search of Lost Time*), ed. by Jean-Yves Tadié (Paris: Gallimard, Pléiade edition, 1987–89), 4 vols, I, p. 3. 'Longtemps, je me suis couché de bonne heure. Parfois, à peine ma bougie éteinte, mes yeux se fermaient si vite que je n'avais pas le temps de me dire: "Je m'endors." Et, une demi-heure après, la pensée qu'il était temps de

chercher le sommeil m'éveillait; je voulais poser le volume que je croyais avoir encore dans les mains et souffler ma lumière; je n'avais pas cessé en dormant de faire des réflexions sur ce que je venais de lire, mais ces réflexions avaient pris un tour un peu particulier; il me semblait que j'étais moi-même ce dont parlait l'ouvrage: une église, un quatuor, la rivalité de François Ier et de Charles-Quint. Cette croyance survivait pendant quelques secondes à mon réveil; elle ne choquait pas ma raison, mais pesait comme des écailles sur mes yeux et les empêchait de se rendre compte que le bougeoir n'était pas allumé. Puis elle commençait à me devenir inintelligible, comme après la métempsycose les pensées d'une existence antérieure; le sujet du livre se détachait de moi, j'étais libre de m'y appliquer ou non; aussitôt je recouvrais la vue et j'étais bien étonné de trouver autour de moi une obscurité, douce et reposante pour mes yeux, mais peut-être plus encore pour mon esprit, à qui elle apparaissait comme une chose sans cause, incompréhensible, comme une chose vraiment obscure'. The translation is taken from *In Search of Lost Time*, ed. by Christopher Prendergast, trans. by Lydia Davies (*Du côté de chez Swann/The Way by Swann's*), James Grieve (*A l'ombre des jeunes filles en fleurs/In the Shadow of Young Girls in Flower*), Mark Treharne (*Le Côté de Guermantes/The Guermantes Way*), John Sturrock (*Sodome et Gomorrhe/Sodom and Gomorrah*), Carol Clark (*La Prisonnière/The Prisoner*), Peter Collier (*Albertine disparue/The Fugitive*) and Ian Patterson (*Le Temps retrouvé/Finding Time Again*) (London: Penguin, 2002), 6 vols, I, p. 7. Subsequent references will be to the Gallimard Pléiade edition, *RTP*, and the Penguin translation.

2. 'Les jours fraîchissent. Il y a moins de roses, moins de boutons de roses. Sur le rosier ancien, le blanc, *Madame de Sévigné*, deux petites têtes casquées, vertes, pointues, debout et droites; petits soldats, parmi les épines et le tétanos et les coups de sécateur qui détachent, d'un claquement, de grosses fleurs abandonnées. Il lui dit que les jours fraîchissent, et qu'il sera peut-être inutile aujourd'hui d'arroser la terrasse; on pourra lire sans étouffer, envolée la vapeur d'été. La cuillère tinte dans la tasse, odeur de café. Elle coupe une jolie rose, deux pétales seulement se sont cambrés hors du bouton, ce n'est pas encore une fleur, deux pétales à demi ouverts. Elle remercie elle ne sait qui ou quoi, elle rend grâce, pour le sursis du matin, le flot de respiration, le bonheur qui est une chose énorme et liquide', Marie Darrieussecq, *Bref séjour chez les vivants* (Paris: Gallimard, 2001), p. 9. Translation is from Marie Darrieussecq, *A Brief Stay with the Living*, trans. by Ian Monk (London: Faber, 2003), p. 1.
3. Proust was born in 1871 and died in 1922; *In Search of Lost Time* was published between 1913 and 1927; Bernanos lived from 1888 to 1948 and published his first novel in 1926; Breton was born in 1896 and died in 1966, beginning his writing career in 1919; Sartre lived from 1905 to 1980 and published his first fiction in 1938; Beckett lived from 1906 to 1989, publishing from the 1930s with a particular concentration of work in the post-War decades; Sarraute's life matched the century from 1900 to 1999, and her writing career lasted from 1939 to the very end of her life; lastly, Darrieussecq was born in 1969, published her first novel in 1996, and continues to publish fiction regularly.
4. 'La vision transparente de la conscience des personnages', Jean-Louis Chrétien, *Conscience et roman, II: la conscience à mi-voix* (Paris: Minuit, 2011), p. 291.
5. David Lodge, *Consciousness and the Novel* (London: Penguin, 2003), p. 10.
6. Antonio Damasio, *Descartes' Error: Emotion, Reason and the Human Brain* (London: Vintage, 2006), pp. 83–113.
7. V. S. Ramachandran, *The Tell-Tale Brain: Unlocking the Mystery of Human Nature* (London: Heinemann, 2011), p. 248.
8. Antonio Damasio, *The Feeling of What Happens: Body, Emotion and the Making of Consciousness* (London: Vintage, 2000), pp. 17–18.
9. Daniel Dennett, *Consciousness Explained* (London: Penguin, 1993), p. 39.
10. Steven Pinker, *How the Mind Works* (New York: Norton, 1997), pp. 134–36; Pinker's model is drawn from R. Jackendoff, *Consciousness and the Computational Mind* (Cambridge: MIT Press, 1987) and Ned Block, 'On a Confusion about a Function of Consciousness', *Behavioural and Brain Sciences*, 18 (1995), 227–87.
11. Phenomenology, the branch of philosophy concerned with the study of mental phenomena as they appear to consciousness, comes to French intellectual life with the first translations of Husserl and Kierkegaard from 1930 onwards.
12. Edmund Husserl, *Logical Investigations* (1900–01), trans. by J. N. Findlay, vol. 2 (London and New York: Routledge and Kegan Paul/Humanities Press, 1970), p. 554, § 10.
13. Henri Bergson, *Essai sur les données immédiates de la conscience* (1927) (Paris: Presses Universitaires de France, 2003), pp. 94–104; Damasio, *The Feeling of What Happens*, pp. 168–233.
14. Sigmund Freud, 'The Unconscious', in *The Standard Edition of the Complete Psychological Works of Sigmund Freud*, trans. by James Strachey, 24 vols. (London: Hogarth Press, 1953–74), XIV, pp. 166–204 (p. 173).
15. Freud, 'The Unconscious', p. 173.
16. Freud, 'The Unconscious', p. 187.
17. For critiques of the Freudian Unconscious, see Jacques Van Rillaer, 'Les Méchanismes de défense des freudiens', in *Le Livre noir de la psychanalyse*, ed. by Catherine Meyer (Paris: Les Arènes, 2005), pp. 413–41 and Richard Webster, *Why Freud Was Wrong: Science, Sin and Psychoanalysis*, 3rd edn. (Oxford: Orwell Press, 2005), pp. 241–58.

18. Ned Block, 'Qualia', in *The Oxford Companion to the Mind*, ed. by Richard L. Gregory, 2nd edn. (Oxford: Oxford University Press, 2004), pp. 785–80 (p. 785).
19. The 'inverted spectrum' thought experiment posits that two people could share the same vocabulary and discrimination with regard to colour, while one's experience of the colour both call 'green' is in fact identical to the other's experience of red, and vice versa. It is first expounded by John Locke in his *Essay Concerning Human Understanding* (1689).
20. Plato, *Phaedo*, trans. by David Gallop (Oxford: Clarendon Press, 1975), pp. 15–46.
21. René Descartes, *Méditations métaphysiques*, ed. by Marie-Frédérique Pellegrin (1641 in Latin, 1647 in French) (Paris: Flammarion, 2009), p. 71.
22. 'Or je suis une chose vraie, et vraiment existante; mais quelle chose? Je l'ai dit: une chose qui pense. Et quoi davantage? J'exciterai encore mon imagination, pour chercher si je ne suis point quelque chose de plus. Je ne suis point cet assemblage de membres, que l'on appelle le corps humain; je ne suis point un air délié et pénétrant, répandu dans tous ces membres; je ne suis point un vent, un souffle, une vapeur, ni rien de tout ce que je puis feindre et imaginer, puisque j'ai supposé que tout cela n'était rien, et que, sans changer cette supposition, je trouve que je ne laisse pas d'être certain que je suis quelque chose', Descartes, pp. 97–8.
23. 'Nous sommes composés de deux natures opposées et de divers genre, d'âme et de corps. Car il est impossible que la partie qui raisonne en nous soit autre que spirituelle; et quand on prétendrait que nous serions simplement corporels, cela nous exclurait bien davantage de la connaissance des choses, n'ayant rien de si inconcevable que de dire que la matière se connaît soi-même', Blaise Pascal, *Pensées* (1669), ed. by Michel Le Guern (Paris: Gallimard, 1977), p. 159.
24. John Heil, 'Introduction', in *Philosophy of Mind*, ed. by John Heil (London: Routledge, 1998), p. 16.
25. 'On n'a jamais employé tant d'esprit à vouloir nous rendre bêtes; il prend envie de marcher à quatre pattes, quand on lit votre ouvrage', Voltaire, letter to Rousseau, 30 August 1755.
26. Webster, *Why Freud Was Wrong*, p. 8.
27. Jacques Lacan, 'Séminaire sur "La letter volée"', in *Écrits* (Paris: Seuil, 1966), pp. 11–61.
28. 'La psychologie ne peut être acceptée dans les études médicales que si elle renonce aux ambitions démesurées et se borne à résumer la conduite et les attitudes des maladies par des termes précis et bien définis en rattachant tous les faits par un déterminisme aussi rigoureux que possible. Ce travail est évidemment très difficile, il ne peut se faire que lentement et nous sommes tentés de dépasser nos observations incomplètes et nos inductions lentes par des généralisations hardies et par des interprétations symboliques et faciles', Pierre Janet, *La Psychanalyse de Freud* (1913) (Paris: L'Harmattan, 2004), pp. 112–13.
29. Shaun Gallagher and Dan Zahavi, *The Phenomenological Mind: An Introduction to Philosophy of Mind and Cognitive Science* (London: Routledge, 2008), p. 2.
30. Francis Crick, *The Astonishing Hypothesis: The Scientific Search for the Soul* (New York: Simon and Schuster, 1995), p. xii.
31. Crick, *The Astonishing Hypothesis*, p. 3.
32. John C. Eccles, *Evolution of the Brain: Creation of the Self* (London: Routledge, 1989), p. 239.
33. Catherine Malabou, *Que faire de notre cerveau?*, 2nd edn. (Paris: Bayard, 2011).
34. Steven Pinker, *The Blank Slate: The Modern Denial of Human Nature* (London: Allen Lane, 2002), pp. 337–50.
35. Adèle King, *French Women Novelists: Defining a Female Style* (Basingstoke: MacMillan, 1989), p. 8; Cordelia Fine, *Delusions of Gender: The Real Science Behind Sex Differences* (London: Icon, 2010); Angela Saini, *Inferior: How Science Got Women Wrong and the New Research that's Rewriting the Story* (London: Fourth Estate, 2017).
36. Hippolyte Taine held the view that nation, environment, and historical period ('race, milieu, moment') had a determining effect on the individual, shaping his or her attitudes, emotions, and behaviour. In literature, the Naturalist movement and its chief exponent, Émile Zola, were strongly influenced by Taine, depicting characters whose inner lives offered themselves to readers' interpretation in terms of their genetic heritage and social circumstances. See Hippolyte Taine, *Histoire de la littérature anglaise*, 5 vols. (Paris: Hachette, 1863), I, p. xxix.
37. Raymond Tallis, *Aping Mankind: Neuromania, Darwinitis and the Misrepresentation of Humanity* (Durham: Acumen, 2011).
38. Perhaps the most notorious misfire in evolutionary psychology was the notion that an 'innate' female attraction to the colour pink might stem from an evolved adaptation for berry-foraging in our ancestral environment. Anya C. Hurlbert and Yazhu Ling, 'Biological Components of Sex Differences in Color Preference', *Current Biology*, 17 (2001), pp. R623–25.
39. Tallis, *Aping Mankind*, p. 293.
40. Peter Stockwell's *Cognitive Poetics* (Routledge: London, 2002) and Gottschall's *Literature, Science, and a New Humanities* offer good introductions to cognitive uses in literary and cultural studies.
41. Martin Daly and Margo Wilson, *Homicide: Foundations of Human Behaviour* (Hawthorne, NY: Aldine, 1988).
42. On incest avoidance, see Pinker, *How the Mind Works*, pp. 455–60.

43. Michelle Scalise Sugiyama, 'New Science, Old Myth: An Evoutionary Critique of the Œdipal Paradigm', in *Evolution, Literature and Film*, ed. by Brian Boyd, Joseph Carrol and Jonathan Gottschall (New York: Columbia University Press, 2010), pp. 306–15.
44. Crick, *The Astonishing Hypothesis*, p. 3.
45. My methods are partly inspired by Jean Starobinski's *La Relation critique*, in which he warns of the distorting effect of an overly prescriptive methodological lens on the object it is supposed to be clarifying (Paris: Gallimard, 1970), pp. 9–33.

1

SELF

Marcel Proust

If we want to understand consciousness in twentieth-century European literature, we have to start with Proust. His three-thousand-page novel, published in seven parts between 1913 and 1927, offers the most sustained introspective analysis of the mind that fiction has to offer. *In Search of Lost Time* explores the workings of memory and perception and the subjective experience of each of them; the differing qualities of consciousness in wakefulness, rapture, obsession, drunkenness, stupor, and despair; the dichotomies of core and social self, or of the intellectual and the instinctive; and, most famously, it explores the temporality of the mind, with its elasticity, its emotional intermittences, and its closed vessels of past time which threaten the continuity of the self. It is a foundation stone of modern culture, and has directly influenced all of the subsequent writers we'll consider here. The publication of the novel also found itself at an important turning-point in discourses of the mind. Proust's novel was published as the topic of consciousness became a new vogue in philosophy, due in large part to the success of Henri Bergson's writings on the subject, and found itself irrevocably, and perhaps detrimentally, linked to the philosopher's name. As well as being an inauguration, the novel also marked the end of an era: It was the last major psychological novel of the pre-Freudian era. Proust writes in ignorance of Freud's new theories of the mind, which were just being translated into French during the later years of the novel's composition. It seems likely that no European writer since that time has represented the mind without at least indirect knowledge of the Œdipus complex, repression, and the Freudian Unconscious.

The unique confluence of artistic and historical factors makes Proust's representation of the mind a literary landmark, and it is a predictably crowded critical territory. Detailed and extensive studies of Proust's view of the mind have been produced by many major critics, drawing on various fields in the framework of their analysis. Predominantly psychoanalytic studies have come from critics such as Julia Kristeva, Jean-Yves Tadié, Malcolm Bowie, and Serge Doubrovsky; phenomenology informs the work of Jean-Pierre Richard and Edward Hughes; while Schopenhauer, Nietzsche, Bergson, and other philosophers of mind offer an interpretative matrix to several critics, including Anne Henry and Joshua Landy. This chapter will set out a sketch of Proust's representation of the mind in the shadow of these critics' analyses, before moving to consider where this representation echoes or differs from the theories of the mind that were already established as Proust wrote, and how far it is compatible with those theories that were to dominate the century that followed. The exploration of Proust's view of the conscious and unconscious mind will also serve to open a dialogue, in which each of the six authors in the subsequent chapters will offer their response. *In Search of Lost Time* holds an ungovernable profusion of ideas on memory, perception, reason, emotion, and the self. Over-abundant and occasionally conflicting views on how the mind works make it very easy for a selective reading to appropriate Proust as an acolyte of a particular school of thought, especially if readers approach armed with critical preconceptions that they are looking to see confirmed.

By way of demonstration, let us indulge in some cherry-picking of the various mindscapes to be found in the novel. Here, for instance, is evidence for the Bergsonian Proust:

> If I always imagined the woman I loved surrounded by the places I longed for most at that time, if I would have liked her to be the one who took me to visit them, who opened the way for me into an unknown world, it was not because of a simple chance association of thoughts; no, it was because my dreams of travel and love were only moments—which I am separating artificially today as if I were cutting sections at different heights of an apparently motionless iridescent jet of water—in a single inflexible upsurge of all the forces of my life.[1]

In this passage, the Narrator is describing how his intellect retrospectively divides up what was, at the time of experience, a desire in which ideas of love and adventure were indivisibly merged together. This is strongly reminiscent of the distinction posited in Bergson's *Essai sur les données immédiates de la conscience* (*Time and Free Will: An Essay on the Immediate Data of Consciousness*, 1889) between the primary consciousness, which receives our sense-impressions from the world, and reflective consciousness, in which we conceptualize our experience. For Bergson, the latter is characterized by a quantifying approach—dividing, measuring, and enumerating as we might divide, measure, or count up physical objects in space—towards impressions that are essentially qualitative in nature. In the intuitive part of our minds, mental states merge like blended colours, within a temporal flow that is akin to our appreciation of a melody we're listening to as an organic whole, rather than our comprehension of it as a sequence of notes on a stave. Bergson expresses it as follows:

> Conscious life presents itself in two ways, depending on whether one perceives it directly or refracted through space. Considered in themselves, fundamental states of consciousness have no relation to quantity; they are pure quality; they merge together in such a way that one cannot tell if they are one or many, nor even examine them in this regard without immediately denaturing them. The duration which they give rise to in this way is a duration in which the moments do not constitute a numerical multiplicity.[2]

Thus we see in the earlier extract that the Narrator's intuitive feelings are to some extent falsified by the intellectual process that distinguishes them in order to give them individual labels.

Within Proust's own lifetime, this passage and others like it were encouraging Bergsonian interpretations of the novel as a whole, to the irritation of its author, who had explicitly rejected the term 'Bergsonian novel' for his work in an interview on the publication of the first volume. Instead, he suggests, the novel might better be thought of as 'a suite of "Novels of the Unconscious"', a choice of words which invites later critics to search for a Freudian or Lacanian Proust.[3] Here, then, is a possible example of such, taken from the final volume, in which the Narrator considers the words spoken by one of a pair of agitated would-be clients on the threshold of Jupien's brothel:

> It was clearly the first time they had been there, somebody must have told them about the place, and they seemed torn between desire, temptation and very cold feet. One of them—a good-looking young man—kept saying every few moments to the other, with a

> smile that was half-enquiring and half intended to persuade: 'Well? After all, what does it matter?' But although he may have meant by that that after all the consequences did not matter, it's likely that it mattered more than he let on, for the remark was followed not by any motion of entering but by another glance towards his friend, followed by the same smile and the same *after all, what does it matter?* This *after all, what does it matter?* was a very good example of that wonderful language, so different from the one we normally speak, in which emotion deflects what we want to say and in its place brings into being a quite different phrase, which emerges from an unknown lake where all these expressions live that are unrelated to thought but which for precisely that reason reveal what we are thinking.[4]

Proust's 'unknown lake' has been seen by psychoanalytic critics as a metaphor for something very like the Freudian Unconscious, a region of the mind inaccessible to consciousness, in which repressed thoughts connected to our strongest emotions proliferate autonomously.[5] Freud makes the point that

> numerous little slips and mistakes people make [. . .] are not accidental, that they require more than physiological explanations, that they have a meaning and can be interpreted, and that one is justified in inferring from them the presence of restrained or repressed impulses and intentions.[6]

The client's words thus seem to offer us an insight into the preoccupations of the Unconscious via an involuntary lapse in conscious control over language.

As a third and final example: Bersani is one critic to note the similarity between the following passage and the intentionality of consciousness that is to form a central concept in Sartre's existentialism:[7]

> Now, as the self lives incessantly thinking about a quantity of things, as it is nothing but the thought of these things, when by chance, instead of having these things before it, it suddenly thinks about itself, it finds only an empty apparatus, something with which it is not acquainted, to which, in order to give it some reality, it adds the memory of a face seen in the mirror. That odd smile, that uneven moustache, these are what will disappear from the surface of the earth. If I killed myself in five years' time, the ability to think all these things that pass unceasingly through my mind would be over and done with. I would no longer be on the surface of the earth and I would never return there, my thoughts would cease forever. And my self seems to have even less substance, to think of it already as something no longer existing.[8]

The passage, which appeared in early versions of *The Fugitive*, and is now confined to the 'Notes et variantes' of the Pléiade edition, suggests that consciousness turned in on itself perceives only a void. This recalls Husserl's concept of intentionality—that consciousness is always consciousness *of* something other than itself—which Sartre adopts in an early philosophical essay:

> Consciousness is purged, it is as clear as a great wind, there is nothing left in it besides a movement to flee itself, a sliding outside of itself; if, impossibly, you found yourself 'inside' a consciousness, you would be seized by a whirlwind and thrown back outside it, by the tree, in the dust, because consciousness has no 'inside'; it is nothing but the outside of itself, and it is this absolute flight, this refusal to be a substance which constitute it as a consciousness.[9]

The 'empty apparatus' Proust's Narrator discovers at the centre of his own mind already appears to him to resemble the non-existence of the self after death; the concept is strikingly close to the 'utter emptiness' of existentialist consciousness, which has no more substance than a beam of light shining onto the object of attention.[10]

Is Proust, then, simultaneously a Bergsonian, a Freudian, and an existentialist in his understanding of the mind, at least insofar as it was possible to be so with a patchy knowledge of Bergson and ignorance of Freud and Sartre? It's certainly true that at these particular points in the text, the Narrator takes a view on the workings of his mind which echoes each of the three thinkers, and, while the first example may present itself as nothing more than a personal phenomenon of the Narrator's youth, the latter two are asserted as if a general law of the mind. The first caveat we must raise is that Proust's discourse is neither philosophical nor scientific, and we are doing it a disservice to reduce its poetic ambiguities to a particular doctrine. The scene on the brothel doorstep, for instance, is not entirely explicit about the mental processes underlying the words and actions of the dithering young man. The episode might on closer inspection appear less like a Freudian slip emerging from the unknown lake of the Unconscious, but rather an inapposite cliché spouting from an inner pool of clichés, the foolishness of which betrays nothing more than the speaker's heightened emotional state. The second caveat is that a point of contact with a philosophical system clearly need not imply any wider endorsement of the philosophy. As we'll discover later in the chapter, scattered similarities between Proust's and Bergson's view of the mind are very much outweighed by major conceptual differences, most notably in the nature of memory and in the experience of time passing. But the last caveat is the most idiosyncratically Proustian: one of the most important themes of his novel is the multiplicity of the self, changing over time as if into a different person, and barely unified into a single entity at any one moment. The insights into the mind expressed in the novel have their source in a composite figure, made up of the Narrator as he writes and his former self at the point in his experience which inspired the insight. The contradictions and developments in these characters, especially the latter, who changes from a child to a mature man and fluctuates between extreme and contrasting emotional states throughout the course of the novel, affect the findings of their introspection, with the result that what appears to the Narrator to be universally true may be superseded by a different understanding emerging from the interrogation of a very different state of mind. (Vincent Descombes suggests that this aspect makes Proust's writing 'not so much a text communicating a system of thought as an instrument for thinking'.)[11] Thus, while the 'empty apparatus' may reflect the inner emptiness felt by the Narrator in the shocking aftermath of Albertine's departure, suddenly deprived of the person who has obsessed his every waking moment, elsewhere he is confident that riches and pleasure are to be discovered from looking inwards, as, for example, here:

> It was only when I was alone that I would be swept on occasion by one of those impressions which brought with them such deeply satisfying feelings. But I only had to be in the presence of someone else, talking with a friend for instance, for my mind to face the wrong way, occupying itself with thoughts directed towards the other person rather than towards myself; and thoughts going in the other direction never afforded me any enjoyment. No sooner had I left the company of Saint-Loup than I sought words with which to tidy up the disordered minutes I had just spent with him. I assured myself that I had a close friend and that a close friend is a rarity; yet in knowing I was the recipient of things difficult to come by, what I felt was the exact opposite of the mode of enjoyment natural to me, the opposite of the pleasure that could come from finding something lying deep within myself, from bringing it out of its inner darkness and into the light of day. Whenever I spent two or three hours talking with Robert de Saint-Loup, and if he was impressed by what I had been

saying, I was overcome by something like remorse, regret or weariness, vexed at not having spent the time alone, at not having got down once and for all to the work that awaited me.[12]

This passage, from an earlier point in the Narrator's life where he is free from obsessive relationships, is in fact the more typical attitude towards introspection expressed in the novel.[13] Far from discovering existentialist nothingness, consciousness turned in on itself finds previously hidden details about the Narrator's individual self and the workings of the mind more broadly. The disparity between the two quotations is one example of the Narrator's tendency to mistake for universal maxims what is only the subjective truth of his mind at that point in his intellectual development, or under the particular emotional pressures he is presently experiencing.

While the Proustian mind may thus reflect all of these models at different points in the text, it can't be relied upon to maintain its allegiances. To gain a clearer understanding of the outline of the mind that Proust presents, we must step away from external theories for a while, and consider the account the text itself makes of consciousness and the unconscious. What aspects of mental activity does the novel itself choose to dwell on, and what explanations of the mind's functioning does it champion to the reader? Only once we have a clearer idea of the principal elements of Proust's view of the mind, taken on its own terms, can we judge the validity of the theories that would seek to elucidate it.

The three elements of the mind that Proust places at the centre of his explorations are memory, perception, and emotion. His novel is now such a marker of psychological literature that it's easy to overlook the fact that these are not the only subjects Proust had at his disposal: reason, language, and imaginative fantasy, for instance, are comparatively under-represented in the author's model of the mind, as are such topics as madness, trauma, or moral judgement, or more abstract philosophical and religious questions like free will or the soul. (It must be noted, however, that while these topics are not a major focus of Proust's attention, every one of them features to at least a small extent in the encyclopaedic novel.)[14] Beyond the famous comparison of voluntary and involuntary memory that opens *In Search of Lost Time*, the theme of memory is explored throughout the length of the novel through its tricks and failings, its fragmentary composite-images, and its networks of associations which link memories to other memories, as well as to present perceptions. Perception itself is coloured by both memory and emotion, as well as being deadened by habit or overridden by preconceptions. The faculty of vision becomes the starting point for meditations on the representation of reality, and on the treachery of surface appearance, a theme which will come to dominate the Narrator's relationship with others. Correspondingly, the topic of emotion is increasingly dominated by jealous desire, part of a realm of uncontrolled instinct that contrasts with the piercing intellect of the Narrator's self-analysis. As we shall see, these three themes of memory, perception, and emotion share characteristics which unite the disparate mental faculties, and run further into other aspects of consciousness. At this more abstract level we will find a second trio of qualities which help to define the Proustian mind: discontinuity, multiplicity, and temporality.

'Combray', the opening section of the first volume, begins with an absence of memory: only the anxious wait for his mother's good-night kiss remains from the adult Narrator's childhood. The image of a brightly lit section of a building surrounded by darkness, as if in the glare of a floodlight or firework (*DCSS*, I, 43; trans. I, 46), which stands as a metaphor for involuntary memory, seems chosen for the extreme contrast between light and darkness, and the sharp dividing line between the two. The products of involuntary memory are by contrast characterized by their blossoming profusion, as the wealth of remembered detail that makes up the second part of 'Combray' attests, but here too a principle of the discrete and discontinuous persists: on finally coming to understand the nature of involuntary memory in the last volume of the novel, the

Narrator conceptualizes these dormant memories as 'a thousand sealed vessels each one of which would be filled with things of a completely different colour, odour and temperature', stacked to the height of our years, and each awaiting the associative stimulus of a present sensation to unseal it once more.[15] Georges Poulet argues that, in this view, recovered memories 'can never reconstitute time, nor endow it with what it is perhaps not in its nature to have, namely continuity'.[16] These are not the only negative aspects to Proust's representation of memory. Much of our experience is not stored at all, and that which *is* retained is consigned to an inaccessible mental 'void' from which only chance may resurrect 'dead recollections', through a process which is itself open to failure, as happens at Hudimesnil when the Narrator feels a recollection stir at the sight of three trees from his carriage, but is unable to call it to mind.[17] When memories are recalled, they may be mistaken, as when the Narrator worries that his memory of seeing le prince de Sagan may be false (*RTP*, III, 118; trans. IV, 123). Even if true, memories may still be an unreliable guide, as when the selectivity and emotional colouring of the Narrator's recollection of his first trip to Balbec match up poorly with the reality on his return, leading him to declare that memory has no better connection to reality than dreams (*RTP*, III, 149; trans. IV, 154).

While memories may be discrete entities, they are not, however, unconnected, and the associative threads that link them are cause for a more positive view. Memories irradiate the present with pleasant or painful associations from the past (*RTP*, IV, 221; trans. V, 607). Lines of associative memory are compared to train lines, some constantly refreshed through current preoccupations, while others fall into disuse (*RTP*, IV, 309; trans. VI, 38), the whole developing with maturity into a vast network of connotations to enrich present experience:

> After a certain age our memories are so interwoven with each other that the object of our thoughts or the book which we are reading has practically no importance. We have left traces of ourselves everywhere, everything is fertile, everything is dangerous, and we can make discoveries every bit as precious in an advertisement for soap as in Pascal's *Pensées*.[18]

Also countering the negative assessments of the faculty of memory is the text itself, and the Narrator's achievement in creating it. Powerful recall combined with creative reimagining build a representation of the Narrator's past that spans a lifetime in scope, and includes such fine detail that a hundred and fifty pages can be devoted to the account of a single evening, as is the case with the Guermantes' dinner-party in *The Guermantes Way*. The Narrator's earlier comments on the possibility of communicating memories to others may be pessimistic, but his final decision to render his past as art demonstrates a confidence that the mind can both retain and express the essence of our experience.[19] And it's in these final pages that the diachronic nature of the novel's reflections on memory is most strongly apparent, for after six volumes in which fragmentation has seemed memory's most prominent characteristic, it is continuity which is emphasized at last, as the Narrator recalls the sound of the garden gate at Combray:

> Then, as I thought of all the events which had to be set in place between the moment when I heard those sounds and this party at the Guermantes', I was frightened to think that the bell could still be ringing in me without my being able to do anything to alter the shrillness of its tinkling, since, no longer remembering very clearly how it faded away, and wanting to rediscover this, and to listen to it properly, I had to try to block out the sound of the conversations which the masks were holding all around me. In order to try to hear it at closer quarters, I was forced to go back down into myself. It must therefore be that this tinkling was always there, and also, between it and the present moment, the whole of this past, unrolled indefinitely, which I did not know that I was carrying. When it tinkled,

> I already existed, and for me still to be able to hear the tinkling there must have been no break in continuity, I must not have ceased for a moment, not taken a rest from existing, from thinking, from being conscious of myself, because this moment from long ago still stuck to me, so that I could still find it again, still go back to it, simply by going more deeply back into myself.[20]

This rediscovered continuity is not a smooth panorama of life: memories remain for the Narrator the intense re-immersion in brief periods of time, separated by gaps, which gives the novel its distinctive structure. Rather, the Narrator's final epiphany concerns the continuity of the self, an unbroken essence that links the child in Combray to the ageing man at the Paris matinée. This hopeful note counters the multiplicity the Narrator has seen in himself through the novel, where he has denied the presence of 'an individual, identical and permanent self', and seen instead a composite self made up of 'these new selves, which should bear a name different from that of their predecessor'.[21] What's more, this multiplicity is not only that of serial selves relayed across time, but also a crowd of simultaneous 'little inner figures' jostling for dominance at any one moment.[22] What the Narrator discovers in the closing pages doesn't sweep away his earlier conception of manifold, discontinuous selves in time, but it does render them less than absolute: through memory, enough of the self persists for us to be able to connect together a life from its disparate parts.

Temporality and multiplicity are also to the fore in Proust's understanding of perception. The Narrator denies that our eyes form 'simply a piece of recording apparatus which takes snapshots', emphasizing instead the active role of the observer in subjective perception.[23] 'The evidence of the senses is itself a mental event in which conviction creates belief,' he declares, describing how what we perceive conforms to our preconceptions.[24] The observer's state of mind thus plays an important role in the shape of his perception, as we see in the novel when the Narrator's state of excitement prevents him from seeing Charlus's drawing-room (*RTP*, III, 841; trans. III, 552), or when Saint-Loup's impression of Albertine's appearance is very different from that of the smitten Narrator (*RTP*, IV, 22; trans. V, 406). 'Habit' is Proust's term for the action of time on perception: 'We only really take cognizance of something which is new, something which abruptly introduces a change of tone that strikes our sensibility, something that habit has not yet replaced with its pale replicas'.[25] The Narrator is ambivalent about the process: habit may deaden us to our surroundings, but unfamiliar impressions excite the senses to a degree that can be intolerable, as the Narrator notes of his unsettled first evening in his Balbec hotel room (*RTP*, II, 27; trans. II, 245). (The theme of habit is also one of the strongest connections between Proust's view of the mind and Beckett's, as we shall see in a later chapter.) A related theory is espoused for the effect of the visual arts on perception. Elstir's paintings allow the Narrator to rediscover 'nature as it is', from which our intellect has estranged us by naming and categorizing what we are accustomed to seeing: 'The names of things always express a view of the mind, which is foreign to our genuine impressions of them, and which forces us to eliminate from them whatever does not correspond to that view', says the Narrator, foreshadowing Sartre's Roquentin.[26] Thus, through art we can learn to reconnect with the raw perception which overlaid connotations have distanced from us. Where perception is linked to literature, it is the refraction of the impression through the unique subjectivity of the observer that comes to the fore. Jean-Pierre Richard explores at length how the subjective connotations imposed on the 'notes' of each individual impression combine in the course of the novel to produce the 'fundamental melody' of the self, noting how abundant food recalls the safety and intimacy of home, or bright colours produce a feeling of euphoria.[27] Rather than being shorn of the accretions of the intellect, the visual impressions which the Narrator records are embellished by metonyms drawn from the surrounding milieu and more personal metaphors which, in Joshua Landy's terms, designate 'their place in Marcel's subjective conceptual framework'. Thus, the flowers and girls he associates with the Martinville steeples connect through a shared status as objects that offer an experience of transcendence.[28] Much emphasis is laid on perception as a process occurring within time. We see this clearly in the movement of the three steeples relative to one another as the Narrator views them from his carriage (*RTP*, I, 179; trans. I, 181), or the changing colours of the sea-gulls as the sun sets over Balbec, which are now white, now yellow, now pink (*RTP*, III, 203, 206, 222; trans. IV, 208, 211, 228). In both cases, objective reality is of little consequence: the gulls are pink, the steeples move. The subjective phenomenon is what interests the Narrator, and his account records not what *is*, but how it seems.

The third of Proust's trio of mental attributes, emotion, is explored primarily through the familial and sexual relationships held by the Narrator and his acquaintances. In the family, the Narrator feels love, anxiety, grief, and guilt towards his mother and grandmother, and outside it, an all-consuming desire that develops into possessive jealousy towards the women he loves. As was the case with perception, the focus stays resolutely with the feeling subject rather than the object of his emotions. Indeed, where sexual relationships are concerned, the Narrator presents the women in question as almost interchangeable. Love is an independent force that we find within ourselves: 'Beneath the outward appearance of the woman, it is to these invisible forces by which she is incidentally accompanied that we address ourselves, as if to obscure divinities'.[29] The similarity of his relationships to Gilberte and Albertine, compounded by the echoes of his own love-affairs he perceives in those of Swann and Saint-Loup, endorses this solipsism. Change over time is more important than ever. The Narrator explores in detail how emotions wax and wane between love and indifference within a relationship with an almost arbitrary 'pendulum swing'.[30] Emotions, or at least those of which we are conscious, can also be oddly dissociated from behaviour. This is especially noticeable in the Narrator's attitude to Albertine, as when he convinces himself he is really in love with Gisèle, or that he is about to end the relationship with Albertine, only to dismiss the rival in a parenthesis, or abruptly decide to marry (*RTP*, II, 244–45; trans. II, 467; *RTP*, III, 514–15; trans. IV, 522). 'Thus something which I had thought meant nothing to me, was quite simply my whole life. How little we know ourselves', he declares when Albertine leaves him.[31] These disparities indicate a tension between the intellectual side of the mind, which is transparent to consciousness and under its control, and the emotional and instinctive side, which is only partly accessible and largely beyond control. The Narrator's self-analysis in the wake of Albertine's departure posits a basic opposition between heart and intelligence:

> [I believed] that I had plumbed the depths of my heart. But however great our intelligence, it cannot conceive all the elements that constitute it and which remain undetected as long as no event capable of isolating them makes them start to solidify out of the volatile state in which they exist for most of the time. I was mistaken when I thought that I saw clearly into my heart. But this knowledge, which the finest insights of my intellect had not given me, had just been brought home to me, as hard, dazzling and strange as crystals of salt, through the sudden stimulus of pain.[32]

The episode of Albertine's departure offers the most sustained exploration of a characteristic of emotional life which suffuses Proust's representation: the inability of the intellect to bring emotional truths to conscious awareness, and the surrogate function of suffering in producing the self-knowledge that intelligence could not. He sums up this view in the final volume of the novel:

> It is only during suffering that our thoughts, in a sense shaken up by endless and shifting impulses, elevate, as in a storm, to a level at which it becomes visible, all that regulated

> immensity, which we, stationed at a badly paced window, do not normally see, because the calm of happiness leaves it smooth and at too low a level.[33]

We may thus be unaware of our own emotions, either because they are too volatile to pin down, or too deep-set beneath consciousness to observe. For Proust, the relationship between intellect and emotion is highly paradoxical. The Narrator speculates that our reason is secretly governed by emotion, and that Bloch is deceived when he believes he has arrived at his political opinions by logical means (*RTP*, II, 593; trans. III, 293). A Nietzschean 'will to ignorance' has been proposed as underlying the Narrator's investigation into Albertine's possible infidelity: while he is conscious only of a desire to learn the truth, his actions betray the influence of an unacknowledged desire to avoid confronting any facts that might damage his love for her.[34] The conventional association of reason with lucidity is shaken in the novel, as the Narrator's desire allows him to rationalize falsehoods. Even when his reason indicates the truth, such as the definitive nature of Albertine's departure, the Narrator is able to override his own judgement with self-serving rationalization to reach the conclusion he desires:

> But, as far as my reason was concerned, the only explanation for some of her bad moods and attitudes had seemed to be, even before I knew anything, that she was planning her final departure; it was difficult to believe, now that this departure had occurred, that it was only pretence. I say for my reason, not for my self. I found the hypothesis of a pretence all the more necessary for being improbable and that it gained in strength what it lost in verisimilitude.[35]

Exploring this episode in the novel, Martha Nussbaum concludes that rational analysis is here trumped by 'love's knowledge' as a means for reaching the truth about the self. 'Cataleptic' knowledge, meaning an emotional understanding gained through suffering, can teach us truth beyond the reach of dispassionate inquiry, which can then be subsumed into the intellect by a cooler head in a quieter moment.[36] Intellect and emotion are thus not opposed in Proust, but rather have a complex interdependence. As Edward Hughes suggests, the true counterpart to the intellect in the Narrator's eyes is not emotion but the kind of instinctive approach to life he sees in the girls of Balbec. His envy of the 'zoophyte' girls, like his attraction to order-obeying military life and his abandonment to the pleasures of music, all suggest that intellect can prove a burden from which he wishes for release.[37]

Emotion in Proust shows us the multiplicity of a self that can debate with and hoodwink its own mind, the emotional discontinuity of an 'intermittent' heart, and the temporal focus of a narrative that tracks in minute detail the ebb and flow of love in the Narrator's feelings. Indeed, a summing up at the end of 'A Love of Swann's' suggests that multiplicity, discontinuity, and temporality together form the essence of our emotional life:

> What we believe to be our love, or our jealousy, is not one identical and continuous passion, indivisible. They are composed of an infinity of successive loves, of different jealousies, which are ephemeral but by their uninterrupted multitude give the impression of continuity, the illusion of unity.[38]

Cognitive discontinuity pervades Proust's representation of the mind: just as emotional states are discrete entities in succession, so the self constantly dies and is replaced, the world is a network of enclosed spaces, and time is remembered as a series of intense experiences, each set apart from the others. Discontinuity is not absolute, but it is endemic to the Proustian mind, particularly when viewed from a temporal perspective, and from these processes of dividing up we inevitably arrive at a state of multiplicity. Swann, Odette, Elstir, Albertine, and the Duchess of Guermantes all appear to the Narrator as different people at different times in their lives, sometimes astonishingly so, as when the Narrator discovers that 'the painter, vacuous and devious' of 'A Love of Swann's' is none other than Elstir, 'such a brilliant man, a solitary, a philosopher who had accumulated wisdom', whom he encounters at Balbec.[39] And as we have seen, the 'countless humble selves that compose us' fragment the Narrator into an inner profusion, while locations double into unfamiliarity on return visits with new eyes.[40] Governing all of this is the mind's temporality, or, to be more precise, its diachronic nature, changing and developing with the onward flow of time. Even the selves which inhabit the mind simultaneously owe their existence to the diverse intellectual and emotional events of the past which brought each of them into being, and each will wax and wane, or vanish entirely, in the future, according to our life's course. The image of the sealed vases of past experience is important not only for the closed nature of the vessels, but also for their great numbers, 'arranged across the full length of our years, during which we have never ceased to change, even if only our thoughts and our dreams'.[41] And on the smaller scale too, mental states are inscribed in duration, like the changing qualities of consciousness as the mind moves into and out of sleep, or the progression from sociable drunkenness to disturbed sleep to morning hangover (*RTP*, I, 3–7; trans. I, 7–11; *RTP*, II, 165–76; trans. II, 388–99). Duration equally pervades perception. Descriptive passages in Proust are not narratorial freeze-frames, as in conventional literature, but rather narratives of the act of perception on the part of the observing protagonist, as Gérard Genette has pointed out:

> Proust's narrative never pauses over an object or a tableau without this stop corresponding to a contemplative pause on the part of the hero himself (Swann in 'A Love of Swann's', Marcel everywhere else), and the descriptive passage thus never escapes the temporality of the story.[42]

The temporal nature of consciousness is thus fundamental to the theory of the mind that the Narrator proposes, explicitly and implicitly, in the novel. What is particularly important to remember, though, is that this temporality applies to the theory itself: the Narrator's model of the mind, and in particular its concept of the mind's multiplicity and discontinuity, will itself develop through time towards the final epiphany of the Guermantes' ball. Thus, as we have seen, the conclusion of the novel will discover unity and continuity in the self through memory and art: what seemed lost was still present deep in memory, and could be recovered and reconnected through literature. What the denouement demonstrates is that *In Search of Lost Time* is not a novel in the service of a thesis on consciousness. Rather, the ideas themselves form the narrative, as the Narrator's changing views structure the development of his story.

*

With the novel's own preoccupations laid out in their broad outline, we are now in a position to measure Proust's view of the mind against other theories from outside the text. One of Proust's clearest alignments is with materialism: he is in no doubt that the mind supervenes on the activity of the physical brain. Just as Morel attributes his own lack of self-control to a physiological cause, claiming 'my nerves are all tied in knots', so the Narrator is apt to see mental events in physical terms.[43] The fading in his memory of Albertine is seen as comparable to the mental consequences of a cerebral stroke:

> That impression of the void which I remember having experienced that day for the first time, that suppression within me of a whole section of the association of my ideas, as in a

> man whose worn-out cerebral artery ruptures and who finds a whole part of his memory erased or paralysed.[44]

The embodied status of the mind is touched on in a number of ways in the novel, through the confusion of emotional and physical pain (*RTP*, IV, 12; trans. V, 396), or the 'involuntary memory of the limbs' that conjures a past lover from a sleeping position.[45] Proust considered the title *The Intermittences of the Heart* for his novel (it survives as a heading to a section of *Sodom and Gomorrah*), attracted by the way the phrase 'alludes to illness of the body in the mental realm', as he wrote to Eugène Fasquelle, thus blurring the distinction between mental and physical.[46] The mind's material nature connects closely to the novel's temporality, in that it makes the deterioration of mental faculties of a piece with the observable physical degradation of the characters in the later parts of the novel. The spectacle of corporeal decline which so shocks the Narrator in the closing Guermantes' ball is not seen as qualitatively different from the 'congestion of her brain' which prevents his grandmother from recognizing him in her final illness, or the dementia which strikes Charlus and Odette in old age.[47] And the physical alteration of the brain can, it seems, be the effect of mental change as well as the cause: Cottard is approvingly cited discussing the theory that psychological trauma can produce 'alterations in the human brain quite comparable to those observable in inanimate matter'.[48] There is an awareness of physicality in Proust's view of the mind to a degree which we will not meet again until the biological metaphors of Nathalie Sarraute and the neuroscience of Marie Darrieussecq.

Proust's interest in the biological substrate of consciousness extends to a nodding acquaintance with Darwinian theory. He discusses his characters' inherited mental and physical characteristics in serious mode, and in comic mode employs evolutionary metaphors to describe the Narrator's grandmother's rise through the animal kingdom in the level of esteem bestowed upon her by the Princesse de Luxembourg (*RTP*, II, 60; trans. II, 279), or the disappearing tail of the 'S' in Gilberte's signature when, as Mme G. S. de Forcheville, she begins to distance herself from her past as Mlle Swann (*RTP*, IV, 167; trans. V, 551). In discussing Morel's abandonment of Charlus for a heterosexual relationship, the Narrator makes explicit reference to Darwin's study of cross-fertilization in flowers, deriving the following analogy to human behaviour:

> Thus the interplay of different psychological laws contrives to compensate, in the flowering of the human species, for everything which, in one way or another, would lead by superabundance or scarcity to its annihilation. As Darwin has shown, a comparable wisdom is to be found among the flowers, governing the methods of fertilization by opposing them successively one to another.[49]

While perhaps betraying an overly teleological view of Darwinian theory, this comment does suggest a broader evolutionary perspective underlying Proust's representation of sexuality, most evident in the famous comparison of gay courting rituals to insect pollination (*RTP*, III, 3–6; trans. IV, 5–8). The discourse of biological science allows Proust to discuss gay relationships in a non-judgmental manner, while making an implicit plea for tolerance through his assertions that same-sex attraction is natural, physiological, and fixed from birth (*RTP*, III, 344, 514; trans. IV, 349, 522).

A materialist stance on the mind brings up an important difference of opinion between Proust and Bergson, which Proust himself details as follows:

> I regret to find myself contradicting on this matter an admirable philosopher, the great Bergson. And among my contradictions, to add the following: it is true that M. Bergson

> claims that consciousness overflows the body and extends beyond it; and indeed, in the sense that one remembers things, or that one thinks about philosophers, etc., this is obvious. But M. Bergson does not mean it in this way. According to him, the soul, extending beyond the brain, can and must survive it. Well, this consciousness can be damaged by any cerebral shock; a simple fainting fit wipes it out. How can we believe that it will survive after death?[50]

As Joyce Megay has discussed, Proust's mind has certain affinities with Bergson's.[51] The centrality of memory and temporal flow to both writers' conceptions of consciousness is itself, of course, a link between them. Both Proust and Bergson also differentiate clock time from time as subjectively experienced, which can race or creep according to the subject's state of mind (*RTP*, I, 601; trans. II, 188). Proust's divided self finds its echo in Bergson, whose distinction between intuitive and reflective consciousness has similarities to Proust's separation of the intellectual self from the instinctive and emotional. Both privilege the subjective and the intuitive over the objective and rational in their attempt to understand the essentials of the self. This, though, is as far as the similarities run. Bergson's central contention on time and consciousness is that states of mind 'succeed each other indistinguishably' within the flow of *durée*, itself defined as 'an organic progression which is not however an increasing quantity'.[52] Time as we live it is immeasurable and indivisible. Only when we come to analyze it with our reflective consciousness do we attempt to figure it in terms of length and quantity, using terms of reference drawn from our understanding of space, which are fundamentally inapposite for describing time. Now, Proust may posit the existence of an intellectual self who has much in common with Bergson's reflective consciousness, but if this intellectual self understands time as a series of discontinuous periods aligned as if in space, this is because time does indeed appear this way to us, at all levels of our consciousness. Early in the novel, the Narrator explicitly assimilates time to space when he writes of Combray's church that it is 'an edifice occupying a space with, so to speak, four dimensions—the fourth being Time'.[53] Time is a dimension like the other three and can be conceptualized in similar ways. The discontinuity of the self across time is anathema to Bergson, for whom discontinuity is itself a spatially derived concept that is inapplicable to true duration. But, as we have seen, the divided, multiple selves and the sealed vessels of experience are at the centre of Proust's view of the mind, and the time his Narrator experiences is, in Poulet's terms, 'spatialized, juxtaposed time'.[54] Elsewhere, Bergson's eccentric idea of memory as a still-existing past which is perceived externally by the mind's eye in a manner analogous to how our real eyes perceive the present is entirely at odds with the modern understanding of memory as traces of experience stored in the brain, which Proust's novel endorses.[55] Superficial kinship in their choice of theme, then, masks deep disagreements between Bergson and Proust. The multiplicity and discontinuity that underlie Proust's model of consciousness are wholly at odds with Bergson's unquantifiable and indivisible mental flow, and we can only sympathize with Proust's discomfort at finding his representation of the mind dubbed 'Bergsonian'.

A more genuine affinity exists between Proust's work and the other major philosophy of consciousness in the early twentieth century, phenomenology. The primacy of visual perception in the thinking of both novelist and philosophers builds a connection between them, and there are interesting parallels between Proust's use of visual description and the phenomenological method. Edward Casey draws out the similarities between descriptive writing in Proust and the phenomenologist Maurice Merleau-Ponty, both of whom explore the act of a perceiving subject in feigned 'reality statements' which aim at finding the essence of the act of perception, thus demonstrating more porous boundaries between fiction and philosophy than is generally the case.[56] Merleau-Ponty in fact acknowledges a debt to Proust, writing in *Le Visible et l'invisible*:

'No one has been further than Proust in fixing the relationship of the visible and the invisible, in the description of an idea which is not the opposite of a sense impression, but which is its shadow and its depth'.[57] Proust's technique of moving from a particular observation to a general maxim anchors his insights in the interaction of the individual self with the world, as Merleau-Ponty and other phenomenologists were attempting to do. From opposed starting points, the novelist and the philosopher converge as each combines the subjective experience of the conventional novel with the abstract laws of traditional philosophy. Julia Kristeva points out the shared philosophical education of the two men, including influence from Lachelier, Ravaisson, Ribot, Egger, and Séailles, as well as from Schopenhauer and his disciples.[58] Proust and Merleau-Ponty connect most closely in their understanding of the interplay of the self and world involved in the process of perception. Merleau-Ponty posits a complex dance of inward reception and outward imposition—'the sensory world returns to me what I lent to it, but what I have to lend originated in that sensory world'—in which memory associations play an important role in conditioning present perceptions.[59] As we have seen earlier, the Narrator's comment on the hidden associative riches of soap advertisements, anticipating his final understanding of the *moments bienheureux* when perceptions trigger involuntary memory, positions Proust squarely in the same territory. More generally, the novel's representation of the world is not a description of reality but an evocation of the unique phenomenal world of the Narrator. Richard's phenomenological reading attempts to reconstruct the characteristics of this world by drawing together perceptions, memory, and imagination in search of the dominant attitudes and associations regarding each of its elements. The sea, for example, is associated with wild strength and agile physiology (notwithstanding the fact that beach resorts on the English Channel form the Narrator's sole maritime experience): waves come 'one after the other, like divers from a board'; the sea in Elstir's paintings is compared by the Narrator to 'a swift and spirited animal' tossing sailors like a rodeo horse; even the individual lexical items—'power', 'burst', 'throw'—contribute to a merged depiction that tells us as much about the Narrator, his confined and convention-bound city life, say, or his attraction to the physicality of the Balbec beach girls, as it does about its ostensible subject-matter.[60] Phenomenological Proust also brings us into contact with recent approaches wedding the philosophical discipline to cognitive science. David Herman offers one such interpretation, arguing that we are wrong to think of modernist fiction like Proust's in terms of an 'inward turn' away from the outside world and into the private sphere of the mind. Rather, he suggests, Proust, Woolf, Joyce, and others present us with minds so embedded within the environments they perceive, and so closely entwined with their physical and social interactions in that environment, that the very distinction between mind and world is dissolved into an all-encompassing *Umwelt*, the lived world as it presents itself to the individual's sensorimotor repertoire.[61]

We shall return to Proust and phenomenology in the fourth chapter, when we examine in greater detail the relationship between his model of the mind and that espoused by Sartre's *Nausea*. Let us leave philosophies of consciousness for now, though, and turn to psychoanalysis, the last great interpretative system of the mind that we will examine here. Proust, it has been established, had no knowledge of Freud's work while he was writing, although he was subject to many of the same cultural influences, and may conceivably have encountered Freud-inspired ideas towards the end of his life as they began to enter the French intellectual *zeitgeist*.[62] Despite the lack of direct contact, it's inarguable that Proust is in tune with Freud on many aspects of mental life. Bowie lists ten areas of common interest between them, including infant sexuality, sadism and masochism, jealousy, homosexuality, dream analysis, theories of consciousness and the unconscious, the 'accidental' emergence of the unconscious in slips and mannerisms, and the role of free association.[63] (Tadié adds a few more, among them jokes, mourning, and adult-child relationships in his own study of the 'consanguinity of minds' between the two men.)[64] Proust's mind does comprise conscious and unconscious parts, with the latter, as in Freud, figured as a vast realm which both stores memories and motivates our actions for reasons unknown to us. Proust's Narrator uses metaphors of things buried underground or in the depths of the sea to describe from where the findings of involuntary memory emerge (*RTP*, I, 45; trans. I, 48; *RTP*, II, 821; trans. III, 531). He searches for insights into his own mind from the interpretation of symbolic dreams (*RTP*, I, 618–19; trans. II, 205), or speculates with hindsight on a motive that may have been 'unconsciously determining' of his actions.[65] Reflecting on such phenomena, he suggests that unconscious root causes may often lie behind our conscious ideas and impressions:

> However clearly we identify our own impressions, as I then believed I saw clearly into my melancholia, we are unable to plumb their deeper meaning: as with those attacks of sickness that a doctor hears his patient describing, but which lead him to detect a deeper cause, unknown to the patient, so our impressions and ideas count only as symptoms.[66]

This representation of the mind suggests an affinity between Proust's principle of mental discontinuity and the Freudian division of the psyche. Proustian multiplicity also finds an echo in psychoanalytic theory: as we saw in the Introduction, Freud's division of the psyche into consciousness and Unconscious, and even more the later partition into superego, ego and id, figure these various faculties as semi-autonomous within the mind. The id, for instance, 'cannot say what it wants' while the ego 'feels itself hated and persecuted by the super-ego'.[67] Proust's *petits personnages intérieurs* act in a similar way, pursuing their own goals, often in conflict with or ignorance of one another. Here, for instance, is the Narrator's indecisiveness on whether he will get down to work posed as an inner debate between selves: 'This one of my selves had kept its scruples and lost its memory. The other self, the one which had conceived his work, on the other hand still remembered'.[68] More Freudian still is the account of the quasi-independent workings of the Narrator's unconscious mind which reconstitute Albertine's phrase, 'smash the pot' without his conscious knowledge:

> But as she talked, my mind was still pursuing, in the waking, creative sleep of the unconscious (a sleep in which things which first passed us by unnoticed now take full shape, in which our sleeping hands grasp the key to secrets hitherto sought in vain), the search for the meaning of the interrupted sentence whose intended conclusion I wished to discover.[69]

As in Freud, the unconscious mind is here associated with sexual taboos. (The phrase in question is a slang term for anal sex.) The central role of sexuality in mental life is the other major element, along with mental discontinuity and multiplicity, which Proust's mind shares with Freud's. Like Freud, Proust makes sexual desire the core of our mental life, and the driving force behind consciously and unconsciously motivated actions. Not only is sexuality given striking prominence for an early-twentieth-century text, it is explored in manifold forms, including such forbidden areas as childhood sexuality, male and female homosexuality, and sado-masochism. In a particularly Freudian move, Proust even draws comparisons between the adult's desire for his lover and the child's for his mother:

> What I experienced with Albertine on those evenings was not the calming effect of my mother's kiss at Combray, but on the contrary, the anguish of the evenings when my mother said good-night to me only hurriedly, or worse, did not come up to my room at all, whether she was cross with me or kept downstairs by guests. That anguish, not its transposition into love, but the anguish itself, which had once been hived off to love, assigned

> to that single passion when the division, the specialization of the passions had taken place, now seemed to spread again over them all, to have returned to its undifferentiated state, as if all my feelings, which trembled at being unable to keep Albertine next to my bed as a mistress, a sister, a daughter all at once, and as a mother whose good-night kiss I was beginning, in childish fashion, to need once more, had begun to coalesce again, to become one in the premature evening of my life, which promised to be no longer than a winter's day. But though I suffered the anguish of my childhood, the changed being who now inspired it, my different feelings about her, the very changes in my own character made it impossible to seek peace from Albertine as I had from my mother.[70]

The possible link between the Narrator's childhood relationship with his mother and his adult sexual relationships is of prime importance to every psychoanalytic study of Proust, of which there were many over the course of the century that followed. Just as this passage appears to invite interpretation of the Narrator's adult sexuality in terms of his formative childhood experiences—Serge Doubrovsky takes it as licence to discuss a hybrid character, 'Albertine-maman'[71]—so psychoanalytic critics have been keen to discover the key to the Narrator's psyche in his childhood reminiscence. Leo Bersani's Freud-inflected study examines the Narrator's dependence on his mother for his own self-image, which the Narrator himself admits, declaring at the end of the novel, 'I noticed that in matters of self-examination, I looked at things from the same point of view as she did'.[72] While Bersani expands this idea to explore the Narrator's 'persistent and fundamental need to merge with a source of strength outside of himself', other psychoanalytic critics fixate on the maternal relationship.[73] Doubrovsky and Kristeva both make the childhood-restoring *petite madeleine* a symbol of the Narrator's mother, supporting this principally by the fact that it is she who offers it to him, along with the *tisane* to drink with it.[74] Both critics proceed to create many-layered interpretative and associative constructs, with Kristeva seeing in the Narrator's consumption of the madeleine hidden references to breast-feeding, and thence to fellatio, and perhaps to an alleged gay practice of eating bread soaked in urine, while Doubrovsky notes linguistic similarities between the madeleine episode and the masturbation scene in *Contre Sainte Beuve* (*Against Sainte Beuve*), and concludes that the Narrator's repressed wish to be rid of his mother is expressed symbolically as both defecating and ejaculating her.[75] These extrapolations are admittedly complemented by other, more sober delvings in the two studies, but they do demonstrate a particular weakness of psychoanalytic criticism, namely that the concept of Freudian repression encourages critical interpretations that bear little relation to what the text, on its 'surface level', declares to be the case. The Narrator's expressed love for his mother can be accepted at face value, or, as the critic desires, be interpreted as a self-deluding cover for repressed feelings with the very opposite signification. Freud's own interpretative methods, which might replace a dream image with a word, then pun on this word to discover the hidden meaning of the image, take him far from the original sense of his material, and similarly read with or against the grain as the interpreter wishes. Freud could at least allege corroborating feedback or salutary effects on his patients' state of mind to support his readings; psychoanalysis in literary criticism has no such limiting factors to its interpretations.

Given that psychoanalysis empowers the critic to declare what the text is 'really' about on the slender evidence afforded by linguistic slips and ambiguous symbols, it's hard to take issue with interpretations we might disagree with on grounds other than simple incredulity. However, if, rather than reading Proust through a Freudian framework, we take the model of the mind elaborated by Proust as our guide to an evaluation of psychoanalytic approaches, we find justification for a certain scepticism. In its broad outlines, the opening of 'Combray' might seem promising territory for a Freudian reading, given that it concerns the recovery of buried memories and a boyhood marked by anxious possessiveness towards the mother. Beyond this caricature, however, it reveals itself as somewhat ill-fitting to a psychoanalytic narrative. The Narrator's childhood consists of a large number of pleasant or neutral memories, plus one traumatic memory, this being the anxious wait for his mother's good-night kiss. Proust's representation of memory, in which the anodyne memories are banished to the 'void' of the unconscious, while the painful one continues to haunt his consciousness, is the opposite of what would be expected according to Freud's theory of repression. For Freud, repression is the process by which consciousness defends itself by sealing traumatic memories away within the Unconscious; indeed, Freud declares that it is by virtue of this process that the unconscious mind comes into existence, and thus considers repression as the 'cornerstone' of his theory.[76] Proust's representation is, however, in tune with the theories of modern psychology, which is dubious about the existence of Freudian repression: in an overview of sixty years of psychological research into the topic, David S. Holmes cites findings that, 'emotionally intense experiences were more likely to be recalled than less intense experiences, regardless of whether they were pleasant or unpleasant'.[77]

The contents of the Narrator's traumatic memory also provide a poor foundation for those who would explicate his inner life in terms of a supposed Œdipus complex. The Freudian psychodrama has three protagonists, with the role of the father as sexual rival to the son taking at least equal importance to that of the mother. In the bedtime drama itself, the Narrator's father does not stand as an obstacle between the son and his mother's affection, but rather the facilitator. Overruling his wife's concerns about indulging the son's emotional fragility, he encourages her to spend the night in the Narrator's room:

> You can see the boy is upset, he seems very sad; look, we're not brutes! You'll end by making him ill, and that won't do us much good! There are two beds in his room; go ahead and tell Françoise to prepare the big one for you and sleep with him tonight.[78]

Hillenaar notes that psychoanalytic criticism tends to sideline analysis of the father, 'reduced to an absence or relegated to the domain of art and creativity', rather than highlighting his failure to fit the Œdipal template.[79] We might similarly note the divergence from Freudian expectations posed by the grandmother's displacement of the mother as the emotional focus of the Narrator's family relationships for much of the novel. While the passage quoted earlier on the adult Narrator's need for a good-night kiss from Albertine does indeed offer the interpretation that his adult sexuality is strongly marked by his childhood relationship to his mother, it is not unequivocal: It might equally well be seen as emphasizing the *differences* between maternal and sexual relationships as drawing connections between them.

The representation of memory also fails to harmonize entirely with the corresponding elements of Freud's theories. For Proust, memories from the unconscious mind come spontaneously, coaxed to the surface in a *moment bienheureux* that has little in common with the slow and sometimes painful process of reconstruction that is the psychoanalytic method. Certainly these memories are previously lost to consciousness, but there is no endorsement in Proust of Freud's distinction between the 'preconscious' store-room into which consciousness can delve at will and the sealed Unconscious, the contents of which can only be extrapolated indirectly. Malcolm Bowie dubs Proust's mind 'the introspective model, in which the mind is transparent from level to level and permeable part by part', in contrast to the Freudian model, 'in which part is radically extrinsic to part and in which barriers and opacities may occasionally be attenuated but never removed'.[80] Equally, unconscious reasons for the Narrator's actions can be uncovered by a process of introspection, which, in cool hindsight, reaches the well-springs of his motivation without the need to bypass an internal censor. Just as the discontinuity of the Narrator's experience of time is tempered by the connection finally wrought by memory and art, so the discontinuity of the self stops short of Freud's rigid compartmentalization: Proust's 'steep slope of introspection' leads to the possibility of a comprehensive understanding of our own minds, rather than ending at the locked door beyond which only the psychoanalyst's interpretations can speculate.[81]

*

Proust lays down foundations for twentieth-century European literature's exploration of the mind through his focus on memory, perception, and emotion (with its counterpart, intellect), and through his understanding of mental life as hallmarked by discontinuity, multiplicity, and temporality. As we have seen, the ideas on consciousness expressed by Proust's Narrator are far from systematic. Rather, they are revised and developed as the Narrator's experience of life grows, creating a profusion of viewpoints which are not always in harmony, and which receives a fundamental reassessment at the novel's denouement with the Narrator's belated appreciation of an underlying continuity of the self. Proust's version of the mind has little time for non-materialist conceptions of consciousness, and has less in common with Bergson's philosophy of mind than has been suggested. His representation does have affinities with the view of consciousness suggested by phenomenology, as well as the psychoanalytic model, although significant differences from this latter cast doubt on the wholesale co-opting of Proust's vision by psychoanalytic literary criticism seen in recent decades. In the third chapter of this book, when we come to explore writing that explicitly aligns itself with elements of Freudian theory in André Breton's *Mad Love*, the distance at which Proust stands from Freud's model will become more apparent in the comparison. What emerges from Proust's novel, despite its profusion and change, is a detailed portrait of a mind looking outward into the world and inward into its own workings. We see consciousness in all its states of alertness, all its colours of emotion, and all its reactions to different stimuli, from art to alcohol. We see the processes by which the mind performs each of the functions of which it is capable, reasoning and rationalizing, perceiving and deluding, recalling and imagining, judging critically and being swept away. We see the experience of living through time, on the small scale of moments and the large scale of a lifetime. And in all of this, Proust works to present us with the unique experience of a particular consciousness, while at the same time extrapolating general laws which the reader is invited to compare with evidence from their own introspection. The model which results is prescient of later findings in psychology, and proves to be, in some aspects, a surer guide to the reality of mental life than the vision of the mind developed contemporaneously by psychoanalysis. Through the century that followed, *In Search of Lost Time* offered any French author venturing into the psychological novel an invitation to dialogue or a challenge to combat. Either way, a response was required, and we shall see in the chapters to come what Proust's successors came up with.

Notes

1. 'Si j'imaginais toujours autour de la femme que j'aimais, les lieux que je désirais le plus alors, si j'eusse voulu que ce fût elle qui me les fît visiter, qui m'ouvrît l'accès d'un monde inconnu, ce n'était pas par le hasard d'une simple association de pensée; non, c'est que mes rêves de voyage et d'amour n'étaient que des moments—que je sépare artificiellement aujourd'hui comme si je pratiquais des sections à des hauteurs différentes d'un jet d'eau irisé et en apparence immobile—dans un même et infléchissable jaillissement de toutes les forces de ma vie', *RTP*, I, 86; trans. I, 89. Full publication details of text and translation are given in the first footnote to the Introduction.
2. 'La vie consciente se présente sous un double aspect, selon qu'on l'aperçoit directement ou par réfraction à travers l'espace.—Considérés en eux-mêmes, les états de conscience profonds n'ont aucun rapport avec la quantité; ils sont qualité pure; ils se mêlent de telle manière qu'on ne saurait dire s'ils sont un ou plusieurs, ni même les examiner à ce point de vue sans les dénaturer aussitôt. La durée qu'ils créent ainsi est

une durée dont les moments ne constituent pas une multiplicité numérique', Bergson, *Essai sur les données immédiates de la conscience*, p. 102.

3. 'Roman bergsonien'; 'une suite de "Romans de l'Inconscient"'. Marcel Proust, Interview with Élie-Joseph Bois, 'Variétés littéraires: *A la recherche du temps perdu*', *Le Temps*, 13 November 1913, p. 4, reprinted in Marcel Proust, *Choix de lettres*, ed. by Philip Kolb (Paris: Plon, 1965), p. 287.
4. 'C'était visiblement la première fois qu'ils venaient là, on avait dû leur indiquer l'endroit et ils semblaient partagés entre le désir, la tentation et une extrême frousse. L'un des deux—un beau jeune homme—répétait toutes les deux minutes à l'autre avec un sourire mi-interrogateur, mi-destiné à persuader: "Quoi! Après tout on s'en fiche?" Mais il avait beau vouloir dire par là qu'après tout on se fichait des conséquences, il est probable qu'il ne s'en fichait pas tant que cela car cette parole n'était suivie d'aucun mouvement pour entrer mais d'un nouveau regard vers l'autre, suivi du même sourire et du même *après tout on s'en fiche.* C'était, ce *après tout on s'en fiche*, un exemplaire entre mille de ce magnifique langage, si différent de celui que nous parlons d'habitude, et où l'émotion fait dévier ce que nous voulions dire et épanouir à la place une phrase toute autre, émergée d'un lac inconnu où vivent ces expressions sans rapport avec la pensée et qui par cela même la révèlent', *RTP*, IV, 401; trans. VI, 130–1.
5. See, for example, Jerry Aline Flieger, 'Proust, Freud and the Art of Forgetting', *SubStance*, 29 (1981), pp. 66–82 (p. 67). Jean-Yves Tadié's *Le Lac Inconnu: Entre Proust et Freud* (Paris: Gallimard, 2012) takes the image as the starting point for a general exploration of parallels between the novelist and psychoanalyst.
6. Sigmund Freud, *An Autobiographical Study*, Standard edn., vol. 20, pp. 7–70 (pp. 46–47).
7. Leo Bersani, *Marcel Proust: The Fictions of Life and Art* (Oxford: Oxford University Press, 1965), pp. 106–7.
8. 'Or, comme le moi vit incessamment en pensant une quantité de choses, qu'il n'est que la pensée de ces choses, quand par hasard au lieu d'avoir devant lui ces choses, il pense tout d'un coup à soi-même, il ne trouve qu'un appareil vide, quelque chose qu'il ne connaît pas, auquel pour lui donner quelque réalité il ajoute le souvenir d'une figure aperçue dans la glace. Ce drôle de sourire, ces moustaches inégales, c'est cela qui disparaîtra de la surface de la terre. Quand je me tuerais dans cinq ans, ce serait fini pour moi de pouvoir penser toutes ces choses qui défilaient sans cesse dans mon esprit. Je ne serais plus sur la surface de la terre et je n'y reviendrais jamais, ma pensée s'arrêterait pour toujours. Et mon moi me parut encore plus nul, de le voir déjà comme quelque chose qui n'existe plus', *Albertine disparue*, IV, 1059–60. These lines appeared in some published versions of *La Fugitive*, but are omitted from current editions of *Albertine disparue* and Collier's translation, and relegated to the 'notes et variantes' of the Pléiade.
9. 'La conscience s'est purifiée, elle est claire comme un grand vent, il n'y a plus rien en elle, sauf un mouvement pour se fuir, un glissement hors de soi; si, par impossible, vous entriez "dans" une conscience, vous seriez saisi par un tourbillon et rejeté au-dehors, près de l'arbre, en pleine poussière, car la conscience n'a pas de "dedans"; elle n'est rien que le dehors d'elle-même et c'est cette fuite absolue, ce refus d'être substance qui la constituent comme une conscience', Jean-Paul Sartre, 'Une Idée fondamentale de la phénoménologie de Husserl: l'intentionnalité', in *Critiques littéraires (Situations* I) (Paris: Gallimard, 1947), pp. 29–32 (p. 30).
10. 'Vide total', Jean-Paul Sartre, *L'Être et le Néant: essai d'ontologie phénoménoloique* (Paris: Gallimard, 1943), p. 23.
11. 'Moins un texte communicant une pensée qu'une sorte d'instrument pour penser', Vincent Descombes, *Proust: philosophie du roman* (Paris: Minuit, 1987), p. 292.
12. 'Seul, quelquefois, je sentais affluer du fond de moi quelqu'une de ces impressions qui me donnaient un bien-être délicieux. Mais dès que j'étais avec quelqu'un, dès que je parlais à un ami, mon esprit faisait volte-face, c'était vers cet interlocuteur et non vers moi-même qu'il dirigeait ses pensées et quand elles suivaient ce sens inverse, elles ne me procuraient aucun plaisir. Une fois que j'avais quitté Saint-Loup, je mettais, à l'aide de mots, une sorte d'ordre dans les minutes confuses que j'avais passées avec lui; je me disais que j'avais un bon ami, qu'un bon ami est une chose rare et je goûtais, à me sentir entouré de biens difficiles à acquérir, ce qui était justement l'opposé du plaisir qui m'était naturel, l'opposé du plaisir d'avoir extrait de moi-même et amené à la lumière quelque chose qui y était caché dans la pénombre. Si j'avais passé deux ou trois heures à causer avec Robert de Saint-Loup et qu'il eût admiré ce que je lui avais dit, j'éprouvais une sorte de remords, de regret, de fatigues de ne pas être resté seul et prêt enfin à travailler', *RTP*, II, 95; trans. II, 315–16.
13. Similar ideas are expressed, for instance, in *RTP*, IV, 48, 146 (trans. V, 433), and *RTP*, IV, 489–93 (trans. VI, 219–23).
14. Examples of each can be found as follows: on reason, *RTP*, II, 593 (trans. III, 293); on imagination, *RTP*, II, 678 (trans. III, 381–2); on language, *RTP*, III, 876–7 (trans. V, 346–47); on madness, *RTP*, IV, 440–1 (trans. VI, 169–70); on trauma, *RTP*, IV, 294 (trans. VI, 22); on moral judgement, *RTP*, II, 585 (trans. III, 285); on free will, *RTP*, II, 179 (trans. II, 402); on the soul, *RTP*, IV, 93 (trans. V, 478).
15. 'Mille vases clos dont chacun serait rempli de choses d'une couleur, d'une odeur, d'une température absolument différentes', *RTP*, IV, 448; trans. VI, 178.

16. 'Ne peuvent jamais reconstituer le temps, ni lui donner ce qui n'est peut-être pas de sa nature d'avoir, une continuité', Georges Poulet, *L'Espace proustien* (Paris: Gallimard, 1982), p. 88.
17. 'Néant';'des souvenirs morts', *RTP*, III, 653; trans. V, 131. The Hudimesnil episode occurs in *RTP*, II, 76–77; trans. II, 297.
18. 'À partir d'un certain âge nos souvenirs sont tellement entre-croisés les uns sur les autres que la chose à laquelle on pense, le livre qu'on lit n'a presque plus d'importance. On a mis de soi-même partout, tout est fécond, tout est dangereux, et on peut faire d'aussi précieuses découvertes que dans les *Pensées* de Pascal dans une réclame pour un savon', *RTP*, IV, 124; trans. V, 508.
19. The Narrator refers to 'the translucent alabaster of our memories, whose colour we cannot show to others as only we can see it so that we can truthfully say to them that they cannot imagine the past, that it was nothing like anything they have seen', ('cet albâtre translucide de nos souvenirs, duquel nous sommes incapables de montrer la couleur qu'il n'y a que nous qui voyons, ce qui nous permet de dire véridiquement aux autres, au sujet de ces choses passées, qu'ils n'en peuvent avoir une idée, que cela ne ressemble pas à ce qu'ils ont vu'), *RTP*, III, 788; trans. V, 262.
20. 'Alors, en pensant à tous les événements qui se plaçaient forcément entre l'instant où je les avais entendus et la matinée Guermantes, je fus effrayé de penser que c'était bien cette sonnette qui tintait encore en moi, sans que je pusse rien changer aux criaillements de son grelot, puisque, ne me rappelant plus bien comment ils s'éteignaient, pour le réapprendre, pour bien l'écouter, je dus m'efforcer de ne plus entendre le son des conversations que les masques tenaient autour de moi. Pour tâcher de l'entendre de plus près, c'est en moi-même que j'étais obligé de redescendre. C'est donc que ce tintement y était toujours et aussi, entre lui et l'instant présent, tout ce passé indéfiniment déroulé que je ne savais pas que je portais. Quand il avait tinté j'existais déjà et depuis, pour que j'entendisse encore ce tintement, il fallait qu'il n'y eût pas eu discontinuité, que je n'eusse pas un instant pris de repos, cessé d'exister, de penser, d'avoir conscience de moi, puisque cet instant ancien tenait encore à moi, que je pouvais encore le retrouver, retourner jusqu'à lui, rien qu'en descendant plus profondément en moi', (*RTP*, IV, 623–4; trans. 356).
21. 'Un moi individuel identique et permanent';'ces nouveaux moi qui devraient porter un autre nom que le précédent', *RTP*, IV, 173–4; trans. V, 558–9.
22. 'Petits personnages intérieurs', *RTP*, III, 522; trans. V, 6.
23. 'Un simple appareil enregistreur qui prend des instantanés', *RTP*, II, 813; trans. III, 524.
24. 'Le témoignage des sens est lui aussi une opération de l'esprit où la conviction crée l'évidence', *RTP*, III, 694; trans. V, 171.
25. 'Nous ne connaissons vraiment que ce qui est nouveau, ce qui introduit brusquement dans notre sensibilité un changement de ton qui nous frappe, ce à quoi l'habitude n'a pas encore substitué ses pâles fac-similés', *RTP*, IV, 110; trans. V, 495.
26. 'La nature telle qu'elle est';'Les noms qui désignent les choses répondent toujours à une notion de l'intelligence, étrangère à nos impressions véritables et qui nous force à éliminer d'elles tout ce qui ne rapporte pas à cette notion', *RTP*, II, 191; trans. II, 415. Christopher Prendergast explores the former phrase in detail, examining the ambiguity in the formulation 'we perceive nature as it is, poetically' ('l'on voit la nature telle qu'elle est poétiquement') to explore the relationship between art and truth in Proust. Christopher Prendergast, *Mirages and Mad Beliefs: Proust the Skeptic* (Princeton, NJ: Princeton University Press, 2013), pp. 118–29.
27. Jean-Pierre Richard, *Proust et le monde sensible* (Paris: Seuil, 1974), p. 7.
28. Joshua Landy, *Philosophy as Fiction: Self, Deception, and Knowledge in Proust* (Oxford: Oxford University Press, 2004), pp. 65–8.
29. 'Sous l'apparence de la femme, c'est à ces forces invisibles dont elle est accessoirement accompagnée que nous nous adressons comme à d'obscures divinités', *RTP*, III, 511; trans, IV, 519.
30. 'Oscillation du pendule', *RTP*, IV, 9; trans. V, 393.
31. 'Ce que j'avais cru n'être rien pour moi, c'était tout simplement toute ma vie. Comme on s'ignore', *RTP*, IV, 3; trans. V, 387.
32. 'J'avais cru bien connaître le fond de mon cœur. Mais notre intelligence, si grande soit-elle, ne peut apercevoir les éléments qui le composent et qui restent insoupçonnés tant que, de l'état volatil où ils subsistent la plupart du temps, un phénomène capable de les isoler ne leur a pas fait subir un commencement de solidification. Je m'étais trompé en croyant voir clair dans mon cœur. Mais cette connaissance que ne m'avaient pas donnée les plus fines perceptions de l'esprit venait de m'être apportée, dure, éclatante, étrange, comme un sel cristallisé par la brusque réaction de la douleur', *RTP*, IV, 4; trans. V, 388.
33. 'Ce n'est que pendant que nous souffrons que nos pensées en quelque sorte agitées de mouvements perpétuels et changeants font monter comme dans une tempête, à un niveau d'où nous pouvons les voir, toute cette immensité réglée par des lois, sur laquelle, postés à une fenêtre mal placée, nous n'avons pas vue, car le calme du bonheur la laisse unie et à un niveau trop bas', *RTP*, IV, 475; trans. VI, 205.
34. Landy, *Philosophy as Fiction*, pp. 85–100.

35. 'Mais pour ma raison, à qui la seule explication de certaines mauvaises humeurs, de certaines attitudes avait paru, avant que je sache rien, le projet formé par elle d'un départ définitif, il était difficile de croire que, maintenant que ce départ s'était produit, il n'était qu'une simulation. Je dis pour ma raison, non pour moi. L'hypothèse de la simulation me devenait d'autant plus nécessaire qu'elle était plus improbable et gagnait en force ce qu'elle perdait en vraisemblance', *RTP*, IV, 18; trans. V, 401–2.
36. Martha Nussbaum, *Love's Knowledge: Essays on Philosophy and Literature* (Oxford: Oxford University Press, 1990), pp. 261–85.
37. Edward J. Hughes, *Marcel Proust: A Study in the Quality of Awareness* (Cambridge: Cambridge University Press, 1983), pp. 185–9. Proust refers to the girls as 'la bande zoophytique des jeunes filles' in *RTP*, II, 210; trans. II, 434.
38. 'Ce que nous croyons notre amour, notre jalousie, n'est pas une même passion continue, indivisible. Ils se composent d'une infinité d'amours successifs, de jalousies différentes et qui sont éphémères, mais par leur multitude ininterrompue donnent l'impression de la continuité, l'illusion de l'unité', *RTP*, I, 366; trans. I, 373–4.
39. 'Le peintre ridicule et pervers'; 'cet homme de génie, ce sage, ce solitaire, ce philosophe', *RTP*, II, 218; trans. II, 441.
40. 'Innombrables et humbles moi qui nous composent', RTP, IV, 14; trans. V, 398.
41. 'Disposés sur toute la hauteur de nos années pendant lesquelles nous n'avons pas cessé de changer, fût-ce seulement de rêve ou de pensée', *RTP*, IV, 448–9; trans. VI, 448.
42. 'Jamais le récit proustien ne s'arrête sur un objet ou un spectacle sans que cette station corresponde à un arrêt contemplatif du héros lui-même (Swann dans *Un amour de Swann*, Marcel partout ailleurs), et donc jamais le morceau descriptif ne s'évade de la temporalité de l'histoire', Gérard Genette, *Figures* III (Paris: Seuil, 1972), p. 134.
43. 'Les nerfs tout entrecroisés les uns dans les autres', *RTP*, III, 699; trans. V, 176.
44. 'Cette impression, que je me rappelle avoir éprouvée ce jour-là pour la première fois, du vide, de la suppression en moi de toute une portion de mes associations d'idées, qu'éprouve un homme dont une artère cérébrale depuis longtemps usée s'est rompue et chez lequel toute une partie de la mémoire est abolie ou paralysée', *RTP*, IV, 172; trans. V, 557.
45. 'Mémoire involontaire des membres', *RTP*, IV, 277; trans. VI, 5.
46. 'Fait allusion dans le monde moral à une maladie du corps', letter dated October 1912 to Eugène Fasquelle, in Proust, *Correspondance*, ed. by Philip Kolb, 21 vols. (Paris: Plon, 1970–1993), XI, p. 257.
47. 'Congestion du cerveau', *RTP*, II, 630; trans. III, 332.
48. 'Dans le cerveau des gens des altérations tout à fait pareilles à celles qu'on remarque dans la matière inanimée', *RTP*, IV, 294; trans. VI, 22.
49. 'Ainsi le jeu des différentes lois psychologiques s'arrange à compenser dans la floraison de l'espèce humaine tout ce qui dans un sens ou dans l'autre, amènerait par la pléthore ou la raréfaction son anéantissement. Ainsi en est-il chez les fleurs où une même sagesse, mise en évidence par Darwin, règle les modes de fécondation en les opposant successivement les uns aux autres', *RTP*, IV, 360; trans. VI, 89. The reference is to Darwin's 1876 study, *The Effects of Cross and Self Fertilization in the Vegetable Kingdom*.
50. 'J'ai le regret d'être ici en contradiction avec un admirable philosophe, le grand Bergson. Et, parmi mes contradictions, ajouter ceci: il est vrai que M. Bergson prétend que la conscience déborde le corps et s'étend au-delà; et certes, dans le sens où l'on se souvient, où l'on pense aux philosophes, etc., cela est évident. Mais M. Bergson ne l'entend pas ainsi. Selon lui, l'âme, s'étendant hors du cerveau, peut et doit lui survivre. Or cette conscience, chaque ébranlement cérébral l'altère; un simple évanouissement l'annihile. Comment croire qu'après la mort elle subsistera?' Marcel Proust, *Cahiers 1 à 75 de la Bibliothèque Nationale de France*, ed. by B. Brun and others, 75 vols (Turnhout: Brepols, 2008), LIX, p. 17.
51. See Joyce Megay, *Bergson et Proust: essai de la mise au point de la question de l'influence de Bergson sur Proust* (Paris: Vrin, 1976).
52. 'Se succèdent sans se distinguer'; 'un développement organique qui n'est pourtant pas une quantité croissante', Bergson, *Essai sur les données immédiates de la conscience*, pp. 170–1.
53. 'Un édifice occupant, si l'on peut dire, un espace à quatre dimensions—la quatrième étant celle du Temps', *RTP*, I, 60; trans. I, 64.
54. 'Du temps spatialisé, juxtaposé', Poulet, *L'Espace proustien*, p. 136.
55. In this regard, A. E. Pilkington points out that 'while both [Bergson and Proust] draw a distinction between two radically different modes of memory, they do not make the same distinction'. Bergson's 'pure memory' is not quite the same as Proust's involuntary memory, and his 'habit memory' has nothing in common with voluntary memory. A. E. Pilkington, *Bergson and His Influence: A Reassessment* (Cambridge: Cambridge University Press, 1976).
56. E. Casey, 'Literary Description and the Phenomenological Method', *Yale French Studies*, 61 (1981), pp. 176–201.
57. 'Personne n'a été plus loin que Proust dans la fixation des rapports du visible et de l'invisible, dans la description d'une idée qui n'est pas le contraire du sensible, qui en est la doublure et la profondeur', Maurice Merleau-Ponty, *Le Visible et l'invisible* (Paris: Gallimard, 1964), p. 195.

58. Julia Kristeva, *Le Temps sensible: Proust et l'expérience littéraire* (Paris: Gallimard, 1994), p. 470.
59. 'Le sensible me rend ce que je lui ai prêté, mais c'est de lui que je le tenais', Maurice Merleau-Ponty, *Phénoménologie de la perception* (Paris: Gallimard, 1945), p. 248.
60. 'L'un après l'autre comme des sauteurs sur un tremplin'; 'un animal fougueux et rapide'; 'force', 'éclater', 'jeter', *RTP*, II, pp. 33, 193; trans., II, 251, 416. Richard's study explores these aspects of the sea in Proust under the category of 'le surgi' ('surging'), and goes on to consider other aspects related to 'le naissant' (nascent) and 'l'écumeux' (foaming). Richard, *Proust et le monde sensible*, pp. 104–14.
61. David Herman, '1880–1945: Reminding Modernism', in *The Emergence of Mind: Representations of Consciousness in Narrative Discourse in English*, ed. by David Herman (Lincoln, NE: University of Nebraska Press, 2014), pp. 243–72.
62. A somewhat controversial exploration of possible influences on Proust from pre-Freudian psychology, including theories of somnambulism and the divided self, is offered by Edward Bizub in his *Proust et le moi divisé: La Recherche: creuset de la psychologie expérimentale (1874–1914)* (Paris: Droz, 2006). Joshua Landy debates the case in 'Proust among the Psychologists', *Philosophy and Literature*, 35 (2011), pp. 375–87.
63. Malcolm Bowie, *Freud, Proust and Lacan: Theory as Fiction* (Cambridge: Cambridge University Press, 1987), pp. 68–9.
64. 'Consanguinité des esprits', Jean-Yves Tadié, *Le Lac inconnu: entre Proust et Freud* (Paris: Gallimard, 2012), p. 12.
65. 'Inconsciemment déterminante', *RTP*, III, 10; trans. IV, 12.
66. 'Nous avons beau voir clair dans nos impressions, comme je crus alors voir clair dans la raison de ma mélancolie, nous ne savons pas remonter jusqu'à leur signification plus éloignée. Comme ces malaises dont le médecin écoute son malade lui raconter l'histoire et à l'aide desquels il remonte à une cause plus profonde, ignorée du patient, de même nos impressions, nos idées, n'ont qu'une valeur de symptômes', *RTP*, IV, 141; trans. V, 525.
67. See especially Freud's 1923 essay, 'The Ego and the Id', *Standard Edition*, XIX, pp. 1–66.
68. 'Ce moi-là en moi avait gardé ses scrupules et perdu sa mémoire. L'autre moi, celui qui avait conçu son œuvre, en revanche se souvenait', *RTP*, IV, 617; trans. VI, 349–50.
69. 'Pendant qu'elle me parlait, se poursuivait en moi, dans le sommeil fort vivant et créateur de l'inconscient (sommeil où achèvent de se graver les choses qui nous effleurèrent seulement, où les mains endormies se saisissent de la clef qui ouvre, vainement cherchée jusque-là), la recherche de ce qu'elle avait voulu dire par la phrase interrompue dont j'aurais voulu savoir quelle eût été la fin', *RTP*, III, 842; trans. V, 313.
70. 'Ce n'était plus l'apaisement du baiser de ma mère à Combray, que j'éprouvais auprès d'Albertine, ces soirs-là, mais, au contraire, l'angoisse de ceux où ma mère me disait à peine bonsoir, ou même ne montait pas dans ma chambre, soit qu'elle fût fâchée contre moi ou retenue par des invités. Cette angoisse—non pas seulement sa transposition dans l'amour—non, cette angoisse elle-même qui s'était un temps spécialisée dans l'amour, qui avait été affectée à lui seul quand le partage, la division des passions s'était opérée, maintenant semblait de nouveau s'étendre à toutes, redevenue indivise de même que dans mon enfance, comme si tous mes sentiments, qui tremblaient de ne pouvoir garder Albertine auprès de mon lit à la fois comme une maîtresse, comme une sœur, comme une fille, comme une mère aussi, du bonsoir quotidien de laquelle je recommençais à éprouver le puéril besoin, avaient commencé de se rassembler, de s'unifier dans le soir prématuré de ma vie, qui semblait devoir être aussi brève qu'un jour d'hiver. Mais si j'éprouvais l'angoisse de mon enfance, le changement de l'être qui me la faisait éprouver, la différence de sentiment qu'il m'inspirait, la transformation même de mon caractère, me rendaient impossible d'en réclamer l'apaisement à Albertine comme autrefois à ma mère', *RTP*, III, 618–19; trans. V, 98–99.
71. Serge Doubrovsky, *La Place de la Madeleine: écriture et fantasme chez Proust* (Paris: Mercure, 1974), p. 121.
72. 'Je m'apercevais que je me plaçais pour me juger au même point de vue qu'elle', *RTP*, IV, 509–10; trans. VI, 240.
73. Bersani, *Marcel Proust*, p. 34.
74. Doubrovsky, *La Place de la Madeleine*, p. 39; Kristeva, *Le Temps sensible*, p. 40. Suzanne Dow draws the same connection via Lacanian psychoanalysis in 'How to Begin a Novel: Proust's *A la recherche du temps perdu* and the Author-Reader Relation', *French Studies*, 63 (2009), 283–94.
75. Kristeva, *Le Temps sensible*, p. 43; Doubrovsky, *La Place de la Madeleine*, p. 49.
76. Freud, 'On the History of the Psycho-Analytic Movement', *Standard Edition*, XIV, pp. 7–66 (p. 16).
77. David S. Holmes, 'The Evidence for Repression: An Examination of Sixty Years of Research', in *Repression and Dissociation: Implications for Personality Theory, Psychopathology and Health*, ed. by Jerome L. Singer (Chicago: University of Chicago Press, 1990), pp. 85–102 (p. 87).
78. 'Tu vois bien que ce petit a du chagrin, il a l'air désolé, cet enfant; voyons, nous ne sommes pas des bourreaux! Quand tu l'auras rendu malade, tu seras bien avancée! Puisqu'il y a deux lits dans sa chambre, dis donc à Françoise de te préparer le grand lit et couche pour cette nuit auprès de lui' *RTP*, I, 36; trans. I, 39.
79. 'Réduit à une absence ou relégué dans le domaine de l'art et de la création', Henk Hillenaar, 'Proust et la psychanalyse', in *Proust Contemporain*, ed. by Sophie Bertho (Amsterdam: Rodopi, 1994), pp. 61–74 (p. 68).
80. Bowie, *Freud, Proust, Lacan*, p. 71
81. 'Pente abrupte d'introspection', *RTP*, IV, 48; trans. V, 433.

2

SOUL

Georges Bernanos and the Catholic Novel

The main author in the second chapter, Georges Bernanos (1888–1948), may be less familiar than some of the other writers in this book, but the view of the mind to which his work gives expression is one of the most widely shared conceptions of the mind during the period: a religiously inflected understanding of consciousness. Bernanos is a psychological novelist and essayist whose distinctive vision combines a strong Catholic faith with highly conservative politics. He views human life as a battleground between divine and satanic influence, with the apparent ascendancy of the latter leading to accusations of Manichaeism in his theological outlook. His eight novels all deal explicitly with religious themes, as the protagonists, who are very often priests, engage in sustained introspection as they wrestle with questions of good and evil. *Diary of a Country Priest* (*Journal d'un curé de campagne*) is his sixth novel, and the one that depicts in greatest detail the inner life of a man of faith. The unnamed protagonist, priest to a small village in north-eastern France, confides his troubles to a private diary as he struggles with suspicious and unwelcoming parishioners, and deals with his own wavering faith and deteriorating health. Notable incidents include the priest restoring the faith of the local Countess, who has turned away from God since the death of her son, as well as bringing stern spiritual guidance to the Countess's daughter, Mlle Chantal, who is consumed with bitterness towards her philandering father. The novel contrasts the priest's timidity and self-doubt with the divine power which works through him, which can bestow miraculous insight and authority when needed to rescue his parishioners from sin or unbelief.

Bernanos also stands here for a broader literary movement, the French Catholic novel, in its most notable flowering between the First and Second World Wars. It was in this period that Bernanos came to the public's attention, along with a number of other Christian writers, including the poet and playwright, Paul Claudel, and the novelists François Mauriac and Julien Green.[1] The cultural phenomenon of the Catholic novel in the early twentieth century is of particular interest, since it is the movement as a whole, rather than *Diary of a Country Priest* specifically, which sets its view of the mind, coherent but not homogenous, against competing secular ideas. It is, for instance, a different novel of Bernanos's, *Un mauvais rêve* (*A Bad Dream*, 1950), which gives us the closest engagement with the psychoanalytic model of mind. And it is Mauriac, rather than Bernanos, who is the author of the most unequivocal attack on Freudian psychotherapy in his 'Thérèse chez le docteur' ('Thérèse at the Doctor's', 1933), and who finds himself on the receiving end of the harshest criticisms from existentialist phenomenology in a devastating attack by Sartre.

The Catholic novel represents the cultural expression of a faith-based understanding of the mind which has been widely held in France throughout the period of our study, but which finds little sympathy from the other writers considered here. Proust, Breton, Sartre, Sarraute, and Darrieussecq are all either indifferent or hostile to religious belief, while Beckett's more thoughtful engagement is hardly an endorsement. Of the major non-literary influences that inform their work, only Bergson's philosophy holds any sympathy for faith: existentialism and Freudian psychoanalysis are overtly atheist in their approach, and the materialist model of contemporary science and 'neurophilosophy' which influences Darrieussecq creates problems for any concept of an immaterial soul. Without Bernanos and his fellow Catholic novelists, the theological viewpoint on the nature and workings of the mind would be almost entirely lacking from our cultural survey.

While faith infuses every text by Mauriac, Bernanos, and Green, none of the three writers was entirely comfortable with the label 'Catholic novelist'. Green found his homosexuality difficult to reconcile with his belief, and replayed the conflict between sexual desire and faith in many of his works. Mauriac objected that only three of his novels—*Les Anges noirs*, *Ce qui était perdu*, and *Le Nœud de vipères* (*The Dark Angels*, 1936; *That Which was Lost*, 1930; *The Knot of Vipers*, 1932)—truly deserved the label 'Catholic novel', as these were 'the only ones to be entirely based on Revelation'.[2] Like Green, Mauriac struggled to reconcile sexuality with Catholic teaching, complaining in 1928 that 'Christianity does not take full account of the flesh', and was viewed with suspicion by Catholic commentators, before a personal crisis and 'conversion' in 1929 led to more orthodox creativity.[3] Bernanos himself rejected the idea that the Catholic novelist should act as a mouthpiece for Church doctrine, declaring:

> Catholic writers cannot be part of the Church and its teachings, and the mistake made by a number of churchmen is to have tried to see in them docile and punctilious collaborators, as a teacher will occasionally have a pupil from the class take his place at the blackboard.[4]

Bernanos was not received uncritically by the Catholic establishment either, which was uneasy with the extent of the power accorded by the writer to Satan. According to Michael R. Tobin, some priests forbade their parishioners to read Bernanos's first novel, *Sous le soleil de Satan* (*Under Satan's Sun*, 1926), on the grounds that it was heretical.[5] We should thus not assume that the Catholic novelists' view of the mind will accord in all aspects with Church doctrine.[6] Nor can we take for granted that the views of the mind expressed in Bernanos's texts will be equally valid for Green and Mauriac. The existence of important differences between them is made clear by Bernanos's contemptuous description of Mauriac's work: 'It sweats carnal despair like damp on a tunnel wall'.[7] The mind's embodiment is for Mauriac an obstacle to salvation—his texts often manifest disgust for the sexual and corporeal—contrasting with Bernanos, whose novels stage demonstrations of incarnate faith, lived out through the body (as with the country priest's exclusive diet of bread and wine as his stomach cancer takes hold) as much as the mind. Nevertheless, there is much common ground between them on matters of mind and faith, which is often brought into relief by the distinctions drawn with other contemporary understandings of the mind.

How closely would the view of the mind expressed in these novels reflect that of their contemporary society? In the 1930s, well over 90 per cent of the French population were baptized Catholic, and a majority of children attended Mass, with many also attending catechism classes before being confirmed at the age of twelve.[8] Education too featured a strong religious presence: at the start of the century, nearly half the boys in secondary education attended Catholic institutions. Despite these influences, France isn't necessarily to be labelled a 'Catholic country' in this period. Since the Revolution, Republican regimes in France had espoused strict policies of *laïcité* (state-enforced secularism) that counter-acted Church influence on the population. Government anti-clericalism had softened considerably in the years following the First World War, but even then it is estimated that no more than a third of the adult population were regular church-goers, a fraction that declined to a quarter or even a fifth, in Maurice Larkin's estimate, by the time *Diary of a Country Priest* was published.[9] Marriages, christenings, and funerals would be the sole contact with formal Catholic worship for very many French people during this period, although this doesn't, of course, imply they were anti-clerical in their politics or atheist in their worldview: the number of people who would consider themselves religious believers is likely to be considerably higher than the number who actually attended church. With the addition of up to a million French Protestants, Christianity in 1930s France remained a significant social and cultural force. Mauriac's and Green's tentative, doubtful faith might well have more in common with typical French attitudes than the supernatural battle between good and evil which Bernanos depicts, but certainly the ideas shared by all three writers of an immaterial soul, divine creation, and external influences of good and evil would have broad currency at the time of writing, as, indeed, they continue to have in our own more secular century.

Let us then draw out the primary characteristics of the mind, as represented in *Diary of a Country Priest* and other Catholic novels of the period. If we begin with the most fundamental ontology of mind, we come first to the belief in a divinely created soul, which is separate from the body and will outlive it. The distinction between mind and soul is not always a clear one: the early Christian author Tertullian affirms 'that the mind coalesces with the soul,—not indeed as being distinct from it in substance, but as being its natural function and agent': the mind is thus associated with consciousness, and the soul with the whole of the self.[10] The *Catholic Encyclopedia* of 1907–14, which offers us a useful insight into the public understanding of doctrine in the early twentieth century, defines the relationship in terms that have striking parallels to the psychoanalytic model: 'It is established beyond doubt the fact that our normal consciousness of everyday life is profoundly affected by subconscious processes of the soul which themselves escape our notice'.[11] Where the concept of the soul distinguishes itself from psychoanalysis, however, and indeed from most other twentieth-century thinking on the mind, is in its immateriality. Dualism is not actually a tenet of Christian belief; as the theologian John W. Cooper points out, a monist understanding of body and mind as being of a single, material substance is by no means incompatible with a belief in the Christian afterlife, which speaks of a physical resurrection of the body.[12] In practice, though, the Cartesian division of the self into a material body and an immaterial mind and soul is generally accepted among believers, and is particularly relevant to the theist conception of an immaterial deity inhabiting a material universe, which mirrors on the large scale the soul/body relationship on the small.[13] Dualism certainly underlies the representation of mind in the French Catholic novel. It is implicit in many passages of the priest's diary in *Diary of a Country Priest*, including the priest's reaction to his sexton's denial of the soul's immortality. When the sexton bluntly asserts, 'when you be dead, everythin' be dead', the priest doesn't argue with him, but privately dismisses the possibility that the sexton might truly consider the death of the body to be the end of consciousness:

> Such blasphemy he really couldn't have meant; he was merely expressing his failure to imagine that eternal life, of which his limited experience denied him proof. But the simple wisdom of his kind yet assured him of its reality, and he believed blindly, without expression.[14]

Death illustrates this Cartesian division between body and mind clearly in the case of one of Bernanos's earlier protagonists, l'abbé Donissan in *Sous le soleil de Satan*:

> His mind had never been more free, his judgment more prompt or more clear, while his body is aware only of the growing pain, of the fixed point from where the acute suffering

> radiates outwards spreading its fantastical branches or running beneath the weft of nerves like a nimble shuttle. It has advanced so far as to appear to have reached the division of body and mind, to make two parts of the same man. The Saint of Lumbres in his death throes now has dealings only with souls.[15]

As Donissan's soul is taking leave of what Bernanos refers to as its 'envelope of flesh',[16] so his mind becomes detached from the nerve impulses sent to his brain, and thus from the sensation of physical pain they cause. We can see the same immaterial self elsewhere in the Catholic novel, such as in Green's *Chaque homme dans sa nuit* (*Each in his Darkness*, 1960), where the hero, Wilfred, is asserted to be present, sentient but disembodied, after his death: a character claims he could have spoken to Wilfred as he sat by his corpse, 'Because he was there, Angus, he was far away and he was close by, so close'.[17] The paradox of simultaneous closeness and distance emphasizes the immateriality of the soul. Wilfred's presence is no longer intelligible in spatial terms, as he exists in a realm that is not physical.

The dualist concept of the self puts Catholic writers at odds with the resolutely materialist Proustian model which we saw in the previous chapter. Proust's novel, labelled 'thoroughly God-less' by Malcolm Bowie, in fact has little truck with souls of any sort: its Narrator declares his own lack of belief in life after death, and expresses scepticism that, deep down, anyone else believes in it either.[18] It is Proust's materialism, rather than Bernanos's dualism, which will dominate literary fiction by the end of the century, as we'll see in the mind-brain model adopted by Darrieussecq. The Catholic writers' dualism also distinguishes them from the quasi-neurological view of mental activity espoused by Freudian psychoanalysis, although, as we shall see in the next chapter, the same isn't necessarily true of psychoanalysis-inspired literature. The most strident opposition in this respect undoubtedly comes not from science or psychoanalysis, but existentialism, where the souls of Catholic writing are sharply distinguished from the minds of atheist philosophy in their relationship to the world.[19] For Bernanos, as for Mauriac and Green, the soul is God's creation, made with the same divine intention as the world it inhabits, and which the mind perceives and acts upon. The idea that the mind is in harmony with the natural world, and that this harmony implies the divinely created status of both, is prevalent in the Catholic novel. In *Diary of a Country Priest*, it is the curé de Torcy who articulates the role of faith in drawing out the link between humanity and nature:

> God has entrusted the Church to keep that soul [of childhood] alive, to safeguard our candour and freshness. Paganism was no enemy of nature, but Christianity alone can exalt it, can raise it to man's own height, to the peak of his dreams.[20]

Encounters with the natural world in the Catholic novel are used to demonstrate sympathetic balance. In Mauriac's *Le Nœud de vipères*, for instance, nature provides the first intimation of the coming conversion of the resolutely anti-Christian Louis:

> One day, on the Lys Valley road, we had got down from the carriage. The stream ran by; I crushed fennel between my fingers; night was gathering on the lower slopes but patches of sunlight lingered on the mountain peaks. . . . I suddenly had the acute feeling, the almost physical certainty that there was another world, a reality of which we knew only the shadow.[21]

The notion of a divine order perceptible in nature, which leads perceivers to infer the existence of God and thus their own status as God's creations, is an important one for Mauriac. In *Souffrances et bonheur du chrétien* (*Anguish and Joy of the Christian Life*, 1931), he recounts the experience which brought him to this belief, an experience with some similarities to Louis's.[22] Earlier, in *Petits essais de psychologie religieuse* (*Short Essays on Religious Psychology*, 1920), he discusses the case of Maurice de Guérin, whose nature-worship led him to what Mauriac sees as Classical paganism, but argues: 'Many men must raise their eyes to God at the sight of the harmony of Creation. Far from being led astray by Nature, as was Maurice de Guérin, they are helped by it to discover and love its Author'.[23]

Green's *Chaque homme dans sa nuit* offers a similar scene to the one from *Le Nœud de vipères*. A few pages after declaring to his agnostic uncle, 'you know that you believe like you know that you are in love', the term 'in love' recurs as Wilfred undergoes an experience in a natural setting that is unmistakably religious:

> He sat on the grass and touched the trunk of one of the great maples that grew along the path. With a fancy to which he often had recourse, he imagined that these trees were alive and that they were watching over him. He was suddenly filled with a delicious feeling of security and he lay down on his back. His hands behind his neck, his gaze wandered deep in the sky that could be seen through the gaps in the leaves, and abruptly it seemed to him that he was in love. With whom, he could not have said. His heart held so much love that there was enough, he thought, for a lifetime, but with all his might he loved someone he did not know. Closing his eyes, he murmured with extraordinary fervour, 'I love you!' These words relieved him of a mysterious burden, and the little phrase strayed across his lips a dozen times. He had never said it in that way to anyone, and he had no one to say it to, but he said it over and over again with a singular joy, of an entirely new kind.[24]

As with Mauriac, the emphasis is here on sensory impressions which lead to the religious epiphany. Green's scene brings out the phenomenological implications of the event: the world is purposeful, loving, and protective, and we can be aware of this protectiveness and reciprocate this love if our perceptions are properly attuned to them. Contrast this with the existentialist phenomenology of Sartre's *Nausea*, which also finds expression in a scene of man perceiving the natural world: the famous centrepiece in the park at Bouville, where Roquentin finally understands the nature of his affliction:

> Existence had suddenly unveiled itself. It had lost its harmless appearance as an abstract category: it was the very stuff of things, that root was steeped in existence. Or rather the root, the park gates, the bench, the sparse grass on the lawn, all that had vanished; the diversity of things, their individuality, was only an appearance, a veneer. This veneer had melted, leaving soft, monstrous masses, in disorder—naked, with a frightening, obscene nakedness.[25]

What Roquentin sees before him is a reality without order and without meaning, which his mind perceives as alien and hostile to its desire to comprehend and categorize, to divide matter into fixed entities with definable attributes. Roquentin is frustrated by the mismatch between his mental faculties and the brute reality with which they are confronted: 'I could not understand it, even if I stayed leaning against the gate for a hundred and seven years; I had learned everything I could know about existence'.[26] This divorce between mind and external reality is the consequence of the absence of any creator's intentions behind the natural world. Conversely, what we see in the Catholic texts is a communion of minds: through nature, the human mind becomes aware of the presence of the divine mind, and the similarities between the two render the world familiar and comprehensible. Let us note in passing how the use of description in the scenes in question bolsters the philosophical outlook of each: leafy sunshine at the riverbank demonstrates to Louis and Wilfred the existence of divine intention in the world; patchy grass in the municipal park proves to Roquentin the opposite.

The idea of a communion of minds is important in the Catholic representation of consciousness through the theme of prayer, and more broadly, through the divine visions and other supernatural mental events which occur in Catholic novels. Overtly supernatural events are most often confined to the mental sphere in these texts, where ambiguity holds sway between a rationalizing psychological explanation and a genuinely divine (or, as the case may be, satanic) intervention from outside the mind itself. Mauriac and Green balance this question carefully. As Mauriac's Louis senses the presence of heaven in a church, or Green's Wilfred hears a divine voice call to him, a purely psychological interpretation remains at the reader's disposal: the presentation of the scenes allows for the possibility that the experiences are the result of nothing more than the workings of a guilty conscience.[27] Indeed, the representation of the mind in both writers might be described as agnostic, at least in terms of the evidence presented for theistic interaction between human and divine minds. Bernanos maintains this ambiguity to some extent: his heroes are still able to doubt whether the mental phenomena they experience are of truly supernatural origin. However, the presence of the supernatural is asserted far more strongly in Bernanos's texts. When God calls out to Bernanos's country priest in a moment of doubt, the divine voice seems real enough to bring the priest out of his house in search of the caller:

> I jumped out of bed, my head throbbing, but my mind horribly clear, with the impression—the certainty, of having heard someone call out my name.
>
> My lamp was still burning on the table.
>
> I looked all round the garden but in vain. I *knew* that I should not find anyone. All that still seems like a dream, yet every detail stands out vividly, lit by a kind of mental clarity, a frozen light, too intense for even the smallest shadow in which I might seek some rest, some safety. . . . It is thus that after death a man must see himself.[28]

Bernanos hesitates between supernatural and psychological explanations for the uncanny event in very much the same manner as traditional fantastic literature.[29] The priest may well have been dreaming when he heard the call, as he himself acknowledges, and despite his search, he is aware that no human voice has called him. Yet the timing of the event, at a point where he has despairingly ceased to pray, combined with the seemingly miraculous lucidity that accompanies it, serve to point us towards divine intervention. Even more strongly indicative is the clairvoyance accorded to the country priest when Mlle Chantal, daughter of an adulterous father and God-hating mother, comes to the confessional:

> Just then a peculiar thing happened. I am not trying to explain it. I shall put it down as it occurred. I am so tired, so overwrought that I may even have dreamt it. Well, as I was staring into the deep shadow where even in full daylight I can barely recognize anyone, the face of Mlle Chantal began to appear to me, by degrees. And this image remained under my gaze, in a wonderful fleeting way, and I kept quite still for fear the slightest movement would have made it disappear. Of course, I never thought of that then. It only occurred to me later. I am wondering if this vision had something to do with my prayer, was it my prayer, in some way? [. . .] And another strange thing happened, which again I can only recount without attempting to explain. It may have been a shot in the dark, yet I knew I was right: 'Give me that letter—that letter in your bag—at once.' She made no attempt to resist. She just sighed deeply and held out the envelope with a shrug.[30]

The priest later casts doubt on this version of events (p. 1144; trans. p. 146), suggesting that he may have imagined his command when Mlle Chantal spontaneously handed over the letter (the contents of which are not revealed, but which forms part of Mlle Chantal's plot of vengeance against her father). However, this later uncertainty does less to undermine our confidence in the supernatural event recounted, than to emphasize its miraculous nature: so extraordinary is it that even its protagonist has difficulty in believing it after the fact.

Such supernatural episodes are a symptom of a broader Catholic conception of mental life as a combination of emanations from the self, influx from the external world, and a third influencing factor which comes from beyond the physical realm. In *Monsieur Ouine*, Bernanos has the curé of Fenouille rebuke the village doctor for his psychological explanations of human morality with the words: 'One day you will have the proof that you are failing to give due consideration to the supernatural'.[31] Prayer is seen literally as the 'soul in touch with God', as the *Diary of a Country Priest* puts it.[32] Such a view accords well with the Bergsonian philosophy of mind, which was to explore mysticism in his later works, and posit the possibility of a mind open to supernatural communication with the divine (proffered by Bergson as evidence of God's existence).[33] This divine influence has implications for free will in the universe of the text. Green's characters see their actions as manipulated by divine intelligence: 'if we are here, you and I, facing each other, it is because He wishes it to be so'.[34] The country priest, too, regards himself as little more than a pawn in God's hands. Recalling the turbulent meeting in which he restored the faith of the Countess, Chantal's mother, shortly before her death, the priest disclaims his own agency in the conversion:

> What could I expect to retain in mind of such strange happenings, through which I tapped my way like a blind man? Our Lord had need of a witness, and I was chosen, doubtless for lack of anyone better, as one calls in a passer-by. I should be crazy indeed to imagine that I had a part, a real part in it. Already it is too much that God should have given me the grace to be present when a soul became reconciled to hope again—these solemn nuptials![35]

Equally, evil deeds may result from malign external influence, rather than from free choice or innate tendencies in the evildoer. This is a theme to be found in Green's writing, where the pounding heart of a man on the point of committing rape and attempted murder 'seemed like the footsteps of an invisible being, marching in his chest',[36] but once again it is Bernanos who most strongly figures evil as an external force. *Sous le soleil de Satan* describes the mind's awareness of sin as 'numb consciousness which gradually becomes aware and takes possession of its sinister guest', a line that foreshadows the climax of the novel, in which the eyes of an apparently dead child reopen, and a satanic consciousness is perceptible in its gaze.[37] The *Diary of a Country Priest* expands on this theme, dubbing Satan 'the enemy in his soul' and suggesting that evil may be a form of demonic possession; the priest cites Luke's gospel as evidence: '"And then the devil entered into him." (Judas)'.[38] When he comes to set down his thoughts on the nature of evil more fully in his diary, it is clearly distinguished from the psychological understanding adopted by secular thinkers:

> The world of evil is so far beyond our understanding! Nor can I really succeed in picturing hell as a world, a universe. It is nothing, never will be anything but a half-formed shape, the hideous shape of an abortion, a stunted thing on the very verge of all existence. I think of those flaccid, translucent pockets in the sea. Does the Monster care that there should be one criminal more or less? Immediately he sucks down the crime into himself, making it one with his own horrible substance, digests it without once rousing from his terrible eternal lethargy. Yet historians, moralists, even philosophers refuse to see anything but the criminal, they recreate evil in the image and likeness of humanity. They form no idea of essential evil, that vast yearning for the void, for emptiness; since if ever our species is to

> perish it will die of boredom, of stale disgust. Humanity will have been eaten up as a beam by invisible fungi, which transform in a few weeks a block of oakwood into spongy matter which our fingers have no difficulty in breaking.[39]

The externality of evil is apparent in Bernanos's choice of metaphors: evil is a predatory jellyfish or a destructive fungus, humanity takes the role of passive victim. The *Catholic Encyclopedia* of 1907–14, while laying more emphasis on individual responsibility than does Bernanos, offers a vision of evil that accords with this view to a large extent:

> There is no reason, indeed, for thinking that all sins and all temptations must needs come directly from the Devil or one of his ministers of evil. [. . .] But [. . .] the activity of Satan does much more than merely add a further source of temptation to the weakness of the world and the flesh; it means a combination and an intelligent direction of all the elements of evil. The whole Church and each one of her children are beset by dangers, the fire of persecution, the enervation of ease, the dangers of wealth and of poverty, heresies and errors of opposite characters, rationalism and superstition, fanaticism and indifference. It would be bad enough if all these forces were acting apart and without any definite purpose, but the perils of the situation are incalculably increased when all may be organized and directed by vigilant and hostile intelligences.[40]

Secular voices who would see in wrongdoing only the freely chosen actions of the wrongdoer are thus blind to the true nature of sin.

If both good and evil actions have their causes in supernatural influences from outside the mind, what room is left for free will? Far from being incompatible with a Catholic worldview, free will is a fundamental part of Christian belief: people are guided into goodness or tempted into evil, but the responsibility for their actions remains their own. None of the Catholic novelists contradicts this view. Even Bernanos describes good and evil as no more than 'seeds on the wind' that can take root in propitious minds. As the country priest strives to revive the Countess's faith (ironically, in the very interview for which he will later disown any active role), he tells her:

> Oh, madame, nobody can see in advance what one bad thought may have as its consequence. Evil thoughts are like good ones: thousands may be scattered by the wind, or overgrown or dried up by the sun. Only one takes root. The seeds of good and evil are everywhere.[41]

The priest's adaptation of the Parable of the Sower may present us as passive recipients of external moral influences, but, as those readers familiar with the original parable would understand, the story implies that a free choice to nurture the implanted idea is required if it is to result in an action.[42] Indeed, when the priest thinks back to the interview, his characterization of the Countess herself is far from passive:

> The memory of her struggle before my eyes, that fight for eternal life from which she emerged victorious, became painful, vivid, shattering.[43]

The strength of these external influences thus doesn't condemn us to passivity, but rather requires of us strenuous activity if we are to resist them. The psychological struggle of a mind wrestling with faith and temptation makes up the basic structure of many of Bernanos's plots, including the *Diary of a Country Priest* and *Sous le soleil de Satan*, which will end with their priest-protagonist victorious, as well as *Un mauvais rêve*, in which the protagonist succumbs.

Curiously, it is in Mauriac's writing where external influence on the mind is barely suggested, that the question of free will becomes controversial, when Sartre publicly declares that its absence in Mauriac's work means that Mauriac is not fit to be called a novelist. In his 1939 essay, 'M. François Mauriac et la liberté' ('M. François Mauriac and Freedom'), Sartre accuses Mauriac of adopting a God-like perspective on his characters, which destroys both narratorial involvement and temporal flow, leaving only 'a languishing truth under the aspect of the eternal'. Bergsonian duration, the conscious experience of time's movement, is regarded as an inconvenience by Mauriac, who takes any opportunity to 'abruptly empty the narrative of its temporal flow', according to Sartre.[44] Where the representation of the mind more generally is concerned, Mauriac's association of freedom with morally good choices, and, conversely, sinfulness with helpless compulsion, means that the 'freedom' of Thérèse Desqueyroux 'no more resembles true freedom than her consciousness resembles true consciousness; and M. Mauriac, who takes such pains to describe Thérèse's psychological mechanisms, suddenly runs out of methods when he wishes to make us feel that she is no longer a mechanism'.[45] Sartre's critique has some validity, and allegedly led to such a crisis of confidence for Mauriac himself that it caused his decade-long literary silence in the 1940s. From our own twenty-first-century perspective, however, criticisms that Mauriac's minds are insufficiently Bergsonian or existentialist indicate not so much an inherent flaw in his writing as a demarcation between competing philosophies of mind of the period, none of which has subsequently attained general endorsement. Mauriac's minute depiction of the cause-and-effect mechanics of psychological motivation do indeed exclude the arbitrariness and anarchy of absolute freedom; the detachment of his narratorial stance may well leave the suggestion of a synchronic perspective on the narrative's time-span. Both of these characteristics may nevertheless be seen as entirely defensible corollaries of a religious conception of mind. Man is 'condemned to be free' in Sartre's atheist universe precisely because of the absence of divine guidance and a divine plan; the theist universe has no need of such absolutes. If such a divine plan existed, it might well justify a writer's decision to take a narrative perspective on his or her own creation which combines the present moment of the human characters with hints of the broader overview of the eternal and omniscient.

Bernanos and his peers are writing in a period when philosophy of mind is not always to be clearly distinguished from psychology. The theorist of consciousness who most obviously straddles this divide is William James, who founded the psychological study of religious belief in his *Varieties of Religious Experience* (1902). James's accounts of the subjective experience of the divine accord well with Bernanos's fiction: he writes of people who feel God's presence, or literally hear his call, 'with an intensity almost like that of an hallucination', which is 'as convincing to those who have them as any direct sensible experiences can be', very much as we saw earlier with the call to the country priest.[46] James analyzes first-hand accounts of religious experiences to infer the dominant mental responses to be conflicting binarisms of solemnity and self-surrendering joy, dread and peace, submission and freedom, which he characterizes as 'moods of contraction and expansion of man's being'. Mystical states of consciousness are, for James, characterized by transience and ineffability; despite their 'noetic' quality of a revelation and new understanding, they are not communicable through language to those who don't share the experience.[47] Both the intimations of the divine that we saw earlier accorded to Louis and in *Le Nœud de vipères* and Wilfred in *Chaque homme dans sa nuit* gesture towards qualities of the experience that can't be rendered on the page: Wilfred feels that he loves but cannot conceptualize the object of his love. And the psychological characteristics of saintliness extrapolated by James also accord well with Bernanos's saintly priests, and Donissan in particular. The attributes of sainthood are virtuous yet excessive, James says, including devotion to the point of fanaticism and a purity and self-sacrifice beyond all reasonable bounds. The self-mortification and extreme asceticism of Donissan's last years testify to a similar conception on

Bernanos's part, as does James's justification for such excess: through their extreme example, saints become 'the great torch-bearers of this belief, the tip of the wedge, the clearers of the darkness'.[48]

James acknowledges that neither science nor philosophy can demonstrate a divine origin to religious experiences, and accepts that 'pathological conditions' may account for the hallucinatory or otherwise extreme states of consciousness involved in mystical incidents. He compares the 'mystical consciousness' of visionaries to his own experience of altered consciousness on nitrous oxide.[49] Psychology and religion, he writes, both admit to the existence of 'forces seemingly outside of the conscious individual that bring redemption to his life'; the divergence comes in the psychologist's attribution to such forces to internal elements developed and incubated in the unconscious mind.[50] However, James ultimately rejects as 'simple-minded' the attempt to reduce religious experience to causes within the mind and brain: 'Medical materialism finishes up Saint Paul by calling his vision on the road to Damascus a discharging lesion of the occipital cortex, he being an epileptic. It snuffs out Saint Teresa as an hysteric, Saint Francis of Assisi as an hereditary degenerate'.[51] While only the believer's private experience can convince of the reality of supernatural intervention, James also points to the permanence of religious conversion once consciousness returns to normal states, and to the beneficial effects of such conversions on the believer's life, as more objective evidence against the sceptical view.

Since James, science and its accompanying philosophers have often taken a less charitable view of religious conceptions of mind. Dualism is attacked by Paul Churchland as scientifically implausible, given the close correlation between mental function with specific areas and observed activity in the brain. He posits that, with an immaterial mind that needed the material brain only for sensory input and volitional output, 'one would expect reason, emotion and consciousness to be relatively invulnerable to direct control or pathology by manipulation or damage to the brain', which is not the case in our experience.[52] Others build on Princess Elisabeth of Bohemia's original objection to Descartes with the premise that causal closure in the physical world renders incoherent the proposition that a soul can cause a neuron to fire; even if it were possible, it would violate the first law of thermodynamics by introducing energy into the physical world from an immaterial source.[53] Other secular voices analyze religion as a natural phenomenon, and it has recently become a topic of interest among evolutionary psychologists. The possibility that religious belief is itself adaptive, increasing fitness for survival and reproduction perhaps by increasing social cohesion or emotional well-being, is considered, but finds less favour than an alternative theory: that religious belief flourishes due to its attractiveness to cognitive attributes that have evolved for quite other purposes. Pascal Boyer, one of the first in this field, speculates that a predisposition to interpret phenomena in terms of agency and intention, along with a similar predisposition towards narrative explanations, prime the human mind for a religious understanding of the world.[54] He is followed by Richard Dawkins, who points out that the propagation of religion through the indoctrination of children is also suggestive of an evolutionary by-product:

> Theoretically, children might learn from personal experience not to go too near a cliff edge, not to eat untried red berries, not to swim in crocodile-infested waters. But, to say the least, there will be a selective advantage to child brains that possess the rule of thumb: believe, without question, whatever your grown-ups tell you.[55]

And a third evolutionary view of faith comes from Daniel Dennett, who offers an intriguing variant in positing that religious memes are parasitic on our evolved capacity for romantic love, with its deliberately costly signals of commitment to our chosen partner.[56] Green's 'in love' would thus be more than simply a metaphor for spiritual devotion: it would be an unwitting reference to the hidden roots of faith.

While the largely naturalistic literary universes of Green and Mauriac allow some scope for theories of this kind, there is little space for a Darwinian or pathologizing view of religion in Bernanos. Here, religious faith is quite clearly not the product of an over-trusting childhood or a misinterpretation of natural phenomena as intentionally produced. Nor is it the emanation of a misfiring cortex. Rather, in Bernanos belief in God is the most rational inference from the available evidence, both subjectively experienced and objectively verifiable. The visions, divine and satanic, accorded to Bernanos's protagonists testify to the supernatural forces battling around them. The opening eyes of the dead child in *Sous le soleil de Satan*, or Mlle Chantal's hidden letter intuited by the country priest, strongly support the inference that such phenomena are more than psychological in origin. More nebulous consequences too, such as the quiet peace of the devout and the despair of the faithless, are used to imply that there must be more than self-delusion in religious belief. Were the phenomena perceived by Bernanos's characters more typical in everyday experience, it's fair to say, the Church would be in a rather healthier position than that in which it currently finds itself: in 2013, the average age of a Catholic priest in France was 75, and less than one per cent of young people regularly attended mass.[57]

While the meme theory of religious belief finds no echo in Bernanos's representation of Christian faith, it does find an uncanny reflection in another aspect of the Catholic novelists' work. In these novels, there is indeed an insidious set of ideas to be seen spreading parasitically through culture by piggy-backing on parts of the human psyche designed for quite another purpose. The meme is psychoanalytic theory, and the host it exploits is a central element of Catholic faith. Psychoanalysis was in the inter-war period a relatively new phenomenon in France, but one whose influence was growing rapidly towards a position of dominance in the understanding of the mind. Freud was himself an atheist, as has been mentioned, and was critical of religion. His ideas on sexuality in particular were seen by Catholic novelists as a threat. Both Bernanos and Mauriac present fictional psychoanalysts in their work, and in both cases the characters function as a warning against doctrines that would dissociate sexuality from sin, or encourage exploration of destructive or shameful urges in the cause of mental hygiene. The country priest despairs at the influence of psychiatry in comparison to religion: 'But alas! We take the psychiatrists' word for it. The unanimous testimony of saints is held as of little or no account'.[58] Elsewhere in Bernanos, psychoanalysts and medical practitioners dabbling in the field deny the existence of the soul and scoff at the idea of a hell awaiting sinners, whilst the materialist view of the mind reduces miracles like Donissan's clairvoyance to mental illness.[59] Moral conflict is tamed by medical labels like 'hyperemotionality' and 'hyperæsthesia', or downgraded to physiological disturbance, as when Donissan's crisis of faith is diagnosed as 'a serious intoxication of the nerve cells, probably of intestinal origin'.[60] Mauriac, whose attitude towards psychoanalysis hardened through his career, finally presents an outright condemnation of the discipline in 'Thérèse chez le docteur'. This short story depicts the psychoanalytic session as a travesty of Catholic confession: Dr Schwartz refers to his couch as his 'confessional', and his patient notes the irony that his title of 'psychiatrist' should translate as 'soul doctor', when he denies the existence of any such entity.[61] The story is focalized through the analyst's wife, whose eavesdropping on his analysis crystallizes her misgivings on psychoanalysis into a decisive rejection of her husband and his calling. As the patient (Thérèse Desqueyroux, in one of three sequel narratives to the eponymous novel) is encouraged to delve into the pain and obsession of her unhappy love-affairs, Mme Schwartz suppresses a desire to cry out to her: 'He has nothing to offer you, he can do nothing for you other than to push you deeper into this mire. I don't know who you should turn to, but not to him, not to him!'[62] Mauriac clearly implies that it is to a priest that Thérèse should turn, a priest who would lead Thérèse away from her sinful promiscuity, rather than rationalize and indulge it as the psychoanalyst does. Both Mauriac and Bernanos are suspicious of the value of psychological introspection, and both criticize its use by Proust as the basis of his novel: Mauriac takes issue with the absence of moral purpose behind Proust's exploration of the psyche, while Bernanos, with more than a hint of homophobia, finds 'the terrible introspection' of Proust and his successors indecent in exposing the most private elements of consciousness.[63] Discussing the contemporary novel, Bernanos refers to 'the most brilliant pupils of the Gide academy and the Proust academy, clutching their diploma in immorality', and declares of them:

> Back in the day, the writer would welcome readers ceremoniously to the threshold of his consciousness, and would indicate prudently from afar, like a suspicious host, the general lay-out of his dwelling and the locations of its most secret rooms. These days he hands over the whole bunch of keys, and gives a little encouraging pat on the shoulder: 'Go right ahead!'[64]

Mauriac equates the absence of judgement on sexual behaviour with amoral permissiveness, and misrepresents psychoanalysis in the short story by having Schwartz actively encourage patients to live out their sexual fantasies: 'As with his other victims, he would incite her to sate herself. Unburdening the mind by satisfying the body: that was what his method boiled down to. The same foul solution served to interpret heroism, murder, sainthood, renunciation'.[65] (Similarly, Dr Gallet in *Sous le soleil de Satan* attempts to convince Mouchette that medical science has disproved Christian sexual morality: 'You and I, we have neither prejudices nor scruples in matters of love. How can one believe in a moral code that medical science, a science as exact as mathematics, refutes every day?')[66] But what finally provokes both Thérèse and Mme Schwartz to turn against the psychoanalyst is his derisive laughter when asked: 'Do you believe in the devil, doctor? Do you believe that evil is a person?'[67] More serious, then, than the discipline's refusal to condemn extra-marital, non-procreative sex, is its understanding of human behaviour in terms of drives that are, in theory, entirely comprehensible in terms of the subject's physiology, present environment, and past experience. It's the same complaint which we saw expressed in the *Diary of a Country Priest*, that secular thought fails to understand the broader nature of good and evil. The self-contained view of mind that sees behaviour in terms of instincts or ethics in terms of hygiene, with no need for outside reference to supernatural influence or divine moral law, is not only misguided, from a Catholic perspective, but actively dangerous, as it provides an apparently rational justification for behaviour that may lead to damnation, and blinds people to the external forces of evil which are luring them into this path.

Despite this irreconcilable difference in outlook, the Catholic novel's view of the mind does have a certain amount of common ground with the psychoanalytic model. The psychological analysis of characters in the work of all three novelists shares its discourse and its interpretation with those of psychoanalysis on occasion. Even Bernanos, whose hostility to psychoanalysis may have been the influence which led Mauriac to turn against it, sometimes appears curiously in harmony with the Freudian view.[68] Within a few pages of each other in *Un mauvais rêve*, for instance, we find these passages of psychological analysis:

> Neither did this justify his sudden flash of hatred towards Mme Alfieri, let alone fleeing absurdly into the night like this. For that, you would no doubt have to go back further, much further, to certain childhood temptations that only chance had allowed him to overcome—but for which the wound was still there, somewhere, in a hidden corner of his brain.

And then, with reference to a different character:

> For the first time her prodigious inner life, which had always turned in on itself and, in the revolting words of old Ganse, had been cooking in its own juices for ten years, this

> mysterious life shared by turns between despair and exaltation, traversed by nightmare figures like a sinister crossroads, this underground river was going to breach the obstacle beneath which its vortexes churned, and break through to daylight.[69]

Whether or not these passages are direct borrowings from Freud—and there is evidence that Bernanos knew his work well—they certainly have much in common with his view of the mind.[70] In the first, we see an interpretation of present behaviour through unconscious motivations linked to events in childhood, the memory of which is inaccessible to consciousness but persists nonetheless in a closed part of the mind. In the second, we have what might be a paraphrase of Freud's discussion of repression: compare Freud's description of repressed drives 'proliferating in the dark' of the unconscious realm until they are strong enough to breach the barrier with 'extreme forms of expression'.[71] Psychoanalysis as an explanatory system is thus not wholly alien to the Catholic novelists' conception of mind, even if it does, in Bernanos's words, neglect the non-material side of characteristics which are 'half-spiritual, half-carnal, as if at the point where body and spirit join'.[72] The real problem is a psychotherapy which encourages patients to unburden themselves of their shameful secrets and desires, while responding with none of the moral strictures of Christian teaching. The psychoanalyst Jacques Lacan emphasizes the same distinction from the other side of the fence:

> Certainly the psychoanalyst directs the treatment. The first principle of this treatment, the one that is spelt out to him before all else, and which he meets throughout his training, to the extent that he becomes utterly imbued with it, is that he must not direct the patient. The direction of conscience, in the sense of moral guidance that a Catholic might find in it, is radically excluded here. If psychoanalysis poses problems for moral theology, they are not those of the direction of conscience, speaking of which I would add that the direction of conscience itself poses problems.[73]

For psychoanalysts, of course, it is the judgmental nature of confession with regard to people's secret urges and private desires which is to be deplored, as it condemns what psychoanalysis sees as involuntary or natural and represses what psychoanalysis believes should be freely explored in the cause of mental health. For Bernanos, however, Catholic confession may offer greater therapeutic benefits than the psychoanalysis which struggles to imitate it:

> Fanatical freethinkers are fools to despise in the Church a method of psychotherapy which they consider excellent and novel in a famous neurologist. This professor, in his clinic, does he really do anything different from a simple priest in the confessional: gaining the confidence of the sick person in order then to take his time to influence them by suggestion while they are calm and relaxed? From how many rotten things in their hearts have people been freed by this effort alone?[74]

These lines, spoken in the closing pages of *Sous le soleil de Satan* by the impersonal narrator, have the gravitas of an authorial pronouncement. There is a degree of ambivalence, in that the priest's methods are essentially similar to the psychoanalyst's, their conceptions of the mind have much in common, and their aims coincide to some extent where the mental well-being of their interlocutor is concerned. Freud himself is in agreement, describing the role of the psychoanalyst as that of 'a father confessor, who gives absolution, as it were, by a continuance of his sympathy and respect after the confession has been made'.[75] For the religious writer, however, these similarities are no grounds for compromise: it is precisely the similarity of its views and methods that makes psychoanalysis such a dangerous surrogate for true Catholic confession.

Bernanos may not explicitly theorize his conception of how the mind works, nor do he and his fellow Catholic novelists present an entirely homogenous view across their work, yet they explore human psychology and the ontology of mind from a Catholic perspective, and in doing so offer a sharply differentiated alternative to the prominent theories of mind that were being developed at this time. As such, their presence alters the cultural landscape of a period in which literary fiction was dominated by questions of consciousness: they are the neglected counterpoint to the inter-war texts that promoted or were inspired by an existentialist, Bergsonian, psychoanalytic or Surrealist understanding of the mind. From our perspective in the twenty-first century, French cultural expression of the nature of consciousness in this period may appear to have been dominated by what was radically new, what was daringly controversial, or what took inspiration from fashionable theories from outside literature. But to writers and readers living through the period itself, the mind was not necessarily to be understood by means of any of these ideas. Bernanos's *Diary of a Country Priest*, along with the other Catholic novels of the mid-twentieth century, shows that the theological view of consciousness was vigorous enough in this period to take on any late-coming rivals who might seek to separate out the mind from the soul.

Notes

1. Jules Barbey d'Aurevilly, J.-K. Huysmans, and Léon Bloy are among the significant figures in the previous generation of Catholic writers, who are important influences on Mauriac, Bernanos, and Green, but the earlier novelists have neither the sustained attention to matters of faith, nor the shared literary preoccupations which will bind the later generation together in the public consciousness.
2. 'Les seuls qui soient tout entiers fondés sur la Révélation', François Mauriac, *Œuvres complètes*, 12 vols. (Paris: Fayard, 1950), III, 'Préface', pp. i–iv (p. ii). Subsequent references are abbreviated to *'OC'*.
3. 'Le christianisme ne fait pas sa part à la chair', François Mauriac, 'Souffrances et bonheur du chrétien' (1931), *OC*, VII, pp. 223–76 (p. 229); first published in 'Souffrances du chrétien' in 1928. Donat O'Donnell cites the contemporary Catholic commentator, Abbé Louis Bethléem, condemning Mauriac's 1920s novels as 'very pernicious' and 'morally base'. Donat O'Donnell, 'François Mauriac: Catholic and Novelist', *Kenyon Review*, 10 (1948), pp. 454–71 (p. 461).
4. 'Un écrivain catholique ne saurait appartenir à l'Église enseignante, et le tort d'un grand nombre de religieux est d'avoir voulu trouver en eux des collaborateurs dociles et ponctuels—comme un professeur se fait parfois remplacer au tableau noir par un des élèves de sa classe', Georges Bernanos, 'L'Écrivain catholique: le rôle qui lui revient' (1943), in *Essais et écrits de combat*, ed. by Yves Bridel and others, 2 vols. (Paris: Gallimard, collection Pléiade, 1946), II, pp. 865–867 (p. 866). Subsequent references are abbreviated to *'EEC'*.
5. Michael R. Tobin, *Georges Bernanos: The Theological Source of his Art* (Montreal: McGill-Queen's University Press, 2007), p. 5.
6. Bernanos's and Mauriac's conflicts with the Catholic Church are detailed in Claire Daudin, *Dieu a-t-il besoin de l'écrivain?: Péguy, Bernanos, Mauriac* (Paris: Cerf, 2006), pp. 14–15.
7. 'Le désespoir charnel transpire comme l'eau au mur d'un souterrain', Georges Bernanos, 'Spiritualisme et circonspection', *EEC*, I, pp. 1237–40 (p. 1237). Bernanos's dispute with Mauriac is discussed in Michael R. Tobin, 'François Mauriac and Georges Bernanos: Two Theologies of the Body', *Christianity and Literature*, 44 (1995), pp. 313–26.
8. Maurice Larkin, *France since the Popular Front: Government and People 1936–1986* (Oxford: Clarendon Press, 1988), p. 18.
9. Maurice Larkin, 'Religion, Anticlericalism and Secularization', in *Modern France 1880–2002*, ed. by James McMillan (Oxford: Oxford University Press, 2003), pp. 203–227 (pp. 207–209); Larkin, *France since the Popular Front*, p. 17.
10. Tertullian examines Classical ideas on mind and soul, before determining that any suggestion of a qualitative distinction between them must be rejected: 'If a separate condition between the soul and the mind is to be admitted, so that they be two things in substance, then of one of them, emotion and sensation, and every sort of taste, and all action and motion, will be the characteristics; whilst of the other the natural condition will be calm and repose and stupor', Tertullian, 'De Anima', in *The Writings of Tertullian*, trans. by Peter Holmes, 3 vols. (Edinburgh: Clark, 1884), II, pp. 410–541 (p. 437).
11. *The Catholic Encyclopedia*, ed. by Charles G. Herbermann and others, 15 vols. (New York: Robert Appleton, 1907–14), s.v. *soul*.

12. John W. Cooper, *Body, Soul and Life Everlasting: Biblical Anthropology and the Monism-Dualism Debate*, 2nd edn. (Michigan and Cambridge: Eerdmans, 2000).
13. See Charles Taliaferro, *Consciousness and the Mind of God* (Cambridge: Cambridge University Press, 1994), pp. 4–6.
14. 'Quand on est mort, tout est mort'; 'Il ne croyait certes pas offenser Dieu par ce blasphème qui n'était que l'aveu de son impuissance à imaginer cette vie éternelle dont son expérience des choses ne lui fournissait aucune preuve valable, mais que l'humble sagesse de sa race lui révélait pourtant certaine et à laquelle il croyait, sans pouvoir rien exprimer de sa croyance', Georges Bernanos, *Journal d'un curé de campagne*, in *Œuvres romanesques*, ed. by Albert Béguin and others (Paris: Gallimard, collection Pléiade, 1961), pp. 1029–259 (p. 1182); trans. 198. Subsequent references abbreviated to *'OR'*. Translations for *Journal d'un curé de campagne* are taken from *The Diary of a Country Priest*, trans. by Pamela Morris (Cambridge, MA: Da Capo, 2002), with page references given after the reference to the French original. All other translations in this chapter are my own.
15. 'Jamais son cerveau ne fut plus libre, son jugement plus prompt, plus net, tandis que sa chair n'est attentive qu'à la douleur grandissante, au point fixe d'où la souffrance aigüe s'irradie, pousse en tous sens ses merveilleux rameaux, ou court sous la trame des nerfs, pareille à une navette agile. Elle a pénétré si avant qu'elle semble atteindre la division du corps et de l'esprit, faire deux parts du même homme. . . . Le saint de Lumbres à l'agonie n'a plus commerce qu'avec les âmes', Georges Bernanos, *Sous le soleil de Satan*, *OR*, pp. 55–308 (p. 275).
16. 'Enveloppe de chair', Bernanos, *Sous le soleil de Satan*, *OR*, p. 211.
17. 'Parce qu'il était là, Angus, il était loin et il était près, tout près', Julien Green, 'Chaque homme dans sa nuit', in *Œuvres complètes*, ed. by Jacques Petit, 8 vols. (Paris: Gallimard, collection Pléiade, 1972), III, pp. 411–708 (p. 708). Subsequent references abbreviated to '*OC*'.
18. Malcolm Bowie, *Proust among the Stars* (London: Fontana, 1998), p. 201; *RTP*, II, 73; trans. II, 293; *RTP*, IV, 196; trans. V, 581.
19. This is not to say, however, that French existentialism begins and ends with the atheist philosophy of Jean-Paul Sartre. The work of Gabriel Marcel (1889–1973) demonstrates that Catholic beliefs and existentialist thought are not incompatible. Sartre acknowledges the presence of a school of Christian existentialism in *L'Existentialisme est un humanisme* (1946) (Paris: Gallimard, 1996), but argues that their shared contention that existence precedes essence creates difficulties for any philosopher who must also argue for the presence of a divine creator's design.
20. 'L'Église a été chargée par le bon Dieu de maintenir dans le monde cet esprit d'enfance, cette ingénuité, cette fraîcheur. Le paganisme n'était pas l'ennemi de la nature, mais le christianisme seul l'agrandit, l'exalte, la met à la mesure de l'homme, du rêve de l'homme', Bernanos, *Journal d'un curé de campagne*, *OR*, p. 1046; trans. p. 20.
21. 'Un jour, sur la route de la vallée du Lys, nous étions descendus de la victoria. Les eaux ruisselaient; j'écrasais du fenouil entre mes doigts; au bas des montagnes, la nuit s'accumulait, mais, sur les sommets, subsistaient des camps de lumière. . . . J'eus soudain la sensation aiguë, la certitude presque physique qu'il existait un autre monde, une réalité dont nous ne connaissions que l'ombre', François Mauriac, *Le Nœud de vipères*, *OC*, III, pp. 343–536 (p. 371).
22. Mauriac derives the following lesson from his observation of the natural world: 'Cybele is purified by Him whom I do not see; she closes up around Him; she hides Him under stones and in leaves; He is within her; the monstrance beams with vines and forests', ('Cybèle est purifiée par Celui que je ne vois pas; elle se referme sur Lui; elle Le cache sous des pierres, dans des feuilles; elle Le contient: l'ostensoir a des rayons de vignes et de forêts'), Mauriac, 'Souffrances et bonheur du chrétien', *OC*, VII, p. 266.
23. 'Sans doute beaucoup d'hommes, à la vue de l'harmonie du monde créé, s'élèvent jusqu'à Dieu. Bien loin d'en être détournés, comme Maurice de Guérin, par la Nature, elle les aide à découvrir et à aimer son Auteur', François Mauriac, *Petits essais de psychologie religieuse de quelques cœurs inquiets* (1920), *OC*, VIII, pp. 1–53 (p. 20).
24. 'On sait qu'on croit comme on sait qu'on est amoureux'; 'Il s'assit sur l'herbe et palpa le tronc d'un des grands érables qui bordaient le chemin. Par un tour d'esprit qui lui était habituel, il se figura que ces arbres étaient des personnes et qu'ils veillaient sur lui. Un sentiment de sécurité délicieuse l'envahit tout à coup et il s'étendit de tout son long sur le dos. [. . .] Joignant les mains sous sa nuque, il laissa ses yeux se perdre au fond du ciel qu'il apercevait par les déchirures du feuillage, et brusquement il lui sembla qu'il était amoureux. De qui, il n'aurait su le dire. Son cœur contenait tant d'amour qu'il y en avait, pensa-t-il, pour une vie entière, mais il aimait de toutes ses forces quelqu'un qu'il ne connaissait pas. Les yeux clos, il murmura avec une ferveur extraordinaire: "Je t'aime!" Ces mots le délivrèrent comme d'un poids mystérieux et plus de dix fois, la petite phrase errait sur ses lèvres. Il ne l'avait jamais dite à personne de cette façon-là et il n'avait personne à qui la dire, mais il la disait et la redisait avec une joie singulière, une joie toute nouvelle', Green, *Chaque homme dans sa nuit*, *OC*, III, pp. 462, 470–1.

25. 'L'existence s'était soudain dévoilée. Elle avait perdu son allure inoffensive de catégorie abstraite: c'était la pâte même des choses, cette racine était pétrie dans de l'existence. Ou plutôt la racine, les grilles du jardin, le banc, le gazon rare de la pelouse, tout ça s'est évanoui; la diversité des choses, leur individualité n'était qu'une apparence, un vernis. Ce vernis avait fondu, il restait des masses monstrueuses et molles, en désordre—nues, d'une effrayante et obscène nudité', Jean-Paul Sartre, *La Nausée* (1938), in *Œuvres romanesques* (Paris: Gallimard, collection Pléiade, 1981), pp. 1–210 (p. 151).
26. 'Je ne *pouvais* pas le comprendre, quand bien même je serais resté cent sept ans appuyé à la grille; j'avais appris sur l'existence tout ce que je pouvais savoir', Sartre, *La Nausée*, p. 160.
27. Mauriac, *Le Nœud de vipères*, *OC*, III, pp. 480–81; Green, *Chaque homme dans sa nuit*, *OC*, III, p. 485.
28. 'Je me suis levé d'un bond, les tempes battantes, le cerveau terriblement lucide, avec l'impression—la certitude—de m'être entendu appeler. . . . Ma lampe brûlait encore sur la table. J'ai fait le tour du jardin, vainement. Je *savais* que je ne trouverais personne. Tout cela me semble encore un rêve, mais dont chaque détail m'apparaît si clairement dans une espèce de lumière intérieure, d'illumination glacée qui ne laisse aucun coin d'ombre où je puisse retrouver quelque sécurité, quelque repos. C'est ainsi qu'au-delà de la mort, l'homme doit se revoir lui-même', Bernanos, *Journal d'un curé de campagne*, *OR*, p. 1140; trans. 140–41, italics Bernanos's.
29. On this hesitation, see Laurence W. Cor, 'Mystical Perception in *Journal d'un curé de campagne*', *Romance Notes*, 12 (1970–71), pp. 244–50.
30. 'À ce moment, il s'est passé une chose singulière. Je ne l'explique pas, je la rapporte telle quelle. Je suis si fatigué, si nerveux, qu'il est bien possible, après tout, que j'aie rêvé. Bref, tandis que je fixais ce trou d'ombre où, même en plein jour, il m'est difficile de reconnaître un visage, celui de Mlle Chantal a commencé d'apparaître peu à peu, par degrés. L'image se tenait là, sous mes yeux, dans une sorte d'instabilité merveilleuse, et je restais immobile comme si le moindre geste eût dû l'effacer. Bien entendu, je n'ai pas fait la remarque sur-le-champ, elle ne m'est venue qu'après coup. Je me demande si cette espèce de vision n'était pas liée à ma prière, elle était ma prière même peut-être? [. . .] Et il s'est passé un autre petit fait que je rapporte avec l'autre, sans l'expliquer non plus. J'ai parlé au hasard, je suppose. Et cependant j'étais sûr de ne pas me tromper. "Donnez-moi la lettre, la lettre qui est là, dans votre sac. Donnez-la-moi sur-le-champ!" Elle n'a pas essayé de résister, elle a seulement eu un profond soupir, elle m'a tendu le papier, en haussant les épaules', Bernanos, *Journal d'un curé de campagne*, *OR*, pp. 1135–37; trans. 133–36.
31. 'Vous aurez un jour la preuve qu'on ne fait pas au surnaturel sa part', Bernanos, *Monsieur Ouine* (1943), *OR*, pp. 1347–562 (p. 1525).
32. 'Ce colloque avec Dieu', Bernanos, *Journal d'un curé de campagne*, *OR*, p. 1209; trans. 232. Bernanos's formulation echoes that of the *Catholic Encyclopedia*, which notes of prayer: 'Nothing that we might obtain in answer to our prayer could exceed in value the familiar converse with God in which prayer consists'.
33. Henri Bergson, *Les Deux Sources de la morale et de la religion* (1932) (Paris: Presses Universitaires de France, édition Quadrige, 2008), pp. 324–38.
34. 'Si nous sommes là, toi et moi, l'un devant l'autre, c'est parce qu'il [Dieu] le veut', Bernanos, *Sous le soleil de Satan*, *OR*, p. 223; Green, *Chaque homme dans sa nuit*, *OC*, III, p. 632.
35. 'Que voudrait-on qui me restât dans l'esprit de circonstances si fortuites à travers lesquelles je me suis dirigé comme à tâtons, en aveugle? Notre-Seigneur avait besoin d'un témoin, et j'ai été choisi, faute de mieux sans doute, ainsi qu'on appelle un passant. Il faudrait que je fusse bien fou pour m'imaginer avoir tenu un rôle, un vrai rôle. C'est déjà trop que Dieu m'ait fait la grâce d'assister à cette réconciliation d'une âme avec l'espérance, à ces noces solennelles', Bernanos, *Journal d'un curé de campagne*, *OR*, p. 1168; trans. 178.
36. 'Ressemblait au pas d'un être invisible, marchant, les pieds dans sa poitrine', Green, *Léviathan* (1929), *OC*, I, pp. 579–814 (p. 673).
37. 'La conscience engourdie [qui] prend peu à peu connaissance et possession de son hôte sinistre', Bernanos, *Sous le soleil de Satan*, *OR*, pp. 208, 267.
38. 'L'ennemi intérieur'; ' "Alors le diable s'empara de lui" (Judas)', Bernanos, *Journal d'un curé de campagne*, *OR*, pp. 1048, 1105; trans. 22, 95.
39. 'Le monde du Mal échappe tellement, en somme, à la prise de notre esprit! D'ailleurs, je ne réussis pas toujours à l'imaginer comme un monde, un univers. Il est, il ne sera toujours qu'une ébauche, l'ébauche d'une création hideuse, avortée, à l'extrême limite de l'être. Je pense à ces poches flasques et translucides de la mer. Qu'importe au monstre un criminel de plus ou de moins! Il dévore sur le champ son crime, l'incorpore à son épouvantable substance, le digère sans sortir un mouvement de son effrayante, de son éternelle immobilité. Mais l'historien, le moraliste, le philosophe même, ne veulent voir que le criminel. Ils refont le mal à l'image et à la ressemblance de l'homme. Ils ne se forment aucune idée du mal lui-même, cette énorme aspiration du vide, du néant. Car si notre espèce doit périr, elle périra de dégoût, d'ennui. La personne humaine aura été lentement rongée, comme une poutre par ces champignons invisibles qui, en quelques semaines, font d'une pièce de chêne une matière spongieuse que le doigt crève sans effort', Bernanos, *Journal d'un curé de campagne*, *OR*, p. 1143; trans. 144–45 (translation modified).

40. *The Catholic Encyclopedia*, s.v. *devil.*
41. 'Oh! Madame, personne ne sait par avance ce qui peut sortir, à la longue, d'une mauvaise pensée. Il en est des mauvaises comme des bonnes: pour milles que le vent emporte, que les ronces étouffent, que le soleil dessèche, une seule pousse des racines. La semence du mal et du bien vole partout', Bernanos, *Journal d'un curé de campagne*, *OR*, p. 1159; trans. 166.
42. The active role of the individual is evident in Jesus's explanation of the original parable, the last verse of which reads: 'But the seed on good soil stands for those with a noble and good heart, who hear the word, retain it, and by persevering produce a crop', *Luke*, 8:15, *New International Version* (London: Hodder and Stoughton, 1987).
43. 'Le souvenir de la lutte qu'elle avait soutenue sous mes yeux, ce grand combat pour la vie éternelle dont elle était sortie épuisée, invaincue, m'est revenu si fort à la mémoire que j'ai pensé défaillir', Bernanos, *Journal d'un curé de campagne*, *OR*, p. 1169; trans. 180.
44. 'Une languissante vérité *sub specie æternitatis*'; 'vider brusquement le récit de sa durée', Jean-Paul Sartre, 'M. François Mauriac et la liberté', in *Critiques littéraires*, pp. 33–52 (pp. 43, 48).
45. 'Ne ressemble pas plus à la vraie liberté que sa conscience à la vraie conscience; et M. Mauriac, qui s'absorbe à décrire les mécanismes psychologiques de Thérèse, manque soudain de procédés lorsqu'il veut nous faire sentir qu'elle n'est plus mécanisme', Sartre, 'M. François Mauriac et la liberté', p. 46.
46. William James, *Varieties of Religious Experience: A Study in Human Nature* (1902) (Marston Gate: Renaissance Classics, 2012), p. 53.
47. James, *Varieties of Religious Experience*, pp. 279–315.
48. James, *Varieties of Religious Experience*, p. 264.
49. James, *Varieties of Religious Experience*, p. 285.
50. James, *Varieties of Religious Experience*, p. 156.
51. James, *Varieties of Religious Experience*, p. 9.
52. Paul Churchland, *Matter and Consciousness* (Cambridge, MA: The MIT Press, 1984), p. 20, italics Churchland's.
53. In correspondence with Descartes, Princess Elisabeth raised the objection that an immaterial mind could not affect changes to a physical brain. The discussion on thermodynamics comes from Stewart Goetz and Charles Taliaferro, *A Brief History of the Soul* (Oxford: Wiley-Blackwell, 2011), pp. 152–81.
54. Pascal Boyer, *Religion Explained: The Evolutionary Origins of Religious Thought* (New York: Basic Books, 2001).
55. Richard Dawkins, *The God Delusion* (London: Bantam, 2006), p. 174.
56. Daniel C. Dennett, *Breaking the Spell: Religion as a Natural Phenomenon* (London: Penguin, 2006), p. 256.
57. Matthew Price, 'Catholic Church "Struggles" to Win over Young People', *BBC Report*, 11 March 2013 www.bbc.co.uk/news/world-europe-21738755.
58. 'Hélas! on en croira sur parole des psychiatres et l'unanime témoignage des Saints sera tenu pour peu ou rien', Bernanos, *Journal d'un curé de campagne*, *OR*, p. 1112; trans. 104.
59. Bernanos, *Un mauvais rêve* (1950), *OR*, pp. 873–1027 (p. 935); *Sous le soleil de Satan*, *OR*, pp. 108, 218.
60. 'Hyperémotivité'; 'Hyperesthésie'; 'une grave intoxication des cellules nerveuses, probablement d'origine intestinale', Bernanos, *Sous le soleil de Satan*, *OR*, pp. 98–9, 231.
61. 'Médecin de l'âme', François Mauriac, 'Thérèse chez le docteur' (1938), *OC*, II, pp. 285–308 (p. 308).
62. 'Il n'a rien à vous donner, il ne peut rien pour vous que de vous enfoncer davantage dans cette boue. J'ignore à qui il faudrait vous adresser, mais pas à lui, pas à lui!', Mauriac, 'Thérèse chez le docteur', *OC*, II, p. 301.
63. Mauriac writes in 1928: 'Ne vouloir connaître de l'homme que son instinct le plus individuel, n'avoir d'autre ambition que d'embrasser d'un regard toujours plus lucide le chaos humain, que d'en enregistrer tous les mouvements confus et transitoires, il y a là une menace redoutable pour le roman moderne et qui pèse singulièrement sur l'œuvre de Marcel Proust'; ('Wanting to know nothing of man besides his most individual instincts, having no other ambition than to capture human chaos with an ever more lucid gaze, these hold a fearsome threat for the modern novel, and one which weighs particularly on the work of Marcel Proust'), 'Le Roman', *OC*, VIII, pp. 261–84 (p. 280). 'La terrible introspection', Bernanos, 'Interview de 1926 par Frédéric Lefèvre', *EEC*, I, pp. 1038–48 (p. 1045). Bernanos goes on to condemn the lack of a moral lesson in the ethically neutral 'observation pure' for which Proust aims.
64. 'Les plus brillants élèves du conservatoire Gide ou du conservatoire Proust, munis de leur brevet d'immoralisme'; 'Jadis l'écrivain recevait cérémonieusement au seuil de sa conscience, et ne désignait que de loin prudemment, ainsi qu'un hôte soupçonneux, le plan général de sa demeure, et l'emplacement de ses chambres les plus secrètes. Aujourd'hui, il nous donne le trousseau de clefs, et une petite tape d'encouragement sur l'épaule: Allez-y!', Bernanos, 'Une vision catholique du réel' (1927), *EEC*, I, pp. 1074–89 (pp. 1079–80).
65. 'Comme ses autres victimes, il la pousserait à s'assouvir. La délivrance de l'esprit par l'assouvissement de la chair: c'était à cela que se ramenait sa méthode. La même clef immonde lui servait pour interpréter l'héroïsme, le crime, la sainteté, le renoncement', Mauriac, 'Thérèse chez le docteur', *OC*, II, p. 302.

66. 'Nous n'avons, toi et moi, dans les choses de l'amour ni préjugés ni scrupules. Comment croire à une morale qu'une science aussi exacte que la mathématique—l'hygiène—dément chaque jour?', Bernanos, *Sous le soleil de Satan*, *OR*, p. 102.
67. 'Croyez-vous au démon, docteur? Croyez-vous que le mal soit quelqu'un?', Mauriac, 'Thérèse chez le docteur', *OC*, II, p. 306.
68. On Bernanos's influence on Mauriac, see Richard Griffiths, *Le Singe de Dieu: François Mauriac entre le 'roman catholique' et la littérature contemporaine, 1913–1930* (Le Bouscat: L'Esprit du temps, 1996), p. 148.
69. 'Cela ne justifiait pas non plus le brusque emportement de sa haine en face de Mme Alfieri, moins encore cette fuite absurde dans les ténèbres. Il fallait sans doute remonter plus haut, beaucoup plus haut, à certaines tentations de l'enfance dont le hasard seul lui avait permis de triompher—mais dont la blessure était encore là, quelque part, dans un repli du cerveau'; 'Pour la première fois, la prodigieuse vie intérieure, toujours repliée sur elle-même et qui, selon un mot ignoble du vieux Ganse, cuisait depuis dix ans dans son jus, cette vie mystérieuse partagée tour à tour entre le désespoir et l'exaltation, traversée de figures de cauchemar ainsi qu'un carrefour suspect, ce flot souterrain allait rompre l'obstacle sous laquelle il creusait ses tourbillons, paraître au jour', Bernanos, *Un mauvais rêve*, *OR*, pp. 977, 985.
70. Pierrette Renard, *Bernanos ou l'ombre lumineuse* (Grenoble: Publications de l'université Stendhal de Grenoble, 1990), p. 41.
71. 'It [the instinctual representative] proliferates, one might say, in the dark, and finds extreme forms of expression', Sigmund Freud, 'Repression', *Standard Edition*, XIV, pp. 141–58 (p. 149).
72. 'Mi-spirituelles, mi-charnelles, comme à la jointure du corps et de l'esprit', Bernanos, *La Joie*, *OR*, pp. 531–724 (p. 571).
73. 'Le psychanalyste assurément, dirige la cure. Le premier principe de cette cure, celui qu'on lui épelle d'abord, qu'il retrouve partout dans sa formation au point qu'il s'en imprègne, c'est qu'il ne doit point diriger le patient. La direction de conscience au sens du guide moral qu'un fidèle du catholicisme peut y trouver est ici exclue radicalement. Si la psychanalyse pose des problèmes à la théologie morale, ce ne sont pas ceux de la direction de conscience, en quoi nous rappelons que la direction de conscience en pose aussi'. Jacques Lacan, 'La Direction de la cure et les principes de son pouvoir', in *Écrits* (Paris: Seuil, 1966), pp. 585–642 (p. 585).
74. 'Les maniaques de la libre pensée sont bien sots de dédaigner à l'église une méthode de psychothérapie qu'ils jugent excellente et nouvelle chez un neurologiste en renom. Ce professeur, dans sa clinique, fait-il autre chose qu'un simple prêtre au confessionnal: provoquer, déclencher la confidence pour suggestionner ensuite, à loisir, un malade apaisé, détendu? Combien de choses pourrissent dans le cœur, dont ce seul effort délivre?', Bernanos, *Sous le soleil de Satan*, *OR*, pp. 303–304.
75. Freud, 'Studies on Hysteria', *Standard Edition*, II, p. 282.

3

SUBJECT

André Breton

In the central chapter of *Mad Love* (*L'Amour fou*), Breton (1896–1966) narrates the uncanny encounter of the 'Sunflower Night' which underpins the book as a whole. His account is prefaced with the following authorial remarks:

> Several times I have recounted a series of facts relating to some intimate circumstances of my life [here, a footnote refers the reader to Breton's earlier works, *Nadja* and *Les Vases communicants*], strange enough to deserve attention. Only a precise and absolutely careful reference to the emotional state of the subject to whom such things happen can furnish any basis for their evaluation. Surrealism has always suggested that they be written like a medical report.[1]

The quasi-medical discourse in which Breton writes is specified in *Nadja* (1928, revised for a new edition in 1963) to be modelled on the plain and objective style of the neuropsychiatric report.[2] Breton's use of the term *subject* in this quotation to refer to himself is a striking instance of this. I have adopted it as the title of this chapter not only because it testifies to Breton's medical background and war-time experiences in psychiatry and neurology, but also because it shadows the practice of another quasi-medical discourse on the mind, psychoanalysis. Breton and Surrealism find their place in this investigation first and foremost from the importance of the movement in the literary representation of dreams, madness, and the irrational, and for their unstinting efforts to access and express the unconscious mind. They also earn our attention for being the first point of contact between French literary culture and Freudian psychoanalysis, and for being the most sustained fellow-travellers of psychoanalytic theory in a century which has seen no shortage of Freudian fictions. With Breton we have the opening chapter in the story of a mutual infatuation between psychoanalysis and French literary culture which will last for the whole of the twentieth century, and recur throughout the remainder of this book. Breton's long engagement with the psychoanalytic model of the mind is fundamental to his work, yet, as we shall see, he is no slavish disciple of Freudian theory, as his prickly relationship with Freud himself demonstrates. Breton's interest in the occult, his belief in prophetic dreams and malignant auras, orient his representation of the mind in a distinctly different direction from Freud's sober materialism, and create some unlikely parallels between the determinedly impious Surrealist and the religious novelists of the previous chapter.

Ian W. Alexander argues that the early decades of the twentieth century see French literature embracing a new depth psychology, as much as a reaction to the lucid consciousness of modernism's inner monologues as a consequence of psychoanalytic infiltration into culture; he cites François Mauriac as emblematic of this trend, along with Georges Duhamel, Pierre Drieu La Rochelle, Jean Giraudoux, and others.[3] Gide, who was also prolific during these years, is another author to direct his attention towards areas of the mind which are, by nature or deliberate intention, concealed from view. His stories revel in irrational, unmotivated acts and self-deluding narrators who use piety, charity, or philosophical doctrine as a front for actions, the true motivations of which are probably unconscious and certainly psycho-sexual in nature. Among many examples, we might cite *Les Caves du Vatican* (1914), in which Lafcadio throws someone from a train in an impulsive 'gratuitous act'; *La Porte étroite* (1909), in which Alissa rejects Jérôme for a cloistered life, in a decision which may stem from her feelings towards her mother's adulterous sexuality; or *La Symphonie pastorale* (1919), in which the married pastor who takes a blind girl into his home has unconscious motivations which extend beyond the charitable. Other twentieth-century writers who have particularly attracted psychoanalytic attention include the French novelists Georges Perec and Marguerite Duras. Perec's texts include *La Boutique Obscure* (1973), a collection of dream-narratives, and the semi-autobiograpical *W ou le souvenir d'enfance* (1975). This latter intersperses childhood recollections of his life before and after his mother's deportation to Auschwitz with episodes from the story of the island of W, in which a society based on sporting ideals gradually comes to appear more and more like a Nazi death camp. Perec emphasizes slips of memory and symbolic imagery, as when a misremembered physical injury is said to stand in place of repressed emotional trauma, while in the fictional chapters, the concentration camp images and echoes of autobiography contaminate the story as if emanations of the narrator's unconscious. Duras is the subject of an essay by Kristeva and an 'hommage' by Lacan, both of which present her fiction as exemplary of psychoanalytic characterization. Lacan's piece (which Duras found patronizing) examined the ambiguity of 'ravissement' in *Le Ravissement de Lol V. Stein* (1964) and explored the interplay of gazes in the text; Kristeva's essay closes her psychoanalytic study of melancholia, and labels Duras's work 'non-cathartic art'. Duras's writing, which forms an important interlocutor for several of the œuvres explored here, show their protagonists in melancholic states, drifting through life at the edge of despair or madness, unable to understand their own behaviour, and compelled to re-enact traumatic love-affairs with new partners in a manner reminiscent of Freudian repetition compulsion.

Writers following Breton who have actively engaged with psychoanalysis in their writing (as opposed to simply attracting psychoanalytic readings) include Michel Leiris, Serge Doubrovsky, Nina Bouraoui, and Marie Cardinal. Doubrovsky and Leiris, a former Surrealist who, like several others, dissociated himself from the movement after falling out with Breton, accompany the more conventional autobiographical or semi-autobiographical narrative of their texts with their own psychoanalytic interpretations of their character and actions, enfolding the traditional task of the psychoanalytic critic within the literary work itself, while thereby forestalling unwelcome readings. This is particularly the case with Doubrovsky's controversial *Le Livre brisé* (1989), the first half of which recounts the author's troubled marriage, and the remainder of which narrates the aftermath of his wife's suicide as the book was in progress. Cardinal's *Les Mots pour le dire* (1975) and Bouraoui's *Mes mauvaises pensées* (2005) present semi-autobiographical accounts of psychoanalytic therapy. The earlier text presents a highly influential and wholly positive account of psychoanalysis, in which distressing psychological and psychosomatic symptoms are dramatically relieved when the psychoanalyst assists the narrator in uncovering repressed memories concerning her mother and father. This is the cultural legacy of Breton's pioneering engagement with Freudian psychoanalysis.

Breton was a founder member and self-proclaimed leader of the Surrealists, other notable members of which include the writers Louis Aragon, Robert Desnos, and Paul Éluard and practitioners of the visual arts such as Max Ernst, Man Ray, and Salvador Dalí. Drawing inspiration from poets like Lautréamont, Rimbaud, and Apollinaire, who coined the term Surrealism, and developing out of the Dada movement in the wake of the First World War, Surrealism was to become a major European cultural force in the inter-war period. Breton was the heart of the movement, embroiled in constant controversy within the group, the history of which is marked by quarrels and splits, and outside it, where his work was accused of being obscene, nonsensical, or even incitement to murder.

Breton's acquaintance with the study of the mind began with his university medical training in 1913, which was interrupted by the outbreak of war. Mobilized as a hospital intern, he was assigned in July 1916 to the neuropsychiatric centre at Saint-Dizier, where he encountered serious mental disorders for the first time, observed the institutional treatment of psychiatric patients, and discovered psychoanalytic theory through a 1914 study by Emmanuel Régis and Angelo Hesnard, *La Psychoanalyse des névroses et des psychoses, ses applications médicales et extra-medicales* (*The Psychoanalysis of Neuroses and Psychoses: Applications in the Clinic and Beyond*), which attempted to present Freud's theories to the French psychiatric establishment. Having abandoned his medical studies in 1920 for the literary life, Breton engaged in experiments with automatic writing and hypnotic slumber with other members of the Surrealist circle, aiming to produce the direct expression of the unconscious mind, bypassing the ordering and censoring processes of consciousness. In this period, Breton began to explore psychoanalytic theory directly, and met Freud himself in Vienna in October 1921, in a brief and ill-starred meeting, written up by Breton in a sneering piece that dismisses Freud as 'a little old man of ordinary appearance'.[4] Automatic writing was soon abandoned by Breton and the other Surrealists in favour of consciously crafted texts, which still dealt with topics of the irrational and unconscious. By the time of the *First Manifesto*, in 1924, he acknowledged a debt to Freud's discoveries; he would continue to express his 'enthusiastic admiration' for the psychoanalyst to the end of his career, while not being afraid to ruffle Freud's feathers with some outspoken criticism.[5] The psychoanalyst is joined by two other thinkers, Hegel and Marx, in Breton's personal pantheon. The former inspires Breton's dialectical approach to the reconciliation of mental oppositions of dreams and waking life, madness and sanity, consciousness and the unconscious; the latter diverts the 'revolutionary' nature of Surrealist art towards explicitly political ends.

Mad Love itself came at the Surrealist movement's creative peak, before the Second World War imposed a hiatus and a diaspora from which it would never fully recover. The book is the third of Breton's three volumes of mingled autobiographical narrative and theoretical essay, interspersed with photographic illustrations. *Nadja* and *Les Vases communicants* (*Communicating Vases*, 1932) are the two which precede it. *Nadja* recounts Breton's relationship with a vulnerable, artistic young woman with schizophrenic tendencies, bookended with considerations on his own unconscious mind and a virulent condemnation of psychiatric care. The three parts of *Les Vases communicants* are more dominated by the essay form: in the first, Breton analyzes the symbolism of one of his dreams, in the second, he describes the dream-like aspects of his waking life during a period of depression, and in the final part, he links the revolutionizing of our understanding of the mind to revolutionary politics. *Mad Love* shares several of the themes of the earlier works each of its parts. Less cohesive than the earlier works, the text is a collection of seven pieces, all but one of which were originally published separately, and with only the last two postdating Breton's decision to create the volume. The text covers a period in Breton's life from April 1934 to September 1936, with the writing roughly contemporaneous. The key events of this period are meeting Jacqueline Lamba, the unnamed woman of the 'Sunflower Night' on 29 May 1934, their marriage the following August, a trip together to Tenerife (where Breton was to present a showing of Buñuel's *L'Âge d'or*) in May 1935, the birth of their daughter, Aube, that December, followed by discord in the relationship through 1936 and a temporary separation in September of that year. The first section of the book, written before the meeting with Lamba, discourses on dreams, chance, and beauty. The second focuses more closely on coincidence, expounding the theory that '*chance is the form making manifest the exterior necessity which traces its path in the human unconscious*'.[6] The thesis is demonstrated in the third section, which recounts Breton's visit to the Saint-Ouen flea-market with Giacometti, where the chance discovery of objects leads Giacometti to overcome a barrier to creativity, and Breton to fulfil an unconscious desire. The first three sections thus set up the themes of coincidence, desire, and the unconscious, which prepare the way for *l'amour fou* itself, which makes its appearance in the fourth section. Here, Breton recounts a night walk around Paris with his new female acquaintance, passing Les Halles, the Tour St Jacques, and the flower market on the bank of the Seine. Some days later, he feels compelled to look up one of his early automatic-writing poems, 'Tournesol', from the collection *Clair de terre* (*Earthlight*, 1923). Line by line, Breton picks out what he believes are uncanny pre-figurations in the poem of the events of that night, more than a decade later. Two scenes from the marriage follow in the next sections. In the fifth part, an account of a hike in Tenerife describes the island's flora in sexualized terms that emphasize its fertile profusion. In the sixth, a rift between the couple during a walk on a Brittany beach is ascribed to the malignant atmosphere as they unwittingly pass the site of a notorious murder. Lastly, Breton addresses the seventh section to his daughter's future sixteen-year-old self, expressing his love for her, and his hopes for the future.

Mad Love offers one of Breton's most intriguing explorations of the irrational and unconscious, coupled with his most mature engagement with Freudian ideas. Where relevant, I shall also refer to *Nadja* and *Les Vases communicants*, along with other texts important to his view of the mind, such as *L'Immaculée Conception* (1930) and *Arcane 17* (1944–47), plus the various poems, essays, and polemics which define his position. We shall see where Breton's ideas on consciousness and the unconscious mind are in tune with Freud's, and where they differ. Some of these points of disagreement interestingly foreshadow later reactions to Freudian orthodoxy within psychiatry, such as R.D. Laing and the anti-psychiatry movement, or Gilles Deleuze's and Félix Guattari's schizoanalysis. We will also explore his relationship to philosophy of mind, with a particular emphasis on Hegel; we shall see how Breton's views compare with scientific views of the mind, and how his interest in the supernatural links him to religious conceptions of consciousness; and, lastly, we shall explore the question of the gendered mind, triggered by Simone de Beauvoir's powerful critique in *Le Deuxième Sexe* of Breton's representation of male and female subjectivity.

Direct references to Freudian theory are abundant in Breton's work. In *Mad Love*, the opening paragraph declares that 'psychoanalysis would have something to say about this' regarding a dream of the sea, presumably alluding to a possible unconscious play on the terms *mer* and *mère*.[7] The only footnote in the book to refer to a non-Surrealist text is a reference to Freud's *The Ego and the Id*, from which Breton takes two quotations on the sex drive and death drive as a postscript to his account of the flea-market finds: Breton's own purchase, a spoon supported by a model shoe on the handle, in which Breton sees symbolism of male and female sex organs, is attributed to the sex drive, while Giacometti's metal mask is linked to the death drive (p. 709; trans. 38). The Tenerife section draws on Freud further, citing him alongside Engels as a champion of sexual love, which, in drawing together people from across social and racial divides, acts as a progressive force (p. 745; trans. 77). These approving sentiments are typical of most of Breton's references to Freud and psychoanalysis. The *First Manifesto* of 1924 declares that 'we must give thanks to Freud's discoveries in this regard' for drawing attention to dreams and the unconscious mind, going on to assert:

> If the depths of our minds harbour strange forces capable of augmenting those of the surface, or struggling against them and winning, there is every interest in capturing them, capturing them first in order later to submit them, if need be, to the control of our reason.[8]

(The nuance afforded by the phrase 'if need be' will prove significant.) On hearing false rumours of Freud's arrest during the annexation of Austria in 1938, Breton writes of the 'pang of anguish' he feels at the news, and praises Freud for 'a whole lifetime of radiant understanding, of exclusive devotion to the cause of human emancipation, conceived in the broadest form that ever was'.[9] The sentiments in both of these statements are to some extent in conflict with other, less positive assessments of psychoanalysis, which we will encounter later.

Direct references aside, there are many connections between Freud and Breton in the latter's representation of the mind, which shares methods of inquiry, topics of focus, and terminology with the psychoanalyst. Which of these links are the result of direct influence, which the product of culturally mediated ideas originating in Freud, and which arise independently in Breton from the medical and cultural background he shares with Freud, is near-impossible to unravel, and need not concern us overly. Many concepts now considered Freudian pre-date Freud himself. In his critique of psychoanalytic theory, Richard Webster offers examples of references to unconscious motivation dating back to Pascal in the seventeenth century ('The heart has its reasons, of which reason knows nothing') and to repression in the Goncourt brothers' diary from 1865, which records Sainte-Beuve making the following confession:

> In my head, I don't know where, here or here—he feels his skull—I have a box, a compartment, that I'm always afraid to allow to open too widely. And my work, everything I do, and all my many articles, are to squash it down. . . . I have stopped it up, crushed it with books, in order not to have the time to think, to not be free to come and go.[10]

Breton and Freud thus share a European cultural heritage, as well as a medical and psychiatric background, which would make a certain convergence in their view of the mind inevitable, even without the growing interest Breton takes in Freud's work through the course of his writing career. Breton's own view of the mind remains largely consistent from his early works, at which point his knowledge of psychoanalysis was often sketchy and second-hand, to his later career, when he had absorbed Freud's work thoroughly. It is also beyond question that Breton's divergences from Freud result not from misunderstandings of psychoanalytic theory, but from genuine differences in his conception of what the mind is, how it relates to the external world, and what its 'healthiest' state might be.

We have noted already Breton's use of scientific discourse in his writing, and it is perhaps surprising, given the Surrealist movement's reputation for anarchic provocation, to see the extent to which Breton's work, like Freud's, takes on the trappings of objective scientific observation and theoretical system-building. The *First Manifesto* attempts to assimilate the methods of Surrealism to those of scientists, claiming that both strike out into uncharted waters without a preconceived plan, avoiding the well-trodden '*sensible* path' and spurred on by 'pure Surrealist joy'.[11] This theme is taken up in *Mad Love* itself, which quotes mathematician and physicist Gustave Juvet on the primacy of astonishment over logic in scientific discovery (751; trans. 83). Elsewhere in the manifesto, Breton defines Surrealism more as a psychological experiment than an artistic movement:

> Surrealism, noun. Pure mental automatism through which one intends to express, either verbally, in writing or by other means, the real functioning of thought. A dictation of thought, in the absence of any control exercised by reason, disregarding any aesthetic or moral concerns.[12]

The text goes on to distance Surrealism further from aesthetic considerations, emphasizing the passivity of the writer in his reception and expression of material emanating from the unconscious:

> But we, who have carried out no filtering, who have made ourselves in our works the dull receptacles of so many echoes, the modest *recording devices* who do not obsess over the design that they [Swift, Baudelaire, Rimbaud, and other precursors of the movement] trace, we perhaps serve a nobler cause. Thus, with integrity we hand back the 'talent' people ascribe to us. Tell me about the talent of this metre rule, this mirror, this door, and of the sky, if you like. We have no talent.[13]

While Surrealism's attempt at an unmediated expression of the unconscious may fall by the wayside in Surrealism's later years, the conception remains of the movement's activities as psychological explorations which contribute to the sum of human knowledge on the mind. The year after the publication of *Mad Love*, Breton's and Éluard's co-produced *Dictionnaire abrégé du surréalisme* (*Shorter Dictionary of Surrealism*, 1938) defines Surrealism itself as 'an instrument of knowledge [which] strives to shine a light on the depths of human consciousness'.[14]

Like psychoanalysis, Surrealism attempts to access the unconscious mind via dreams, free association and uncontrolled language. Breton's equivalent of the Freudian slip is the 'waking sentence', words which appear spontaneously in the mind at a point between sleep and wakefulness, as if 'tapping on the window-pane of consciousness'.[15] Like Freud, Breton sees mental life as dominated by desire, primarily sexual in nature, which operates in an unconscious conceived as a near-autonomous entity within the mind. *Mad Love* puts it as follows, drawing on similar imagery to the Proustian 'unknown lake' that we saw in the opening chapter:

> What I have wanted to do above all is to show the precautions and the ruses which desire, in search of its object, employs as it wavers in preconscious waters, and, once this object is discovered, the means (so far stupefying) it uses to reveal it through consciousness.[16]

The nature and function of dreams is understood in a largely Freudian sense: in *Mad Love*, Breton's dream-images 'possess the *keys to situations*'; *Nadja* labels certain dream-impressions as '"overdetermining" in the Freudian sense' in their symbolic value.[17] *Les Vases communicants* accepts Freud's notion of abstruse sexual symbolism in banal dream-images: 'sexually, it is known that a laid table symbolizes woman', Breton asserts, following Freud's *The Interpretation of Dreams* (1899), and makes several further references to Freud's study in the course of Breton's own dream interpretation, including Freud's claim that a neck-tie must symbolize the penis both due to its similarity (both hang downwards and are owned by men) and difference (ties can be changed at will).[18] As in Freud, such cryptic significations may be linguistic as well as visual: the 'Sunflower Night' is heralded in *Mad Love* by a punning play on the words *l'on dine* ('one dines') and *l'ondine* ('water sprite') overheard on the street, the latter recalling water-tank cabaret turn performed by Jacqueline Lamba.

For Freud, dream symbolism is a consequence of gatekeeper censorship at the borders of consciousness, which forbids entry to repressed material, and thus requires the unconscious to smuggle such thoughts through in disguise at a moment when vigilance is relaxed. Specifically, Freud considers dreams to be 'disguised fulfilments of repressed wishes', and advances the following hypothesis as to their formation:

> In our mental apparatus there are two thought-constructing agencies, of which the second enjoys the privilege of having free access to consciousness for its products, whereas the activity of the first is in itself unconscious and can only reach consciousness by way of the second. On the frontier between the two agencies, where the first passes over to the second, there is a censorship, which only allows what is agreeable to it to pass through and holds back everything else. According to our definition, then, what is rejected by the censorship is in a

> state of repression. Under certain conditions, of which the state of sleep is one, the relation between the strength of the two agencies is modified in such a way that what is repressed can no longer be held back. In the state of sleep this probably occurs owing to a relaxation of the censorship; when this happens it becomes possible for what has hitherto been repressed to make a path for itself to consciousness. Since, however, the censorship is never completely eliminated but merely reduced, the repressed material must submit to certain alterations which mitigate its offensive features. What becomes conscious in such cases is a compromise between the intentions of one agency and the demands of the other. Repression—relaxation of the censorship—the formation of a compromise, this is the fundamental pattern for the generation not only of dreams but of many other psychopathological structures; and in the latter cases, too, we may observe that the formation of compromises is accompanied by processes of condensation and displacement and by the employment of superficial associations, which we have become familiar with in the dream work.[19]

Many of these ideas are echoed in Breton, for whom the self is 'a false-bottomed box', the unconscious levels of which are working independently of consciousness, and sending forth coded therapeutic messages during sleep.[20] Breton asks: 'Can dreams too not be put to work in resolving the fundamental questions of life?'[21] The answer comes in *Les Vases communicants* by the example of a dream which enables Breton to move on from his fixation on a failed relationship with Suzanne Muzard through dream-images which denigrate monogamy in general and Muzard in particular: 'Everything happens as if [the sleeper] wished to resolve in this way a particularly complex affective problem, which, due to its overly emotive character, defies the elements of conscious appreciation which determine, for one part, the way we conduct our lives'.[22]

Similarly, the idea of a censoring function within conscious thought is prominent in Breton's writing. He rails against self-censorship in art, condemning the pressures that lead artists into 'correcting, *self*-correcting, polishing, touching up, finding fault and not drawing blindly on our subjective treasure'.[23] The Surrealists' use of hypnotic trances in their own writing is described as an attempt to 'escape from the constraints that burden those thoughts which are watched over'. Breton names two such constraints: our 'subordination to immediate sensory perceptions, which to a large extent make the mind the plaything of the external world' and the constraint 'which makes the *critical mind* weigh on language, and more generally, on the most diverse modes of expression'.[24] Later in the same interview he refers to three psychological limits to creativity which the Surrealists sought to overcome:

> These shackles were of the order of *logic* (rationalism of the narrowest kind saw to it that nothing be let past that did not receive its stamp), of the order of *morality* (in the form of sexual and social taboos), and lastly of the order of *taste*, governed by the sophistic conventions of 'good form', which may be the worst of all.[25]

We could continue at length on cataloguing the affinities between Breton's view of the mind and the psychoanalytic model. From *Mad Love* alone there are numerous other points of contact, such as the psychoanalytic sketch of maternal and paternal influences which, Breton speculates, may have caused Michel Henriot, the Brittany murderer, to develop his criminal tendencies, or the tribunals of men and women who judge Breton in the mental theatre of his dreams, with their air of a psychoanalytic superego, or the element of the Freudian uncanny in the overlaying of the events of the 'Sunflower Night' with the memories of the poem written long before.[26] The resemblances that we have seen are sufficient to demonstrate the fundamental area of common ground between Breton and psychoanalysis: both describe a decentred subject whose conscious mind is figured as only part of a larger self, in which the unconscious mind, characterized by the irrational and the taboo, harbours desires and motivates actions without our awareness.

Already, though, in the examples given, we have begun to see some of the differences between Breton and Freud. Breton's unconscious is more porous and accessible than Freud's: absenting yourself from everyday distractions can be enough to escape the censorship of conscious thought. Indeed, the strict division between conscious and unconscious mind is itself put into question by Breton's work, which aims to reconcile the two domains and consciously employ to creative ends the taboos, dream-logic, madness, and irrationality associated with the unconscious. Breton's interpretation of dreams, too, betrays on closer inspection some important differences from Freudian orthodoxy. Breton's dream in *Les Vases communicants* is interpreted, as we saw, as offering guidance in moving on from a relationship. We note first the future-orientation of Breton's reading: for him, the dream is concerned with his present situation and the future development of it. This despite the fact that the central scenes of the dream are one of conflict with his father, immediately followed by a scene involving a young boy. Freudian analysis would naturally relate such material to the analysand's childhood, and to a putative Œdipus complex, but Breton gives no consideration to such a possibility. Indeed, Breton's unconscious is not so much the vault of hidden traumas from the past, as an anarchic co-pilot of the self, focused on the same contemporary problems as the conscious mind, but unconstrained by the latter's self-censorship of logic, taste, and morality. While Freud's dream interpretation may also involve the actions of the unconscious aiding the dreamer to resolve a problem, such problems in psychoanalysis often originate in the unconscious itself. The clues encoded in the dream teach us about the nature of repressed material in the unconscious, which the conscious mind can then recover and attend to. In Breton's dream, the unconscious offers the solution, but doesn't hold the problem, making Breton's dream interpretation closer to the folk-wisdom, cited in his text, that 'night brings counsel'.[27]

In *Mad Love* the reciprocal gaze of Breton and his baby daughter symbolizes the communication between the conscious and unconscious mind (p. 784; trans. 117). In *Nadja*, 'the absence of a borderline, as is well known, between *non-madness* and madness' lays out a no-man's land between reason and irrationality that synthesizes the two halves of the mind and provides the narrative with a territory of its own.[28] (This is also the territory that Duras will adopt for many of her characters.) In *Les Vases communicants*, the title itself refers to the connecting realms of 'the world of reality' and 'that of dreams', and the text itself attempts 'conciliation' between the two.[29] Breton's images of interconnection clearly distinguish his idea of mental architecture from Freud's:

> In closely examining the content of the most unconsidered activity of the mind, if we pass beyond the extraordinary and hardly reassuring frothing at the surface, it is possible to reveal *capillary tissue*, without the knowledge of which we would strive in vain to conceptualize mental circulation. The role of this tissue is, as we have seen, to assure the constant exchange which needs to occur in thought between the external and internal worlds, an exchange which necessitates the continuous interpenetration of waking and sleeping activity. My whole ambition has been to offer here an insight into its structure.[30]

Breton's capillary tissue (read as a metonym for mental functioning rather than as dubious neuroanatomy), lays out a more dynamic vision of the mind than the psychoanalytic model, with a constant and substantial two-way traffic between the conscious and unconscious mind, the latter of which is thereby a more tangible presence for the self. In a conference speech from 1938, Breton announces that the task Surrealism has been keenest to tackle is 'ending the opposition between reality and dreams', and goes on to declare that psychoanalysis, while appreciating that the nature of a dream depends partly on conscious activity from the previous day, has failed to notice that the reverse is also true: 'waking activity proceeds, at least partially, from the earlier dream activity'.[31] Elsewhere, Breton discusses his former depressive state in which he finds his waking life held a 'striking analogy' with the dream state, or makes reference to monasticism, a life in which men prioritize hallucination over reality, in order to emphasize the presence of the irrational mind, beyond conscious control, as part of our waking experience.[32]

Breton not only conceives the relationship between the rational and irrational mind differently from psychoanalysis, he also offers a different value judgement. Where psychoanalysis wishes to purge the Unconscious, Surrealism will celebrate it. The collapse of reason in Nadja's schizophrenic episodes is likened to Surrealist creativity: when Nadja hallucinates a fiery hand on the surface of the Seine, when she imagines a fountain as composed of her thoughts combined with Breton's, or sketches delusional images, Breton quotes her words and reproduces her drawings, demonstrating clearly the similarity with the art and poetry which the Surrealists strove to produce. (Similarly, in the essay, 'L'Art des fous, la clé des champs' ['Mad People's Art, The Open Road', 1948–49], Breton praises the 'total authenticity' of mental patients' art, which constitutes 'a reservoir of moral health', unfettered by the limitations of normal life.)[33] At the end of the relationship with Nadja, Breton declares that he would like to remember only her poetic phrases, of which he reproduces nine, any of which would be at home as a line of Surrealist poetry, such as: 'The lion's claw grasps the breast of the vine'.[34] He notes that as her sanity falters, 'her thoughts became still clearer, and her manner of expression gained lightness, originality and depth'.[35] Even her final descent into madness is viewed ambivalently. Breton declares that she served the only worthy cause there is, that of 'human emancipation *in all respects*, let it be understood, *according to means available to every one of us*', and that her means of doing so was 'by putting her head and then an arm through the bars of logic, that most hateful of prisons, which she had bent apart in this way'.[36] The Surrealists are held back from sharing her fate only by their 'instinct for self-preservation' as they venture beyond the bounds of reason in the course of their work. Breton's attitude to psychoanalytic therapy in regard to Nadja's case is somewhat conflicted. At the end of the text, he suggests that Nadja might have been saved by a proper talking cure which allowed her to regress to the source of her trouble. Elsewhere in the book, though, Breton sneers at psychoanalysis's 'achievements worthy of a bailiff', and claims the discipline aims at 'nothing less than evicting man from himself'.[37] The implication is that the contents of the unconscious, taboos, traumas, irrationality, and all, are not monsters to be tamed but an integral part of the self to be embraced, and a potential source of insight and creativity.

While Breton is in two minds about Freudian psychotherapy, he is in no doubt where the methods of conventional psychiatry are concerned. The final pages of *Nadja* are given over to a tirade against psychiatric care, in which Breton declares that mental institutions drive their patients insane just as prisons harden criminals, that internment is arbitrary and without justification, and that his own reaction to confinement would be to 'coldly assassinate one of them, preferably the doctor, who might fall into my hands'.[38] Breton responds to the outrage of the medical profession at these words by reprinting their condemnations at the head of his second manifesto and heaping insults on them in the article, 'La Médecine mentale devant le surréalisme' ('Psychiatry and Surrealism', 1930), which denounces psychiatrists as having 'the primary function of being used as instruments of social repression', and claims they treat patients like dogs and are surprised not to have the right to put them down at will.[39]

Breton's intemperate language may be deliberately provocative, but the ideas expressed both in his re-evaluation of mental illness and his criticism of psychiatric care will find strong echoes in the second half of the twentieth century among notable thinkers on mental illness, in particular, Michel Foucault, in his first published work, *Histoire de la folie à l'âge classique* (*Madness and Civilization*, 1972); the influential analyst R.D. Laing and his associates in the anti-psychiatry movement of the 1960s; and the 'schizo-analysis' of Deleuze and Guattari. Foucault describes the insane asylum as 'an instrument of moral uniformity and of social denunciation'.[40] Laing disclaims for himself the term 'anti-psychiatry', coined by his friend and collaborator, David Cooper, but declares: 'I agree with the anti-psychiatric thesis that by and large psychiatry functions to exclude and repress those elements society wants excluded and repressed'.[41] Like Foucault, Laing adopts a relativist view of madness and sanity, claiming that we cannot take an 'unequivocal view of the sanity of common sense, or of the madness of the so-called madman'.[42] As with Foucault, the relationship between the 'sane' and the 'insane' is seen in terms of an imbalance of power: 'The psychiatrist, as ipso facto sane, shows that the patient is out of contact with him. The fact that he is out of contact with the patient shows that there is something wrong with the patient, but not with the psychiatrist'.[43] Deleuze and Guattari in turn take inspiration from Laing, quoting his assertion that madness can be a 'breakthrough' rather than a 'breakdown' in *L'Anti-Œdipe* (*Anti-Œdipus*, 1972).[44] Deleuze and Guattari's work has broader similarities with Breton's views in their celebration of creative and liberating aspects of mental disorder, and in their attempt to adapt a psychoanalytic understanding of the mind for revolutionary, rather than therapeutic, aims. Breton too strives to connect his Marxist and Freudian influences: the *Second Manifesto* signs Surrealism up to the principles of historical materialism and declares the willingness of the movement to fulfil their revolutionary duties, while at the same time bemoaning the suspicion with which Surrealists are viewed by the Communist Party.[45] This commitment is allied in *Les Vases communicants* to the study of the mind, since, in Breton's words, 'any mistake in the interpretation of man entails an error in the interpretation of the universe: it subsequently becomes an obstacle to its transformation'.[46] He goes on to claim that 'corrupting germs' in the mind are an obstacle to social progress, and that this corruption takes the form of 'cloudy, distorting bubbles which constantly rise from the swampy depths of the individual's *unconscious*'.[47] Thus, he concludes, we must understand the unconscious in order to control it. Elsewhere, though, Breton takes a different tack, explicitly linking the socialist liberation of the masses to the Surrealist liberation of the unconscious mind:

> Today more than ever the *liberation of the mind*, which is the express aim of Surrealism, requires in the eyes of the Surrealists as its primary condition the *liberation of mankind*, which implies that whatever obstructs this end must be fought with desperate energy, and that today more than ever the Surrealists are counting on the Revolution of the proletariat for this definitive liberation of mankind.[48]

Breton won't be the last writer here to blur his theories of the mind with his political convictions. The two areas are combined only with difficulty, and usually with some distortion of the theory of mind, the better to fit it to the required ideology. Here, as the scepticism of the Communist Party towards Surrealism confirms, there is a basic incoherence in the stance Breton proposes. The embrace of madness and anarchic creativity is a very different kind of revolution from that envisaged by the far left in the Soviet era. The politicizing of Breton's view of the mind brings to the fore the tension between liberation and control, which has always been present in his work through the competing demands of the Surrealist rejection of all constraints and the psychoanalytic aim to normalize extreme mental states.

Politics aside, the relativist approach to madness and sanity found in Foucault, Laing, Deleuze, and Guattari is most clearly prefigured in Breton through his expressed attitudes to specific mental disorders: 'hysteria', paranoia, and the five disorders whose discourses are imitated in the 'Possessions' section of *L'Immaculée conception*. These last—'simulation attempts' of mental retardation, mania, general paralysis of the insane, interpretative delirium, and dementia praecox, co-written with Paul Éluard—are of sufficient verisimilitude to earn the endorsement of psychiatrist Alain Rauzy, and were a strong influence on Lacan.[49] Breton alone wrote the preface to the five pieces, in which he explains that the aim of the texts is to 'prove that the mind, *poetically* trained in the normal man, is capable of reproducing in their broad outlines the most paradoxical verbal manifestations', such as the discourses of the insane.[50] He declares that the work has consequences both for our understanding of mental illness and for our appreciation of poetry. On mental illness, he writes:

> It would be all over for the arrogant categories into which we amuse ourselves by consigning those who have a score to settle with human reason, this same reason that daily denies us the right to express ourselves by the means which are instinctive to us.[51]

On poetry, he blithely signs off the introduction with the recommendation: 'Suffice it to say that we would very much recommend that the practice be generalized, and that, as far as we can see, the "simulation attempt" of certifiable illnesses would profitably replace ballads, sonnets, epics, nonsense poems and other outmoded forms'.[52] 'Hysteria' is similarly reconfigured from an illness to a poetic gift in the article Breton writes with Louis Aragon to mark the fiftieth anniversary of the discovery of the alleged disorder: 'Hysteria is not a pathological phenomenon and may in all respects be considered a supreme means of expression'.[53] The terms of sexual attraction by which Breton and Aragon refer to the sufferers in the article, and the accompanying images of partly clothed young women in the throes of an attack, reproduced from Jean-Martin Charcot's *Iconographie photographique de la Salpêtrière* (*Photographic Iconography from the Salpêtrière Asylum*, 1876–80), recall the idea of 'convulsive beauty' with which Breton ends *Nadja*, and which the opening section of *Mad Love* explores.

Paranoia, lastly, is less overtly discussed in Breton's work, but it is nonetheless a pervasive presence. In interview, Breton discusses Salvador Dalí's 'paranoid-critical activity', in which delirious over-interpretation of an image creates stories from its content, and agrees that a similar process is at work in certain of the 'Possessions' texts.[54] But the excessive interpretation of experience is found widely in Breton's work. He declares in *Nadja*: 'It may be that life asks to be decoded like a cryptogram'.[55] In *Les Vases communicants*, he shows awareness of the delusions that such an attitude may bring:

> It will be understood that all the intermediate stages can exist between pure and simple recognition of the outside world for what it is and negation of the world in favour of a system of representations which are favourable (or unfavourable) to the human individual who stands before it. Ideas of persecution, or of megalomania, are not far from being in play here.[56]

But it is in *Mad Love* that this profusion of personal significance in the world around Breton is most clearly displayed. We see it in the *trouvailles* of the flea-market that commend themselves to Breton's and Giacometti's attention while secretly holding the key to their desires. We see it in the coincidence of the two novels, *The Fox* and *The Woman Changed into a Fox*, at Breton's and his wife's bedside on the day they fall under the malignant spell of the house where the murderer Henriot bred silver foxes. Most of all we see it in the 'Sunflower Night', where the streets Breton walks with Lamba, the postmark on a letter received a few days beforehand, the chirping cricket he hears several days later, and a host of other perceptual details are marshalled in the cause of demonstrating the prophetic nature of the Sunflower poem. Breton is equivocal about how far this significance is present in the world, and how far it's imposed on perception by the unconscious. Discussing the phenomenon in the opening section of the text, he distinguishes it from the interpretative delirium of paranoia:

> I am profoundly persuaded that any perception registered in the most involuntary way—for example, that of a series of words spoken to no one in particular—bears in itself the solution, symbolic or other, of a problem you have with yourself. You have only to know how to get along in the labyrinth. Interpretative delirium begins only when man, ill-prepared, is taken by a sudden fear in the *forest of clues*. But I maintain that for anyone, watchfulness would do anything rather than pay a second's notice to whatever remains exterior to his desire.[57]

The emphasis here is on a psychological rather than supernatural understanding of the 'forest of clues' that is the world around us. (The phrase riffs on Baudelaire's sentient 'forests of symbols' in his famous sonnet, 'Correspondances', which offers a similarly mystical vision.) Breton highlights what emerges from within us—the words we speak only to ourselves, or the desires that guide the focus of our attention—over what impinges from outside. But, here, as elsewhere in Breton, a dialectic is in play, and we will shortly see the other side to Breton's uncanny.

In his attitude to mental illness and his views on psychiatric care, then, Breton prefigures several of the ideas of Foucault, Laing, Deleuze, and Guattari. If any of the four theorists was aware of Breton's views, though, they fail to acknowledge his contribution. Laing cites Foucault, and Deleuze and Guattari cite both these predecessors, but there are no references to Breton in *Histoire de la folie*, *Capitalisme et schizophrénie*, or any of Laing's work (which displays an impressively broad knowledge of French literature).[58] It seems likely that at least one of these influential thinkers was aware of their Surrealist precursor, but either dismissed his inflammatory rhetoric as histrionics, or thought it unwise to link their own re-evaluation of mental illness and its treatment in our society to that of a man who counselled murdering psychiatrists.

The mention of dialectics brings us to the other major influence on Breton's thought beside Freud, which is the philosophy of Hegel, and we should pause to consider how these ideas shape Breton's understanding of the mind. The re-evaluation of madness is itself a Hegelian idea. His *Philosophy of Mind* (1817) posited that madness was the consequence of a healthy mind's encounter with an experience of pain that it found unendurable. Madness was thus, in Hegel's view, paradoxically therapeutic, in that it represented a retreat from reality in order to heal 'wounds of the spirit'.[59] Hegel's conviction that the mentally ill have not lost the faculty of reason, but rather have it embroiled in internal contradictions, as well as his assertion that an element of madness plays a necessary role in the development of the mind, were an influence on Breton and Éluard in the composition of *L'Immaculée conception*.[60] *Mad Love* makes reference to Hegel at several points, notably in the concepts of objective chance and of the 'sublime point' (p. 780). This latter is the point at which, Breton will later explain, 'all the antinomies that gnaw at us and lead us to despair are called to resolve themselves'.[61] This notion, which Breton says is 'incontestably Hegel', is the essential element Breton takes from Hegelian dialectic: Surrealism will be a 'conducting wire' between reason and madness, intellect and passion, the inner and outer worlds, and, most of all, it will offer 'a possibility of drastic conciliation between the two terms which tend to oppose the world of reality to that of dreams, in favour of a philosophy that confuses the two'.[62] The same objective is expressed for *L'Immaculée conception:* 'Our major preoccupation is to reduce the antinomy of reason and unreason, which, among other things, has been one of the permanent ambitions of Surrealism'.[63] The dialectical approach here is a significant departure from the psychoanalytic method: Breton is not attempting to explain the world of dreams by using the rational faculties of waking consciousness, as Freud has done. Rather, he is searching for a synthesis of the two realms, which will also entail the refiguring of the conscious world with the logic of dreams.

Objective chance is one means by which Breton will achieve this. He attributes the concept to Hegel (although others doubt its provenance), and defines it as follows:

> Objective chance is that kind of chance through which is manifested in a way which is still very mysterious to man a necessity which escapes him, despite the fact that he has a vital sense of it as necessary. While order and ends in nature do not objectively coincide with what they are in the minds of men, it may nevertheless occur that natural necessity falls in harmony with human necessity in a rather extraordinary and troubling manner such that the two determinations prove indistinguishable.[64]

These are the coincidences and prophecies which make up the uncanny elements of Breton's world, and Breton asserts that such phenomena need not arise by the action of the mind alone, but may be brought about by the action of the mind and world together. The concept of the 'magic-circumstantial', expressed in *Mad Love* (p. 687; trans. 19) as one of the qualities of convulsive beauty, contains within it the tension between randomness and design in Breton's view of these events. This brings us, at last, to the supernatural, and the parallels between Breton's view of the mind and that of religious writers like Bernanos, Green, and Mauriac.

Breton is no friend of religion, describing God as a pig, and condemning Christianity for reclassifying mental disorders from divine delirium to satanic possession.[65] He inverts Christian sexual morality, dismissing in *Mad Love* 'the infamous Christian idea of sin', and going on to declare that 'there has never been any forbidden fruit. Only temptation is divine'.[66] But the supernatural in its broader sense is an object of fascination for him. Breton takes an interest in telepathy and alchemy, and consults astrological charts. *Mad Love* notes the occultation of Venus by the moon on the day of the *ondine* incident (p. 686; trans. 16), and suggests the conjunction of Mars and Venus at Breton's birth may partly account for the discord in love experienced on the Brittany beach, (p. 765; trans. 99). It is in clairvoyance, though, that Breton places his greatest faith. He reports in *Nadja* that the fortune-teller Mme Sacco 'has never been wrong where I am concerned', and he and Max Ernst accept her vaguely worded warning as a reason not to paint Nadja's portrait: 'this counter-indication seemed sufficient to us', he declares.[67] He argues in *Les Vases communicants* that 'Freud is again very definitely wrong in concluding that prophetic dreams do not exist'.[68] In *Mad Love*, he describes how he reads his own future in cards, which he believes are influenced by a mandrake root in his possession:

> Taking into account the rule of probability and any hesitation I might have about it, nothing prevents my declaring that this last object, mediated by my cards, has never told me about anything other than myself, bringing me back always to the living centre of my life.[69]

This hesitant, scrupulous tone of the objective observer is common in Breton's discussions of the supernatural: he prefers the stance of the reluctantly convinced sceptic to that of the impassioned believer. After recounting an incident in which Nadja correctly predicts that a darkened window is about to turn red, he offers the reader the following justification:

> I am sorry, but if this perhaps passes the bounds of credibility, I can do nothing about it. However, on such a subject, I would blame myself for taking sides: I limit myself to accepting that from black, this window then became red, and that is all.[70]

The description of the fear that overcomes both of them at this uncanny event suggests that Breton's view of the event isn't entirely neutral, as does the tucking away in a footnote, 'for those who like simple answers', of the fact that the window faces Nadja's former apartment.

Predictions and coincidences, *trouvailles* and prophetic dreams would seem to suggest a providential understanding of reality, in which apparently chance events occur for a purpose, which is mysteriously aligned with the inner realm of the mind. Breton is reticent about his own interpretation, and is concerned to avoid the label of superstition for his ideas. In summing up the uncanny experiences of *Nadja*, he says that they leave him disposed to 'a certain finalism' in his outlook on life, which is then qualified with a footnote declaring that 'any idea of teleological justification in this area being, as you may well imagine, ruled out in advance'.[71] Breton's distinction is unclear, since finalism and teleology are virtual synonyms, both referring to the notion of a purpose behind naturally occurring events. The stronger religious connotations of the latter, with its implication of a divine plan, are the likely reason for its rejection. Breton's finalism is elsewhere expressed as a confluence between 'human necessity' and 'natural necessity', again drawing on the concept of objective chance, for which Breton rejects the label of mysticism, but is prepared to accept the interviewer's suggestion of a 'magical virtue' in coincidence.[72] When he is judged by a critic, J.-P. Samson, to be a closet mystic with 'a state of mind that his atheism should not prevent being characterized as religious', Breton's response is to note the coincidence that Samson's article arrived on a day he was to have lunch with a girl 'with Delilah eyes'.[73] The providential nature of many of Breton's coincidences is suggested in *Mad Love's* Edenic garden scene in the Orotava valley, which reminds Breton of the 'arbre à pain' ('bread[fruit] tree') image that frequently appeared in sessions of automatic writing: 'One myth among all the others, clear and without harshness, is developed starting with this tree: that of the inexhaustible natural generosity able to see to the most diverse human needs'.[74] While we shouldn't overstate the similarities between Breton's view and the communion of mind and world we saw in the divinely ordered universe of the Catholic novel, there is certainly a parallel to be found between Breton and the religious writers in the mysterious congruence Breton posits between his own inner life and the reality he perceives.

There is, however, an even closer connection between Bernanos and Breton to be found in the belief the writers express in the permeability of the mind to outside forces, which in both cases will be primarily malevolent ones. The penultimate section of *Mad Love*, in which Breton and Lamba experience discord as their stroll on the beach passes the murderer's house, offers a view of consciousness which even Breton concedes may appear 'medieval' to some readers (p. 776; trans. 110). The events of the narrative, briefly, are that a groundless feeling of separation from Lamba afflicts Breton, along with a panicked desire to turn back, as they approach the Henriot house. Walking apart from his wife, Breton uncharacteristically throws stones at sea-birds. Later, he is reminded by his parents that the house was the scene of a notorious murder, in which the fox-breeder Henriot killed his wife. Breton remarks on the further coincidences of the two novels with foxes in their titles at either side of his own marital bed, and on the murderer's alleged propensity for shooting sea-birds. Returning to the scene, he is shocked to see a solid wall blocking his view of the metal fox-cages, of which he believed he had an uninterrupted view on his previous visit, leading him to speculate that the wall had appeared transparent to him. He attempts to explain the events as follows:

> Above all I could not detach myself from another detail, of the greatest subjective importance for me: the little fort that I had found myself in front of after crossing the stream was no other, they assured me, than the provisional dwelling that Michel Henriot and his wife had chosen during the time that it took to construct the 'Villa of the Loch' for them. Thus the space between these two buildings, which had been for me that afternoon such an exceptional place of disgrace, revealed itself, *in its very limits*, to be the previous theatre of a singular tragedy. Everything had occurred as if I had undergone, as if I had not been alone in undergoing, precisely from one to the other, the effects of deleterious emanations attaching the very principle of moral life. Should we admit that the curse had fallen on this

> place after the crime, or see, already in the crime itself, the accomplishment of that curse? This question remained, naturally, without an answer.[75]

Breton and his wife thus found themselves by chance in a 'malevolent place' where each became 'victim of a learned machination on the part of powers which remain, until things change, highly obscure'.[76] The parallels are clear with the depiction in Bernanos of consciousness as vulnerable to infiltration and possession by satanic forces, which we saw in the previous chapter. Breton shuns religious references, making his own dark forces more of a pagan or animist phenomenon in keeping with his interest in the occult, but the notion of free will overwhelmed by a hostile supernatural intelligence is the same in both. The idea of an external intelligence in contact with our own is found throughout Breton's work, including the more benign version seen in *Nadja*, where Breton talks of seeing 'signals' in the world around him 'which convince me of my illusion every time I think myself alone at the ship's helm'.[77]

The involuntary nature of the rift between Breton and Lamba is strongly emphasized in the *Mad Love* tale, which opens with the suggestion that what follows will be the result of 'a series of arbitrary causes, unrelated to love', and asserts this twice more in the final paragraphs of the piece, declaring that the event was caused by 'circumstances totally foreign to love', and then, a few lines further on, that their emotional state in that place was '*in total contradiction* to our real feelings'.[78] The book as a whole presents the Brittany incident as an inexplicable anomaly in a passionate love story which begins with the magic of the 'Sunflower Night', blossoms in the paradise of Tenerife, and is sealed with the birth of their daughter, Aube. Breton's biography presents a rather different story: Jacqueline walked out on her husband in May 1936, two months before the Brittany episode, taking their five-month-old daughter with her. On that occasion, they were reconciled by the end of the month, but in September she left again, this time leaving Aube with Breton to take a job in Ajaccio. Breton wrote the final section of the book in her absence, before her return in mid-October. The couple finally separated in 1942 and divorced three years later, at which point Breton married his third wife, Elisa Claro. Critics have seized on this discrepancy to suggest that, despite his interest in psychoanalysis, Breton's self-analysis doesn't go far enough (ironically, the very fault of which Breton accuses Freud).[79] Jean-Luc Steinmetz casts doubt on Breton's claim that he was unaware of the Henriot house's history at the time of the incident, and speculates that tensions aroused by their recent parenthood, combined with Jacqueline's difficult relationship with Breton's parents (with whom they were staying), and a possible untold story of Breton's jealousy towards the unnamed friend who lent Jacqueline the fox novels, can amply account for an afternoon of silent resentment.[80] Supernatural forces thus offer a convenient cover to allow personal relationship difficulties to remain private, while at the same time publicly absolving Breton of any responsibility for what happened. Other, similar cases of the marvellous possibly standing in place of a more complex personal explanation can be found elsewhere in Breton's work. Earlier in *Mad Love*, for example, the flea-market *trouvaille* that unblocks Giacometti's creativity offers a demonstration of the efficacy of Surrealist belief in objective chance. Unmentioned is Breton's well-founded anxiety that Giacometti is about to leave the Surrealist group, along with his active attempts to retain him.[81] On similar lines, the celebration of the uncanny powers and poetic creativity which emerge in Nadja in her moments of mental disturbance might in part be motivated by Breton's guilt at his possible exacerbating role in her decline into madness. The pre-emptive abuse of those who might accuse him of playing such a role as 'low-level cretins', along with the condemnation of the psychiatrists to whom Nadja's care is eventually entrusted as the true wreckers of sanity, adds weight to such suspicions.[82] We see in such moments possible divergences between the real-life André Breton and the version presented to us in his autobiographical texts, whether by conscious omissions and distortions or perhaps an unconscious form of wishful thinking, which prefers explanations rooted in the fantastic to those rooted in personal resentment, anxiety, and guilt. Whatever the reason, the consequence is that we are presented with a Breton, real or fictional, for whom external forces invade the mind with benign and malevolent intent, for whom unconscious desires are mysteriously in harmony with events in the world, and for whom the distinction between madness and sanity, along with the value judgment attached to each, is heavily blurred.

There remains one final aspect of Breton's representation of the mind for us to deal with, which, like psychoanalysis, will become increasingly important in cultural discourse as the century progresses. It is the issue of gender, and in particular, the question of whether men's and women's minds are intrinsically different, and whether any such differences stem primarily from genetic predispositions or social conditioning. The matter is forcefully raised with respect to French literature by Simone de Beauvoir in her 1949 essay, *Le Deuxième Sexe*, and Breton is singled out for criticism. At the end of the 'Mythes' section of the essay, Beauvoir examines the representation of women by five male writers, including Breton. She too discovers paradoxical similarities between Surrealist and religious writing: woman in Breton 'is an element of disruption; she tears man from his immanent sleep; mouth, key, doorway, bridge, she is Beatrice initiating Dante into the beyond'.[83] Beauvoir accuses Breton of according subjectivity only to men in his texts. His representation of women may lack the overt misogyny of a writer like Henri Montherlant, but his praise of women figures them as mystic incarnations of beauty or of nature, and the role he sees for them as the salvation of mankind reduces them to the instruments by which men achieve transcendence:

> Breton does not talk of women as subjects. [. . .] Woman only interests him because she is a privileged 'mouth'. Deeply rooted in nature, close to the earth, she also appears as the key to the beyond. [. . .] Truth, Beauty, Poetry, she is Everything: once again, everything in the guise of the other, Everything apart from oneself.[84]

Reading Breton from a twenty-first-century perspective, it's hard to disagree with Beauvoir's assessment. In *Mad Love* we note the oddly passive invocation to his daughter that ends the text: 'I want you to be madly loved', the assimilation of the pregnant Jacqueline to the fertile profusion of Tenerife flora, and the complete absence of reference to Jacqueline's own perspective on events, or to her view of the relationship.[85] *Arcane 17* is the text in which Breton engages most fully with questions of gender and consciousness, but it is here too that the focus on male salvation through an idealized femininity is at its most pronounced, perhaps due to the absence of the individualizing presence of a Nadja or a Jacqueline in the text. Breton evokes 'the idea of *terrestrial salvation by woman*, of woman's transcendent vocation' in the context of Goethe's 'eternal feminine', the mystic intercessionary power through which his Faust is finally redeemed.[86] Breton may call for society to 'assert the ideas of women over those of men' and distance himself from those who would label women with a 'so-called female "irrationality"', but it's quickly clear that Breton is attempting to revalorize, rather than contest, the irrationality of the 'child-woman'.[87] The masculine mind is associated with order, logic, and strength; female consciousness is relegated to the realm of dreams, childhood, and imagination. Breton's celebration of women may be well-meaning, but his insistence that 'male psychology [. . .] *is utterly invalid for women*' sets up a relationship of extreme difference which conforms to the worst stereotypes of the era.[88] What is more, while Breton's view of women excludes them from the domains of reason and intellect, he accepts no such limitations for male consciousness: he and his fellow Surrealists stand as evidence that these 'feminine' characteristics can be appropriated and exploited by the male mind in the service of creativity. The surreal art and poetry which was for Nadja little more than an involuntary symptom of her disordered mind is harnessed by Breton and his male colleagues into an aesthetic revolution.

*

Finally, then, beyond the mutual misunderstandings that lead Freud to declare that he has no idea what Surrealism is or what it wants, and Breton to announce on behalf of the Surrealists that, despite their adoption of a psychoanalytic understanding of dreams and the unconscious, 'We nonetheless reject the greater part of Freud's philosophy as *metaphysical*', we have in Breton's work the inauguration of the psychoanalytic century in European literary culture.[89] Breton's aims may be very different from those of psychoanalysis, moving from an early, orthodox Freudian position that the exploration of the unconscious mind might allow us to better understand and control it to an extreme anti-psychiatric position that views rationality as an oppressive censorship from which the mind is to be liberated. His belief in supernatural forces orchestrating events and infiltrating consciousness also distinguishes his view of the mind from the psychoanalytic mainstream, despite Freud's private interest in the occult and the mystic bent of his successor, Carl Jung. Yet such differences are far outweighed by the confluence of outlook between psychoanalysis and Surrealism on the nature of the unconscious mind and its relationship to consciousness. For the first time, the conscious mind is displaced as the primary focus of interest, and as the defining element of the self. The dangerous, fascinating chaos of the unconscious is brought to the fore in Breton's work. Its creative potential is displayed in anarchic literature that transgresses moral and aesthetic conventions and displays a dream-logic that is familiar to us all but alien to our waking life. Most importantly, it posits a model of the mind in which the irrational plays a far greater role in the mental life of those of us who consider ourselves sane than we might like to admit. Beneath a veneer of order seethes an unacknowledged mass of thoughts, images, and desires, of which we may be largely unaware, and which, should we come to know them, we might very well refuse to accept as part of ourselves, so at odds are they with the self-image we have created. For Breton, this submerged part of the mind, more accessible than in Freud's model, but scarcely less mysterious, holds the key to who we are, indeed, it *is* who we are, vastly outweighing the tiny area of consciousness and the memory and imagination it has at its ready disposal. Our failure to communicate with this hidden side of ourselves, or our active repression of it, amounts to a denial of the self, and of the extraordinary, perhaps even magical potential it harbours.

In Breton's 'medieval' malignant auras, which betoken a concept of mind that in fact predates the middle ages by many centuries, we have an aspect of his representation which draws on older ideas about consciousness even than those inspired by Christian doctrine in Bernanos. And these religious aspects of Bernanos's mind themselves pre-date the materialist representation we saw in Proust, with his strong interest in the states of the brain and their relationship to mental experience. These ancient ideas inhabit Breton's writing alongside the enthusiastic espousal of the very latest theories of the mind to emerge in Western thought, a Freudian cutting edge that was revolutionizing understanding of the mind in Breton's day with at least the same controversy and excitement that cognitive science has generated in the first decades of our own century. We are far from a simple chronological progression here. While new conceptions of mentality from science, philosophy, and psychoanalysis would successively infiltrate literary creativity as the century continued, older modes of thought endured and coexisted with the new, often within the work of a single writer. It's true, of course, that irrational beliefs, religious faith, and ancient superstitions coexist in many minds with more rigorous conceptions of consciousness inspired by psychology or neuroscience. An intellectual appreciation that there is a relationship between electro-chemical activity among the neurons and the thoughts we experience may sit alongside faith-based intuition that, say, the self we feel within us is a divinely implanted soul, and for many the two modes of understanding do not conflict. So it is in the cultural history of consciousness. Sometimes radically different understandings of mental life will exist in harmony, as when Breton interprets dreams using both psychoanalytic method and mystical belief in their prophetic potential. At other times, we see bitter condemnation despite underlying similarities between the two outlooks, as we saw with the confessional and the psychiatrist's couch in the previous chapter. We are dealing here, not with serial developments in understanding through the century, but with an overlaid arrangement of simultaneous perspectives which rise and fall in dominance across the decades. No rise and fall in the course of the century will be more dramatic than that of psychoanalysis, as we shall see.

Notes

1. 'À maintes reprises j'ai été amené à situer, par rapport à diverses circonstances intimes de cette vie, une série de faits qui me semblaient de nature à retenir l'attention psychologique, en raison de leur caractère insolite. Seule, en effet, la référence précise, absolument consciencieuse, à l'état émotionnel du sujet au moment où se produisirent de tels faits, peut fournir une base réelle d'appréciation. C'est sur le modèle d'observation médicale que le surréalisme a toujours proposé que la relation en fût entreprise', André Breton, *L'Amour fou*, in *Œuvres complètes*, ed. by Marguerite Bonnet, 4 vols. (Paris: Gallimard, Pléiade edition, 1988–2008), II, pp. 673–785 (p. 710). Subsequent references to the *Œuvres complètes* will be given as *OC*. Translations from *L'Amour fou* are taken from André Breton, *Mad Love*, trans. by Mary Ann Caws (Lincoln, NE: Bison, 1987). All other translations are my own.
2. Breton, *Nadja*, *OC*, I, pp. 643–753 (p. 645).
3. Ian W. Alexander, *French Literature and the Philosophy of Consciousness: Phenomenological Essays* (Cardiff: University of Wales Press, 1984), p. 128.
4. 'Un petit vieillard sans allure', Breton, 'Interview du Professor Freud', *OC*, I, pp. 255–6 (p. 255).
5. 'Admiration enthousiaste', Breton, *Entretiens 1913–1952*, *OC*, III, pp. 423–649 (p. 474). In this interview Breton also expresses regret for his discourteous account of the 1921 meeting.
6. '*Le hasard serait la forme de manifestation de la nécessité extérieure qui se fraie un chemin dans l'inconscient humain*', *OC*, II, p. 690; trans. 23, italics Breton's.
7. 'La psychanalyse aurait son mot à dire', *OC*, II, p. 675; trans. 5.
8. 'Il faut en rendre grâce aux découvertes de Freud'; 'Si les profondeurs de notre esprit recèlent d'étranges forces capables d'augmenter celles de la surface, ou de lutter victorieusement contre elles, il y a tout intérêt à les capter, à les capter d'abord, pour les soumettre ensuite, s'il y a lieu, au contrôle de notre raison', Breton, 'Manifeste du surréalisme', *OC*, I, pp. 309–46 (p. 316).
9. 'Grand serrement de cœur'; 'toute une vie de compréhension rayonnante, de dévouement exclusif à la cause de l'émancipation humaine, conçue sous la forme la plus large qui fut jamais', Breton, 'Note à propos de l'arrestation annoncée de Freud', *OC*, II, pp. 1213–14 (p. 1213).
10. 'Le cœur a ses raisons, que la raison ne connaît point'; 'j'ai dans la tête, je ne sais où, là ou là—il se tâte le crâne—une loge, une case, que j'ai toujours peur de laisser trop ouvrir. Et mes travaux, et tout ce que je fais, et mes excès d'articles, c'est pour la comprimer. . . . Je l'ai bouchée, écrasée avec des livres, de façon à ne pas avoir le loisir de réfléchir, de n'être pas libre d'aller et de venir', Quoted in Webster, *Why Freud Was Wrong*, pp. xii–xiii. The Pascal quotation is from Article IV of the *Pensées*; Sainte-Beuve's confession is taken from Edmond and Jules de Goncourt, *Journal des Goncourt: Mémoires de la vie littéraire*, 9 vols. (Paris: Charpentier, 1891), II, entry for 27 March 1865.
11. 'Chemin *raisonnable*'; 'la joie surréaliste pure', 'Manifeste du surréalisme', *OC*, I, pp. 345–46, italics Breton's.
12. 'Surrealisme, n. m. Automatisme psychique pur par lequel on se propose d'exprimer, soit verbalement, soit par écrit, soit de toute autre manière, le fonctionnement réel de la pensée. Dictée de la pensée, en l'absence de tout contrôle exercé par la raison, en dehors de toute préoccupation esthétique ou morale', 'Manifeste du surréalisme', *OC*, I, p. 328.
13. 'Mais nous, qui ne nous sommes livrés à aucun travail de filtration, qui nous sommes faites dans nos œuvres les sourds réceptacles de tant d'échos, les modestes *appareils enregistreurs* qui ne s'hypnotisent pas sur le dessin qu'ils tracent, nous servons peut-être une plus noble cause. Aussi rendons nous avec probité le "talent" qu'on nous prête. Parlez-moi du talent de ce mètre en platine, de ce miroir, de cette porte, et du ciel, si vous voulez. Nous n'avons pas de talent', 'Manifeste du surréalisme', *OC*, I, p. 33, italics Breton's.
14. 'Un instrument de connaissance [qui] travaille à mettre à jour la conscience profonde de l'homme', André Breton and Paul Éluard, *Dictionnaire abrégé du surréalisme* (1938), *OC*, III, pp. 787–862 (p. 846).

15. The term 'waking sentence' ('phrase de réveil') comes from *L'Amour fou*, *OC*, II, p. 701; trans. 33. The window-tapping image is from 'Manifeste du surréalisme', *OC*, I, p. 324; Breton further discusses the phenomenon in 'Le Message automatique', *Point du jour* (1934), *OC*, II, pp. 263–392 (pp. 375–92) and in *L'Amour fou*, p. 723; trans. 54.
16. 'Je ne me suis attaché à rien tant qu'à montrer quellesl précautions et quelles ruses le désir, à la recherche de son objet, apporte à louvoyer dans les eaux pré-conscientes et, cet objet découvert, de quels moyens, stupéfiants jusqu'à nouvel ordre, il dispose pour le faire connaître par la conscience', *OC*, II, p. 696; trans. 24–25. Freud himself maintained a strict terminological distinction between the accessible 'preconscious' mind and the Unconscious proper, a distinction which Breton seems less concerned about.
17. 'Portent les *clés des situations*'. *OC*, II, p. 675, italics Breton's; trans. 5 (translation modified); '"surdéterminant" au sens freudien', *Nadja*, *OC*, I, p. 675.
18. 'Sexuellement on sait que la table mise symbolise la femme', *Les Vases communicants*, *OC*, II, pp. 118–34.
19. Sigmund Freud, 'On Dreams' (1901), *Standard Edition*, V, pp. 631–86 (p. 676).
20. 'Une boîte à multiple fond', 'Second Manifeste du surréalisme' (1930), *OC*, I, pp. 775–837 (p. 810).
21. 'Le rêve ne peut-il être appliqué, lui aussi, à la résolution des questions fondamentales de la vie?', 'Manifeste du surréalisme', *OC*, I, p. 318.
22. 'Tout se passe comme si [le dormeur] entendait résoudre de la sorte un problème affectif particulièrement complexe qui, en raison même de son caractère trop émouvant, défie les éléments d'appréciation consciente qui déterminent, pour une part, la conduite de la vie', *Les Vases communicants*, *OC*, II, p. 127.
23. 'Corriger, *se* corriger, polir, reprendre, trouver à redire et non puiser aveuglement dans le trésor subjectif', 'Le Message automatique' (1933), *Point du jour*, *OC*, II, pp. 375–92 (p. 376).
24. 'Échapper aux contraintes qui pèsent sur la pensée surveillée'; 'l'assujettissement aux perceptions sensorielles immédiates qui, dans un grand mesure, fait de l'esprit le jouet du monde extérieur'; 'qui fait peser *l'esprit critique* sur le langage et, d'une manière générale, sur les modes les plus divers d'expression', *Entretiens*, *OC*, III, p. 476.
25. 'Ces entraves étaient de l'ordre de *la logique* (le rationalisme le plus étroit veillait à ne rien laisser passer qui n'eût été estampillé par ses soins), de l'ordre de *la morale* (sous forme de tabous sexuels et sociaux), de l'ordre enfin du *goût*, régi par les conventions sophistiques du "bon ton", peut-être les pires de toutes', *Entretiens*, *OC*, III, p. 477, italics Breton's.
26. On the Henriot case, Breton remarks that the judiciary carried out 'a whole series of investigations which never got very far, chiefly because a psychoanalytic examination had not been carried out. But these investigations, almost left to chance, had nevertheless furnished a few interesting details having to do with the personality of the criminal: a neurotic heredity on the mother's side—she loved to shoot, and her extreme attachment to her child had contrasted utterly with the professional indifference and the impassivity of the father'; ('Toute une suite d'investigations qui sont très loin d'avoir été menées à bout puisque, notamment, un examen psychanalytique n'a pas été pratiqué mais qui, livrées presque au hasard, ont fourni néanmoins quelques éléments d'appréciation intéressants, touchant la personnalité du criminel: hérédité névropathique du côté de la mère, éprise de tir et dont la faiblesse extrême pour son enfant avait contrasté autant que possible avec l'indifférence et la morgue toutes professionnelles du père'), p. 774; trans. 108.
27. 'La nuit porte conseil', *Les Vases communicants*, *OC*, II, p. 127.
28. 'L'absence bien connu de frontière entre la *non-folie* et la folie', *Nadja*, *OC*, I, p. 741, italics Breton's.
29. 'Le monde de la réalité'; 'celui du rêve', *Les Vases communicants*, *OC*, II, p. 104.
30. 'En examinant de près le contenu de l'activité le plus irréfléchie de l'esprit, si l'on passe outre à l'extraordinaire et peu rassurant bouillonnement qui se produit à la surface, il est possible de mettre à jour un *tissu capillaire* dans l'ignorance duquel on s'ingénierait en vain à vouloir se figurer la circulation mentale. Le rôle de ce tissu est, on l'a vu, d'assurer l'échange constant qui doit se produire dans la pensée entre le monde extérieur et le monde intérieur, échange qui nécessite l'interpénétration continue de l'activité de veille et de l'activité de sommeil. Toute mon ambition a été de donner ici un aperçu de sa structure', *Les Vases communicants*, *OC*, II, p. 202.
31. 'Faire cesser l'opposition de la réalité et du rêve'; 'l'activité de veille procède, au moins partiellement, de l'activité de rêve antérieure', 'Conférences de Mexico', *OC*, II, pp. 1260–85 (p. 1279).
32. *Les Vases communicants*, *OC*, II, pp. 177, 185.
33. 'Authenticité totale'; 'un réservoir de santé morale', *La Clé des champs*, *OC*, III, pp. 651–959 (p. 887).
34. 'La griffe du lion étreint le sein de la vigne', *Nadja*, *OC*, I, p. 719.
35. 'Sa pensée s'est éclaircie encore, et son expression a gagné en légèreté, en originalité, en profondeur', *Nadja* *OC*, I, p. 718.
36. 'L'émancipation humaine *à tous égards*, entendons-nous bien, *selon les moyens dont chacun dispose*'; 'en passant la tête, puis un bras entre les barreaux ainsi écartés de la logique, c'est-à-dire la plus haïssable des prisons', *Nadja*, *OC*, I, p. 741, italics Breton's.
37. 'Exploits d'huissier'; 'rien moins qu'à expulser l'homme de lui-même', *Nadja*, *OC*, I, p. 653.

38. 'Assassiner avec froideur un de ceux, le médecin de préférence, qui me tomberait sous la main', *Nadja*, *OC*, I, p. 740.
39. 'Avant tout pour fonction de servir d'instruments à la répression sociale', 'La Médecine mentale devant le surréalisme' (1930), *OC*, II, pp. 322–5.
40. 'Un instrument d'uniformisation morale et de dénonciation sociale', Michel Foucault, *Histoire de la folie à l'âge classique* (Paris: Gallimard, 1972), p. 613.
41. R. D. Laing, *Wisdom, Madness and Folly: The Making of a Psychiatrist 1927–1957* (London: MacMillan, 1985), p. 9.
42. R. D. Laing, *The Politics of Experience, and, the Bird of Paradise* (London: Penguin, 1967), p. 12. A footnote in Laing's text at this point invites the reader to explore further in Foucault's *Histoire de la folie.*
43. Laing, *The Politics of Experience*, p. 90.
44. Gilles Deleuze and Félix Guattari, *Capitalisme et Schizophrénie 1: L'Anti-Œdipe* (Paris: Minuit, 1972), p. 156.
45. *Seconde Manifeste*, *OC*, I, p. 795.
46. 'Toute erreur dans l'interprétation de l'homme entraîne une erreur dans l'interprétation de l'univers: elle est, par la suite, un obstacle à sa transformation', *Les Vases communicants*, *OC*, II, p. 196.
47. 'Germes corrupteurs'; 'bulles troubles, déformantes qui se lèvent à toute heure du fond marécageux de l'*inconscient* de l'individu', *Les Vases communicants*, *OC*, II, p. 196, italics Breton's.
48. 'Aujourd'hui plus que jamais la *libération de l'esprit*, fin expresse du surréalisme, aux yeux des surréalistes exige pour première condition la *libération de l'homme*, ce qui implique que toute entrave à celle-ci doit être combattue avec l'énergie du désespoir, qu'aujourd'hui plus que jamais les surréalistes comptent pour cette libération de l'homme en tout et pour tout sur la Révolution prolétarienne', *Qu'est-ce que le surréalisme?*, *OC*, II, pp. 223–62 (p. 230), italics Breton's.
49. Rauzy's thesis, *À propos de* L'Immaculée conception *d'André Breton et Paul Éluard. Contribution à l'étude des rapports du surréalisme et de la psychiatrie* (University of Paris Faculty of Medicine, 1970), is discussed by Marguerite Bonnet and Étienne-Alain Hubert in *OC*, I, 1640–41. Lacan's interest in the text is attested by Elisabeth Roudinesco, who claims Lacan's 1932 thesis on paranoia was heavily inspired by Surrealism, particularly *L'Immaculée Conception.* Roudinesco, *Jacques Lacan: Esquisse d'une vie, histoire d'un système de pensée* (Paris: Fayard, 1993), p. 85.
50. 'Prouver que l'esprit, dressé *poétiquement* chez l'homme normal, est capable de reproduire dans ses grands traits les manifestations verbales les plus paradoxales', *L'Immaculée Conception*, *OC*, I, pp. 839–84 (p. 848).
51. 'C'en serait fait alors des catégories orgueilleuses dans lesquelles on s'amuse à faire entrer les hommes qui ont eu un compte à régler avec la raison humaine, cette même raison qui nous dénie quotidiennement le droit de nous exprimer par les moyens qui nous sont instinctifs', *L'Immaculée Conception*, p. 848.
52. 'C'est assez dire que nous en proposerions fort bien la généralisation et qu'à nos yeux l' "essai de simulation" de maladies qu'on enferme remplacerait avantageusement la ballade, le sonnet, l'épopée, le poème sans queue ni tête et autres genres caducs', *L'Immaculée Conception*, p. 849.
53. 'L'hystérie n'est pas un phénomène pathologique et peut, à tous égards, être considérée comme un moyen suprême de l'expression', Louis Aragon and André Breton, 'Le Cinquantenaire de l'hystérie, 1878–1928', *OC*, I, pp. 948–50 (p. 950).
54. *Entretiens*, *OC*, III, p. 530.
55. 'Il se peut que la vie demande à être déchiffrée comme un cryptogramme', *Nadja*, *OC*, I, p. 716.
56. 'On conçoit que tous les intermédiaires puissent exister entre la reconnaissance pure et simple du monde extérieur pour ce qu'il est et sa négation au profit d'un système de représentations favorables (ou défavorables) à l'individu humain qui se trouve placé devant lui. Les idées de persécution, de grandeur ne sont pas très loin d'entrer en jeu', *Les Vases communicants*, *OC*, II, p. 183.
57. 'Je suis intimement persuadé que toute perception enregistrée de la manière la plus involontaire comme, par exemple, celle de paroles prononcées à la cantonade, porte en elle la solution, symbolique ou autre, d'une difficulté où l'on est avec soi-même. Il n'est encore que de savoir s'orienter dans le dédale. Le délire d'interprétation ne commence qu'où l'homme mal préparé prend peur dans cette *forêt d'indices.* Mais je soutiens que l'attention se ferait plutôt briser les poignets que de se prêter une seconde, pour un être, à ce que le désir de cet être reste extérieur', p. 685, trans. 15 (translation modified), italics Breton's.
58. Laing co-wrote a volume on Sartre's philosophy, and cites Artaud, Baudelaire, Camus, Cocteau, Fanon, Genet, Mallarmé, Proust, and Rimbaud, among others, in his work.
59. G.W.F. Hegel, *Philosophy of Mind*, trans. by W. Wallace and A. V. Miller (Oxford: Clarendon Press, 2006), § 408.
60. Discussed in *OC*, I, p. 1639.
61. 'Sont appelées à se résoudre toutes les antinomies qui nous rongent et nous désespèrent.' Breton's gloss on the concept comes from *Entretiens*, *OC*, III, 525.

62. 'Fil conducteur'; 'une possibilité de conciliation extrême entre les deux termes qui tendent à opposer, au bénéfice d'une philosophie confusionnelle, le monde de la réalité à celui du rêve', *Les Vases communicants*, *OC*, II, pp. 164, 104.
63. 'La préoccupation majeure est de réduire l'antinomie de la raison et de la déraison, qui, parmi d'autres, a été une des ambitions permanentes du surréalisme', *Entretiens 1913–1952*, OC, III, 531.
64. 'Le hasard objectif est cette sorte de hasard à travers quoi se manifeste encore très mystérieusement pour l'homme une nécessité qui lui échappe bien qu'il l'éprouve vitalement comme nécessité. L'ordre, la fin dans la nature ne se confondant pas objectivement avec ce qu'ils sont dans l'esprit de l'homme, il arrive cependant que la nécessité naturelle tombe d'accord avec la nécessité humaine d'une manière assez extraordinaire et agitante pour que les deux déterminations s'avèrent indiscernables', *Conférences de Mexico*, *OC*, II, 1280. On the provenance of the concept, see Denis Lejeune, *The Radical Use of Chance in Twentieth-Century Art* (Amsterdam: Rodopi, 2012), pp. 106–9.
65. *Le Surréalisme et la peinture* (1926), note 2; *La Clé des champs*, OC, III, p. 886.
66. 'L'infâme idée chrétienne du péché. Il n'y a jamais eu de fruit défendu. La tentation seule est divine', *OC*, II, p. 760; trans. 93.
67. 'Ne s'est jamais trompé à mon sujet'; 'cette contre-indication nous paraît suffisante', *Nadja*, *OC*, I, pp. 693, 710.
68. 'Freud se trompe encore très certainement en concluant à la non-existence du rêve prophétique', *Les Vases communicants*, *OC*, II, p. 111. In context, the passage is ambiguous, perhaps deliberately so, as to whether Breton is arguing that dreams can be prophetic in a supernatural sense, or merely that they can be speculative about the future.
69. 'Tout compte tenu du calcul des probabilités, et quelque hésitation que j'aie à avancer un témoignage semblable, rien ne me retient de déclarer que ce dernier objet, par l'intermédiaire des cartes, ne m'a jamais entretenu de rien d'autre que de moi, qu'il m'a toujours ramené au point vif de ma vie', p. 686; trans. 16.
70. 'Je regrette, mais je n'y puis rien, que ceci passe peut-être les limites de la crédibilité. Cependant, à pareil sujet, je m'en voudrais de prendre parti: je me borne à convenir que de noire, cette fenêtre est alors devenue rouge, c'est tout'; 'pour les amateurs de solutions faciles', *Nadja*, *OC*, I, p. 695.
71. 'Un certain finalisme'; 'toute idée de justification téléologique dans ce domaine étant, on pense bien, écartée d'avance', *Nadja*, *OC*, I, p. 719.
72. 'Nécessité humaine'; 'nécessité naturelle'; 'vertu magique', *Entretiens*, *OC*, III, 514–16.
73. 'Un état d'esprit que son athéisme ne doit pas empêcher de qualifier de religieux', *Les Vases communicants*, *OC*, II, 168.
74. 'Un mythe entre tous clair et dénué de sévérité se développe à partir de cet arbre: celui de l'inépuisable générosité naturelle susceptible de pourvoir aux besoins humains les plus divers', p. 748; trans. 80.
75. 'Par-dessus tout je ne parvenais pas à me détacher d'une autre donnée, celle-ci pour moi de la plus grande importance subjective: le petit fort devant lequel je m'étais trouvé après le passage de ruisseau n'était autre, on m'en assurait, que l'habitation provisoire qu'avaient élue Michel Henriot et sa femme, pendant le temps qu'on mettait à construire pour eux la "villa du Loch". Ainsi l'espace compris entre ces deux bâtiments, qui m'avait été l'après-midi un lieu si exceptionnel de disgrâce, se révélait, *dans ses limites mêmes*, le théâtre antérieur d'une tragédie des plus particulières. Tout s'était passé comme si j'avais subi, je n'avais pas été seul à subir, précisément de l'un à l'autre, les effets d'émanations délétères, d'émanations s'attaquant au principe même de la vie morale. Fallait-il admettre que la malédiction était tombée sur ce lieu à la suite du crime ou voir déjà dans le crime l'accomplissement de la malédiction? Cette question restait, naturellement, sans réponse', p. 775; trans. 109, italics Breton's.
76. 'Lieu maléfique', p. 777; trans. 111; 'victime d'une machination des plus savantes de la part de puissances qui demeurent, jusqu'à nouvel ordre, fort obscures', pp. 776–7; trans. 111.
77. 'Qui me convainquent de mon illusion toutes les fois que je me crois seul à la barre du navire', *Nadja*, *OC*, I, p. 652.
78. 'Une série de causes occasionnelles, sans rapport avec l'amour', p. 768; trans. 100 (translation modified); 'circonstances totalement étrangères à l'amour', p. 776; trans. 110; '*en totale contradiction avec nos sentiments réels*', p. 776; trans. 111, italics Breton's.
79. *Les Vases communicants*, *OC*, II, p. 117. Freud responds to the charge with a protestation that his own and his family's privacy required protection.
80. Jean-Luc Steinmetz, *André Breton et les surprises de L'Amour fou* (Paris: Presses Universitaires de France, 1994), pp. 81–92.
81. Steinmetz, *André Breton et les surprises de L'Amour fou*, p. 35.
82. 'Crétins de bas étage', *Nadja*, *OC*, I, p. 736.
83. '[La femme] est une élément de perturbation; elle arrache l'homme au sommeil de l'immanence; bouche, clé, porte, pont, c'est Béatrice initiant Dante à l'au-delà', Simone de Beauvoir, *Le Deuxième Sexe I: les faits et les mythes* (Paris: Gallimard, 1949), p. 366.

84. 'Breton ne parle pas de la femme en tant qu'elle est sujet. [. . .] La femme ne l'intéresse que parce qu'elle est une "bouche" privilégiée. Profondément ancrée dans la nature, toute proche de la terre, elle apparaît aussi comme la clé de l'au-delà. [. . .] Vérité, Beauté, Poésie, elle est Tout: une fois de plus tout sous la figure de l'autre, Tout excepté soi-même', Beauvoir, *Le Deuxième Sexe I*, p. 375.
85. 'Je vous souhaite d'être follement aimée', *OC*, II, p. 785; trans. 119.
86. 'L'idée du *salut terrestre par la femme*, de la vocation transcendante de la femme', *Arcane 17*, *OC*, III, pp. 35–113 (p. 59).
87. 'Faire valoir les idées de la femme aux dépens de celles de l'homme'; 'prétendu "irrationnel" féminin'; 'femme-enfant', *Arcane 17*, *OC*, III, p. 65.
88. 'La psychologie de l'homme [. . .] *n'est aucunement valable pour la femme*', *Arcane 17*, *OC*, III, p. 68, italics Breton's.
89. 'Nous n'en rejetons pas moins la plus grande partie de la philosophie de Freud comme *métaphysique*.' Freud's remark is in a letter reprinted by Breton at the end of *Les Vases communicants*, *OC*, II, pp. 210–15; Breton's comment comes from the *Dictionnaire abrégé du surréalisme* (1938), ed. by André Breton and Paul Éluard, *OC*, II, pp. 787–862 (p. 812), italics Breton's. Entry for 'Freud, Sigmund', signed 'A.B.'. On the 'metaphysical' nature of Freud's theory of the mind, see Michel Onfray, *Crépuscule d'un idole: l'affabulation freudienne* (Paris: Grasset, 2010), pp. 309–23.

4

BEING-FOR-ITSELF

Jean-Paul Sartre

For a decade or two in post-war Europe, Sartre's philosophy of consciousness caught the public imagination like no other before or since. Fresh, challenging, and provocative for those who took the trouble to understand it properly, attractively relevant and radical for the thousands more who skimmed off buzz-words and half-digested theories, his philosophy developed an unlikely characteristic in those years which sets it apart from the other approaches to the mind we are investigating here: it was *cool*. Sartre took his primary influence from the phenomenology of Husserl and fashioned from it and other philosophical and literary inspirations the French existentialist model, which swept across Western culture. Sartre's vision was of a self-created self, absolutely free and absolutely responsible for its own choices, grappling with a Godless, purposeless world and the hostile gaze of the Other. *Nausea*, his only stand-alone novel, dramatized several of the principal ideas of his early philosophical essays and prefigured those of *L'Être et le Néant* (*Being and Nothingness*), with which he would make his mark as a philosopher five years later in 1943.[1] The novel includes some social commentary, but Sartre was not yet the politically committed literary activist he would become following his experiences as soldier, prisoner, and Resistance-sympathizer in the Second World War. Rather, in *Nausea*, the focus is on the individual, and our attention is directed towards the workings of consciousness itself, its relationship with the raw, physical reality it confronts through the senses, with the other minds it encounters, and with the self it conjures intermittently into existence from present feelings and the records of memory.[2] Melding philosophical discourse with literary narrative, *Nausea* played an essential role in the rise of French existentialism in the post-war decades, not only as a vivid illustration of a philosophical worldview, but also as a demonstration that Sartre's philosophy is a philosophy of experience, and one that may be applied to our own perceptions and interactions with the world as much as those of its protagonist, Roquentin. The novel, along with the essays, plays, and stories that followed it, was the trigger for a movement that would come to dominate mid-twentieth-century intellectual life in France and beyond.

The genesis of *Nausea* between philosophy and fiction has been well documented in the letters and memoirs of Sartre and Simone de Beauvoir. Sartre began to write an essay described as a 'factum on contingency' in 1931 at the age of twenty-six, having completed his military service and taken up the post of philosophy teacher at a *lycée* in Le Havre, the clear model for *Nausea*'s Bouville. The following year (the year in which the story is set), the essay had become, with Beauvoir's encouragement, a philosophical novel.[3] Much of the writing was done during a year's research leave in Berlin, during which Sartre spent his working day alternating between the novel and a text which would become *La Transcendance de l'Ego* (*The Transcendence of the Ego*, 1937). The central ideas of this essay, along with those of other early pieces such as *Esquisse pour une théorie des emotions* (*Sketch for a Theory of the Emotions*, 1939) and *L'Imaginaire* (*The Imaginary*, 1940), are perceptible at certain points in the novel's narrative. When the novel was accepted by Gallimard on Sartre's second attempt, it was entitled *Melancholia* and substantially longer: the present title, along with cuts of around fifty pages, were imposed by the publisher. The novel's success was immediate, well received by critics, and a contender, if not laureate, for the major French literary prizes of 1938.[4] Sartre always considered it 'the best thing I ever did'.[5]

Nausea takes the form of the diary entries for the first two months of 1932 by Antoine Roquentin, who is researching the life of an eighteenth-century marquis in the port town of Bouville. His diary recounts the distressing incidents of nausea he experiences from certain sense-impressions, such as the touch of a half-dry, half-muddy pebble on the shore, or the sight of purple braces against a blue shirt. In the famous epiphany scene in Bouville park, which I touched on earlier in this study, Roquentin comes to understand this nausea as the effect of an unmediated apprehension of existence.[6] The world is stripped of the intellectual categories through which the mind habitually encounters it, and appears monstrous in its excess and contingency. Roquentin realizes that names and definitions, such as those of the chestnut tree root that captivates him, can only describe things inadequately and incompletely, rather than capturing an essence as a geometric definition defines a circle. The chaos and randomness of the physical world, and the failure of our mental capacities to comprehend it, is overwhelming. The absurdity of human existence is revealed by the same token, and Roquentin rails against the bourgeoisie who convince themselves and others that their lives are lived in the mode of necessity, that their status in life is theirs by right. Through the course of the story, Roquentin encounters and rejects means by which he might attempt to justify his absurd existence, such as the humanism offered by the autodidact, or the possibility of a loving relationship with Anny. He is finally inspired by the unreal, abstract beauty of a jazz tune to seek his own salvation in art, although the status of the text as 'found' documents leaves the outcome of this project in doubt.

Like the volumes of Beckett's trilogy, and unlike most of the other texts mentioned in this study, *Nausea* finds the term *psychological novel* something of an imperfect fit. We are indeed concerned here with the representation of a mind, and one for which subjective experiences are rendered in vivid and exact detail. But Roquentin's psyche is in many respects a blank canvas. We know nothing of his childhood and early influences. What we do know of his former life as a lover and international adventurer is sketchy and contradictory, and provides only a schematic and somewhat implausible opposition to the isolated and humdrum existence led by the Roquentin we meet. His likes and dislikes are not emphasized, beyond those that strike him in the moment of perception, and his personality traits are muted. His experiences in the course of the novel are, it's true, extraordinary—existential nausea is a phenomenon not even shared by Sartre—yet they imply nothing extraordinary about Roquentin himself. He is simply the recipient of a revelation, one that admittedly appears to him in dramatically heightened form, but one that presents a truth about existence which is available to anyone. While we may fail to recognize the fact, or deliberately conceal it from ourselves, Sartre implies, our own minds are capable of apprehending reality in the same way. As Sartre says of his hero: 'He's a character who had an intuition, but who was privileged in that he had the intuition that others ought to have had'.[7] All seven of the writers considered in this study aim to express general truths about human minds, rather than merely the particular mind of their fictional creations. Proust's maxims on love and jealousy, or Sarraute's nameless, faceless characters, are only the most overt examples. But, in moving from a psychology to a *phenomenology* of consciousness, Sartre takes us to a new level of generality. Where Sarraute dissects a particular emotion down to the nameless psychical movements of attraction or repulsion from which it is constituted, Sartre works toward a theory of emotion which will explain what emotions are and what they are for. Where Proust's Narrator gazes on hawthorn blossom to evoke the minutiae of the visual impressions received and the nuances of the feelings produced, Sartre's narrator stares at a tree root to understand what it means for a material object to exist. Sartre lays out his conception of the differences between psychological and phenomenological investigation in *L'Imagination* (1936):

> Psychology remains for Husserl, like physics or astronomy, 'a science of the natural attitude', that is, a science that entails spontaneous realism. Phenomenology, on the other hand, begins at the point where 'we put aside the general position of existence which belongs to the essence of the natural attitude'. [. . .] Phenomenology is a description of the structures of transcendental consciousness founded on the intuition of the essences of these structures. Naturally, this description operates on the plane of reflection. But reflection is not to be confused with introspection. Introspection employs a special mode of reflection which seeks to grasp and fix empirical facts. To convert its results into scientific laws, one must *then* pass inductively to the general. But the phenomenologist employs a different kind of reflection: one which seeks to grasp essences. That is to say, it begins by placing itself on the grounds of the universal from the very start.[8]

Roquentin does have unique experiences and an individual psychology of course, but the novel also makes use of him to present general insights into existence as a conscious being, and into the relationship of that consciousness with the world. With an eye for this slightly different alignment of Sartre's text, then, let us begin by briefly outlining the sort of mind *Nausea* presents to us. While the nausea itself may initially strike its victim as a possible 'attack of insanity', it will turn out not to be a phenomenon of consciousness alone, but rather, an effect of the relationship between consciousness and the world (the relationship, in fact, by which phenomenology is defined).[9] The principal element of this relationship, and the crux of Sartre's early philosophy, is its intentionality, the proposition that consciousness must always be consciousness *of* something. Recalling his experience in the park as he organizes his thoughts that evening, Roquentin writes:

> How long did that spell last? I *was* the root of the chestnut tree. Or rather I was all consciousness of its existence. Still detached from it—since I was conscious of it—and yet lost in it, nothing but it.[10]

We see here the famous *nothingness* of Sartre's being-for-itself, the mode of existence unique to human consciousness. In an almost pathological heightening of the intentional stance, Roquentin's mind is wholly directed towards the tree root, yet it still retains an awareness that it is *not* that tree root, and through this negation distinguishes itself from the world. One consequence of intentionality is that the conscious mind can never be free of an object of thought, an inescapability that Roquentin experiences as a burden in his bleakest moment:

> My thought is *me*: that is why I can't stop. I exist by what I think. . . . and I can't prevent myself from thinking. At this very moment—this is terrible—if I exist, *it is because* I hate existing. It is I, *it is I* who pull myself from the nothingness to which I aspire: hatred and disgust for existence are just so many ways of *making me* exist, of thrusting me into existence. Thoughts are born behind me like a feeling of giddiness, I can feel them being born behind my head. . . . If I give way, they'll come here in front, between my eyes—and I go on giving way.[11]

Descartes's *cogito* is here turned on its head—'I exist therefore I must think'—and presents itself as a life sentence with no hope of escape. Intentional consciousness must always focus on something, even if that something is the desire for oblivion.

Sartrean intentionality has another, more significant difference from the Cartesian model however, a difference which Sartre was elaborating in *La Transcendance de l'Ego* while writing *Nausea*. 'The Cogito affirms too much', he wrote in the essay. 'The sure and certain content of the pseudo-"cogito" is not "I am conscious of this chair", but "*there* is consciousness of this chair"'.[12] Departing from Husserl's original conception of intentionality, Sartre makes the ego—the 'autobiographical self' of durable character-traits which we consider ourselves to be—external to the 'impersonal spontaneity' which is consciousness.[13] It is simply another object onto which consciousness may direct its spotlight, just like an object of our perception in the external world.[14] So while consciousness without thought is inconceivable, consciousness without ego is a possibility, and as if to demonstrate the theory in action, Sartre gives us an example of Roquentin without his self: 'And suddenly the I pales, pales and finally goes out. Lucid, motionless, empty, the consciousness is situated between the walls; it perpetuates itself. Nobody inhabits it any more'.[15] Perceptions and imaginings drift through the ego-less consciousness until, after a short time, the sense of self is reborn: 'There is knowledge of the consciousness. It sees right through itself, peaceful and empty between the walls, freed from the man who inhabited it, [. . .] and the I surges into consciousness'.[16] Jean-Marc Mouillie suggests that this displacement of the ego from the centre of the mind helps to found a 'radical deconstruction of the subject' which will accompany much French poststructuralist thought on human nature in the latter parts of the century, including that of Jacques Derrida and Michel Foucault.[17] We'll see a still more radical displacement shortly in Beckett's *The Unnamable*.

Where intentionality is directed outwards, into the physical world, it encounters the passive existence Sartre labels *being-in-itself*, and it's in this encounter that Roquentin's nausea is generated. Through his nausea, Roquentin becomes aware of two characteristics of perception which usually serve to keep the pounding immediacy of existence at bay. First, there is the division of the stuff of the world into nameable, countable objects. As the tram-seat beneath him seems to metamorphose into the swollen hide of a dead donkey, Roquentin realizes: 'Things have broken free from their names. They are there, grotesque, stubborn, gigantic, and it seems ridiculous to call them seats or say anything at all about them: I am in the midst of Things, which cannot be given names'.[18] Our mental categories not only separate out the things of the world, but also reconnect them in new orders through the attribution of shared qualities: 'I was thinking *appurtenances*, I was saying to myself that the sea belonged to the class of green objects, or that green formed part of the sea's qualities'.[19] Not only do we categorize the world, but we also perceive it in terms of our own ideas and intentions: as both Heidegger and Bergson had argued previously, we see objects in terms of their utility for our projects. As the filter of practical interpretation abandons him, Roquentin protests: 'Objects ought not to *touch*, since they are not alive. You use them, you put them back in place, you live among them: they are useful, nothing more'.[20] Even our most familiar tool, the human hand, similarly transforms from being an extension of conscious will to 'a reddish flash covered with white hairs'.[21] Elsewhere in Sartre's œuvre, we see a change in the status of the perceived object as the situation of the perceiving subject changes. In *Le Sursis* (1945), second volume of Sartre's unfinished *Chemins de la liberté* cycle, Mathieu sees peace-time Paris, with its café-lined boulevards, transformed into war-time Paris, where the roads are oriented with respect to distant international borders, and homes take on the status of 'dormitory-refectories for those eligible to be called up, for the families of those called up already', ready to further transform in the future into 'strategic points' and thence to 'targets'.[22] The central moments of *Nausea* involve the shearing away of such reflective overlays to perception to leave the unrefined spectacle of reality itself. Roquentin experiences his new perspective on the world as 'the collapse of the human world, of measures, of quantities, of bearings'.[23] As we saw in the Bernanos chapter, in the scene in Bouville park, the very concept of a distinguishable object begins to falter, leaving only horrifying and incomprehensible chaos.

This, then, is Sartre's basic conception of consciousness, lived through the mode of being-for-itself, as it confronts the being-in-itself of the world around it.[24] While psychology isn't Sartre's primary concern, his fiction and philosophy do construct a detailed model of the existential mind. It is a model that frequently ventures onto the same territory as Freudian, Darwinian, religious, or cognitive theories of mind, and overlaps with the concerns of our other six authors. Like Bergson, Sartre envisages two different degrees of sophistication in consciousness. Basic consciousness, the intentional 'spotlight' of sentience, is self-aware to the extent that it distinguishes itself from the object of its attention, but has no real sense of that self as a person: 'There is no *I* on the unreflected level'.[25] We see this not only in extreme states like Roquentin's loss of identity, but also in more ordinary situations where our attention is focused outside of ourselves. To take a non-visual example, in *L'Âge de raison*, first volume of the *Chemins de la liberté* cycle, Boris's consciousness is consumed by touching Lola's body: 'He was nothing more than a hand stretched out over silky skin'.[26] Psychology itself deals rather with the more complex *reflective* consciousness, which is reflective in the sense that it involves intellectual thought, but also more literally in that the mind takes itself as its object. It is reflective consciousness which holds reality at arm's length with its intellectual processing of our raw impressions, as Sartre writes in *L'Imaginaire*: 'Judgment rectifies, organizes, stabilizes perception'.[27] For Rhiannon Goldthorpe, commenting on the importance of the transcendent ego in *Nausea*, the apparent unity and stability of the ego constructed over time by reflective consciousness masks the true liberty and spontaneity of consciousness, leading to an apprehension of 'jerky incoherence' and 'dizzying freedom' when the mask finally slips.[28] Psychology is thus for Sartre a dubious discipline to begin with, being in his eyes the study of a construct of consciousness that has no real existence and is inclined to deceive us about our true nature.

Beauvoir's memoirs characterize Sartre as being against the introspective approach of the psychological novel: 'In these gardens where high-class souls cultivate delicate secrets, *they* [Sartre and his friends] saw stinking swamps: this was where all the trafficking of bad faith quietly took place, this was where the stagnant morsels of narcissism were consumed'.[29] Roquentin appears to share the opinion. He scoffs, 'I am neither a virgin nor a priest, to play at having an inner life', and, as he embarks on the task of understanding his nausea, he is uncomfortable about the prospects for self-analysis via traditional categories of character: 'I don't think the profession of historian fits a man for psychological analysis. In our work, we have to deal only with simple feelings to which we give generic names such as Ambition or Interest'.[30] (Later, we will see how Sarraute and Darrieussecq make this problem the heart of their own literary projects.) The idea that the truth about ourselves can be captured in the clumsy labels of character is attacked in Sartre's novel via two of its supporting characters: Anny, who has escaped such illusions, and the autodidact, who continues to labour under them. Anny is now disabused of her former belief in the independent existence of abstract entities like emotions:

> I used to think that hate, love, or death descended on us like tongues of fire on Good Friday. [. . .] Yes, I really thought that 'Hate' existed, that it settled on people and raise them above themselves. Naturally, I am the only one, I am the one who hates, I am the one who loves[31]

The autodidact, on the other hand, has already amply demonstrated his faith in the possibility of grasping the world second-hand through artificial orders and concepts with his methodical progress through the volumes of Bouville library from A to Z. It's little surprise to see that he also considers mental life a suitable subject for labels, listing and measured comparison, as he shows in his thoughts inspired by Roquentin's travels: 'If I were to go on a voyage, I think I should like to make written notes of every aspect of my character before leaving, so that on my return I could compare what I used to be and what I have become'.[32]

As both his fiction and his philosophy strive to displace the autobiographical self from the heart of our being, Sartre defines his stance in opposition to conventional psychological description, and his primary point of reference in this is Proust. While Sartre in later life will come to acknowledge Proust's genius, and the strong influence that the earlier writer had on his work, at this point in his career Proust offers Sartre a helpful shorthand for all that is wrong in the conventional view of the mind.[33] In 'Une idée fondamentale de la philosophie de Husserl: l'Intentionnalité' ('A Fundamental Idea in Husserl's Philosophy: Intentionality'), published the year after *Nausea* in 1939, Sartre sets up an explicit opposition between the outward-looking intentional model of the mind and the 'digestive' internalization of the introspective approach. It ends with an anti-Proustian thrust as cutting as the attack on Mauriac that will follow a month later:

> Husserl reinstalled horror and charm in things. He gave us back the world of the artists and the prophets: frightening, hostile, dangerous, with havens of grace and love. He made room for a new treaty on the passions which would be inspired by a truth which is so simple yet so profoundly misunderstood by our sophisticates: if we love a woman, it is because she is lovable. At a stroke we are free of Proust. Free at the same time from 'inner life': we would search in vain, like Amiel, like a child kissing his own shoulder, for the caresses, the pampering, of our own private sphere, because in the end everything is outside, everything, even ourselves: outside, in the world, among other people.[34]

The choice of love for a woman as an example is clearly not accidental, given how limited the active role of the loved one is in Proust's psychodramas of desire and jealousy, as we have seen in the opening chapter. But it is also the processes of this inward-looking psychology, not only the inwardness itself, that Sartre takes issue with. Proust's view of the mind, aside from being hopelessly bourgeois, is criticized by Sartre as mechanistic and associationist.[35] Bergson's *Essai sur les données immédiates de la conscience* has already offered Sartre a strong critique of associationist psychology: 'The associationist reduces the self to an aggregate of phenomena of consciousness, sensations, feelings and ideas. But if he sees in these various states nothing more than what their name expresses, if he retains from them only the impersonal aspect, he will be able to juxtapose them indefinitely without ever obtaining anything but a phantom self, the shadow of the self projected into space'.[36] Sartre takes Proust to task in this regard over a passage from *The Way by Swann's* describing Swann's fluctuating feelings for Odette between desire, jealousy, revulsion, and tenderness. It will help to unravel the arguments by which Sartre distances himself from Proust if we first examine the Proust passage for ourselves:

> Because as soon as Swann could picture her without horror, as soon as he again saw kindness in her smile, and as soon as the desire to take her out of reach of all other men was not added by jealousy to his love, that love again became above all a predilection for the sensations that Odette's person gave him, for the pleasure he took in admiring like a spectacle or questioning like a phenomenon the dawn of one of her glances, the evolution of one of her smiles, the emission of an intonation of her voice. And this pleasure, different from all the others, had ended by creating in him a need for her that she alone could satisfy by her presence or her letters. [. . .] and so, with the very chemistry of his disease, after he had created jealousy with his love, he began again to manufacture affection, pity for Odette.[37]

According to Sartre, 'Proust by means of intellectualistic distinctions is perpetually trying to find bonds of rational causality between psychic states in the temporal succession of these states'.[38] He seizes on Proust's phrase 'by the very chemistry of his disease' as evidence of a naïve understanding of mental phenomena as individual substances that can be combined 'like milk in coffee'.[39] Proust is wrong (Sartre believes) in taking the constructed ego for the centre of mental life, missing as he does so the flux of consciousness which constructed it and which now perceives it. Hazel Barnes offers a useful précis of Sartre's own theory of self, which can be used to distinguish it from Proust's position:

> Our psychic life, the object of our introspection, can indeed be grasped by a consciousness, however inadequately, either my own or that of a therapist or biographer. Yet despite our familiarity with our autobiography, we recognize the sense of frustration that accompanies our attempt to pin down the real me or true self. The explanation lies in the fact that I apprehend an object where I sought to lay hands on a subjectivity. What is original about Sartre's rediscovery that the subject who thinks is not the subject thought of is precisely the fact that the original self-consciousness is not the personalized self.[40]

Swann's love is conceived of as an entity existing within his mind. Such durable states are, for Sartre, outside consciousness (since we continue to love someone even when we are not thinking about them). They are components of the transcendent ego we intermittently set up when consciousness reflects on itself, and are to be distinguished from our *intentional* feelings. Consciousness does not 'contain' love; rather, it has a loving apprehension, in thought or perception, of the person in question. Love is thus the manner in which we relate to the external object: it is not a substance within us but a mode of engagement in the phenomenological interplay of self and world. Furthermore, Proust's emotional chemistry implies a deterministic causality to mental processes which is at odds with the Sartrean conception of human freedom. For Proust, Swann's jealousy *adds* a possessive element in his love; his pleasure in admiring Odette *creates* a need for her presence; the waning of his jealousy *manufactures* new tenderness. Sartre declares that such chains of cause and effect misrepresent the mind's activity and fail even to offer a clearly understandable temporal model of emotions in transition:

> Proust here attempts to constitute a symbolic *chemistry*, but the chemical images which he uses are capable only of disguising the motivations and irrational acts. It is an attempt to draw us towards a mechanistic interpretation of the psychic which, without being any more intelligible, would completely distort its nature. And yet Proust cannot keep from showing us between estranged states almost interhuman relations (to create, to manufacture, to add), which would almost allow us to suppose that these psychic objects are animated agents.[41]

Proust thus connects up mental events into a coherent narrative and thereby, as Sartre writes elsewhere, transforms the mind's contingency into necessity.[42] In Proust's defence, the passage Sartre has selected discusses change within Swann's relatively stable autobiographical self over an extended period of time. Elsewhere, Proust offers an abundance of examples of the moment-to-moment processes of consciousness, as it gazes outwards on the body of a sleeping lover, or inwards on the barely perceptible eddies of sensation and thought which herald a returning memory. And while the figurative chemistry of emotions in the selected passage may have a determinist flavour, the Narrator's capricious fluctuations of desire in the wider novel show his mind to be far more unpredictable in its reaction to circumstances than those of the classic Realist heroes of a generation earlier.[43]

Sartre may do Proust an injustice in setting him up as an opposing pole to his view of the mind, but he does at least thereby clarify his own view, which is then borne out in his own creative practice. The spontaneity of mental phenomena, and the focus on the immediacy of consciousness rather than the familiar psychological elements of the constructed ego, are clearly in evidence in *Nausea.* There is a gratuitous element to Roquentin's thoughts, moods, and actions. The nausea comes over him at unpredictable times, and his sunnier and darker moods, as well as his moments of horror and panic, are under-determined by the circumstances in which they arise. His thoughts are sometimes beyond his control: the notion that the absent café-owner may be lying dead upstairs is 'a floating idea of which I could neither convince myself nor rid myself'.[44] Behaviour can similarly lack cause or motive. Both Roquentin and Mathieu in *L'Âge de raison* stab knives into their own hands, in both cases a futile gesture without reason or consequences.[45] Two incidents in *Nausea*, one life-changing, one trivial, show Roquentin at a loss to understand the causes of his own actions. His decision to leave France for a life of adventure, and his sudden decision, six years later, to return, are both described as a 'sudden impulse'.[46] The latter, in particular, goes against his rational analysis of the situation in which the decision was made: invited to continue his travels with an archaeological mission to Bengal, Roquentin notes 'I had always wanted to go to Bengal. [. . .] I could see no reason to refuse', and a possibly untrustworthy companion needing to be watched was only 'another reason to accept enthusiastically'.[47] His reaction to the invitation, however, is to stare, 'paralyzed' at a Khmer statuette on the desk in front of him, while the slow realization dawns that he does not know why he is there or why he should continue: 'I felt I was terribly bored. I couldn't understand why I was in Indo-China. What was I doing there?'[48] He returns home the following day. The second example occurs in the narrative present of the novel, and concerns Roquentin's habit of picking up dirty pieces of paper he comes across in the street. In the days following his first attack of the nausea, he finds himself strangely inhibited:

> I bent down, already looking forward to touching this fresh and tender pulp which would roll into grey balls in my fingers . . . I couldn't do it. I stayed in the bent position for a moment, I read: 'Dictation: The White Owl', then I straightened up, empty-handed. I am no longer free, I can no longer do what I want.[49]

While they certainly demonstrate spontaneity and the absence of determinist causality in the mind, the presence of these incidents in *Nausea* may seem surprising. Sartre is, after all, the philosopher of autonomy and transparency, who denies the existence of the unconscious and dismisses as incoherent the theory that the mind may contain knowledge or motivations to which consciousness may not accede. Yet the lapses in self-knowledge and self-control that we see in these examples appear distinctly Freudian in nature, and have indeed been interpreted as such by psychoanalytic critics. Josette Pacaly reads Roquentin's paper-habit as an 'anal drive', and his inhibition as rooted in repressed castration anxiety linked to masturbation: 'It is little surprise to find the Nausea projected "in my hands". It is the hands which touch that which must not be touched'.[50] How can Roquentin be unaware of the factors which appear to compel and restrict his actions, unless he is being influenced by the hidden contents of an unconscious mind?

To answer that question properly, we'll need first to take a short excursus into the wider relationship between Sartre's existentialism and psychoanalysis. Sartre's opinion on psychoanalysis, like much of his thought, changed significantly as his career progressed. In his pre-war writing, where his attitude is largely marked by indifference or hostility, Sartre's most overt literary engagement with psychoanalysis comes in the short story, 'L'Enfance d'un chef' ('A Leader's Childhood', 1939). Written immediately following the publication of *Nausea*, and in many ways a pendant to the novel, the story recounts the development of its protagonist, Lucien, from child to adult, during which time he rejects the insights afforded to Roquentin, instead asserting his own rights and necessity as he transforms from bohemian dilettante to bourgeois capitalist and nationalist thug.[51] Lucien is introduced to psychoanalysis by his friend Berliac, and at first joyfully discovers in the theory a simple explanation for his feeling of emptiness and indefinability: '"My goodness," he thought, "I have a complex"'.[52] Later, he will see in Freudian theory the inevitability of his mental degradation into a self he considers hateful: '"It's the slippery slope", he thought. "I started with an Œdipus complex, then I turned anal-sadistic, and now, to cap it all, I'm a homosexual"'.[53] In fact, the story makes clear that all three of these characterizations are very wide of the mark. Lucien isn't gay, as his aggressive heterosexuality later makes clear, but has been seduced and sexually abused by the predatory Surrealist Achille Bergère. Nor is he 'anal-sadistic', but is labelled as such by the freeloading Berliac to imply he is ungenerous with his money: 'Berliac stared at him gravely and said, "I thought as much: you're an anal type" and explained to him the Freudian relationship: fæces = gold and the Freudian theory of avarice'.[54] The idea of the Œdipus complex is even more clearly exploited for comic effect. Berliac, his face shiny with saliva-coated acne, solemnly tells Lucien, 'I desired my mother up to the age of fifteen', and asserts that Lucien must also have sexual feelings towards his own mother. Lucien is 'enchanted by the scientific turn their confidences had taken', although disconcerted by the idea that the warty Mme Berliac might be an object of desire.[55] The Œdipus complex becomes for Lucien a secret bond with his best friend ('We've got first-rate complexes!'), but also a pseudo-explanation for his own 'strange impression of not existing, this void he had had for a long time in his consciousness', an affliction which, the text strongly implies, is not in fact psycho-sexual at all but a confused awareness of the contingency of his own existence. Roquentin will come to understand this contingency and attempt to face up to it; Lucien, we infer, is blocking it out with Freudian fairy-tales. When his former philosophy tutor dismisses psychoanalytic theory as 'twaddle', Lucien feels released from a burden: 'It was a nightmare, he thought, but it's completely gone now'.[56] The rejection of psychoanalysis does mark a further stage in Lucien's development towards the extreme right, however: he considers that he has returned to 'moral health' from a psychoanalytic milieu in which the 'vices' of homosexuality and marijuana-smoking were indulged. The story as a whole may mock Freud for his implausible ideas on human nature, but the worldview he engenders is presented as a more open and tolerant one than the repressive ideology for which Lucien exchanges it.[57]

Later in life, Sartre's views on psychoanalysis mellowed. *L'Être et le Néant* in 1945 attempted to co-opt certain concepts and methods for an 'existentialist psychoanalysis'; in 1958, Sartre accepted a commission from John Huston to write a screenplay for a biopic of Freud, although his eight-hundred-page script proved unfilmable; and towards the end of his life the mediation of Freud's ideas through Lacan found some favour with Sartre: his biography of Flaubert, *L'Idiot de la famille*, ascribed to its subject's early development something which very much resembles the Lacanian mirror stage.[58] Sartre's most fundamental misgivings about the psychoanalytic view of the mind were never allayed, however, as he made clear in a late interview:

> To come back to Freud, I'd say that I was incapable of understanding him because I was a Frenchman brought up in the Cartesian tradition, full of rationalism, to whom the idea of the unconscious was profoundly shocking. But I wouldn't *only* say that. In fact, I'm still shocked today by something that was inevitable in Freud: his recourse to physiological and biological language to express ideas that could only be communicated through this medium. The result is that the way he describes the analytic object suffers from a sort of mechanistic cramp.[59]

Freud's quasi-medical terminology of aetiologies, excitation, and energy discharge, while they may be no more than metaphors, align his view of the mind with the physical sciences, in which the uncaused causation of free will has no place. The same issue arises when the Sartrean mind comes up against Darwinian and cognitive models of consciousness, as we shall see shortly. As for the 'shocking' unconscious, Sartre's more Cartesian alternative uses bad faith to explain much of what psychoanalysis ascribes to unconscious impulses: the agoraphobia of absolute freedom causes us to hide behind fictions of compulsion and inevitability, but the fundamental awareness that our behaviour is a choice always remains. Predictably, given these views, Sartre has little time for André Breton (who shares initials with Sartre's Achille Bergère) or the Surrealists and their flirtations with psychoanalysis.[60] *Qu'est-ce que la littérature? (What is literature?*, 1948) accuses Surrealism of doing away with consciousness altogether to make the mind a haunted house of ownerless voices, and further takes issue with their attempts to break through to a supposed Unconscious or to blur together the real and the imagined.[61]

Two further elements of the Sartrean psyche allow for deficient or erroneous self-knowledge, without conceding the existence of an unconscious or a lack of transparency in consciousness itself. The first is the transcendent ego which we saw earlier. If my autobiographical self is not part of consciousness, but rather a thing in the world that I understand in the same way as I understand other people, then I can be mistaken in my beliefs about my own self just as I can be mistaken about others. Sartre illustrates this with the neat question: 'Am I lazy?'[62] He points out that the best way to discover the answer to this question is to ask other people, and that, even if I attempt to answer the question through introspection, then I must attempt to evaluate myself objectively as if from the stance of an external observer, with, of course, no guarantee of success.[63] The second deficiency of self-knowledge is summed up in the distinction Sartre makes between *conscience* and *connaissance* (awareness and knowledge). As part of the outline of his alternative, existential version of psychoanalysis that occupies some of the final pages of *L'Être et le Néant*, Sartre envisages the possibility of a fully conscious subject who nevertheless doesn't fully know his or her own mind:

> Empirical psychoanalysis in fact is based on the hypothesis of the existence of an unconscious psyche, which on principle escapes the intuition of the subject. Existential psychoanalysis rejects the hypothesis of the unconscious; it makes the psychic act coextensive with consciousness. But if the fundamental project is fully experienced by the subject and hence wholly conscious, that certainly does not mean that it must by the same token be *known* by him; quite the contrary.[64]

We can thus be aware of something without having knowledge of it: its presence in our unreflected consciousness does not mean that it is grasped and understood intellectually, as Sartre goes on to illustrate:

> [Reflection] is penetrated by a great light without being able to express what this light is illuminating. We are not dealing with an unsolved riddle as the Freudians believe; all is there, luminous; reflection is in full possession of it, apprehends all. But this 'mystery in broad daylight' is due to the fact that this possession is deprived of the means which would ordinarily permit *analysis* and *conceptualization*.[65]

Sartre claims that the evidence from Freudian psychotherapy itself supports this view over Freud's interpretation. Since analysands recognize their complex when it is shown to them by the analyst, they must, Sartre contends, have been conscious of it, even if their reflective consciousness had not understood it.[66]

We are now in a position to return to Roquentin, his Asian adventures and his litter-picking habits. The question, as you may remember, is how these episodes of what seem like blind compulsion or unconscious motivation fit with the Sartrean model of the mind. The end of Roquentin's foreign travels can be seen as a matter of a lack of self-knowledge and a misreading of the ego. Roquentin considers himself to be an adventurer, and, out of genuine enthusiasm for adventure in his early travels, he has constructed an identity which outlasts his conscious enjoyment of the adventuring life. Due to lack of reflection, he has failed to conceptualize his current feelings as boredom, and failed to observe that his identity as the happy traveller no longer coheres with his conscious experience. As he admits in hindsight: 'The thing is that I very rarely think; consequently a host of little metamorphoses accumulate in me without my noticing it, and then, one fine day, a positive revolution takes place'.[67]

The decision to return surprises him, just as Mathieu in *L'Âge de raison* is surprised to find himself telling Marcelle he no longer loves her, having intended to say the opposite.[68] As Christina Howells comments:

> Sartre's characters are as complex as his theory of freedom: 'will', 'decision', 'deliberate' choice are mistrusted as simplifications which tend to involve the masking of a genuine project and choice in the bad faith of rationalization. Real choices and apparent decision-making are not identical and may at times be at odds.[69]

This masking of the truth of the self also applies to the advent of the nausea. Roquentin worries that his consciousness has been too outward-facing and unreflective, and he has failed to recognize the development of his autobiographical self which has led to these feelings. The lesson he takes from his recollection of the Asian episode is, 'I should like to understand myself properly before it is too late', and he resolves to reflect on and comprehend the nausea, rather than simply enduring it.[70] Closer examination of the litter scene similarly weakens the case for a Freudian unconscious at work. At the most basic level, Roquentin knows quite well why he cannot (or, more precisely, is unwilling to) pick up the piece of paper: he is afraid. 'I am afraid of entering in contact with [objects], just as if they were living animals'.[71] What gives him pause is not so much repressed castration anxiety as the memory of his recent attack of nausea with the pebble from the beach, and a foreshadowing that the paper will affect him in the same way.[72] In other words, the outward exercise of his freedom is constrained by his situation, as another key passage from *L'Être et le Néant* explains:

> In addition, it is necessary to point out against 'common sense' that the formula 'to be free' does not mean 'to obtain what one has wished' but rather 'by oneself to determine oneself to wish' (in the broad sense of choosing). In other words success is not important to freedom. [. . .] Thus we shall not say that a prisoner is always free to go out of prison, which would be absurd, nor that he is always free to long for release, which would be an irrelevant truism, but that he is always free to try to escape (or get himself liberated); that is, that whatever his condition may be, he can project his escape and learn the value of his project by undertaking some action.[73]

Just as our actions are constrained by our past, our environment, or the actions of others, so Roquentin is inhibited by the nausea, which, let us not forget, is an acute reaction to an *external* phenomenon, the existence of the material world. Roquentin remains free in his choices and aware of his own mind, even though he doesn't yet reflectively grasp the nature of his nausea. In saying 'I am no longer free, I can no longer do what I want', he is either simply mistaken, or else he is referring to the constraints put on him by his situation, rather than the limitations of his mind.

The differences between the Sartrean and Freudian conceptions of mind amount to more than semantics. It is not simply a recasting of the conscious/unconscious dichotomy into a new division between the known and the conscious-but-not-known. What I have tried to illustrate here is a profound difference of opinion with regard to the mind's availability to itself, and with regard to the subject's responsibility for his or her own decisions. For Sartre, our consciousness has free access to everything our minds can hold, even if we may not pay attention to it, may not understand it, or may prefer to ignore it. Equally, although circumstances may thwart our actions, nothing limits our decisions, the responsibility for which is all our own. It must be borne in mind, however, that this exegesis comes from applying onto Sartre's fiction ideas taken from his philosophical essays. The explanations of Roquentin's sudden impulses and mysterious inhibitions are not a part of the novel itself, and even if they were, they would have only the authority of speculations on the part of Roquentin-as-narrator as to the possible ontological underpinnings of his subjective experience. For the text to presume any greater authority than this over the nature of consciousness would require a divine perspective, and recourse to such a perspective would, of course, invalidate one of the founding premises of Sartre's atheist existentialism.[74] If we accept the reader's right to freedom of interpretation, then, the existentialist reading has no monopoly over the meaning of the novel, and psychoanalytic critics like Pacaly have been undeterred by Sartre's hostility from drawing up their own analyses of the novel as a whole. François George, Andrew Leak, and Serge Doubrovsky are among others to have taken this route.[75] Doubrovsky is predictably the most flamboyant, reading a fear of sodomy in the 'smashed-in bench' on which Roquentin sits in the café, and an Œdipus complex in the trumped king of the nearby card-players. More promisingly, psychoanalytic criticism draws attention to a possibly inadvertent sexual aspect to Sartre's philosophical metaphors, suggesting a feminine element in metaphors of contingency, often accompanied by disgust for the flesh, and a masculine, often phallic, one in metaphors of transcendence.[76] It is worth also noting in passing that Sartre's ideas on the mind found much greater favour with the rival psychiatric movement founded by R.D. Laing and David Cooper, which I discussed in the previous chapter. Laing and the anti-psychiatrists adopt Sartre's political concern to consider the individual in the context of his or her social situation, as well as his critique of the unequal relationship between analyst and patient.[77] Sartre in turn contributes an approving preface to Laing's and Cooper's co-authored book on his philosophy, in which he praises their work as working towards 'a truly *human* psychiatry', and agrees that mental illness is the '"way out" that the free organism, in its total unity, invents in order to be able to live through an intolerable situation'.[78]

One last element of the litter-picking episode will lead us into a final confrontation for the existentialist model of the mind, which is its on-going encounter with scientific psychology. As we saw, it is Roquentin's memory of the recent distressing nausea from picking up the pebble, along with similar incidents with a door-handle and his pipe, which makes him hesitate when faced with the paper. 'Now I see; I remember better what I felt the other day on the sea-shore when I was holding that pebble [. . .]: a sort of nausea in the hands'.[79] His previous bad experiences induce him to avoid behaviour which might bring about a recurrence of a similarly negative episode. Roquentin has, in other words, been conditioned, not unlike a lab rat in a behaviourist psychological experiment. Once again, this may seem surprisingly un-Sartrean, given that Sartre's doctrines are opposed to all determinist conceptions of the mind, Freudian or otherwise. In fact, Sartre never denied the existence of conditioning, and, while it was given little consideration in his early work, it would come to preoccupy him more and more in his later years. His childhood memoir, *Les Mots* (*The Words*, 1964), reads as an extended meditation on the conditioning effect of his middle-class, intellectual, and literary upbringing. In a 1969 interview, he defined freedom as 'this small movement which makes an entirely conditioned social being into a person who does not entirely recreate the totality of what he has received from his conditioning'.[80] Even here, the insistence is still on the non-absolute nature of conditioning, however, and the swerve of freedom which makes a person's thoughts and actions differ, if only slightly, from what their upbringing, environment, and past experience would predict. A comparative study of Sartre's and the behaviourist B. F. Skinner's models of the mind by Martin E. Morf concludes that superficial connections mask fundamental differences of emphasis, and particularly so in Sartre's early work, where he is more interested in freedom's possibilities and consequences than its limits.[81] *L'Être et le Néant* does in fact discuss behaviourism briefly, but does so only to dismiss it as solipsistic:

> If animals are machines, why shouldn't the man whom I see pass in the street be one? Why should not the radical conception of the behaviourists be the right one? What I apprehend on that face is nothing but the effect of certain muscular contractions, and they in turn are the effect of a nervous impulse of which I know the course. Why not reduce the ensemble of these reactions to simple or conditioned reflexes? But the majority of psychologists remain convinced of the existence of the Other as a total reality of the same structure as their own.[82]

Striking to the modern reader here is Sartre's casual adoption of the Cartesian assumption that animals are machines. Derived from the Christian distinction between ensouled humans and soulless animals, Descartes's inference is that conscious life is restricted to humans, and that all other animal life must be insentient automata. This then leads Sartre unfairly to assimilate behaviourism to the abolition of consciousness, and to attribute to it the absurd position that everyone is an automaton apart from the one person whose sentience is undeniable: me. (A more thoughtful and detailed engagement with behaviourism, though no less strongly opposed, is to be found in Sarraute's work, as we shall see later.)

The implied dichotomy between the minds of human beings and those of the rest of the animal kingdom suggests we'll find little common ground between the Sartrean and Darwinian views of life. Equally, his incredulous rhetoric on 'muscular contractions' and 'nervous impulses' doesn't bode well for a rapprochement with neuroscientific approaches to the mind. The *Chemins de la liberté* cycle refers to people as animals on two occasions. In *Le Sursis*, Irène thinks, 'we are animals, we put words on an instinct,' as she sits through Marc's clumsy seduction.[83] In *La Mort dans l'âme*, Sarah sees the stream of people fleeing Paris as the German army approaches as 'thinking animals'.[84] As for the mind-as-brain, a character in the short story 'La Chambre' ('The Room', 1939) does propose a genetic understanding of the madness afflicting the protagonist, who has 'a terribly burdened heredity', and who has carried 'this flaw' within himself from birth.[85] None of these examples helps to build a very convincing case, however. The concept of a 'thinking animal' is immediately labelled 'against nature' by Sarah, and Irène's meditation is clearly in the context of sexual desire, and very much in the lineage of pre-Darwinian religious and philosophical divisions of human nature into 'divine' reason and 'bestial' urges, in which the latter have no more than a metaphorical resemblance. In 'La Chambre', the character who expresses the genetic view, M. Darbédet, is hardly a mouthpiece for authorial opinion. His insensitive and judgmental attitudes towards the insane Pierre are implicitly condemned in the course of the story. While the progressive deterioration of Pierre's mental condition supports the view that his affliction is neurological, the story itself skates over this aspect to explore the attempts to understand Pierre's subjective experience of his condition by those around him.[86] As for *Nausea* itself, the gulf separating it from scientific perspectives on the mind is betrayed by one of Roqeuntin's rare mentions of the wider animal kingdom, in which he refers in passing to 'the immutable forms of animal species'. The phrase suggests a Platonic conception of life on his part, in which the minor variations of individual members of a species cluster around the fixed ideal that is their template, and which has remained unchanged since Creation. The immediate context of Roquentin's remark is also illuminating:

> I looked in alarm at these unstable creatures which, in another hour, in another minute, were perhaps going to collapse: yes, I was there, I was living in the midst of these books crammed full of knowledge, some of them describing the immutable forms of animal species, and others explaining that the quantity of energy in the universe remained unchanged; I was there, standing in front of a window whose panes had an established index of refraction. But what weak barriers![87]

For Roquentin, then, the Platonic model of life is an example of the scientific ordering of reality, to be set alongside the refractive index of glass or the first law of thermodynamics as a bulwark against the horrifying chaos that he now perceives in existence. In fact, he has it quite the wrong way around. By the time Sartre was writing, the Darwinian revolution had replaced the eternal order of the Classical model with a scientific model which presents life in constant flux, and reduces the labels by which species and genera are categorized to useful fictions within a continuum of creeping evolutionary change. So inviting is the analogy that it seems rather a shame Sartre did not make use of it to evoke the collapse of Roquentin's own ordered view of the world into purposeless, meaningless disorder. Instead, zoology stands in *Nausea*, like music, geometry, and mathematics, for the purity of an ideal realm, in opposition to the mess that confronts us in the real world.

If Sartre has little time for the human mind as the product of our evolutionary past, he has scarcely more concern for its present status as the creation of the physical brain. We have seen already Sartre's aversion to doctrines that connect mind and brain too closely, since the physical laws which govern the processes of the latter would seem to leave scant room for the operation of free will in the former. The fascination and revulsion with which *Nausea* and the stories of *Le Mur* treat the human body, coupled with Sartre's critique of the religiously inspired psychology of Mauriac in his notorious essay, led critic André Rousseau in two articles of 1939 to characterize Sartre as a materialist. Sartre's response sets out his position clearly:

> You accuse me of materialism, which is precisely the doctrine that is most repugnant to my reason. [. . .] [F]urthermore, since you cite a line of mine in *La Revue universelle*: 'Only things exist, consciousness does not exist, it acts itself out', I imagine that it is precisely this sentence which has confused you. Perhaps it is indeed unclear. You understood it to mean, I suppose, that I was asserting that only material things have reality and the consciousness is created out of them. But what I meant was quite the opposite. I intended to say: only things have that passive and inert existence that we ordinarily call *being*. The existence of consciousness is of another kind: it is an absolute free spontaneity which determines itself to exist. Can you still call me a materialist after this profession of faith?[88]

If not a materialist, is Sartre then a dualist, positing an immaterial substance of consciousness akin to the immortal souls of Bernanos, Mauriac, and Green? Unsurprisingly, he is positing no such thing. Rather than distinguishing between material and immaterial substances, Sartre's theory of consciousness distinguishes between different modes of existence. What he here objects to under the term *materialist* is the idea that consciousness might be *composed of* the molecules and electrical impulses of the brain. That consciousness might be *brought about* by the activity of this physical substrate—that it might be, in Hazel Barnes's words, 'a doing and not a being'—is entirely acceptable to his theory.[89] As Matthew Eshleman notes, this philosophical stance would today be considered to fall within the scope of materialism.[90] It is, to be precise, property dualism, the theory which claims, as we saw in the Introduction, that only material substances exist, but that the properties of the mind are not reducible to the properties of the brain that gives rise to it. Sartre himself is prepared to concede this point in his later writings.[91]

Sartre does give some consideration to the question of consciousness outside that of the adult human. *L'Âge de raison* contains a rare reference to infant mentality in a scene where Mathieu meets the gaze of Sarah's young son, Pablo:

> Pablo's gaze was not yet human and yet it was already more than just alive: it had not been long since the kid had emerged from a belly and that was plain to see: he was there, indistinct, very small, he still retained the unwholesome downiness of something that has been vomited up; but behind the cloudy humours that filled his eye-sockets, a greedy little consciousness had infiltrated itself.[92]

As well as displaying Sartre's care to avoid the pitfall of sentimentality in the representation of small children, the passage contains an interesting combination of the relative and the absolute with regards to consciousness. The infant Pablo may not yet have attained a fully 'human' degree of mental sophistication, but his existence is already qualitatively different from that of other living things. Consciousness itself, it seems, is not a matter of degree, but simply present or absent, like a soul. And, like the soul, it's something hard to reconcile with a developmental model of the mind, which would imply a continuum of increasing levels of consciousness through the stages of embryonic progress, just as a similar continuum is implied in our evolutionary development.

Towards the end of his life, Sartre does make reference in an interview to 'animal consciousness'.[93] As Barnes points out, though, this off-the-cuff remark doesn't bear scrutiny in the context of Sartre's wider philosophical system, which assumes a self-aware subject consciously taking free decisions, and has little or no application to instinctive or genetically programmed behaviours in the animal kingdom.[94] The *Esquisse d'une théorie des emotions*, published the year after *Nausea*, well illustrates the incompatibility between the Sartrean mind and evolutionary psychology. Emotions, according to Sartre's theory, are directed outwards at the world, and are related to a goal we consciously hope to achieve. However, they result from the failure of rational means to attain this goal, and instead consist in an attempt to magically reconfigure the world to suit our own ends:

> I see a ferocious beast coming towards me: my legs give way under me, my heart beats more feebly, I turn pale, fall down and faint away. No conduct could seem worse adapted to the danger than this, which leaves me defenceless. And nevertheless it is a behaviour of *escape* [. . .]. The real meaning of fear is now becoming apparent to us. It is a consciousness whose aim is to negate something in the external world by means of magical behaviour, and will go so far as to annihilate itself in order to annihilate the object also.[95]

The essay offers a similar sketch of the processes of melancholy, which is said to transform the world into a bleak arena where no useful action is possible, as a means of avoiding the necessity to act in circumstances that I wish were otherwise: 'Lacking the ability and the will to carry out the projects I formerly entertained, I behave in such a manner that the universe requires nothing more of me'.[96] This idea has interesting implications for *Nausea*, the title of which, we should remember, was imposed by Gallimard in preference to Sartre's own *Melancholia*. In such a reading, Roquentin's apathy, his abandonment of his historical work, and his half-hearted attempt to reconnect with Anny, might be seen at least in part as an emotional response to the arrival of the nausea. With his life blighted by this mysterious new affliction, Roquentin is no longer able to interact with the world as he once did, and so he makes it a place where there is nothing to be done, and nothing to be gained. Only when he has understood the nature of the nausea can he rediscover a purpose for himself and see life afresh, as he does in the novel's final pages.

My point, though, is to draw attention to how fundamentally anti-Darwinian this all is. If we examine Sartre's analysis of fear a little more closely, then—aside from the question of whether swooning in the face of peril is a sufficiently widespread phenomenon to warrant a general theory in the first place—there appears to be no good reason why playing dead shouldn't, in fact, be a perfectly adaptive third alternative in situations where the more usual 'fight or flight' responses prove unfeasible. (Darrieussecq offers precisely this view in *A Brief Stay with the Living*: 'instinctively you play dead hands over your neck as the bear attacks'.)[97] Sartre's characterization of emotion as the last recourse of a rational subject for whom rational means have failed commits the error, from a post-Darwinian perspective, of taking higher cognitive functions as its premise, and then asking why they should call older and more basic mental phenomena into being. Freud's theory of the formation of the Unconscious makes the same mistake. Rather than ask, as modern psychologists do, how unconscious mental activity should have come to produce consciousness over the course of our evolution from simpler life forms and over the course of our fœtal (and perhaps early infant) development, Freud asks instead why a fully developed consciousness should need to equip itself with an Unconscious. His answer, that repression creates the Unconscious as a store-house for what the conscious mind doesn't wish to contemplate, is ontogenetically and phylogenetically backwards.[98] In the same way, Sartre posits reasoned responses as prior to emotional responses, without considering that, in our evolutionary history and in our own lives, emotional responses pre-date intellectual ones, and are in no way dependent on them.[99]

Attempts have been made to build bridges between other areas of Sartre's thought and contemporary theories of consciousness. Barnes, a life-long Sartre scholar, devoted one of her final essays to uncovering connections between Sartrean existentialism and twenty-first century neuroscientific theory. She points out that, while Sartre does not engage with Darwin in his thought or his fiction, the purposelessness and contingency of natural selection bring forth a world and a humanity that are very much in accord with Sartre's philosophical vision.[100] While Barnes's essay (published when she was nearly ninety years old) breaks new ground in Sartre studies, she arguably picks the wrong cognitive scientist on which to focus her comparison. Gerald M. Edelman, a Nobel prize-winner for immunology and a leading figure in consciousness studies, has views on the mind which closely resemble epiphenomenalism—the doctrine that brain activity causes consciousness, but consciousness has no causal effects on the brain (or, indeed, anything else). Neural activity, in Edelman's view, causes me to believe I am choosing to raise my hand, and causes my hand to rise, but the event in my consciousness is not the cause of the action of my body. Edelman's conception of neural activity itself as governed by a highly deterministic internal Darwinism, a 'survival of the fittest neural impulse', further underlines his difference from Sartre. Other scientific thinkers, some of them writing after Barnes's death, offer closer links to the free self of existentialism. Among the philosophers, Jean-Marc Mouillie, Kenneth Williford, Dan Zahavi, and Shaun Gallagher reinvigorate Sartrean phenomenology with new perspectives from cognitive science.[101] Mouillie attempts to go beyond the 'dialogue of the deaf' which often transpires between philosophy and neuroscience due to their different approaches to consciousness. His proposed *rapprochement* is again a form of property dualism, although he doesn't label it as such. Acknowledging that Sartrean freedom entails the irreducibility of the *being-for-itself* of mind to the *being-in-itself* of brain, he argues that no such reduction is implied in the supervenience of mind on brain: 'The fact that certain physiological equipment is needed to think *in the way* that we do does not authorize us to say that it is this equipment that thinks *what* we are thinking'.[102] Meanwhile, among the scientists, Damasio offers a model of consciousness with some striking similarities to Sartre's. 'Self, of course, is not a thing', Damasio writes in *Self Comes to Mind* (2010); 'it is a dynamic process, held at some fairly stable levels during most of our waking hours but subject to variations, big and small, during that period, especially at the tail ends'.[103] Like Sartre's transcendent ego, Damasio's autobiographical self is 'treated like any other object' of attention, and called intermittently into being when consciousness reflects on itself, or, in Damasio's terminology, when our extended consciousness fits our core consciousness into a broader mental arena of ideas, imagination, and thoughts of past and future.[104] These concepts of core and extended consciousness themselves correspond closely to Sartre's pre-reflective consciousness, with its non-positional awareness of self, and reflective consciousness, in which the mind takes itself as object.[105] While Damasio's Darwinian and neurological theory of the development of the mind has no counterpart in Sartre, his conception of the nature of mature human consciousness has arrived at very much the same destination as Sartre's phenomenological enquiry.

*

In *Nausea*, then, we have seen a mind that is radically distinct from the world it looks out on and the body that houses it, and yet in other ways is inextricably melded to both. The very mode of existence of consciousness, being-for-itself, is qualitatively different from the inert being-in-itself of the material world, a world which includes the body of the conscious subject and the brain that gives rise to that consciousness. The pure realm of the intellect is a harmonious space in which the human abstractions of art, music, or mathematics can be contemplated with serenity. The world outside, on the other hand, threatens to dissolve into chaotic horror as it escapes the order Roquentin imposes on it. The body too is an object of revulsion once he perceives it as a physical existent in itself, rather than as a function of the consciousness within it. And yet he is no immaterial soul dwelling temporarily in an envelope of flesh before departing for a higher realm. Roquentin *is* a body, and he feels his embodiment keenly:

> I exist. [. . .] There is some frothy water in my mouth. I swallow it, it slides down my throat, it caresses me—and now it is starting up again in my mouth, I have a permanent little pool of whitish water in my mouth—unassuming—touching my tongue. And this pool is me too. And the tongue. And the throat is me.[106]

When assailed by the nausea, Roquentin may wish to escape to an intellectual plane: 'To have neither blood, nor lymph, nor flesh', he thinks as he recovers from an attack. 'To be nothing but coldness'.[107] Yet this is no more than a fantasy. The reality of his life is that his consciousness must live in constant confrontation with physical reality in which it is embodied and embedded.

We have also seen in *Nausea* a novel that rejects the psychological chains of cause and effect of the traditional realist novel. Instead, it is a representation of spontaneity, which is not psychological randomness but psychological freedom, in which a choice may be guided by the mental and environmental events which lead up to it, but it is not finally determined by them. In taking this path, while restricting himself to the viewpoint of his protagonist, Sartre leaves himself open to a reading against the grain, which would see Roquentin's choices not as freely taken, but as determined by an unconscious mind that he doesn't even believe exists. Reading with rather than against Sartre, though, by using his philosophy as a key to his conception of the mental architecture underlying the subjective experience with which the novel presents us, we see a mind with full access to all of its parts, even while there may be parts it doesn't focus on or cannot fully comprehend. It is a mind whose freedom is unfettered by the (apparently) deterministic electro-chemical processes in the brain on which it supervenes, but for all that, it is a natural product of these processes, with no immaterial substances or supernatural entities required to explain it. There are no souls and no ghosts in Sartre, beside the hallucinations of delirious minds like Pierre's angels in 'La Chambre'. There is also, though, little interest on the part of the writer in tracing the origins of our complex consciousness, neither in the matter of the brain, nor in the developing infant mind, nor yet in the slow crawl to sentience which is our evolutionary history. Sartre, of course, was writing at a time when the 'hard problem' of how physical processing gives rise to conscious experience was fit only for idle speculation.[108] It is not until the end of the century that these questions would create interest in the sciences, and from there begin to be seriously addressed in literature, as we'll see in the final chapter. *Nausea* may have been the spark that began the wildfire sweep of existentialism across Western intellectual life in the mid-twentieth century, but in the cultural history of the mind it nevertheless represents an ending. It is the last hurrah of the Cartesian conception of the mind as a consciousness transparent to itself, equipped for self-knowledge, and untrammelled in its liberty. Already as Sartre was writing *Nausea*, the murkier image of Freudian psychoanalysis, with its hidden Unconscious and primal drives, was growing in influence in European thought. Later in the century would come the similarly deterministic overtones of Darwinian psychology, uncovering the urges of our selfish genes beneath our apparently rational self-governance, or downgrading our conscious life to an accidental by-product of electro-chemical activity in our brains. Never again would the freedom, clarity, and autonomy of the individual seem such a persuasive model for mental life as it did at the zenith of Sartre's fame.

We are now past the half-way point. In the first chapter, we saw Proust's novel as an invitation to the reader to see the world through another person's eyes. Proust's Narrator, whose subjectivity we are invited to share, is a unique individual, but neither he nor the life-experiences he traverses are presented as abnormal or even atypical. The characteristics of his mind and its activity are able to be generalized, and, in many cases, are intended to be equally applicable to the reader's own mind. Our experiences of love and jealousy, of the joys of art and nature, and the complexities of social interaction, are solicited for comparison with the Narrator's, in a process that may offer us new insights into our own mentality. This isn't quite the case with Bernanos and Breton. While neither Bernanos's fictional protagonists nor Breton's autobiographical persona are presented as mentally extraordinary, the experiences to which they are subjected are not representative of typical life-experiences. Bernanos's novels are structured around moments in which the hero's perceptual capacities defy rational explanation, the better to suggest a miraculous connection between human and divine minds. Breton's narratives of the self are not autobiographies in any conventional sense, but a series of carefully selected incidents of the uncanny and coincidental, presented to emphasize their supernatural potential and downplay any possible rational explanations. Like Bernanos, Breton has a thesis to advance, in this case the mystic confluence of mind and world through 'objective chance'. But with Sartre we have taken a step further still from showing the reader a typical consciousness in action. Here, for the first time, we have the depiction of a starkly unusual mind, which experiences the world through a state of consciousness that in all likelihood none of the novel's readers will ever experience. The mind Sartre represents in *Nausea* is not a reflection of our own consciousness back to us. It is a radical 'what if?' scenario. What might the world look like to our eyes if we could apprehend it directly, rather than through the categories, attributes, and personal projects through which our reflective consciousness orders our perceptions? Sartre's attempt to render a pre-reflective phenomenal experience, like the Surrealists' efforts to evoke the uncensored contents of a Freudian Unconscious, aims at presenting the reader with a model of mental activitity which is, in the author's view, no less real for its inaccessibility than is the conscious life typically experienced. We are some distance here from the *raison d'être* David Lodge posits for the psychological novel. Lodge suggests we read such books simply 'because they give us a convincing sense of what the consciousness of people other than ourselves is like'.[109] He is not wrong, of course, where writers such as Proust or his own example of Henry James are concerned. But novels of the mind are not restricted to the narrow band in the spectrum of mental activity that is everyday awareness. Sartre shows us clearly how the representation of an extraordinary, perhaps even an impossible subjectivity can still offer a convincing account of aspects of mind that may be present in all of us.

Notes

1. Sartre's three other novels, *L'Âge de raison* (*The Age of Reason*, 1945), *Le Sursis* (*The Reprieve*, 1945) and *La Mort dans l'âme* (*Iron in the Soul*, 1949), with the fragment, 'Drôle d'amitié' ('Strange friendship', 1949), form the unfinished novel sequence, *Les Chemins de la liberté* (*The Roads to Freedom*). His other prose fiction consists of the five short stories collected in *Le Mur* (*The Wall*, 1939). His screenplays for *Les Jeux sont faits* (*The Chips Are Down*, 1947) and *Le Scénario Freud* (*Freud Screenplay*, 1984) have also been published as *romans-scénarios*, and, of course, his œuvre also includes major bodies of work in the genres of drama, philosophy, literary criticism, biography, and autobiography.
2. Looking back in a late interview, Sartre contrasts the person he was at the time of writing *La Nausée* with the committed author his war-time experiences would make of him: 'Before the War I thought of myself simply as an individual. I failed to see the link between my individual existence and the society in which I lived. By the time I left the École Normale, I had built a whole theory around it: I was "the lone man", which is to say the individual who sets himself against society by the independence of his thought, but who owes society nothing, and on whom society can have no effect, because he is free. That was the self-evident point on which I founded everything I thought, everything I wrote and everything I lived before 1939', 'Autoportrait à soixante-dix ans' (1975), in *Situations X* (Paris: Gallimard, 1976), pp. 133–226 (p. 176).
3. Jacques Deguy suggests that the novel is nevertheless structured as an argument in support of the thesis, 'the essential thing is contingency', Jacques Deguy, *La Nausée de Jean-Paul Sartre* (Paris: Gallimard, 1993), p. 49.
4. Extracts from the novel's early reviews can be seen in *OR*, 1701–11.
5. 'Ce que j'ai fait de meilleur', in a 1971 interview with Michel Contat and Michel Rybalka, *OR*, p. 1669.
6. The incident with the pebble was in part inspired by Paul Valéry's *Eupalinos ou l'Architecte* (1921), in which questions on existence are inspired by intense consideration of a white object picked up on the shore. Pilkington demonstrates that several elements of Sartre's thinking on consciousness are anticipated in Valéry's writing, including the 'nothingness' of consciousness, its intentionality, and the 'negation' by which it distinguishes itself from the object of its perception. A. E. Pilkington, 'Valéry and Sartre: The Nature of Consciousness', *French Studies*, 43 (1989), pp. 182–94.
7. 'C'est un personnage qui avait une intuition, mais qui était privilégié en cela qu'il avait l'intuition que les autres auraient dû avoir', *OR*, p. 1700.
8. 'La psychologie, pour Husserl, reste, comme la physique ou l'astronomie, une "science de l'attitude naturelle", c'est-à-dire une science qui implique un réalisme spontané. Au contraire, la phénoménologie commence lorsque "nous mettons hors de jeu la position genérale de l'existence qui appartient à l'essence de l'attitude naturelle". [. . .] La phénoménologie est une description des structures de la conscience transcendantale fondée sur l'intuition des essences de ces structures. Naturellement, cette description s'opère sur le plan de la réflexion. Mais il ne faut pas confondre réflexion avec introspection. L'introspection use un mode spécial de réflexion qui cherche à saisir et à fixer les faits empiriques. Pour convertir ses résultats en lois scientifiques il faut *ensuite* un passage inductif au général. Or il est un autre type de réflexion dont use le phénoménologue: celle-là cherche à saisir les essences. C'est-à-dire qu'elle débute en se plaçant d'emblée sur le terrain de l'universel', Jean-Paul Sartre, *L'Imagination* (1936) (Paris: Presses universitaires de France, 1948), pp. 139–40, italics Sartre's.
9. 'Crise de folie', Jean-Paul Sartre, *La Nausée* (1938), in *Œuvres romanesques* (Paris: Gallimard, Pléiade edition, 1981), pp. 1–210 (p. 6; trans.10). Translation references are to *Nausea*, trans. by Robert Baldick (London: Penguin, 1965).
10. 'Combien de temps dura cette fascination? J'*étais* la racine du marronnier. Ou plutôt j'étais tout entier conscience de son existence. Encore détaché d'elle—puisque j'en avais conscience—et pourtant perdu en elle, rien d'autre qu'elle', *OR*, p. 156, trans. 188, italics Sartre's.
11. 'Ma pensée c'est moi: voilà pourquoi je ne peux pas m'arrêter. J'existe parce que je pense . . . et je ne peux pas m'arrêter de penser. En ce moment même—c'est affreux—si j'existe, *c'est parce que* j'ai horreur d'exister. C'est moi, *c'est moi* qui me tire du néant auquel j'aspire: la haine, le dégoût d'exister, ce sont

autant de manières de *me faire* exister, de m'enfoncer dans l'existence. Les pensées naissent par-derrière moi, comme un vertige, je les sens naître derrière ma tête . . . si je cède, elles vont venir là devant, entre mes yeux—et je cède toujours', p. 119, trans. 145, italics Sartre's.

12. 'Le Cogito affirme trop. Le contenu certain du pseudo "Cogito" n'est pas "*j'ai* conscience de cette chaise" mais "il y a conscience de cette chaise"', Sartre, *La Transcendance de l'Ego* (1936), in Sartre, *La Transcendance de l'Ego et autres textes phénoménologiques*, ed. by Vincent de Coorebyter (Paris: Vrin, 2003), p. 104, italics Sartre's.
13. Sartre, *La Transcendance de l'Ego*, p. 127.
14. 'The Ego appears to consciousness as a transcendent in-itself, as an existent in the human world, not as *of the nature* of consciousness', Jean-Paul Sartre, *L'Être et le Néant* (Paris: Gallimard, 1943), p. 140, italics Sartre's.
15. 'Et soudain le Je pâlit, pâlit, et c'en est fait, il s'éteint. Lucide, immobile, déserte, la conscience est posée entre des murs; elle se perpétue. Personne ne l'habite plus', p. 200; trans. 241.
16. 'Il y a connaissance de la conscience. Elle se voit de part en part, paisible et vide entre les murs, libérée de l'homme qui l'habitait, [. . .] le Moi jaillit dans la conscience', p. 202; trans. 242–3.
17. 'Déconstruction radicale du sujet', Jean-Marc Mouillie, *Sartre: Conscience, ego et psychè* (Paris: Presses universitaires de France, 2000), p. 117.
18. 'Les choses se sont délivrées de leurs noms. Elles sont là, grotesques, têtues, géantes et ça paraît imbécile de les appeler des banquettes ou de dire quoi que ce soit sur elles: je suis au milieu des Choses, les innommables', p. 148; trans. 180.
19. 'Je pensais l'*appartenance*, je me disais que la mer appartenait à la classe des objets verts, ou que le vert faisait partie des qualités de la mer', p. 150; trans. 182.
20. 'Les objets, cela ne devrait pas *toucher*, puisque cela ne vit pas. On s'en sert, on les remet en place, on vit au milieu d'eux: ils sont utiles, rien de plus', p. 16; trans. 22.
21. 'Un éclair rougeaud couvert de poils blancs', p. 26; trans. 34.
22. 'Dortoirs-réfectoires pour les mobilisables, pour les familles des mobilisés'; 'points stratégiques'; 'cibles', Jean-Paul Sartre, *Le Sursis* (1945), in *Œuvres Romanesques*, pp. 731–1133 (p. 1045).
23. 'L'écroulement du monde humain, des mesures, des quantités, des directions', p. 152; trans. 184.
24. The Husserlian and Cartesian conceptions of the mind are undoubtedly the most important influences on the novel, and on Sartre's ideas more generally at this stage of his career, but they are not the only ones. Rhiannon Goldthorpe points to a telling line from Nietzsche's *Birth of Tragedy* that appears to précis the plot of Sartre's novel: 'The truth once seen, man is aware everywhere of the ghastly absurdity of existence [. . .] nausea invades him. Then, in this supreme jeopardy of the will, art, that sorceress expert in healing, approaches him; only she can turn his fits of nausea into imaginations with which it is possible to live', Friedrich Nietzsche, *The Birth of Tragedy*, trans. by Francis Golffing (New York: Doubleday, 1956), pp. 51–2; quoted in Rhiannon Goldthorpe, *La Nausée* (London: HarperCollins, 1991), p. 22. The 'coteau vert' scene as Roquentin looks down over Bouville and its benighted inhabitants also suggests a Nietzschean influence, with the initiate Roquentin separated from the common man by his possession of the secret truth of existence. Bergson too was a major influence on Sartre's thinking at this time, despite the reservations Sartre held about Bergson's conception of the 'inner self'. Bergson's defence of free will, and his method of intuiting the nature of consciousness through exploration of subjective experience both make their mark on Sartre's thought. For Reidar Due, Sartre's faith in the structural and temporal unity of all an individual's conscious activities also finds its source in Bergson (Reidar Due, 'Freedom, Nothingness, Consciousness: Some Remarks on the structure of *Being and Nothingness*', in *Sartre Today: A Centenary Celebration*, ed. by Adrian van den Hoven and Andrew Leak [New York: Berghahn, 2005], pp. 31–42.) Lastly, as he writes *La Nausée*, Sartre is beginning to discover Heidegger, who will have a major impact on his thought. The novel does suggest some Heideggerian influence, albeit possibly second-hand, such as the affinity between Roquentin's ideas on existence and Heidegger's concept of *Dasein*. Heidegger is certainly part of Sartre's philosophical repertoire by the following year, where he is discussed and quoted in the *Esquisse d'une théorie des emotions*.
25. 'Il n'y a pas de *Je* sur le plan irréfléchi', *La Transcendance de l'Ego*, p. 102.
26. 'Il ne fut plus qu'une main étendue sur une chair de soie', Jean-Paul Sartre, *L'Âge de raison* (1945), in *OR*, pp. 391–729 (p. 427).
27. 'Le jugement rectifie, organise, stabilise la perception', Jean-Paul Sartre, *L'Imaginaire* (Paris: Gallimard, 1940), p. 58.
28. Rhiannon Goldthorpe, *La Nausée* (London: HarperCollins, 1991), p. 80.
29. 'Dans ces jardins où les âmes de qualité cultivent de délicats secrets, ils voyaient, eux, de puants marécages; c'est là que s'opèrent en douce tous les trafics de la mauvaise foi, c'est là que se dégustent les délices croupies du narcissisme', Simone de Beauvoir, *La Force de l'âge*, 2 vols. (Paris: Gallimard, 1960), I, pp. 29–30.

30. 'Je ne suis ni vièrge ni prêtre, pour jouer à la vie intérieure', p. 15; trans. 21; 'Je ne pense pas que le métier d'historien dispose à l'analyse psychologique. Dans notre partie, nous n'avons affaire qu'à des sentiments entiers sur lesquels on met des noms génériques comme Ambition, Intérêt', p. 8; trans. 13.
31. 'Je croyais que la haine, l'amour ou la mort descendaient sur nous, comme les langues de feu du Vendredi saint. [. . .] Oui, vraiment, je pensais que ça existait "La Haine", que ça venait se poser sur les gens et les élever au-dessus d'eux-mêmes. Naturellement, il n'y a que moi, moi qui hais, moi qui aime', p. 177; trans. 214.
32. 'Si jamais je devais faire un voyage, il me semble que je voudrais, avant de partir, noter par écrit les moindres traits de mon caractère pour pouvoir comparer, en revenant, ce que j'étais et ce que je suis devenu', p. 43; trans. 54.
33. Echoes of Proust can clearly be seen in the ending of *La Nausée*, as Roquentin turns to salvation through art, and perhaps in other incidents of significance to both narrators, such as listening to a particular tune or gazing in fascination at a tree. However, none of these references have the same meaning in *Nausea* as in *In Search of Lost Time*, and perhaps seem more parody than homage. A shared interest in the temporality of conscious experience similarly fails to establish much common ground. Unlike Proust, Sartre's principle concern is the contingency of experience, the randomness and lack of direction of which is contrasted with the imposed order and purpose of a life recounted in narrative. Beauvoir nevertheless records Sartre saying at the end of his life that he discovered Proust 'with delight', and that Proust was a major influence on his writing (Simone de Beauvoir, *La Cérémonie des adieux* (Paris: Gallimard, 1971), pp. 167, 178, 249). Recent essays on Sartre's relationship to Proust include Christie McDonald, 'Sartre Rereading Proust', *Journal of Romance Studies*, 6 (2006), 197–207, Young-Rae Ji, 'Sartre, admirateur secret de Proust', *L'Esprit créateur* 46.4 (Winter 2006), 44–55, and, in the same volume, Shawn Gorman, 'Sartre on Proust: Involuntary Memoirs', 56–68.
34. 'Husserl a réinstallé l'horreur et le charme dans les choses. Il nous a restitué le monde des artistes et des prophètes: effrayant, hostile, dangereux, avec des havres de grâce et de l'amour. Il a fait la place nette pour un nouveau traité des passions qui s'inspirerait de cette vérité si simple et si profondément méconnue par nos raffinés: si nous aimons une femme, c'est parce qu'elle est aimable. Nous voilà délivrés de Proust. Délivrés en même temps de la "vie intérieure": en vain chercherions-nous, comme Amiel, comme une enfant qui s'embrasse l'épaule, les caresses, les dorlotements de notre intimité, puisque finalement tout est dehors, tout, jusqu'à nous-mêmes: dehors, dans le monde, parmi les autres', Jean-Paul Sartre, 'Une idée fondamentale de la philosophie de Husserl: l'Intentionnalité' (1939), in *Critiques littéraires (Situations I)*, pp. 27–32 (p. 32). The article is dated in the January of that year; the Mauriac article, discussed in the second chapter of this study, in the February.
35. *L'Imaginaire*, p. 93.
36. 'L'associationniste réduit le moi à un agrégat de faits de conscience, sensations, sentiments et idées. Mais s'il ne voit dans ces divers états rien de plus que ce que leur nom exprime, s'il n'en retient que l'aspect impersonnel, il pourra les juxtaposer indéfiniment sans obtenir autre chose qu'un moi fantôme, l'ombre du moi se projetant dans l'espace', Bergson, *Essai sur les données immédiates de la conscience*, p. 124.
37. 'Car sitôt que Swann pouvait se la représenter sans horreur, qu'il revoyait de la bonté dans son sourire, et que le désir de l'enlever à tout autre n'était plus ajouté par la jalousie à son amour, cet amour redevenait surtout un goût pour les sensations qui lui donnait la personne d'Odette, pour le plaisir qu'il avait à admirer comme un spectacle ou à interroger comme un phénomène, le lever d'un de ses regards, la formation d'un de ses sourires, l'émission d'une intonation de sa voix. Et ce plaisir différent de tous les autres avait fini par créer en lui un besoin d'elle et qu'elle seule pouvait assouvir par sa présence ou ses lettres [. . .]. Ainsi, par le chimisme même de son mal, après qu'il avait fait de la jalousie avec son amour, il recommençait à fabriquer de la tendresse, de la pitié pour Odette', *RTP*, I, p. 299; trans. I, pp. 306–7. The ellipsis appears in Sartre's own quotation of Proust.
38. 'Proust cherche perpétuellement à retrouver par décomposition intellectualiste dans la succession temporelle des états psychiques des liens de causalité rationnelle entre ces états', *L'Être et le Néant*, p. 203.
39. 'À la façon d'une tasse de café avec un nuage de lait', *L'Être et le Néant*, p. 202.
40. Hazel E. Barnes, 'Sartre's Concept of the Self', in *Sartre and Psychology*, ed. by Keith Hoeller (Atlantic Highlands, NJ: Humanities Press International, 1993), pp. 41–65 (p. 44).
41. 'Proust tente de constituer ici un "chimisme" symbolique, mais les images chimiques dont il se sert sont simplement capables de masquer des motivations et des actions irrationnelles. On essaie de nous entraîner vers une interprétation mécaniste du psychique, qui, sans être plus intelligible, déformerait complètement sa nature. Et pourtant, on ne peut s'empêcher de nous montrer entre les états d'étranges relations presque interhumaines (créer, fabriquer, ajouter) qui laisseraient presque supposer que ces objets psychiques sont des agents animés', *L'Être et le Néant*, p. 204.
42. 'Proust les analysait [i.e., les passions], les rattachait à des états antérieurs et, par là, les rendait nécessaires', 'À propos de John Dos Passos', in *Critiques littéraires*, pp. 14–24 (p. 17).

43. Some of the clearest examples of the Narrator's caprice involve Albertine: in *À l'ombre des jeunes filles en fleurs* (II, 244–5; trans. II, 467–8) his affections move between Albertine and Gisèle with bewildering speed, and the closing pages of *Sodome et Gomorrhe* (III, 510–15; trans. IV, 518–22) see him switch from an intention to end his relationship with Albertine to an intention to marry her.
44. 'Une idée flottante dont je ne pouvais ni me persuader ni me défaire', p. 91; trans 112.
45. In *La Nausée*, Roquentin stabs his hand in *OR*, p. 119; in *L'Âge de raison*, Mathieu does the same at *OR*, p. 610.
46. 'Un coup de tête', p. 9; trans. 14.
47. 'J'avais toujours désiré aller au Bengale [. . .] je ne voyais aucun motif de refus'; 'une raison de plus pour accepter avec enthousiasme', p. 9; trans. 14.
48. 'Je sentis que je m'ennuyais profondément. Je ne parvenais pas à comprendre pourquoi j'étais en Indochine. Qu'est-ce que je faisais là?', p. 10; trans. 15.
49. 'Je me suis baissé, je me réjouissais déjà de toucher cette pâte tendre et fraîche qui se roulerait sous mes doigts en boulettes grises. . . . Je n'ai pas pu. Je suis resté courbé, une seconde, j'ai lu "Dictée: le Hibou blanc", puis je me suis relevé, les mains vides. Je ne suis plus libre, je ne peux plus faire ce que je veux', p. 16; trans. 22.
50. 'Pulsion anale'; 'Nous ne serons pas étonnés de voir la nausée projetée "dans les mains". Ce sont elles qui touchent ce qu'on ne doit pas toucher', Josette Pacaly, *Sartre au miroir: une lecture psychanalytique de ses écrits biographiques* (Paris: Klincksieck, 1980), p. 129.
51. The parallel with *Nausea* is emphasized by Lucien's own ontological encounter with a chestnut tree, in which he kicks the trunk, calls it a 'filthy chestnut tree' ('sale marronnier'), and announces to his mother his discovery that trees are made of wood. 'L'Enfance d'un chef', in *Le Mur*, *OR*, pp. 211–388 (p. 321).
52. 'Parbleu, pensa-t-il, j'ai un complexe', 'L'Enfance d'un chef', *OR*, p. 339.
53. 'C'est la pente fatale, songeait-il, j'ai commencé par le complexe d'Œdipe, après ça je suis devenu sadico-anal et maintenant c'est le bouquet, je suis pédéraste', 'L'Enfance d'un chef', *OR*, p. 356.
54. 'Berliac le regarda avec profondeur et lui dit: "Je m'en doutais: tu es un anal" et il lui expliqua le rapport freudien: fèces = or et la théorie freudienne de l'avarice', 'L'Enfance d'un chef', *OR*, p. 342.
55. 'J'ai désiré ma mère jusqu'à l'âge de quinze ans'; 'très séduit par le tour scientifique qu'avaient pris leurs confidences', 'L'Enfance d'un chef', *OR*, pp. 338–9.
56. 'Nous avons des complexes maison!'; 'impression étrange de ne pas exister, ce vide qu'il avait eu longtemps dans sa conscience'; 'fariboles'; 'c'était un cauchemar, pensa-t-il, mais il n'en reste plus rien!', 'L'Enfance d'un chef', *OR*, pp. 339, 359.
57. This ideology is particularly embodied in Maurice Barrès (who also makes a memorable appearance in *La Nausée* when Roquentin dreams of spanking him). Lucien reads Barrès's *Les Déracinés* and contrasts its view of the mind with that of Freud: 'The Œdipus complex, Mental Disarray, what childishness . . . he was seduced from the very first pages: to begin with, this was not psychology—Lucien had had more than enough of psychology already—the young people Barrès was talking about were not abstract individuals, deadbeats like Rimbaud or Verlaine, nor were they invalids like all those idle Viennese who had themselves psychoanalyzed by Freud. . . . But how he preferred the unconscious filled with rustic smells offered to him by Barrès to Freud's squalid and lewd beasts. To grasp it, Lucien had only to turn away from sterile and dangerous contemplation of himself', 'L'Enfance d'un chef', *OR*, p. 372.
58. 'Mirrors fascinate him. If he catches himself in one he will be the object for himself that he is to everyone else', *L'Idiot de la famille*, I, p. 678. Sartre's relationship with Lacanian psychoanalysis, and the discipline more generally, is discussed in detail in Christina Howells, *Sartre: The Necessity of Freedom* (Cambridge: Cambridge University Press, 1988), pp. 145–64.
59. 'Pour revenir à Freud, je dirai que j'étais incapable de le comprendre parce que j'étais un Français nourri de tradition cartésienne, imbu de rationalisme, que l'idée d'inconscient choquait profondément. Mais je ne dirais pas *seulement* cela. Aujourd'hui encore, en effet, je reste choqué par une chose qui était inévitable chez Freud: son recours au langage physiologique et biologique pour exprimer des idées qui n'etaient pas transmissibles sans cette médiation. Le résultat, c'est que la façon dont il décrit l'objet analytique souffre d'une sorte de crampe mécaniste', 'Sartre par Sartre', interview in *Le Nouvel Observateur*, 26 January 1970, reprinted in *Situations IX* (Paris: Gallimard, 1972), p. 105.
60. Geneviève Idt points out the shared initials, although any libellous undertones are mitigated by the fact that, within 'L'Enfance d'un chef', Bergère mentions Breton by name as an exemplary individual (*OR*, p. 347). Sartre himself denied that Bergère was based on a real individual (in conversation with the editors, *OR*, p. 341n.). Geneviève Idt, Le Mur *de Jean-Paul Sartre: techniques et contexte d'une provocation* (Paris: Larousse, 1972), p. 180.
61. Jean-Paul Sartre, *Qu'est-ce que la littérature?* (Paris: Gallimard, 1948), p. 323. Michel Beaujour speculates that Sartre's traumatic brush with hallucinatory psychoses while experimenting with mescaline

may have contributed to his aversion to Surrealism. An exception is nevertheless made for Aimé Césaire, whose politically committed Surrealism earns Sartre's praise. Michel Beaujour, 'Sartre and Surrealism', *Yale French Studies*, 30 (1963), pp. 86–95.

62. *La Transcendance de l'Ego*, p. 122.
63. The importance of Sartre's third mode of being, *l'être-pour-autrui*, in our sense of self is also suggested in *La Nausée*. The episode we saw earlier in which Roquentin's ego is temporarily snuffed out is triggered when, after final encounters with Anny and the Autodidacte, he realizes that he lost his last meaningful acquaintances and has fallen into 'utter oblivion' ('oubli total', p. 200). Earlier, Roquentin sardonically notes of the single men in the café Mably: 'They too need to group together in order to exist' ('Eux aussi, pour exister, il faut qu'ils se mettent à plusieurs', p. 11). *La Nausée*, concerned as it is with 'l'homme seul', does not yet evoke the complex interactions of freedoms and subjectivities theorized in *L'Être et le Néant*. The essay's pessimistic view of human interactions characterized by conflict and power imbalances is to be found in much of his subsequent writing, however, perhaps most evidently in the play *Huis clos*.
64. 'La psychanalyse empirique part, en effet, du postulat de l'existence d'un psychisme inconscient qui se dérobe par principe à l'intuition du sujet. La psychanalyse existentielle rejette le postulat de l'inconscient: le fait psychique est, pour elle, coextensif à la conscience. Mais si le projet fondamental est pleinement *vécu* par le sujet et, comme tel, totalement conscient, cela ne signifie nullement qu'il doive être du même coup *connu* par lui, tout au contraire', *L'Être et le Néant*, p. 616, italics Sartre's.
65. '[La réflexion] est pénétrée d'une grande lumière sans pouvoir exprimer ce que cette lumière éclaire. Il ne s'agit point d'une énigme indevinée, comme le croient les freudiens: tout est là, lumineux, la réflexion jouit de tout, saisit tout. Mais ce "mystère en pleine lumière" vient plutôt de ce que cette jouissance est privée des moyens qui permettent ordinairement l'*analyse* et la *conceptualisation*', *L'Être et le Néant*, p. 616, italics Sartre's. The phrase 'mystère en pleine lumière' is taken from Barrès.
66. *L'Être et le Néant*, p. 619.
67. 'Je dois reconnaître que je suis sujet à ces transformations soudaines. Ce qu'il y a, c'est que je pense très rarement; alors une foule de petites métamorphoses s'accumulent en moi sans que j'y prenne garde et puis, un beau jour, il se produit une véritable révolution', p. 9; trans. 14.
68. *OR*, p. 704.
69. Howells, *Sartre: The Necessity of Freedom*, p. 54.
70. 'Je voudrais voir clair en moi avant qu'il ne soit trop tard', p. 10; trans. 15.
71. 'J'ai peur d'entrer en contact avec [les objets] tout comme s'ils étaient des bêtes vivantes', p. 16; trans. 22.
72. Pacaly's Freudian reading argues that Roquentin's reaction to the pebble, with its disturbingly 'damp and muddy' underside, could be equally psycho-sexual in nature. To sustain this interpretation, however, Roquentin would need to be mistaken in his later epiphany about the cause of his nausea in unmediated exposure to the true nature of existence.
73. 'Il faut, en outre, préciser contre le sens commun que la formule "être libre" ne signifie pas "obtenir ce qu'on a voulu", mais "se déterminer à vouloir" (au sens large de choisir) par soi-même. Autrement dit, le succès n'importe aucunement à la liberté. [. . .] Ainsi ne dirons-nous pas qu'un captif est toujours libre de sortir de prison, ce qui serait absurde, ni non plus qu'il est toujours libre de souhaiter l'élargissement, ce qui serait une lapalissade sans portée, mais qu'il est toujours libre de chercher à s'évader (ou à se faire libérer)—c'est-à-dire que quelle que soit sa condition, il peut projeter son évasion et s'apprendre à lui-même la valeur de son projet par un début d'action', *L'Être et le Néant*, pp. 528–9.
74. Roquentin's own unbelief is mostly only implicit in the novel, detectable in the chaotic vision of existence revealed in his nausea, which leaves no room for divine purpose or providence, and perhaps in his indictment of a smug bourgeoisie, who are unjustified in seeing their place in the world as being necessary and in order. A more direct reference comes as Roquentin contrasts other people's view of the beauty of the surface of the sea 'which speaks of God' ('qui prouve l'existence de Dieu') with his own view of 'the *real* sea' ('la *vraie* mer'), which is 'cold and black and full of creatures' ('froide et noire, pleine de bêtes', p. 147; trans. 178–9). The novel also takes a swipe at religiously inspired literature through Roquentin's savage caricature of the Catholic humanist' who writes 'for the edification of the angels, long, sad, beautiful novels which frequently win the [all-women juried] prix Femina' ('pour l'édification des anges, de longs romans tristes et beaux, qui obtiennent fréquemment le prix Femina', p. 138; trans. 168). Georges Bernanos, while not a perfect fit for Roquentin's characterization, did win the prix Femina in 1929 for *La Joie*.
75. Serge Doubrovsky, '*La Nausée*: Fragment of an Analytic Reading', in *Sartre*, ed. by Christina Howells (London: Longman, 1995), pp. 49–57; François George, *Deux Études sur Sartre* (Paris: Bourgois, 1976); Andrew Leak, 'Nausea and Desire in Sartre's *La Nausée*', *French Studies*, 43 (1989), 61–72.
76. George, *Deux Études sur Sartre*, pp. 373–406
77. Max Charlesworth, 'Sartre, Laing and Freud', in *Sartre and Psychology*, ed. by Keith Hoeller (Atlantic Highlands, NJ: Humanities Press International, 1993), pp. 23–39 (p. 28). Sartre also suggests that his

biography of Flaubert, *L'Idiot de la famille*, might be seen as a work of anti-psychiatry. 'Sur *L'Idiot de la famille*', in *Situations X*, pp. 91–115 (p. 100).

78. Sartre's forward to R. D. Laing's and David Cooper's *Reason and Violence: A Decade of Sartre's Philosophy 1950–1960* (New York: Random House, 1964), p. 7. The existentialist psychology of Ludwig Binswanger and others, in which psychological problems are considered to result from the confrontation of the self with the fundamentals of existence, such as contingency, freedom, mortality, and the Other, also demonstrates the influence of existentialism (although not exclusively Sartre's in this case) in the applied study and treatment of mental life.
79. 'Maintenant je vois; je me rappelle mieux ce que j'ai senti, l'autre jour, au bord de la mer, quand je tenais ce galet [. . .]: une sorte de nausée dans les mains', p. 16; trans. 22.
80. 'Ce petit mouvement qui fait d'un être social totalement conditionné une personne qui ne restitue pas la totalité de ce qu'elle a reçu de son conditionnement', 'Sartre par Sartre', in *Situations IX*, pp. 99–134 (pp. 101–2).
81. Martin E. Morf, 'Sartre, Skinner and the Compatibilist Freedom to Be Authentically', *Behavior and Philosophy*, 26.1/2 (Spring/Fall, 1998), pp. 29–43.
82. 'Si les animaux sont des machines, pourquoi l'homme que je vois passer dans la rue n'en serait-il pas une? Pourquoi l'hypothèse radicale des béhaviouristes ne serait-elle pas la bonne? Ce que je saisis sur ce visage n'est rien que l'effet de certaines contractions musculaires et celles-ci à leur tour ne sont que l'effet d'un influx nerveux dont je connais le parcours. Pourquoi ne pas réduire l'ensemble de ces réactions à des réflexes simples ou conditionnés? Mais la plus grande partie des psychologues demeurent convaincus de l'existence d'autrui comme réalité totalitaire de même structure que la leur propre', *L'Être et le Néant*, p. 262.
83. 'On est des bêtes, on met des mots sur un instinct', *Le Sursis, OR*, p. 1050.
84. 'Bêtes qui pensent', *La Mort dans l'âme, OR*, p. 1152.
85. 'Une hérédité terriblement chargée'; 'cette tare', 'La Chambre', in *Le Mur, OR*, p. 241.
86. While the story does not linger on the physiological basis of Pierre's condition, it nevertheless presents a portrait of mental illness which is difficult to reconcile with the 'anti-psychiatric' position of such illness as a mental response to an intolerable situation proposed by Sartre in his preface to Laing's and Cooper's book. Philippe Cabestan's 'lecture psycho-phénoménologique' of the story suggests it reveals an inconsistency in Sartre's theory of madness, in that the 'captive consciousness' of dreams, hallucinations, and involuntary or unshakeable emotions is not entirely compatible with the absolute freedom of the existential mind. Philippe Cabestan, 'Rêve, obsession, hallucination: qu'est-ce qu'une conscience captive?', in *Sartre et la phénoménologie*, ed. by Jean-Marc Mouillie (Fontenay-aux-roses: Éditions ENS, 2000), pp. 21–76. Cabestan explores the issue more broadly in *L'Être et la conscience: recherches sur la psychologie et l'ontophénoménologie sartriennes* (Brussels: Ousia, 2004).
87. 'Je regardai avec effroi ces êtres instables qui, dans une heure, dans une minute allaient peut-être crouler: eh bien oui; j'étais là, je vivais au milieu de ces livres tout pleins de connaissances, dont les uns décrivaient les formes immuables des espèces animales, dont les autres expliquaient que la quantité d'énergie se conserve intégralement dans l'univers; j'étais là, debout devant une fenêtre dont les carreaux avaient une indice de réfraction déterminé. Mais quelles faibles barrières!', p. 93; trans. 113–14, translation modified.
88. 'Vous m'accusez de *matérialisme* et c'est précisément la doctrine qui répugne le plus ma raison. [. . .] Comme vous citez par ailleurs dans *La Revue universelle* une de mes phrases: "Seules les choses sont, la conscience n'est pas, elle se fait", j'imagine que c'est précisément cette phrase qui vous a trompé. Peut-être en effet n'est-elle pas claire. Vous l'avez comprise, je suppose, comme si j'affirmais que seules les choses matérielles ont de la réalité et que la conscience se fabrique à partir d'elles. Or c'est juste le contraire que j'entendais. Je voulais dire: seules les choses ont cette existence passive et inerte qu'on appelle ordinairement *l'être*. L'existence de la conscience est d'une autre sorte: c'est celle d'une spontanéité absolue et libre qui se détermine elle-même à exister. Pourrez-vous encore me traiter de matérialiste après cette profession de foi?', Undated letter to André Rousseau, discovered among Sartre's papers (and thus possibly unsent), *OR*, 'Dossier de presse' for *Le Mur*, pp. 1810–17 (p. 1813).
89. Hazel E. Barnes, 'Sartre's Ontology', in *The Cambridge Companion to Sartre*, ed. by Christina Howells (Cambridge: Cambridge University Press, 1992), pp. 13–38 (p. 17). Howells herself notes elsewhere that Sartre's definition of consciousness as a *néant* may also help to side-step the choice between materialism and dualism: the 'nothingness' of consciousness has no material substance, yet does not require us to posit the existence of immaterial substances. Howells, *Sartre: The Necessity of Freedom*, p. 15.
90. Matthew C. Eshleman, 'What Is It Like to Be Free?', in *Reading Sartre: On Phenomenology and Existentialism*, ed. by Jonathan Webber (London: Routledge, 2011), pp. 31–47 (p. 33).
91. Sartre, *Critique de la raison dialectique, précedé de Question de méthode*, I: *théorie des ensembles pratiques* (Paris: Gallimard, 1960), p. 248.

92. 'Le regard de Pablo n'était pas encore humain et pourtant c'était déjà plus que de la vie: il n'y avait pas longtemps que le môme était sorti d'un ventre et ça se voyait: il était là, indécis, tout petit, il gardait encore un velouté malsain de chose vomie; mais derrière les humeurs troubles qui remplissaient ses orbites, une petite conscience goulue s'était embusquée', *L'Âge de raison*, *OR*, p. 437.
93. 'There are other kinds of consciousness than human ones, there is animal consciousness, or insect consciousness'; ('Il y a d'autres consciences que les consciences humaines, il y a des consciences des animaux, des insectes, par exemple'), Beauvoir, *La Cérémonie des Adieux*, p. 555. *L'Idiot de la famille* also considers domestic animals' awareness of human being-for-itself, without being able to transcend their natures towards human existence. Sartre, *L'Idiot de la famille*, 3 vols. (Paris: Gallimard, 1971), I, pp. 145–46.
94. Hazel Barnes, 'Sartre as Materialist', in *The Philosophy of Jean-Paul Sartre*, ed. by Paul Arthur Schilpp (La Salle: Open Court, 1981), p. 40.
95. 'Je vois venir vers moi une bête féroce, mes jambes se dérobent sous moi, mon cœur bat plus faiblement, je pâlis, je tombe et je m'évanouis. Rien ne semble moins adapté que cette conduite qui me livre sans défense au danger. Et pourtant c'est une conduite d'évasion [. . .]. Ainsi le véritable sens de la peur nous apparaît: c'est une conscience qui vise à nier, à travers une conduite magique, un objet du monde extérieur et qui ira jusqu'à s'anéantir, pour anéantir l'objet avec elle', Jean-Paul Sartre, *Esquisse d'une théorie des émotions* (1939) (Paris: Hermann, 1965), p. 43.
96. 'Comme nous ne pouvons et ne voulons pas accomplir les actes que nous projetons, nous faisons en sorte que l'univers n'exige plus rien de nous', *Esquisse d'une théorie des émotions*, p. 47.
97. 'Instinctivement fait-on le mort mains sur la nuque sous l'attaque de l'ours', Darrieussecq, *Bref séjour chez les vivants*, p. 223.
98. Ontogeny is the process of fœtal development, phylogeny of evolutionary development.
99. This is not to claim that *irrational* responses pre-date rational ones. The hungry infant's wail and the desperate flight of the prey from the predator are both emotional responses, and both entirely rational ones in the circumstances, although not, of course, consciously reasoned. Sartre's claim, however, is that emotional responses are an irrational fall-back which comes into being for use in circumstances where a reasoned response is in some way inadequate.
100. Hazel E. Barnes, 'Consciousness and Digestion: Sartre and Neuroscience', in *Sartre Today: A Centenary Celebration*, ed. by Adrian van den Hoven and Andrew Leak (Oxford: Berghahn, 2005), pp. 117–32. Barnes's discussion focuses on two works by Edelman, *Bright Air, Brilliant Fire: On the Matter of the Mind* (London: Penguin, 1994) and *Wider than the Sky: A Revolutionary View of Consciousness* (London: Penguin, 2004).
101. See Mouillie, *Sartre: Conscience, ego et psychè*; Kenneth Williford, 'Pre-Reflective Self-Consciousness and the Autobiographical Ego', in *Reading Sartre*, ed. by Jonathan Webber, pp. 195–210; Dan Zahavi, *Subjectivity and Selfhood: Investigating the First-Person Perspective* (Cambridge, MA: The MIT Press, 2005); Gallagher and Zahavi, *The Phenomenological Mind*.
102. 'Dialogue des sourds'; 'Qu'un certain équipement physiologique soit nécessaire pour penser *comme* nous le faisons n'autorise pas à dire que c'est cet équipement qui pense *ce que* nous pensons', Mouillie, *Sartre: Conscience, ego et psyche*, pp. 120–1, italics Mouillie's.
103. Antonio Damasio, *Self Comes to Mind: Constructing the Conscious Brain* (London: Heinemann, 2010), p. 165.
104. Damasio, *The Feeling of What Happens*, pp. 196, 221.
105. The relationship between Sartre's and Damasio's theories is further discussed in Kenneth Williford, 'Pre-Reflective Self-Consciousness and the Autobiographical Ego', in *Reading Sartre*, pp. 195–210.
106. 'J'existe. [. . .] Il y a de l'eau mousseuse dans ma bouche. Je l'avale, elle glisse dans ma gorge, elle me caresse—et la voilà qui renaît dans ma bouche. J'ai dans la bouche à perpétuité une petite mare d'eau blanchâtre—discrète—qui frôle ma langue. Et cette mare c'est encore moi. Et la langue. Et la gorge, c'est moi', p. 117; trans. 143.
107. 'N'avoir ni sang, ni lymphe, ni chair. N'être que du froid', p. 34; trans. 44.
108. The 'hard problem' of consciousness was formulated by David Chalmers in the article, 'Facing up to the Problem of Consciousness', *Journal of Consciousness Studies*, 2 (1995), 200–19.
109. Lodge, *Consciousness and the Novel*, p. 30.

5

SENTIENCE

Samuel Beckett

One of Beckett's earliest works is his essay on Marcel Proust, written in 1931. The study highlights many of the shared preoccupations of Beckett and Proust, as well as distorting several of Proust's preoccupations, the better to align them with Beckett's. Beckett explores how Proust's Narrator turns away from friendship in order to devote his time to introspection that will give him the insights into the self that he seeks for his art. He comments approvingly:

> The only fertile research is excavatory, immersive, a contraction of the spirit, a descent. The artist is active, but negatively, shrinking from the nullity of extracircumferential phenomena, drawn in to the core of the eddy.[1]

Years later this image of the inward swirl will recur in the first and most sustained of the inset narratives of Beckett's *The Unnamable* (1953), the novel which follows *Molloy* and *Malone Dies* (both published in 1951) to complete his post-war trilogy. The episode concerns Mahood, whose mysterious relationship to the eponymous narrator we shall consider shortly, and his return home from his travels to his family. He finds himself in a vast yard surrounded by high walls, the ground covered in ashes. At the centre of the yard is a small windowless rotunda, from which his family watch his approach through gaps in the woodwork. Mahood moves slowly with the help of crutches, having lost a leg in the course of his travels, and ostensibly for this same reason, is unable to proceed in a straight line:

> I had already advanced a good ten paces, if one may call them paces, not in a straight line I need hardly say, but in a sharp curve which, if I continued to follow it, seemed likely to restore me to my point of departure, or to one adjacent. I must have got embroiled in a kind of inverted spiral, I mean one the coils of which, instead of widening more and more, grew narrower and narrower and finally, given the kind of space in which I was supposed to evolve, would come to an end for lack of room.[2]

His motivation for struggling onwards is not love. Indeed, he refers to his waiting relatives exclusively in crude and hateful terms. Rather, he is obeying some obscure compulsion to continue towards his goal:

> Though now close at hand, as the crow flies, to my goal, I did not quicken my step. I could have no doubt, but I had to husband my strength, if I was ever to arrive. I had no wish to

> arrive, but I had to do my utmost, in order to arrive. A desirable goal, no, I never had the time to dwell on that. To go on, I still call that on, to go on and get on has been my only care, if not always in a straight line, at least in obedience to the figure assigned to me. There was never any room in my life for anything else.[3]

The spiral, which the English version also refers to as an 'orbit', as well as, more bluntly, 'screw[ing] myself to a standstill', proves too roundabout a method for a successful reunion, as the waiting family dies of food-poisoning before Mahood can arrive.[4] Opinions differ as to the conclusion of the episode, with Mahood claiming to have turned back on the family's death, but the Unnamable itself preferring to believe that the journey to the rotunda was completed: 'There completed my rounds, stamping underfoot the unrecognizable remains of my family [. . .] I like to fancy, even if it is not true, that it was in my mother's entrails I spent the last days of my long voyage'.[5]

Mahood's spirals are echoed in other parts of the trilogy. Molloy, in the first volume, also travels in spirals, due to his own afflicted leg, as he struggles onwards towards his own mother in the sway of a similar imperative.[6] The setting of *The Unnamable* itself, at least initially, is one of orbital motion, with Malone and other characters from the trilogy and Beckett's previous works appearing to circle around the Unnamable at the centre of their gyre. The inward-turning spiral, getting ever smaller as it approaches a zero-point, is emblematic of Beckett's work more broadly. Like the spiral, his narratives come back around to repeat themselves with variations, people, and language decline and degrade, content is gradually pared away, until incident, character, and setting are all left behind, and we head deep into the self. Northrop Frye compares Beckett's fiction to peeling an onion, penetrating layer by layer as we proceed through his novels, until:

> In *The Unnamable* we come as near to the core of the onion as it is possible to come and discover of course that there is no core, no undividable unit of continuous personality.[7]

Vivian Mercier describes the trilogy as resembling an asymptotic curve (a figure that also receives a mention, if a passing one, within the novels themselves), its content decreasing as it heads ever closer to silence and nothingness without ever quite reaching the destination.[8] The mote dancing in the dark, the membrane thin as foil, the creature made of silence: these are the infinitesimal objects and barely existent beings to which we are drawn within the eddy of Beckett's stories.

In this chapter we will be taking the spiral path into Beckett's representation of consciousness and the self, principally through the trilogy, but also looking at the works that precede and follow it in his œuvre. We will examine the nature of the mind that we encounter on the journey, exploring the literary, philosophical and other influences that shape it. Unlike most writers considered here, however, Beckett is less concerned to produce a portrait of the mind as to take us on through it, heading for what lies at the heart of the spiral. As we approach this singularity, I shall be arguing, it is not consciousness but sentience that is Beckett's ultimate concern.

*

Beckett wrote the three novels of his trilogy between 1946 and 1951, a period of intense creativity in the early post-war years that also saw the writing of *En attendant Godot*, *Mercier and Camier*, and several shorter texts. Previous to this point in his life, Beckett has published literary criticism on Dante, Joyce, and Proust, all three of whom would remain major influences on his own writing. He had also published several works in English: the poem, *Whoroscope* (1930), the stories of *More Pricks than Kicks* (1934), and the novel, *Murphy* (1938), with a second English-language novel, *Watt*, written during the war years but not to be published until after the trilogy in 1953. Besides literature, Beckett's understanding of the mind was also shaped by psychoanalysis. In his twenties,

Beckett underwent nearly two years of psychoanalysis with Wilfred Bion, coming away with a thorough knowledge of the major concepts of the discipline. We have perhaps already seen one example of its use in his writing in the image of Mahood's journey home ending in the 'bas-ventre' of his mother, the original French term connoting both womb and genitals. More important than psychoanalysis, though, in forming Beckett's view of mind and self, is the long tradition of Western philosophical thought on the topic, from the pre-Socratics, through Classical and early Christian philosophy, Cartesian thought, the Enlightenment, the nineteenth-century phenomenologists, and their twentieth-century successors. Philosophers who are quoted or referred to in Beckett's fiction begin with Democritus and Plato among the ancients, followed by St Augustine as the inaugural thinker in a long line of theological speculation. Early-modern philosophers figure with particular prominence in Beckett's work, including Leibniz and Berkeley, but most especially Descartes, who appears in person in *Whoroscope* and haunts all of Beckett's subsequent work, along with his disciple, Geulincx. Kant is also present, as is Schopenhauer, and the German phenomenological lineage through Hegel and Heidegger. The period in which the trilogy was written is, of course, the time in which existentialism was rising to dominate French cultural life. Beckett was acquainted with Sartre from the period when both men were at the École Normale Supérieure in the late 1920s, and several critics have been tempted to read Beckett's work as infused with existentialist theory.[9] Beckett is also an influence on the philosophers who followed him: Gilles Deleuze, Theodor Adorno and Alain Badiou are among those to have written essays on him. Yet when asked about philosophy, Beckett is quick to dissociate himself: 'When Heidegger and Sartre speak of a contrast between being and existence, they may be right, I don't know, but their language is too philosophical for me. I am not a philosopher'.[10] And despite the immense number of philosophical references, explicit and veiled, in his works, it is not possible to read his texts as illustrating philosophical concepts, much less adopting a philosophical system. Rather, we have in Beckett a profusion of philosophical fragments, shored by his narrators against the ruins of their understanding, and more often than not mockingly dismissed as soon as spoken.

More than with any other writer here, the question presents itself with Beckett of whether it's possible to know the nature of the minds he represents at all. In the trilogy and much of his later work, Beckett's narrations are first person, allowing no firmer authority on the validity of the representation of the mind than the subjective impressions of its owner. In the trilogy, the owners of these minds do little to inspire the reader's confidence in their assertions. Moran, the agent sent by the mysterious Youdi to find Molloy in the second part of the first novel, disconcerts us with a mention that he has lied about certain details of his 'report' that we are reading, before pulling the rug in the final lines of the novel with the implication that everything we have been reading has been mendacious from the start: 'Then I went back into the house and wrote, It is midnight. The rain is beating on the windows. [The opening words of the 'report'.] It was not midnight. It was not raining'.[11] The Unnamable in the final volume implies that its monologue may not only be deceitful but also nonsensical: it refers to its narration as 'perjury' and admits at one point, 'it is not that their meaning [of the figures he perceives moving through the darkness] escapes me, my own escapes me just as much'.[12] Where they are not making deceitful or meaningless utterances, the narrators tell us their perceptions are unclear. Molloy admits: 'When I wake I see the first things quite clearly [. . .]. Then in my eyes and in my head a fine rain begins to fall'.[13] They tell us they are unsure whether what they perceive is there at all. The Unnamable sees lights of varying intensity, but admits, 'they are perhaps unwavering and fixed and my fitful perceiving the cause of their inconstancy'.[14] And they tell us that when they do perceive something, they often don't comprehend it. Moran watches his bees dance, and declares, 'with rapture, here is something I can study all my life, and never understand'.[15] And this is only the beginning of it. Whenever the narrators do bring themselves to assert a truth about themselves or their situation, it may be only to deny it, cast doubt or otherwise undermine it later in the text. The trilogy begins, for instance, with Molloy's remembered account of watching two men on a road from the vantage point of a rock. One of the men, we are told, is wearing sand-shoes, smoking a cigar, and carrying a Pomeranian. This precise image once established, Molloy proceeds to cast doubt: 'But was not perhaps in reality the cigar a cutty, and were not the sand-shoes boots, hobnailed and dust-whitened, and what prevented the dog from being one of those stray dogs that you pick up and take in your arms?'[16] And once doubt has arrived, it corrodes Molloy's recollections comprehensively, until the episode is reduced to a series of disparate fragments: 'And perhaps it was A one day at one place, then C another at another, then a third the rock and I, and so on for the other components, the cows, the sky, the sea, the mountains'.[17] Malone's account in the second novel is prey to similar uncertainty, leading him to confess that 'my notes have a curious tendency [. . .] to annihilate all they purport to record'.[18] Even the Unnamable's spiral story is undermined in this way. The narrator breaks off the account of Mahood's journey home with a curt 'enough of this nonsense. I was never anywhere but here'. Later, it denies even that the spiral is an apt metaphor for its journey through life—'my course is not helicoidal, I got that wrong too, but a succession of irregular loops'—before reaffirming a few pages on that the central idea of the inward spiral does indeed underlie its sense of its own existence: 'I have dwindled, I dwindle'.[19] The pattern of assertion followed by doubt or denial pervades the trilogy, as well as *Comment c'est* (*How It Is*, 1961) and most of the later texts. We are left almost nothing of the narrators' worlds, inner or outer, that we can grasp with any certainty.

The uncertainty about what we are told is compounded by uncertainty over who is doing the telling. Ostensibly in the trilogy we have four different narrators, Molloy and Moran in *Molloy*, Malone in *Malone Dies* and the Unnamable in *The Unnamable*. Added to these are the inset characters of the narrators' tales: the character variously named Saposcat, Sapo, and MacMann in *Malone Dies*, and Mahood (originally named Basil) and Worm in *The Unnamable*. Almost immediately, however, these identities begin to blur, as uncanny similarities arise between the principal narrators. At the start of his narrative, Molloy is shambolic, decrepit, destitute, and aimless, dawdling and drifting in his 'quest' to reach his mother's house, which may equally well be found in the town he leaves behind him at the start of it. Moran, at the start of his, is in many ways his antithesis: brutally efficient in his need for order and obedience, self-satisfied and incurious in outlook, living with his housekeeper and son in bourgeois comfort on the wages of his missions, the latest of which is to track down Molloy. As the mission progresses, Moran takes on ever more of Molloy's attributes. His physical health declines, his leg stiffens, he acquires first a bicycle, later crutches, and sports a hat with a strap. Like Molloy, he meets and apparently beats to death a stranger in an act without cause or consequence. By the end of their tales, both men are ruined and alone in the former family home, their quests having petered out into stasis from which they required rescue, occupied with writing an account of their journey on the orders of a mysterious outside party. Malone's situation closely resembles this end point of Molloy and Moran: bed-ridden in a house, writing his account, employing a stick as Molloy used his crutch, and obsessed as Molloy was with drawing up an inventory of his goods and possessions as a final act. Malone even repeats some of the opening lines of Molloy's monologue: 'I do not remember how I got here. In an ambulance perhaps, a vehicle of some kind certainly'.[20] While names remain a distinguishing factor, Malone tacks a parenthesis to his own, '(since that is what I am called now)', that shakes its authority as a marker of identity.[21] The Unnamable has no such marker of course, nor any stable setting or physical attributes, but has links to its predecessors nevertheless: the crutches and progressive bodily deterioration reappear when it speaks as Mahood, and it claims at one point to have been born in Bally, Molloy's hometown.[22]

While some elements of the characters suggest they are different people, and others that they are the same, others still suggest a Russian-doll hierarchy of existence among them. Long before

Moran has come to resemble Molloy, his thoughts on his quarry are suggestive of a more primal inner self—perhaps a Freudian id—escaping the bonds of Moran's rigid self-control. He says of his 'inner Molloy': 'He panted. He had only to rise up within me for me to be filled with panting'.[23] Curiously, Moran lists Murphy, Watt, and Mercier, protagonists of previous Beckett novels, as the targets of his earlier missions, and wonders if the object of his current one might be his own creation: 'Perhaps I had invented him, I mean found him ready made in my head'.[24] In the next novel, when Malone offers a similar list, now including Molloy and Moran, he associates them with the stories he tells, as if they were invented characters. He also includes his own name in the list, and associates himself with the protagonists of his stories. 'I wonder if I am not talking yet again about myself?', he says as he narrates the tale of Saposcat, and later seems to be talking partly of real people and partly of his fictional creations when he remarks: 'I watched them come and go, then I killed them, or took their place, or fled'.[25] (He also, it must be noted, claims at an early point that 'nothing is less like me' than Saposcat, but the similarities grow as the tale progresses, as with Molloy and Moran.)[26] It is with the Unnamable, however, that the absorption of identities is most pronounced. At the start of the text, the narrator sees Malone, or perhaps Molloy wearing Malone's hat, orbiting about it, as well as two figures who may be Mercier and Camier, and expresses the belief that, 'they are all here, at least from Murphy on, I believe we are all here'.[27] (The possibility is hereby raised that the head we are in is that of the author of these characters, and that Beckett joins Breton and Sarraute in making the mind under investigation his own.) The new named character, Basil/Mahood, also appears initially as an external figure who visits and speaks to the narrator. From the start, however, we are warned by contradictory statements not to take the existence of these others at face value: 'I shall not be alone, in the beginning. I am of course alone'.[28] Within pages, the narrator is suggesting that not only Basil, but the narrators of the previous novels too, are figments of its imagination:

> All these Murphys, Molloys and Malones do not fool me. They have made me waste my time, suffer for nothing, speak of them when, in order to stop speaking, I should have spoken of me and of me alone. [. . .] Let them be gone now, them and all the others, those I have used and those I have not used, give me back the pains I lent them and vanish, from my life, my memory, my terrors and shames. There, now there is no one here but me, no one wheels about me [. . .]. And Basil and his gang? Inexistent, invented to explain I forget what.[29]

The Unnamable goes on to refer to the others as its delegates, mannequins, or vice-existers, using both first and third person to merge and differentiate itself from them. It considers the possibility that it has lived the life of Mahood—the spiral walk, and a later phase as a limbless body in a jar: 'what if we were one and the same after all [. . .]. And I have been in the places where he says I have been?'[30] This opens the alternate possibility that the Unnamable isn't a storyteller who has invented Molloy and company, but a being who has existed 'in the land of the living' within their linked consciousnesses. It does, after all, have knowledge of the world, including the existence of Pulitzer Prizes and Toussaint Louverture. If it prefers to conclude that it was 'never anywhere but here', then the matter is scarcely settled, since 'here' does not seem to have any characteristics that would suggest a physical space. Near the end of the novel, and four hundred pages into the trilogy, the Unnamable remarks that 'it has not yet been our good fortune to establish with any degree of accuracy what I am'.[31]

There are two conclusions to be drawn from all of these contradictions and uncertainties. The first, and more obvious, is that they present an obstacle, perhaps an insuperable obstacle, to any attempt to extract from Beckett's texts an understanding of the nature of mind in his fiction. Almost everything that is proposed in the texts about the narrators' conscious or unconscious minds, their perceptions, memories, and mental life, is undermined or denied elsewhere, and the narrators themselves can't even be said with any confidence to be individual human beings with a mind of their own. The second conclusion, if I may be permitted a contradiction of my own, is that these uncertainties do not present an obstacle to our understanding of mind in Beckett's fiction. This is because they are an inherent, not to say essential, part of it. Beckett is not offering an objective, third-person study of consciousness, mind, and self. He is presenting us with a first-person exploration of a self thinking about its own existence, examining its conscious experience and spinning hypotheses about what lies behind that experience, and what brings it into being. If the possibilities raised are left hanging, sometimes in conflict with each other, and if some lines of thought lead only to aporia and bafflement, then this is a necessary reflection of the human condition, and to do otherwise would be fraudulent.

Bearing in mind, then, that contradiction and uncertainty may be what we are seeking, rather than what we are seeking to overcome, let us see what shared characteristics we can discover in the minds represented in Beckett's trilogy and beyond. We can begin by despatching rapidly a couple of areas in which he has relatively little interest. One of these is gender. While Beckett did explore female subjectivity in several of his dramas, including *Oh les beaux jours (Happy Days,* 1961) and *Pas moi* (*Not I,* 1972), it is less in evidence in his prose fiction. The narrators' attitudes to women vary from indifference—Malone dismisses MacMann's love interest with the words 'our concern here is not with Moll, who after all is only a female'—to violent misogyny: the Unnamable refers to Mahood's waiting wife and mother in the middle of the spiral as 'the two cunts'.[32] If I refer to the Unnamable here as an 'it' rather than a 'he', it's not because the text offers a compelling distinction from the masculine voices and attitudes in the novels that preceded it. Like Sartre, Beckett is not so much concerned with minds in their variation, such as particularities of gender difference, but rather with the human mind at its most essential and general. And like Sartre, his template for investigation into this subject was male, perhaps because of a philosophical and cultural tendency among many of his sources and in the zeitgeist of his era to elide the masculine with the universally human, or perhaps simply because the primary source for his investigation into the human mind was his own. Whatever the reason, we find little consideration of women's minds in the texts we are focusing on, nor of the masculinity of the minds we inhabit and the possibility that this may bias or limit the findings of the inquiry. Evolutionary theory also holds a similar place in Beckett's œuvre as in Sartre's: a smattering of references displays at least an acquaintance with Darwinian ideas, but they seem to have little bearing on questions of the nature of the human mind and its place in the world. The Unnamable refers to evolution on several occasions, talking, for instance, of its 'longing to have floundered however briefly, however feebly, in the great life torrent streaming from the earliest protozoa to the very latest humans', while Molloy attributes his longevity to the 'lousy unconquerable genes' inherited from his mother.[33] Darwinian views of man are spoken of unfavourably: Mahood refuses to parrot his 'lesson' that 'Man is a higher mammal'.[34] They are mixed with other, incompatible understandings of life, as when MacMann is driven onwards by 'the élan vital or struggle for life', the former concept referring to the mystical life-force proposed by Bergson.[35] Most often, they are simply rejected. Moran insists: 'I still think I am cleverer than things. There are men and there are things, to hell with animals'.[36] This division is often reinforced by the classic Cartesian distinction of the possession of an immaterial soul: Malone comments on the death of a pig that the animal has no soul and therefore no afterlife, while the Unnamable links together the walking and limbless Mahoods with a reference to the Cartesian indivisibility of the soul (a topic we shall return to in the final chapter). Mahood on crutches and Mahood in the jar are adjudged to be 'two phases of the same carnal envelope, the soul being notoriously immune from deterioration and dismemberment'.[37]

Do Beckett's characters, then, have souls? We are clearly not going to assimilate the author of *En attendant Godot* too closely to the worldview of Bernanos and the Catholic authors, but nor will we find in his work the confident rejection of faith-based understanding that we saw in Sartre. Beckett's personal views, as Mary Bryden has discussed, were on the agnostic edge of atheism, seasoned with a rich cultural awareness of faith from his background in Irish Protestantism and his philosophical studies.[38] Beckett told Tom Driver, 'I have no religious feeling. Once I had a religious emotion. It was at my first Communion. No more'.[39] Later, though, he declared he was neither Christian nor atheist, and, towards the end of his life, when asked if he had left religious influence behind him, he responded: 'in my outward behaviour, probably. . . . But as for the rest'.[40] The texts offer us uncertainty and contradiction on their narrators' faith in God and the likelihood that such faith might have a real foundation. Moran, for instance, starts his tale a committed Christian, seeing, like Mauriac's Louis, 'a superfetatory proof of the existence of God' in the natural world.[41] (The 'superfetatory' implies that such proof was unnecessary as no doubts existed beforehand.) Shortly into his new mission, however, he finds that God is 'beginning to disgust me', and by the end of his quest he is reciting a bleak parody of the Lord's Prayer, beginning, 'Our Father who art no more in heaven than on earth or in hell'. Despite this, there are hints of the divine in the world he occupies, both in the God(ot)-like status of the unseen Youdi, whose name might be a burlesque *verlan* of the word 'Dieu', and in the mysterious voice that comes to replace Youdi's orders as his guiding force: 'the voice I listen to needs no Gaber to make it heard. For it is within me and exhorts me to continue to the end the faithful servant I have always been'.[42]

Voices within the mind are widespread in Beckett's prose. Molloy, Moran, and the Unnamable all hear them, as do the protagonists of the later prose works, *Comment c'est* and *Compagnie* (1980, first published in English as *Company* in 1979). The texts toy with the question of whether they are internal or external in origin, and if the latter, perhaps divine. *Compagnie* takes its structure from the phenomenon, opening with the hopeful line, 'A voice comes to one in the dark', only to end with the 'company' of an external voice dismissed as a fable, 'And you as you always were. Alone'.[43] In *Comment c'est*, the protagonist perceives 'scraps of an ancient voice in me not mine', and wonders if the voice might belong to 'an intelligence somewhere a love' with 'exceptional powers' and 'assistants innumerable', before concluding finally, 'this voice quaqua yes all balls yes only one voice here yes mine yes'.[44] The Unnamable, which similarly moves towards a final acknowledgement of the internal nature of the other voice it perceives, links the voice at one point to a 'master', which it assimilates both to Moran's Youdi and directly to God through the line, 'his will is done as far as I'm concerned'.[45] As in Bernanos, the possibility of the permeability of the mind to supernatural outside intelligence is floated, and never entirely dismissed, but Beckett's fictions conclude by understanding these inner voices in closer alignment to a Proustian view of the multiplicity of the self.

One further religious influence on Beckett is the Christian belief in the immortality of the soul. Malone on his deathbed declares himself 'almost resigned' to it, and the Unnamable, whose narrative might be read as picking up from the point of Malone's death at the end of the previous novel, may have knowledge of earthly life, but does not seem to be partaking in it as it speaks to us.[46] Several of the situations of Beckett's texts suggest an afterlife, notably *Comment c'est*, in which the mud-crawling protagonist has memory flashes of an ordinary life 'up there in the light', and the play *Comédie* (1970, first performed as *Play* in 1964) in which three figures in urns endlessly recount what sounds like an adulterous love-triangle in their past. The Unnamable remarks wryly that Hell would make an acceptable 'distant analogy' for its own situation, emphasized in its early presentation by its darkness, depth (it is referred to as a 'pit') and the circles formed by those who surround it.[47] The hypothesis that the words we read are issuing from a posthumous consciousness very much requires to be taken seriously, despite the ambivalence towards the broader religious implications of such a situation that we see in Beckett's work. It must be said, though, that even if Beckett did set some of his fiction in an afterlife, this doesn't necessarily mean that the immortality of the soul was a tenet of his worldview (an unlikely prospect, given his public statements on religion), or even a major concern in his thinking. After all, Sartre's *Huis clos* is unambiguously set in Hell, but is self-evidently not a play about the nature of the hereafter: rather, Hell is a useful setting in which to imprison three disparate characters, and a vivid metaphor for Sartre's view of interpersonal relations. Equally, Beckett's inward spiral may progressively deprive his characters of sex lives and social lives, sucking stones and bicycles, mobility, corporeality, and deprive them by the end even of a name, and the fact that the last twists of this spiral are reminiscent of Hell or purgatory may be a consequence of this dwindling rather than the goal of the journey. The goal may be to examine what is left when all of these are stripped away, and the question of where that remnant can exist, and how it survives in isolation, may not be the most relevant. In any case, the question is not answered, and we lack sufficient evidence to answer it for ourselves.

Despite these hints of dualism, it can scarcely be said that Beckett neglects the embodied nature of the mind. Rather, he revels in corporeal existence, the more vivid and revolting the better. For Molloy, the eyes are not the windows on the soul; rather, the arsehole is 'the true portal of our being'.[48] Molloy's relish in the physical—'the finger in the nose, the scratching of the balls, digital emunction and the peripatetic piss'—is mirrored by Moran's 'horror of the body and its functions', but both horror and celebration give the body a central role in the characters' sense of self.[49] This role is only reinforced when physical ailments and declining strength make the suffering, impotent body impinge ever more inescapably on consciousness. For Malone, the final stages of this decline make death itself a gradual shutting down of the body (from the feet upwards)—'my head will be the last to die'—rather than exclusively concerning the snuffing out of the mind.[50] Even the Unnamable, who seems to have left corporeality behind, spends much of its monologue describing imagined or remembered bodies of itself and its avatars, where once again, stoic acceptance of physical suffering and disability are defining psychological characteristics.

Cartesian echoes in Beckett will recur as we draw nearer to the centre of the spiral and deal with his philosophical engagements in earnest. Before we get there, though, let us dwell a little longer on Beckett's relationship with his most clearly acknowledged literary influence, Proust. Were it not for Beckett's early essay on Proust, and for the numerous sly allusions in the trilogy—Molloy encounters a hawthorn hedge in full bloom but remarks only that he dislikes the smell—the style and content of the two writers' work might seem so fundamentally different as to preclude meaningful connections.[51] But they are united in their introspective search for the self, and, it transpires, in some of their findings. In particular, the multiplicity of the self and the importance of habituation to mental life feature prominently in the work of both men. Beckett's essay makes explicit the link between the two phenomena and between the two writers' interest in them:

> Habit is a compromise effected between the individual and his environment, or between the individual and his own organic eccentricities, the guarantee of a dull inviolability, the lightning conductor of his existence. Habit is the ballast that chains the dog to his vomit. Breathing is habit. Life is habit. Or rather life is a succession of habits, since the individual is a succession of individuals.[52]

Beckett is particularly thinking here of the Balbec episode of *In Search of Lost Time*, in which the Narrator's initial anxiety over sleeping in the high-ceilinged hotel bedroom gradually wanes as he becomes habituated to the unfamiliar room. Proust describes the process as follows:

> It is those parts of us, even the most insubstantial and obscure of them, such as our attachment to the dimensions or the atmosphere of a particular room, which take fright, withhold consent and engage in rebellions which must be seen as a covert and partial yet tangible and true mode of resistance to death, that lengthy, desperate, daily resistance to the sporadic but non-stop dying which attends us throughout our lives, stripping off bits of us at every moment, which have no sooner mortified than new cells begin to grow. For a nervous disposition such as mine (that is, one in which the functioning of the intermediaries, the nerves, is impaired, so that they fail to stifle the voice of the lowliest elements of self doomed to decease, and their harrowing many-headed lament, in all its sorrow, rises unmuted to the wearied ears of consciousness) the anguish and alarm I felt when lying beneath a ceiling that was unknown and too high was nothing but the protest of my surviving attachment to a ceiling which was known and lower. No doubt that attachment would end and be replaced by another: first death, then a new life, would have done their dual work at the behest of Habit.[53]

As Beckett notes, the Proustian idea of serial selves, which we explored in the first chapter, is central to his understanding of habit. Habituation, for Proust, is the death of the self for whom the high ceiling is anxiety-inducing, and its replacement by one to whom it has come to seem normal. Like our contemporary understanding of habituation as a form of non-associative learning, the process in Proust (and Beckett's reading of Proust) is unconscious. The Narrator's initial sense of unease doesn't depend on a conscious comparison of his bedroom ceiling with that of the hotel room—indeed, the understanding of its cause comes only later—and equally, the comforting sense of familiarity after habituation has occurred requires no conscious understanding of the change that has occurred with the 'death' of the anxious self and the birth of its successor.

Beckett's own view of habit leans more heavily on Schopenhauerian pessimism than does Proust's—indeed, Beckett evokes Schopenhauer explicitly in his discussion of habit.[54] In Beckett it is life itself, rather than the sensory overload of the unfamiliar, which causes suffering, and towards which habit, the 'great deadener' can dull our senses.[55] J. D. O'Hara suggests that in Beckett, as in Schopenhauer, the endless struggle imposed on the self by the will to live and the desires it strives to satisfy make self-conscious individuality a source of pain in itself.[56] The abolition of our awareness would thus be seen primarily a release from pain, and therefore something to be welcomed. In the meantime, habituation, which 'paralyses our attention, [and] drugs those handmaidens of perception whose co-operation is not absolutely essential' may blind us to the raw truth and beauty to be found in existence, but will insulate our minds from the suffering inherent in the engagement.[57] The shift in emphasis from Proust is very clear in Beckett's fiction, where habituation is most often linked with physical pain. The term itself occurs when the Unnamable fantasizes about being whipped with increasing violence to counter the 'habituation factor', and is explored at greatest length with regard to new pain in Molloy's, and later Moran's good leg, which, while no different in quality or intensity from the pain in the bad leg, nevertheless causes greater suffering:

> For the old pain, do you follow me, I had got used to it, in a way, yes, in a kind of way. Whereas to the new pain, though of the same family exactly, I had not yet had time to adjust myself.[58]

Beckett's representation of habituation is consistent with scientific research that finds awareness of stimulation is greatest when the stimulation is novel and declines on repetition, as is Proust's, although here with greater detail on the subjective and unconscious elements of the phenomenon.[59] It is only in Beckett, though, that habituation leads from the psychological to the philosophical, and becomes both shield and blindfold against the nature of our existence.

The multiple self is for both Proust and Beckett a fundamental part of their conception of the nature of the mind, which extends well beyond the realm of habit. As with Proust, Beckett's multiple selves may be serial, replacing each other as personality changes over time, and may also be contemporaneous with each other, although this latter leads to a far more radical alienation of the subject from itself in the later writer than in his predecessor. Molloy inaugurates the topic of serial selves after his scrape with the police force, remarking: 'I'll meet again the sergeant and his merry men. And if, too changed to know it is they, I do not say it is they, make no mistake, it will be they, though changed'.[60] It is Moran, though, who embodies the principle, becoming almost literally a different person by the end of his account. The change begins quickly, coming to his awareness as soon as he accepts the mission to find Molloy: 'the poison was already acting on me. [. . .] The colour and weight of the world were changing already'.[61] Towards the end of his mission he finds himself 'so changed from what I was' through a process he first compares to rapid ageing, then to 'a crumbling, a frenzied collapsing of all that had always protected me', and finally to 'a clawing towards a light and countenance I could not name, that I had once known and long denied'.[62] Moran's transformation appears to combine the Proustian replacement self with a Freudian return of the repressed, emphasizing the breakdown of self-control and the release of a more violent, more wretched, but also more self-aware Moran at the end of his journey.

Proust's multiple 'little inner figures' jostling for control of the mind at any one time are echoed throughout Beckett's trilogy, for instance in Molloy's conception of his personality: 'For in me there have always been two fools, among others, one asking nothing better than to stay where he is and the other imagining that life might be slightly less horrible further on'.[63] However, what in Proust was a benign metaphor for changing moods becomes in Beckett a disturbing sense of displacement. Moran comes to consider he has been 'dispossessed of self', and observes his own behaviour as that of a stranger.[64] Malone and the Unnamable, as well as the later narrators of *Compagnie* and *Comment c'est*, talk of other presences or foreign voices that turn out to emanate from within themselves, yet are not recognized as being part of the self. Malone has an inner stranger of his own, and expects at some point in the future 'to feel, behind my closed eyes, other eyes close'.[65] This deeper, simpler self in some respects resembles the Unnamable, who perhaps relates to Malone in the way that Worm will relate to the Unnamable itself. The various avatars with which the Unnamable populates its existence before dismissing them as puppets are the most obvious example in the trilogy of the confusion of self and other, but even the voice which speaks the text of the novel is dissociated from the mind that hears it—the voice 'fills me, it clamours against my walls, it is not mine'—before being acknowledged as the product of that same mind: 'this voice that is not mine, but can only be mine, since there is no one but me. [. . .] So it is I who speak, all alone'.[66] These inner strangers retain a Proustian kernel: it is when he is between sleep and waking that Molloy will 'forget who I am and strut before my eyes, like a stranger'.[67] But there is little in common with Proust in the development of this idea into the self as a foreigner in its own mind, as the Unnamable asserts at the outset: 'I seem to speak, it is not I, about me, it is not about me'.[68]

Understanding this phenomenon requires us to distinguish the concepts of self and mind to a greater extent than some previous writers, Proust included, felt necessary. One of the most developed attempts by any of Beckett's narrators to understand its own nature comes at the very end of the trilogy, in the last pages of *The Unnamable*, and employs 'self' and 'mind' as distinct entities. It is worth examining in some detail:

> Perhaps that's what I feel, an outside and an inside and me in the middle, perhaps that's what I am, the thing that divides the world in two, on the one side the outside, on the other the

> inside, that can be as thin as foil, I'm neither one side nor the other, I'm in the middle, I'm the partition, I've two surfaces and no thickness, perhaps that's what I feel, myself vibrating, I'm the tympanum, on the one hand the mind, on the other the world, I don't belong to either.[69]

While it must not be ignored that, in typical Beckett fashion, this self-analysis is denied almost as soon as uttered ('no, that's not it, I feel nothing at all of that'), it is nevertheless given weight in Beckett's text both by its placement at the end of the trilogy and its vivid and sustained image. I am not my mind; rather, the self is the foil-thin division between mind and world.

We have seen a similar distinction already in Sartre's transcendence of the ego, and passages like this one have led several critics to read Beckett's model of the mind in terms of existentialist theory or its phenomenological antecedents. For Sartre, as you may recall, consciousness is nothing more than a direction of attention, and the complex autobiographical self with its memories and personality traits is a temporary construct which can be conjured up by the application of attention, only to evaporate when the attention is elsewhere. The two-dimensional nature of Beckett's tympanum strongly recalls Sartre's contentless consciousness, as does the symmetry of mind and world as equivalent objects, contiguous but external to it and available for its attention.

Phenomenology and existentialism are very much part of Beckett's philosophical repertoire. Watt, in the novel written previous to the trilogy, undergoes a crisis that is recognizably related to Roquentin's as concepts detach from the objects they label, just as they did in *Nausea*:

> For it was not a pot, the more he looked, the more he reflected, the more he felt sure of that, that it was not a pot at all. It resembled a pot, it was almost a pot, but it was not a pot of which one could say, Pot, pot, and be comforted.[70]

Earlier still in Beckett's œuvre, before the first stirrings of French existentialism, we see a stripping away of the paraphernalia of the mind towards consciousness without content in *Murphy* (1938 in English, 1947 in French translation). While the interlude describing the zones of Murphy's mind parodies various philosophies of consciousness, among them Descartes, Leibniz, and Spinoza, the comedy fades when we reach the third and final zone of the mind. In the first and second zones, Murphy is free to reimagine the world as he might wish it to be or leave the world behind in purely aesthetic contemplation; in the third zone he is not free, but rather exists as 'a mote in the dark of absolute freedom'.[71] Murphy's mote removes further dimensions from the Unnamable's tympanum to leave a single point of awareness, and its association with absolute freedom similarly recalls (or prefigures) existentialist consciousness. However, the paradox of being within freedom yet not free, an unmoving point in the 'ceaseless unconditioned generation and passing away of line',[72] seems mysteriously to bring Murphy's absolute freedom full circle towards determinism, perhaps suggesting some affinity with the Sarrautean stance, which we will encounter shortly, in which control and decision-making dissolve as we venture beyond language and rational thought to more primal levels of the mind.

Roger Scruton is one critic to see an evocation of being-for-itself in Beckett's fiction. He suggests that Beckettian subjectivity is 'a perspective on the world, and not an item in it', and that it is negation that provides the means to approach an understanding of it.[73] Molloy certainly expresses an enthusiasm for disciplines that define man 'in terms of what he is not', and both Malone and the Unnamable are more confident in negating falsehoods about their existence than asserting positives.[74] Here is Malone, for instance, rejecting the findings of first the senses then of introspective thought as evidence of the nature of the self:

> All my senses are trained full on me, me, Dark and silent and stale, I am no prey for them. I am far from the sounds of blood and breath, immured. [. . .] Somewhere in this turmoil,

> thought struggles on, it too wide of the mark. It too seeks me, as it always has, where I am not to be found.[75]

On this reading, the cautious hypotheses and swift rejections about who, where, and why the narrators are don't simply erase themselves to leave us back where we started. Rather, they discard failed hypotheses about the nature of the self and wear away at the inessential elements, leading us gradually closer to the core. In this way, the trilogy itself may be read as a slow, progressive phenomenological reduction, 'reduction' here in the sense of a 'leading back' through the objects of the external world, through the psychological complexities of the autobiographical self and individual perception, thought and memory, towards pure consciousness. The existentialist critic David H. Hesla sees in Beckett's minds the 'unhappy consciousness' of Hegelian phenomenology. In this conception, the conscious being is aware of its existence as being-for-itself and as being-in-itself, both free and determined, static and in flux.[76] Our consciousness is in fact a double consciousness, one self-consciousness gazing into another, desiring unity but unable to achieve it.[77] The musing of the Unnamable as to whether 'the two retinae' of its putative eyes might not be facing each other is suggestive of this view.[78] Certainly, the trilogy appears to develop—or devolve—ever more towards the narrative instance of a consciousness looking at itself.

As we have seen, Beckett's indeterminacy allows his texts to be assimilated to various philosophical doctrines, many of which are teasingly referenced in the novels themselves, but we must be careful not to co-opt him into phenomenology or existentialism simply on the grounds that his stories don't explicitly rule out such a reading. As L.A.C. Dobrez has pointed out, there are at least two areas in which the Beckettian mind is perceptibly different from the existentialist one: free will and complexity.[79]

There is more to free will in Beckett than Murphy's mote, and much of it is deeply pessimistic. Murphy himself, as we have just seen, has freedom in the self-controlled zones of his mind and a curious passivity-within-freedom in the zone beyond, yet outside his mind, his freedom is in doubt. Only when his body is neutralized, ideally by being bound naked to his rocking chair, and his existence is reduced to the mental sphere, can he experience freedom: 'Soon his body would be quiet. Soon he would be free', he thinks as he rocks.[80] Malone offers a suggestive metaphor for a freedom that extends only to the limits of your own skull in the image of a cab-passenger 'as helpless to act on the course of events as the dark box that encloses him, abandons himself to the pleasant feeling of being freed from all responsibility'.[81] This image itself has an antecedent in the Occasionalist thought of Arnold Geulincx, a philosopher whose name occurs twice in Beckett's novels, and to whom Beckett advised readers to turn in interpreting his work. Malone's cab-rider appears to be a variation on Geulincx's image of a ship-passenger, an image which makes an appearance in *Molloy*. When the question of why he stayed with Lousse brings Molloy to the question of whether he could possibly have done otherwise, the topic of free will is invoked:

> I who had loved the image of old Geulincx, dead young, who left me free, on the black boat of Ulysses, to crawl towards the East, along the deck. That is a great measure of freedom, for him who has not the pioneering spirit. And from the poop, poring upon the wave, a sadly rejoicing slave, I follow with my eyes the proud and futile wake. Which, as it bears me from no fatherland away, bears me onward to no shipwreck.[82]

Geulincx's passenger, free to move eastwards along the deck of a westward-travelling ship, symbolizes a freedom of thought that does not extend to the physical realm. Similar to Leibniz's more famous concept of the monad, it is a consequence of Cartesian dualism, and a response to the problem of how an immaterial mind might interact with a material body. Descartes insisted that it could, by mechanisms unknown involving the pineal gland, as we saw earlier. Geulincx, and later Leibniz, explored the possibility that it could not. Geulincx's Occasionalism and Leibniz's 'pre-established harmony'—a concept that also appears in Beckett's trilogy—both posit God as the means to connect thought and action across a gulf that direct causation cannot bridge.[83] Beckett's narrators are less optimistic about God, but attached to the idea of the monadic isolation of consciousness. The closed rooms in which his narrators dwell remind them of an enclosed skull, their isolation from the external world standing as a metaphor for consciousness divided from physical existence. Perhaps it is more than a metaphor, as Malone speculates: 'Sometimes it seems to me I am in a head and that these eight, no, six, these six planes that enclose me are of solid bone'.[84] In the 'ivory dungeon' of the skull, as one of the narrators of the *Textes pour rien* (*Texts for Nothing*, 1958) puts it, the outside world is held at bay, incomprehensible and uncontrollable, the failing body a poor means of interaction, and the worry always present that life in the world, if it is not illusory, may be running along a predetermined track.[85] There is a flirtation, too with epiphenomenalism, the idea that free will doesn't exist inside or outside consciousness, as may be gleaned from the Unnamable's dry observation that 'the problem of liberty too, as sure as fate, will come up for my consideration at the pre-established moment'.[86] Finally, though, the understanding of will with which Beckett's fiction has greatest affinity is probably Schopenhauer's, whose Hindu- and Buddhist-inflected worldview sidesteps the question of determinism to explore a conception of the Will as harmful desire, apparently externally imposed, and leading only to suffering without being assuaged. Schopenhauer describes what it might be like to be free of willing:

> He now looks back calmly and with a smile on the phantasmagoria of this world which was once able to move and agonize even his mind, but now stands before him as indifferently as chess-men at the end of the game, or as fancy-dress cast off in the morning, the form and figure of which taunted and disquieted us on the carnival night.[87]

Molloy's and Moran's pleasure in losing their consciousness in contemplation of things they can't understand—the knife-rest in Molloy's case, the bees in Moran's—as an escape from the world has intimations of a Schopenhauerian worldview.[88] The sense of obligation in the tasks the narrators pursue, like Molloy's journey, Malone's stories and inventory, and the Unnamable's 'pensum' of self-description are reminiscent of Schopenhauer's view of the Will as an imposition, and the narrators' longing for release and oblivion, particularly in the last of the trilogy, accords closely with Schopenhauer's pessimistic view of life.

The other significant difference between Beckett's minds and those of Sartrean existentialism is the level at which attention is focused. Sartre may see consciousness as a pure beam of directed attention, but this consciousness is in the service of a rational intelligence, complex in thought and emotion, empowered by cognition and language, and existing within an intricate network of intersubjective relations. (Note also that Sartrean intentionality strives to abolish the division between the subject and the world, which Beckett's immured consciousnesses and tympanum of self appear to reinstate.) Beckett's characters too have language, emotion and intelligence, human lives and relationships to others. For Beckett, though, this is so much psychological detritus to be worked through in order to discover what remains when you have left them all behind. Both would seem to agree that the *cogito* affirms too much, that, as we saw Sartre claim, the subjective experience of consciousness tells us only 'there is consciousness of this chair' rather than 'I am conscious of this chair'. The Unnamable grumbles that it has had 'enough of this cursed first person, it really is too red a herring' and suggests outside parties are trying to deceive it 'to make me believe I have an ego all my own, and can speak of it'.[89] Similarly, *Nausea* does indeed at one point stage the snuffing out of Roquentin's own ego, leaving only an impersonal consciousness without a first person, as we saw in the previous chapter. However, this is not the main focus of Sartre's creative endeavours, which for the most part prefer to work up from this starting point in order to explore human interactions in a world where the freedom of consciousness is absolute and personality traits are contingent constructs of the mind with illusory stability. Beckett heads for the core, and is not as sure as Sartre that intelligence, reason, and language will accompany him right to the end of the journey. Nor is he so confident that everything that constitutes the self, which Sartre bundled into his transcendental ego and jettisoned from consciousness, will be lost.

Time, then, to place ourselves at the centre of Beckett's spiral. Let us attempt to sum up the nature of what we find here, and finish by examining how it compares to current thinking on consciousness.[90] By the time we reach the Unnamable, we have left behind the names and personalities of the previous narrators, the incidents of their lives and their interactions with others. A little further in and we have also left behind the physical body that the Unnamable briefly conjures up for itself, the perception of a physical space outside of the self, and the presence of other minds. We have not, of course, left behind language and the conceptual thought underlying it, at least not until we reach the final line of text, which suggestively announces 'I'll go on', as if the Unnamable might continue beyond the point where its words end. Does the spiral lead beyond language? It certainly seems so. The Unnamable considers for a moment the possibility that it is 'in words, made of words,' but decides almost immediately that the words emanate from it and describe it but that 'I'm something quite different, a quite different thing, a wordless thing in an empty place'.[91] This aligns with Molloy's confession at the start of the trilogy that rendering his mental activity on the page as an inner monologue is in fact a misrepresentation:

> Every time I say, I said this, or I said that, or speak of a voice saying, far away inside me, Molloy, and then a fine phrase more or less clear and simple, [. . .] I am merely complying with the convention that demands you either lie or hold your peace. For what really happened was quite different. And I did not say, Yet a little while, at the rate things are going, etc., but that resembled perhaps what I would have said, if I had been able. In reality I said nothing at all, but I heard a murmur, something gone wrong with the silence, and I pricked up my ears, like an animal I imagine, which gives a start and pretends to be dead. And then sometimes there arose within me, confusedly, a kind of consciousness, which I express by saying, I said, etc., [. . .]. Or which I express without sinking to the level of oratio recta, but by means of other figures quite as deceitful, as for example, It seemed to me that, etc., or, I had the impression that, etc., for it seemed to me nothing at all, and I had no impression of any kind, but simply somewhere something had changed, so that I too had to change, or the world too had to change, in order for nothing to be changed.[92]

The point is not that language is absent from mental life, but that it isn't the essential medium of mental activity that literature sometimes claims it to be. As we shall see in greater detail in the work of Sarraute and Darrieussecq, non-linguistic thought is increasingly a focus of the French psychological novel as the century progresses, and with it the question of how best to represent it through language in the text. Molloy declares that some of the thought he narrates as monologue in his text (*oratio recta* means 'direct speech') was not language in his head, and, furthermore, that some of it was not conceptualized at all. The references to wrongness in the silence and changes in the world and self attempt to render thought that is not unconscious but *non-conceptual*: cognition that uses neither words nor images, nor other means to crystallize itself. The incident that sparks this meditation is Molloy's realization that his forward progress through the forest is slowing down towards a standstill, initially expressed in the text as follows: 'I also said, Yet a little while, at the rate things are going, and I won't be able to move, but will have to stay, where I happen to be unless someone comes and carries me'.[93] What the subsequent meditation lays out for us is that the thought, when it occurred to him, did not consist of this sentence, nor of any word or fragment of it. Nor was the thought an image or inner film-show of Molloy's future halt and putative rescue, nor any other means by which the two situations might be rendered as a recognizable idea. And yet it was a realisation nonetheless.

Recent approaches to non-linguistic thought in cognitive science will be explored more thoroughly in the final chapter, but let us note for now that the field of conceptual semantics finds itself largely in agreement with Beckett on this point. Damasio contends that consciousness is non-verbal, but creates a narrative, a non-languaged map of logically related events. Humans convert this narrative into a verbal translation, which is what leads theorists to the wrong conclusion that consciousness requires language.[94] Evidence is growing to support this view. Language acquisition appears to map words onto pre-existing basic concepts of causality, agency, and spatial relations in the infant mind. Our memories store the gist of what we read or hear rather than the words themselves, such that experimental subjects shown a sentence expressing in different words the same meaning as a sentence they have seen previously will falsely recall having seen it before. The high level of polysemy in all languages, with many common words having half a dozen definitions and usages that are concrete and virtual, particular or collective, points to mental functioning at the level of concept over that of language.[95] Our thoughts frequently break out of the 'prison house' of language, and readily resort to metaphor or new coinages to do so, or sometimes fail to fit themselves to language, as in *Comment dire* (*What is the Word*, 1989), Beckett's devastating final poem. Molloy and the Unnamable would appear to be right in proposing that the mental level on which they must present themselves to us, that of language, is not yet the most fundamental level of their consciousness.

What then can be said about the pre-linguistic self towards which the narrators gesture? Malone's stranger, the 'one in the dark' of *Compagnie*, and most notably, the Unnamable's 'Worm' all suggest an inner self beyond the shell of language, and in the case of Worm, lacking other characteristics as well. The Unnamable returns to describing Worm at several points in the later parts of *The Unnamable*. On first 'baptizing' the avatar Worm, the Unnamable comments that the name 'will be my name too, when the time comes, when I needn't be called Mahood any more', suggesting that Worm may lie further along the spiral of dwindling than the linguistic text can reach.[96] He is described as 'inexpugnable', in contrast to all the other selves the narrator takes on and discards. Worm exists, we are told, and is conscious in at least a rudimentary way, and yet lacks the quality of *self*-consciousness that is an essential part of human awareness:

> Worm, to say he does not know what he is, where he is, what is happening, is to underestimate him. What he does not know is that there is anything to know. His senses tell him nothing, nothing about himself. Nothing about the rest. And this distinction is beyond him. Feeling nothing, knowing nothing, he exists nevertheless, but not for himself, for others, others conceive him and say, Worm is.[97]

Worm is elsewhere described as a being which 'can't take thought', suggesting conceptual cognition is beyond him as well as language and self-awareness.[98] Worm has no knowledge of anything beyond himself, and due to this lack, has no knowledge *of* himself as an individual being distinct from the world around him. The Unnamable equivocates as to whether it is, can be or will be Worm itself: 'I'm Worm, no, if I were Worm, I wouldn't know it, I wouldn't say it, I wouldn't say anything, I'd be Worm. [. . .] I'm Worm, that is to say I am no longer he, since I hear'.[99] It feels 'Worm inside. Feeling nothing, knowing nothing, capable of nothing, wanting nothing. Until the instant he hears the sound that will never stop. Then it's the end. Worm no longer is'.[100] Language, either in its production or reception, and the higher conceptual functions of mind that attend it, form a threshold beyond which the Unnamable is no longer Worm. In the silences between language, however, and perhaps the long silence that follows the final word of the trilogy, 'then it will be he, it will be I'.[101]

Dobrez sees the narrator's transition to Worm as a process in which consciousness is 'left behind' for another realm of being, a kind of void beyond consciousness.[102] Northrop Frye says something similar, suggesting that *The Unnamable* is a '"stream of consciousness" from which real consciousness is somehow absent'.[103] This, though, is to misread Beckett's spiral. We are not taken into pure consciousness only to be taken back out again and away somewhere else. The continuity that we have seen from Molloy's reflections on his non-linguistic awareness through to the Unnamable's inner Worm shows that this centre-point of the mind persists from the most psychologically developed of Beckett's characters to the most austere. In Molloy's meditation it is specifically referred to as 'a kind of consciousness', and Worm too, it's clear, is not an unconscious being: he is without sensory input, without memory or prior knowledge, and yet he is aware. His mind is available to receive sense-impressions, we are told, and if ever they should come he will cease to be Worm and elaborate around his consciousness the knowledge of self and other that is the beginning of a human nature. The difficulty is perhaps a terminological one: a consciousness without knowledge, memory or perception is such a different state of existence from normal adult human mentality that Dobrez and Frye cannot conceive it as consciousness at all. But it is a form of consciousness. In fact, it is the purest and most fundamental element of consciousness: it is sentience.

The idea that the psychologically complex Proustian self is the basis of our conscious existence has been under attack for some time now. Dennett presents the image of a homunculus inside a 'Cartesian theatre' of the brain to encapsulate this intuitive misunderstanding of mental life. The Cartesian theatre is seen as 'a crucial finish line or boundary somewhere in the brain, marking a place where the order of arrival equals the order of "presentation" in experience because *what happens there* is what you are conscious of'.[104] The self resides in this theatre, envisaged as a homunculus replicant of the mind's owner, receiving sense data and issuing commands.[105] The man-inside-a-skull image that we have seen in the trilogy—and which Beckett doodled on the manuscript of *The Unnamable*—shows that Beckett is familiar with the venerable philosophical idea of the homunculus. We might see in it an acknowledgement of the subjective intuition of the self as a person within us, or perhaps attribute it to the vast philosophical bric-a-brac Beckett's narrators have accumulated, and which they let fall into their accounts in teasing shreds. In either case, there's little encouragement for us to take the suggestion literally. (Beckett would in any case undoubtedly be aware of the paradox of infinite regression—heads within heads within heads—which makes the homunculus a deliberately absurd idea.) Dennett's replacement for the inner homunculus is the 'multiple drafts theory' in which the unified self is an illusion created by mental events occurring at different times and places within the brain.[106] Other thinkers, including Damasio and Block, are closer to Beckett in looking for a simpler, more rudimentary form of consciousness within the elaborations of the Proustian self. We have already seen mention of Damasio's distinction between the core self and autobiographical self of consciousness (along with the nonconscious 'proto-self' composed of reflexes to stimulus and somatic regulation, and present in simpler organisms), and explored the similarities between the autobiographical self and Sartre's transcendent ego. Damasio himself illustrates the difference as follows:

> Minimal scope [in consciousness] allows a sensing of the self, say when one is drinking a cup of coffee at home, unconcerned with the provenance of either the cup or the coffee,

> or with what it will do to your heartbeat, or with what you have to do today. You are quietly present in the moment, that's all. Now suppose you are sitting down for a similar cup of coffee at a restaurant to meet with your brother, who wishes to discuss your parents' inheritance and what is to be done with your half sister, who has been acting strangely. You are still very present and in the moment, as they say in Hollywood, but now you are also transported, by turns, to many other places, with many other people besides your brother, and to situations that you have not experienced yet that are products of your informed and rich imagination. [. . .] I have given names to those two kinds of consciousness. The minimal-scope kind I call *core* consciousness, the sense of the here and now, unencumbered by much past and by little or no future. It revolves around a core self and is about personhood but not necessarily identity. The big-scope kind I call *extended* or *autobiographical* consciousness, given that it manifests itself most powerfully when a substantial part of one's life comes into play and both the lived past and anticipated future dominate the proceedings. It is about both personhood and identity. It is presided over by an autobiographical self.[107]

Damasio argues that the term *consciousness* is more often associated with extended consciousness, and core consciousness is neglected. This would certainly account for Dobrez's contention that the final whorls of Beckett's spiral move through too ascetic a medium to warrant the term, and must take place somewhere other than consciousness. Damasio also suggests that core consciousness, bereft of extension and autobiography, is not only to be found in moments of coffee-drinking absent-mindedness, but may also be a more stable mental state, for instance in infants and animal minds. Beckett's dwindling spiral is suggestive in some respects of a transition from extended consciousness and the autobiographical self towards core consciousness alone. Worm might well be described as being 'quietly present in the moment', and indeed, as being incapable of being otherwise, since here and now are all he knows, without even conceiving that here is a place or that now is a time.

Coming from a philosophical background, but closely engaged with contemporary neuroscience, Block also considers consciousness to be a 'mongrel concept' in need of dissection, and proposes to distinguish 'Phenomenal Consciousness' from 'Access Consciousness' (abbreviated to 'P-consciousness' and 'A-consciousness'). He defines them by explaining their differences from one another:

> P-conscious content is phenomenal, whereas A-conscious content is representational. It is of the essence of A-conscious content to play a role in reasoning, and only representational content can figure in reasoning. Many phenomenal contents are also representational, however, so it would be better to say that it is in virtue of its phenomenal content or the phenomenal aspect of its content that a state is P-conscious, whereas it is in virtue of its representational content, or the representational aspect of its content, that a state is A-conscious. [. . .] The P-conscious content of a state is the totality of the state's experiential properties, what it is like to be in that state. One can think of the P-conscious content of a state as the state's experiential 'value' by analogy with the representational content as the state's representational 'value'. In my view, the content of an experience can be both P-conscious and A-conscious, the former in virtue of its phenomenal feel and the latter in virtue of its representational properties. A closely related point: A-conscious states are necessarily transitive: A-conscious states must always be states of consciousness of. P-conscious states, by contrast, sometimes are and sometimes are not transitive. P-consciousness, as such, is not consciousness of.[108]

Block goes on to explain that phenomenal consciousness broadly deals in sensations while access conscious deals with propositions (thoughts or beliefs *that* something is something), but acknowledges that the boundary between the two is often blurred. I may, for instance, have a perception of redness in phenomenal consciousness and a proposition that the object in front of me is red in access consciousness.

Like Damasio's theory, Block's offers a stripped-down consciousness, shorn of the cognitive complexity which is often thought to be integral to it. Linking this basic sentience to phenomenal experience might appear problematic for Beckett's Worm, who seems to have the former but not the latter. However, Block is thinking of minds in the world, not Worm's utter isolation, and it is in any case clear from Beckett's text that Worm is available for phenomenal experience, but not capable of thinking *about* any such experience without ceasing to be Worm and entering a more complex state of mind. Both Block and Damasio have as their central argument the contention that everyday human consciousness, in all its cognitive sophistication, conceals a more rudimentary awareness, which complements it in Block's view and is included within it in Damasio's. Beckett's dwindling narrators take us as close as their narrations can bring them to such raw sentience, and gesture onwards so that we can catch a glimpse of it further down the path.

*

Beckett's trilogy of novels was a triumph in the French and the English literary spheres, but it left him in something of a creative impasse. Some time later, he would tell an interviewer:

> At the end of my work [the trilogy], there was nothing left but dust: the namable. In the last work, *The Unnamable*, there is total disintegration. No *I*, no *Have*, no *Be*, no nominative, no accusative, no verb. There's no way to go on. The last thing I wrote, *Texts for Nothing*, was an attempt to get out of this attitude of disintegration, but it was a failure.[109]

The grammatical breakdown he describes is at the same time an arrival at the extreme limit of the self. Subjects can no longer perform actions on objects as there is nothing to act upon, no means of acting, and nobody left to act. There is no first person, dismissed by Beckett, as by Sartre, as a presumptuous extrapolation from the presence of a consciousness, which may once have had a name, a body, and a life, but has since shrunk down to a bare existence. There is nothing to have, and while something might yet continue to be, the means of communicating that existence has dwindled away, leaving only an uncertain silence. From the effusive comedy of Murphy, through the more austere humour of Watt, Mercier, and Camier, to the trilogy with its steady drain of narrative content with each of the four narrators, Beckett has written his way to the nothingness of pure sentience and the silence of pre- (or post?) linguistic mentality. Later prose works will rebuild new worlds of imagination and memory, like the endless chain of abusive Pims and Boms in *Comment c'est* or the autobiographical fragments of *Compagnie*, before breaking them down once more to return to a single consciousness alone in the dark. No other writer in the century, not even Sartre with his obsessive focus on consciousness as nothingness, will come as close as Beckett to clearing away the extraneous detail of the mind and putting sentience itself, sentience and nothing else, on the page.

Notes

1. Samuel Beckett, *Proust, and Three Dialogues with Georges Duthuit* (1931, 1949) (London: Calder, 1965), pp. 65–6.
2. 'J'avais déjà fait une bonne dizaine de pas, si on peut appeler ça des pas, non pas en ligne droite, bien sûr, mais selon une courbe fort prononcée, laquelle, sans peut-être me ramener précisément à mon

point de départ, semblait destinée à me le faire frôler de fort près, pour peu que je m'y maintinsse. Je m'etais probablement empêtré dans une sorte de spirale renversée, je veux dire dont les boucles, au lieu de prendre de plus en plus d'ampleur, devaient aller en rétrécissant, jusqu'à ne plus pouvoir se poursuivre, vu l'espèce d'espace où j'etais censé me trouver,' Samuel Beckett, *L'Innommable* (Paris: Minuit, collection 'double', 1953/2004), p. 49; *Three Novels: Molloy, Malone Dies, The Unnamable* (New York: Grove Press, 1958), p. 310. Minuit publishes each of the three volumes in two editions, with slightly different pagination. I shall be using the more widely available 'double' edition for references. All translations are Beckett's own.

3. 'Quoique tout près, à vol d'oiseau, du point mort, je ne pressais pas le pas. Je l'aurais pu sans doute, mais je devais me ménager, si je tenais à arriver. Je n'y tenais pas, mais j'étais obligé de faire de mon mieux, pour arriver. Un but désirable, je n'ai jamais eu le temps de réfléchir à cela. Aller de l'avant, j'appelle ça de l'avant, sinon en ligne droite, tout au moins selon la figure qui m'avait été assignée. Il n'y a pas eu de place dans ma vie pour autre chose', *L'Innommable*, pp. 55–6; trans. 314.
4. *L'Innommable*, pp. 49, 51; trans. 312, 310. The French version has simply 'tournait' and 'après m'être serré à bloc'.
5. 'J'y parachève mes girations, en piétinant les restes méconnaissables des miens [. . .]. J'aime à penser, quoique je n'en aie pas la certitude, que c'est dans le bas-ventre de maman que j'ai terminé, pendant des journées entières, mon long voyage', *L'Innommable*, pp. 60–1; trans. 317.
6. 'Je repris mes spirales' ('I resumed my spirals'), Samuel Beckett, *Molloy* (Paris: Minuit, collection 'double', 1951/1982), p. 63; trans. 63.
7. Northrop Frye, 'The Nightmare Life in Death', in *Northrop Frye on Twentieth-Century Literature*, ed. by Glen Robert Gill (Toronto: University of Toronto Press, 2010), pp. 159–67 (p. 165).
8. Vivan Mercier, 'The Mathematical Limit', *Nation*, 14 February 1959, pp. 144–5 (p. 145). The term appears in *Molloy*, p. 205; trans. 143, where Moran imagines organizing his dwindling food supplies into 'a series of menus asymptotically approaching nutritional zero' ('une série de menus s'approchant asymptotiquement du néant alimentaire').
9. See, for instance, Roger Scruton, *The Aesthetic Understanding* (London: Methuen, 1983) or L.A.C. Dobrez, *The Existential and Its Exits: Literary and Philosophical Perspectives on the Works of Beckett, Ionesco, Genet & Pinter* (London: Athlone, 1986).
10. Samuel Beckett and Tom F. Driver, 'Beckett by the Madeleine' (Interview), *Columbia University Forum*, 4 (1961), pp. 21–5 (p. 25).
11. 'Alors je rentrai dans la maison, et j'écrivis, Il est minuit. La pluie fouette les vitres. Il n'était pas minuit. Il ne pleuvait pas', *Molloy*, p. 241; trans. 170.
12. 'Ce n'est pas que leur sens m'échappe, car le mien m'échappe tout autant', *L'Innommable*, p. 70; trans. 323.
13. 'Les premières choses qui s'offrent à moi, à mon réveil, je les vois avec assez de netteté [. . .]. Puis dans mes yeux et dans ma tête une pluie fine se met à tomber', *Molloy*, p. 37; trans. 24.
14. 'Elles sont peut-être permanentes et fixes, perçues par moi avec vacillation et par intermittence', *L'Innommable*, p. 12; trans. 288.
15. 'Avec ravissement, Voilà une chose que je pourrai étudier toute ma vie, sans jamais la comprendre', *Molloy*, p. 232; trans. 163.
16. 'Mais ce cigare n'était-il pas en réalité un brûle-gueule peut-être, et ces espadrilles des chaussures cloutées blanchies par la poussière, et ce chien qu'est-ce qui l'empêchait d'être un chien errant qu'on ramasse et prend dans ses bras?', *Molloy*, p. 14; trans. 8.
17. 'Et ce fut peut-être un jour A à tel endroit, puis un autre B à tel autre, puis un troisième le rocher et moi, et ainsi de suite pour les autres composants, les vaches, le ciel, la mer, les montagnes', *Molloy*, p. 17; trans. 10.
18. 'Mes notes ont une fâcheuse tendance, je l'ai compris enfin, à faire disparaître tout ce qui est censé en faire l'objet', *Malone meurt* (Paris: Minuit, collection 'double', 1951/2004), p. 138; trans. 252.
19. 'Laissons tout ça. Je n'ai jamais été ailleurs qu'ici', *L'Innommable*, p. 61; trans. 317; 'ce n'est pas une spirale, mon chemin, là aussi je me suis gouré, mais des boucles irrégulières', p. 66; trans. 320; 'Je diminuais. Je diminue', p. 73; trans. 325.
20. 'Je ne me rappelle pas comment j'y suis arrivé. Dans une ambulance peut-être, un véhicule quelconque certainement', *Malone meurt*, p. 13; trans. 177; *Molloy*, p. 7; trans. 3 (Molloy's version is 'I don't know how I got there. Perhaps in an ambulance, certainly a vehicle of some kind', with similar minor differences between the French versions.)
21. '(C'est en effet ainsi que je m'appelle à présent)', *Malone meurt*, p. 216; trans. 216.
22. *L'Innommable*, p. 18; trans. 292.
23. 'Il haletait. Il n'avait qu'à surgir en moi pour que je m'emplisse de halètements', *Molloy*, p. 156; trans. 108.
24. 'Peut-être l'avais-je inventée, je veux dire trouvée toute faite dans ma tête', *Molloy*, p. 154; trans. 107.
25. 'Je me demande si ce n'est pas encore de moi qu'il s'agit', *Malone meurt*, p. 23; trans. 183; 'je les suivais des yeux en geignant d'ennui, puis je les tuais, ou me mettais à leur place, ou m'enfuyais', p. 32; trans. 188.

26. 'Rien ne me ressemble moins', *Malone meurt*, p. 30; trans. 187.
27. 'Je les crois tous ici, à partir de Murphy tout au moins, je nous crois tous ici', *L'Innommable*, p. 10; trans. 287.
28. 'Je ne serai pas seul, les premiers temps. Je le suis bien sûr. Seul', *L'Innommable*, p. 8; trans. 286.
29. 'Ces Murphy, Molloy et autres Malone, je n'en suis pas dupe. Ils m'ont fait perdre mon temps, rater ma peine, en me permettant de parler d'eux, quand il fallait parler seulement de moi, afin de pouvoir me taire. [. . .] Que maintenant ils s'en aillent, eux et les autres, ceux qui m'ont servi, ceux qui attendent, qu'ils me rendent ce que je leur ai infligé et disparaissent, de ma vie, de mon souvenir, de mes hontes, de mes craintes. Voilà, il n'y a plus que moi ici, personne ne tourne autour de moi [. . .]. Et Basile et consorts? Inexistants, inventés pour expliquer je ne sais plus quoi', *L'Innommable*, pp. 27–8; trans. 297–98.
30. 'Si après tout nous ne faisions qu'un [. . .]? Si j'avais passé par là où selon lui j'ai passé?', *L'Innommable*, p. 47; trans. 309.
31. 'Chez les vivants', *L'Innommable*, p. 209; trans. 405; 'il n'a pas été donné encore d'établir avec le moindre degré de précision ce que je suis', *L'Innommable*, p. 168; trans. 382.
32. 'Il ne s'agit pas ici de Moll, qui n'est après tout qu'une femelle', *Malone meurt*, p. 144; trans. 256; 'des deux cons', *L'Innommable*, p. 59; trans. 316.
33. 'L'envie de m'être débattu, même brièvement, même faiblement, dans la grande trombe animée qui va des premiers protozoaires jusqu'aux hommes les plus récents', *L'Innommable*, p. 58; trans. 315; 'indéfectibles saloperies de chromosomes', *Molloy*, p. 110; trans. 75.
34. 'L'homme est un mammifère supérieur', *L'Innommable*, p. 83; trans. 331.
35. '*Struggle for life* ou élan vital', *Malone meurt*, p. 111; trans. 236, italics Beckett's.
36. 'Je me crois toujours plus malin que les choses. Il y a les hommes et les choses, ne me parlez pas des animaux', *Molloy*, p. 227; trans. 159.
37. 'Deux aspects d'une seule et même enveloppe charnelle, l'âme étant notoirement à l'abri des ablations et délabrements', *L'Innommable*, p. 72; trans. 324.
38. See Mary Bryden, *Beckett and the Idea of God* (London: MacMillan, 1998).
39. Tom Driver 1961 interview, quoted in Bryden p. 1.
40. 'Dans mon comportement extérieur sans doute. . . Mais pour le reste. . .', in conversation with Charles Juliet, quoted in Bryden, p. 1.
41. 'Une preuve superfétatoire de l'existence de Dieu', *Molloy*, p. 137; trans. 94.
42. 'Quant à Dieu, il commence à me dégouter', *Molloy*, p. 145; trans. 100; 'Dieu qui n'êtes pas plus au ciel que sur la terre et dans les enfers', p. 229; trans. 161; 'la voix que j'écoute, je n'ai pas eu besoin de Gaber pour me le transmettre. Car elle est en moi et elle m'exhorte à être jusqu'au bout ce fidèle serviteur que j'ai toujours été', p. 181; trans. 126. There is also possible symbolic meaning in the name of Youdi's messenger, Gaber, which recalls the Angel Gabriel.
43. 'Une voix parvient à quelqu'un dans le noir'; 'toi tel que toujours. Seul', *Compagnie* (Paris: Minuit, 1980), pp. 7, 88; Samuel Beckett, *Company, Ill Seen Ill Said, Worstward Ho, Stirrings Still*, ed. by Dirk Van Hulle (London: Bloomsbury, 2009), pp. 3, 42. David Ellison sees in *Compagnie* a homage to the opening *In Search of Lost Time*, with a narrator in each dissociated from self and lost in memory as he lies in bed. David Ellison, 'Proust and posterity', in *The Cambridge Companion to Proust*, ed. by R. Bales (Cambridge: Cambridge University Press, 2001), pp. 200–15.
44. 'Bribes d'une voix ancienne en moi pas la mienne'; 'une intelligence quelque part un amour [. . .] des pouvoirs exceptionnels [. . .] des aides sans nombre'; 'cette voix quaqua oui de la foutaise oui qu'une voix ici oui la mienne oui', *Comment c'est* (Paris: Minuit, 1961), pp. 9, 214, 224; trans. 3, 120, 127.
45. 'Sa volonté est faite', *L'Innommable*, p. 42; trans. 306.
46. 'Presque qu'on se résigne', *Malone meurt*, p. 87; trans. 222.
47. 'Lointaine analogie', *L'Innommable*, p. 14; trans. 289.
48. 'Le vrai portail de l'être', *Molloy*, p. 74; trans. 109.
49. 'Le doigt dans le nez, la main sous les couilles, le mouchage sans mouchoir et la pissade ambulante', *Molloy*, p. 32; trans. 21; 'horreur du corps et de ses fonctions', p. 162; trans. 113.
50. 'Ma tête mourra en dernier', *Malone meurt*, p. 177; trans. 276.
51. *Molloy*, p. 35; trans. 22.
52. *Proust*, pp. 18–19.
53. 'Ce sont [ces parties de l'ancien moi],—même les plus chétives, comme les obscurs attachements aux dimensions, à l'atmosphère d'une chambre—qui s'effarent et refusent, en des rébellions où il faut voir un mode secret, partiel, tangible et vrai de la résistance à la mort, de la longue résistance désespérée et quotidienne à la mort fragmentaire et successive telle qu'elle s'insère dans toute la durée de notre vie, détachant de nous à chaque moment des lambeaux de nous-mêmes sur la mortification desquels des cellules nouvelles multiplieront. Et pour une nature nerveuse comme était la mienne, c'est-à-dire chez qui les intermédiaires, les nerfs, remplissent mal leurs fonctions,—n'arrêtent pas dans sa route vers la

conscience, mais y laissent au contraire parvenir, distincte, épuisante, innombrable et douloureuse, la plainte des plus humbles éléments du moi qui vont disparaître—, l'anxieuse alarme que j'éprouvais sous ce plafond inconnu et trop haut, n'était que la protestation d'une amitié qui survivait en moi, pour un plafond familier et bas. Sans doute cette amitié disparaîtrait, une autre ayant pris sa place (alors la mort, puis une nouvelle vie auraient, sous le nom d'Habitude, accompli leur œuvre double)', Proust, *À la recherche du temps perdu*, II, p. 32; trans. 250.

54. *Proust*, p. 19.
55. 'Grande sourdine', Beckett, *En attendant Godot* (Paris: Minuit, 1952), p. 128; *Waiting for Godot* (New York: Grove Press, 1954), p. 58.
56. J. D. O'Hara, 'Where There's s Will There's a Way Out: Beckett and Schopenhauer', *College Literature*, 8.3 (1981), pp. 249–70 (p. 250).
57. *Proust*, p. 20.
58. 'L'accoutumance', *L'Innommable*, p. 110 ; trans. 347 ; 'Car l'ancienne souffrance, vous comprenez, je m'y étais en quelque sorte habitué, oui, en quelque sorte. Mais la nouvelle, quoique de la même famille exactement, je n'avais pas encore eu le temps de m'y ajuster', *Molloy*, pp. 104–105; trans. 71.
59. On the science of habituation, see, for instance, Larry R. Squire and Eric R. Kandel, *Memory: From Mind to Molecules*, 2nd edn (Greenwood Village, CO: Roberts and Company, 2009), pp. 28–30.
60. 'Je retrouverai le commissaire et ses aides. Et si j'ai trop changé pour les reconnaître, je ne précise pas que ce sont les mêmes, ne vous y trompez pas, ce seront les mêmes, quoique changés', *Molloy*, p. 36; trans. 23. In the English version, Molloy does indeed encounter a second 'sergeant' only a few pages further on, after running over Lousse's dog, and fails to make any comment on the man's identity.
61. 'Le poison me travaillait [. . .]. Le monde changeait déjà de couleur et de poids', *Molloy*, p. 133; trans. 92.
62. 'Changé'; 'un émiettement, [. . .] un effondrement rageur de tout ce qui depuis toujours me protégeait'; 'une sorte de forage de plus en plus rapide vers je ne sais quel jour et quel visage, connus et reniés', *Molloy*, p. 204; trans. 142.
63. 'Car en moi il y a toujours eu deux pitres, entre autres, celui qui ne demande qu'à rester là où il se trouve et celui qui s'imagine qu'il serait un peu moins mal plus loin', *Molloy*, p. 65; trans. 43–4.
64. 'Combien il m'était indifférent de me posséder', *Molloy*, p. 205; trans. 143.
65. 'Sentir, derrière mes yeux fermés, se fermer d'autres yeux', *Malone meurt*, p. 34; trans. 190.
66. 'Sort de moi, elle me remplit, elle clame contre mes murs, elle n'est pas la mienne'; 'cette voix qui n'est pas la mienne, mais qui ne peut être que la mienne, puisqu'il n'y a que moi [. . .]. C'est donc moi qui parle, tout seul', *L'Innommable*, pp. 33–4; trans. 301.
67. 'J'avais oublié qui j'étais (il y avait de quoi) et parlé de moi comme j'aurais parlé d'un autre', *Molloy*, p. 56; trans. 37.
68. 'J'ai l'air de parler, ce n'est pas moi, de moi, ce n'est pas de moi', *L'Innommable*, p. 7; trans. 285.
69. 'C'est peut-être ça que je sens, qu'il y a un dehors et un dedans et moi au milieu, c'est peut-être ça que je suis, la chose qui divise le monde en deux, d'une part le dehors, de l'autre le dedans, ça peut être mince comme une lame, je ne suis ni d'un côté ni de l'autre, je suis au milieu, je suis la cloison, j'ai deux faces et pas d'épaisseur, c'est peut-être ça que je sens, je me sens qui vibre, je suis le tympan, d'un côté c'est le crâne, de l'autre le monde, je ne suis ni de l'un ni de l'autre'; 'non, ce n'est pas ça, je ne sens rien de tout ça', *L'Innommable*, p. 376; trans. 377.
70. 'Car ce n'était pas un pot, plus il le voyait, plus il y pensait, plus il était sûr que ce n'était pas un pot, mais alors pas du tout. Ca ressemblait à un pot, c'était presque un pot, mais ce n'était pas un pot à en pouvoir dire, Pot, pot et en être réconforté', Samuel Beckett, *Watt* (Paris: Minuit, 1968), p. 8; original English version (Paris: Olympia, 1953), p. 78.
71. 'Un atome dans le noir de la liberté absolue'; 'dans une génération et dans un effondrement, sans cesse ni condition, de ligne', *Murphy* (Paris: Minuit, 1947), p. 100; original English version (London: Routledge, 1938), p. 112.
72. 'Dans une generation et dans une effondrement, sans cesse ni condition, de lignes', *Murphy* (Paris: Minuit, 1947), p. 100; original English version (London: Routledge, 1938), p. 112.
73. Roger Scruton, *The Aesthetic Understanding* (London: Methuen, 1983), p. 235.
74. 'En termes de ce qu'il n'est pas', *Molloy*, p. 52; trans. 35.
75. 'C'est sur moi que mes sens sont braqués. Muet, obscur et fade, je ne suis pas pour eux. Je suis loin des bruits de sang et de souffle, au secret. [. . .] Quelque part dans cette confusion, la pensée s'acharne, loin du compte elle aussi. Elle aussi me cherche, comme depuis toujours, là où je ne suis pas', *Malone meurt*, p. 19; trans. 180.
76. David H. Hesla, *The Shape of Chaos: An Interpretation of the Art of Samuel Beckett* (Minneapolis: University of Minnesota Press, 1971), p. 199.
77. On 'unhappy consciousness' ('unglückliche Bewuβtsein'), see G.W.F. Hegel, *The Phenomenology of Spirit*, trans. by A. V. Miller (Oxford: Oxford University Press, 1977), pp. 455-7.

78. 'Les deux rétines', *L'Innommable*, p. 23; trans. 295.
79. See Dobrez, pp. 63–84.
80 'Bientôt son corps serait tranquille, bientôt il serait libre', *Murphy*, p. 16; English version, p. 9.
81. 'Se sachant aussi impuissant à agir sur le déroulement des événements que la case sombre qui le renferme, se laisse aller peut-être à l'agréable sentiment de s'être dégagé de toute responsabilité', *Malone meurt*, p. 91; trans. 224.
82. 'Moi j'avais aimé l'image de ce vieux Geulincx, mort jeune, qui m'accordait la liberté, sur le noir navire d'Ulysse, de me couler vers le levant, sur le pont. C'est une grande liberté pour qui n'a pas l'âme des pionniers. Et sur la poupe, penché sur le flot, esclave tristement hilare, je regarde l'orgueilleux et inutile sillon. Qui, ne m'éloignant de nulle patrie, ne m'emporte vers nul naufrage', *Molloy*, p. 68; trans. 46. Geulincx is also mentioned in *Murphy*, p. 153.
83. 'L'harmonie préétablie', *Molloy*, p. 84; trans. 57.
84. 'Il me semble souvent que je suis dans une tête, et que ces huit, non, ces six parois sont en os massif', *Malone meurt*, p. 75; trans. 215.
85. 'Oubliette d'ivoire', *Nouvelles et Textes pour rien* (Paris: Minuit, 1958), p. 125 (Texte ii).
86. 'Le problème de la liberté, j'en traiterai aussi, c'est couru, au moment préétabli', *L'Innommable*, p. 85; trans. 332.
87. Arthur Schopenhauer, *The World as Will and Representation*, trans. by E.F.J. Payne, 2 vols (New York: Dover, 1966), i, p. 390.
88. See J. D. O'Hara, 'Where There's a Will There's a Way Out: Beckett and Schopenhauer', *College Literature*, 8.3 (1981), pp. 249–70 (p. 249).
89. 'Assez de cette putain de première personne, c'en est trop à la fin'; 'pour me faire croire que j'ai un moi à moi et que je peux en parler', *L'Innommable*, pp. 92, 97; trans. 336, 339.
90. Marco Bernini is one critic to have ventured into this territory, comparing the Unnamable's pared-down mentality to the 'centre of narrative gravity' in Daniel Dennett's model of consciousness. Marco Bernini, 'Gression, Regression and Beyond: A Cognitive Reading of *The Unnamable*', in *Samuel Beckett Today/Aujourd'hui: Revisiting Molloy, Malone meurt/Malone Dies, L'Innommable/The Unnamable*, ed. by David Tucker, Mark Nixon and Dirk Van Hulle (Amsterdam: Rodopi, 2014), pp. 193–209.
91. 'Je suis en mots, je suis fait de mots'; 'je suis tout autre chose, une chose muette, dans un endroit dur, vide', *L'Innommable*, p. 164; trans. 379–80.
92. 'Chaque fois que je dis, Je me disais telle et telle chose, ou que je parle d'une voix interne me disant, Molloy, et puis une belle phrase plus ou moins claire et simple, [. . .] je ne fais que me plier aux exigences d'une convention qui veut qu'on mente ou qu'on se taise. Car c'est tout autrement que les choses se passaient. Je ne me disais donc point, Du train où ça va, d'ici très peu de temps, etc., mais cela ressemblait peut-être à ce que je me serais dit, si j'en avais été capable. En fait je ne me disais rien du tout, mais j'entendais une rumeur, quelque chose de changé dans le silence, et j'y prêtais l'oreille, à la manière d'un animal j'imagine, qui tressaille et fait le mort. Et alors, quelquefois, il naissait confusément en moi une sorte de conscience, ce que j'exprime en disant, Je me disais, etc., [. . .]. Ou que j'exprime sans tomber aussi bas que dans l'oratio recta, mais au moyen d'autres figures, tout aussi mensongères, comme par exemple, Il me semblait que, etc., ou J'avais l'impression que, etc., car il ne me semblait rien du tout et je n'avais aucune impression d'aucune sorte, mais il y avait simplement quelque chose de changé quelque part, qui faisait que moi aussi je devais changer, ou que le monde lui aussi devait changer, afin que rien ne fût changé', *Molloy*, pp. 119–20; trans. 82.
93. 'Mais je me disais aussi, D'ici très peu de temps, du train où ça va, je ne pourrai plus me déplacer, mais où que je me trouve je serai obligé d'y rester, à moins d'être porté', *Molloy*, p. 119; trans. 82.
94. Damasio, *The Feeling of What Happens*, p. 185.
95. See, on this topic, Steven Pinker, *The Stuff of Thought: Language as a Window into Human Nature* (London: Allen Lane, 2008), pp. 148–50.
96. 'Ce sera mon nom aussi, au moment voulu, quand je n'aurai plus à m'appeler Mahood', *L'Innommable*, p. 84; trans. 331.
97. 'L'inexpugnable', *L'Innommable*, p. 100; trans. 341; 'Worm, dire qu'il ne sait pas ce qu'il est, où il est, ce qui se passe, c'est trop peu dire. Ce qu'il ignore, c'est qu'il y ait quelque chose à savoir. Ses sens ne lui apprennent rien, ni sur lui, ni sur le reste, et cette distinction lui est étrangère. Ne sentant rien, ne sachant rien, il existe pourtant, mais pas pour lui, pour les hommes, ce sont les hommes qui le conçoivent et qui disent, Worm est là', *L'Innommable*, p. 98; trans. 340.
98. 'De ne pouvoir faire attention', *L'Innommable*, p. 121; trans. 353.
99. 'Je suis Worm, non, si j'étais Worm je ne le saurais pas, je ne le dirais pas, je ne dirais rien, je ne saurais rien, je serais Worm. [. . .] Je suis Worm, c'est-à-dire que je ne le suis plus, puisque soudain j'entends', *L'Innommable*, pp. 100–3; trans. 341–3.

100. 'Et Worm dedans. Ne sentant rien, ne sachant rien, ne pouvant rien, ne voulant rien. Jusqu'au moment où il entend ce bruit qui ne cessera plus. Alors c'est la fin, Worm n'est plus', *L'Innommable*, p. 102; trans. 342.
101. 'Alors ce sera lui, ce sera moi', *L'Innommable*, p. 209; trans. 406.
102. Dobrez, p. 69.
103. Frye, 'The Nightmare Life in Death', p. 166.
104. Dennett, *Consciousness Explained*, p. 107.
105. See, for instance, Dennett, *Freedom Evolves*, p. 249: 'The centrepiece metaphor of this coevolved human user-illusion is the Self, which appears to reside in a place in the brain, the Cartesian Theatre, providing a limited, metaphorical outlook on what's going on in our brains'.
106. Dennett's Darwinian view of the origins of consciousness also has some resonance for Beckett's Worm, who resembles a phylogenetic throwback to an earlier stage in our mental development: 'Intentionality doesn't come from on high: it percolates up from below, from the initially mindless and pointless algorithmic processes that gradually acquire meaning and intelligence as they develop', *Darwin's Dangerous Idea*, p. 205.
107. Damasio, *Self Comes to Mind*, pp. 168–9.
108. Ned Block, 'On a Confusion about a Function of Consciousness', *Behavioral and Brain Sciences*, 18 (1995), pp. 227–87 (p. 232).
109. 'À la fin de mon œuvre, il n'y a rien que poussière: le nommable. Dans le dernier livre, *L'Innommable*, il y a complète désintégration. Pas de *Je*, pas de *Avoir*, pas de *Être*, pas de nominatif, pas d'accusatif, pas de verbe. Il n'y a pas moyen de continuer. La toute dernière chose que j'ai écrite, *Textes pour rien*, a été une tentative pour sortir de cette attitude de désintégration, mais ce fut un échec', Interview with Israël Shenker, *New York Times*, May 1956, quoted in Pierre Mélèse, *Samuel Beckett* (Paris: Seghers, 1986), p. 137.

6
TROPISM
Nathalie Sarraute

Nathalie Sarraute (1900–99) devoted her life to tropisms. Her unique view of the mind is the central concern of each of her thirteen prose works and six plays, and of almost all of her essays. From *Tropismes*, first published in 1939, to her final work, *Ouvrez* (*Open*, 1997), Sarraute focuses on the depiction of these 'faint inner movements which slip quickly by at the threshold of consciousness', which she figures as the origin of the conscious feelings we can label and the thoughts we can express in language.[1] My choice of *Childhood* as the central text of this chapter is to some degree an arbitrary one: every one of her texts offers a wealth of examples of her conception of mental life and her method of representing it, with a remarkable consistency of theory and technique, and I shall therefore be sampling widely across her œuvre. *Childhood* recommends itself largely for being her best-known and most widely read text, perhaps because its autobiographical subject matter is more accessible than her sometimes disorienting fiction with its anonymous voices and undetermined situations. It is also highly representative of Sarraute's concerns, combining the detailed evocation of tropisms from her earliest work with the concern for language as both cause and effect of tropistic activity from later texts, and the interest in the multiplicity of the self which will dominate her final texts. Being a memoir of childhood, *Childhood* offers Sarraute's most sustained exploration of the workings of memory, with interesting parallels and contrasts with Proust, whose own representation of the mind is one of Sarraute's primary reference points in her essays. *Childhood* is also Sarraute's only non-fiction narrative, which means that, like Breton's *Mad Love*, it is not only a creative imagining of consciousness, but also a declaration that the representation reflects the workings of a real mind, that tropisms are not poetic fancy but genuine mental phenomena that exist in Sarraute's mind, and, by implication, in our own. While links with Breton and Proust will be of interest, it is with Sartre that Sarraute has the most direct engagement among her precursors: Sartre was the first champion of Sarraute's work (although he would later take a more critical stance), and his presentation of Sarraute's first novel had a long-lasting effect on the reception of her work, to the author's occasional irritation. While much divides their conceptions of the mind, Sartre and Sarraute are united in their interest in intersubjectivity, the being-for-others of a mind which interacts with other minds, in a process which, for both thinkers, is characterized as a primarily hostile struggle for self-assertion. Sarraute sees her creative influences largely in terms of the literary, rather than philosophical, heritage of her work through Dostoevsky, Proust, Joyce, and Woolf. She is, however, very much aware of the two major rival theories of consciousness in twentieth-century culture. She is dismissive of psychoanalysis, which is nevertheless widely used by critics to interpret her work. But it is scientific psychology, in the form of the theories of behaviourism developed by B. F. Skinner and others that dominated psychology in the mid-century, which excites her particular disapproval, and in some of her essays she goes so far as to present her own project as a reaction to behaviourist influence on literature.

Childhood is Sarraute's tenth prose work, published when the writer was in her early eighties, although still with sixteen years of creativity, three further prose texts and a play ahead of her. Although autobiographical material had appeared in her work before, as certain familiar episodes in *Childhood* reveal, this was Sarraute's first overt foray into the genre, and her anxieties that it might be seen as a signal of her retirement, or a retreat from experimentation, are expressed in the opening pages. Any fears are quickly dispelled that this writer, whose uncompromising radicalism left her early work struggling to find publishers and readers, and whose essays on literature provide a rallying cry for the revolutionary ambitions of the New Novelists in the 1950s, may have mellowed with age. Even the form in which her opening anxieties are expressed testifies to the fact that this is no conventional memoir: two voices are in dialogue, one expressing the desire to explore the tropisms of her own childhood memories, the other expressing scepticism about the wisdom or feasibility of such a project. Both voices, it soon becomes clear, are avatars of Sarraute herself, and the dialogue is a staged conversation within her own mind between the impulse to narrate and the scruples which give her pause. The two voices will continue to produce the text between them, the one narrating, while the other questions, doubts, confirms, and extrapolates. For Valerie Minogue they are a 'burrower' and a 'sifter'; for Philippe Lejeune, a voice to narrate and a voice to check, listen, and collaborate.[2] For Sarraute, they are herself and her double, who is 'a more sensible side, a side that re-reads and asks, "why do you say this?"'[3] Between them, the narrator and her double unearth and dissect seventy individual fragments of memory, taken from Sarraute's life between the ages of two and twelve, during which time she lives alternately with each of her divorced parents in Paris and Russia. The book focuses particularly on the years 1909–12 at the end of this period, when the young Sarraute ('Natacha') is living in Paris with her father, stepmother Véra, and half-sister Hélène, and her mother is an increasingly distant figure in her life. Many of the fragments examine Natacha's interactions with her family, her increasing bond with her father, a fractious relationship with the stepmother who would like to be rid of her, and jealousy towards her favoured half-sister. Arcs of narrative can be recuperated from the text, as Natacha becomes ever closer to her father and more disillusioned with her mother, or as her relationship with Véra deteriorates, then moves towards a more sympathetic understanding, and as Natacha herself becomes a more autonomous individual, gaining control over her ideas and emotions, and taking the first steps of self-expression. However, the presentation of this material gives the reader little help or encouragement in this direction. Names, dates, and places are mentioned only as if in passing between the two voices, both of which have full access to Sarraute's memories. Episodes invariably open *in medias res* with the memory itself, which is often a fleeting impression or a single spoken phrase that has lingered in the narrator's mind. Rather than taking these moments as a starting point for an unfolding chronology, Sarraute generally prefers to remain within the moment itself, exploring the effects of the experience on the child's mind, with the two voices working in tandem to unearth the emotional repercussions triggered, and cautiously disentangling the impressions of the child who lived through the experience from the more sophisticated adult she has become. The goal of the narrating voices is, as ever in Sarraute, to recover the tropisms of the experience and evoke them in the text. The problem, as ever for the writer, is that tropisms are, by the very definition Sarraute gives them, non-linguistic. Sarraute's primary interest in *Childhood*, and throughout her œuvre, is to find the means to render these fleeting and amorphous mental phenomena through language, and to trace how they are sparked by, and how they themselves develop into the clear, crude primary colours of traditional psychology or the ill-fitting and socially inhibited conventions of spoken discourse.

The term *tropism* is taken from biological science, where it refers to movement or growth in an organism, particularly in plants, in response to an environmental stimulus, such as turning towards a light source. For Sarraute's adoption of the term as metaphor, the three significant elements are the status of tropisms as a biological process, their involuntary nature, and the external source of the stimulus: Sarraute's tropisms are always a reaction to something impinging on consciousness from outside, generally another human being, which makes her principal object of study not so much the mind itself as the interaction of minds. Although tropisms are now indelibly associated with her work, Sarraute isn't the first literary writer to make use of the term. In *Les Caves du Vatican* (*The Vatican Cellars*, 1914), André Gide has a character conduct scientific experiments into animal behaviour, partly based on the work of Jacques Loeb, who originally coined the word:

> While waiting to get stuck into the human, Anthime Armand-Dubois claimed simply to reduce all the behaviour of the animals he was observing to 'tropisms'. Tropisms! The term was no sooner minted than already nobody understood anything else any more; a whole category of psychologists would no longer have anything other than *tropisms*. Tropisms! What sudden illumination emanated from these syllables! Clearly organisms reacted to the same stimuli as does the sunflower when the plant involuntarily turns its face to the sun (which is easily reducible to a few simple laws of physics and biochemistry). The cosmos was finally endowed with a reassuring benignancy. In the most surprising movements of a creature one could plainly recognize perfect obedience to the active force.[4]

Gide's intentions are satirical. Anthime's school of 'psycho-physiology' is bent on reducing the mind to a mechanistic system of stimulus-response, which will expose free will as an illusion and banish the concept of the human soul. (His stance is, in fact, the set-up for a dramatic conversion to equally extreme religious belief later in the story.) The experiments in animal conditioning by which he lays the foundations for his theory are strongly reminiscent of those carried out by Loeb, who taught the 'father of behaviourism', John B. Watson, at the University of Chicago. The experiments on tropisms in animals carried out by Loeb and Watson formed the foundation of Watson's 1925 study, *Behaviorism*, which was the formative influence on Skinner's thought. In Anthime, arguably we have literature's first behaviourist.

Sarraute is quite aware of the term's heritage when she adopts it (she herself employs the example of plants responding to light in her explanations),[5] but makes clear that she is neither using it in its strict scientific sense, nor bound by its behaviourist implications:

> This word 'tropism' was a compromise solution. I was looking for a title for my first book which might evoke as best I could all these indefinable feelings and, and the time, 'tropism' was in the air. I thought it might apply to those kinds of instinctive movements which are independent of our will, which are provoked by external stimuli.[6]

She is, however, happy to appropriate the scientist's attitude of objective observation and recording to describe her methods. She tells Simone Benmussa that *Tropismes* itself consisted of 'soundings by which I reached a certain level of consciousness where I settled myself in'.[7] Of her later work, she says:

> My site of investigation lies right on the edge of the subconscious, anyone can find it if they take the time to stop there, to put effort in, but generally people have other things to do [. . .]. For my part, I stop precisely there. I set up my microscope, I film in slow-motion and I watch what happens.[8]

The siting of tropisms at the very limits of conscious perception is an important aspect of Sarraute's concept of mind. If these mental phenomena are 'the secret source of our existence', as Sarraute says in her most famous definition of them, and if they are involuntary and quasi-physiological, more akin to reflex actions than intellectual thought, then there would seem to be little room for a complex and semi-autonomous unconscious mind lying beneath them.[9] Rather, tropisms are presented as if they were the lowest level of mental activity before we come to the basic mechanisms of bodily regulation, like the neural impulses that have us recoil from pain or the adrenaline floods that make us tremble with fear, and this proximity is reinforced by the use of precisely such physiological processes as metaphors for the mind's reactions to the words or perceptions which impinge on it. Take, for example, the very first tropism to appear in *Childhood*, where the young Natacha wields her governess's scissors with the intention of slashing the sofa upholstery, and is sternly forbidden to do so:

> 'No, you're not to do that' . . . these words flow in a heavy, massive tide, what it carries with it sinks into me in order to crush what is stirring in me, what is trying to rise . . . and under this pressure, it braces itself, rises more vigorously, rises higher, grows, and violently projects out of me the words . . . 'Yes, I'm going to do it'.[10]

The governess's prohibition is an invasive flow into the child's body; her attempt to suppress Natacha's misbehaviour is represented as downward pressure, in opposition to the upward stirrings of the child's rebellious desire, which reacts violently to expel the interdiction with a forthright declaration of will. The imagery calls to mind the vomit reflex, but deliberately mixes in other, incompatible images from biology and the natural world in order that the mental processes described shouldn't be reducible to a simple metaphor, such as 'rebellion against oppression is like vomiting out food'. Rather, the tropistic movement is a unique entity, which is reminiscent of physiological processes but has no direct counterpart among them.

In situating tropisms at the most basic level of mental functioning, Sarraute distances them from higher-level cognitive processes, including language. She holds that they can therefore be neither labelled nor explained with words, and, consequently, 'it was possible to communicate them to the reader only through images which might give equivalents to them and make the reader experience analogous sensations'.[11] (There's an echo here of the 'love's knowledge' found in Proust, except in this case it is the reader, rather than the character, who intuits understanding through means other than the intellectual.) The range of metaphors Sarraute employs to this end is wide. From biology come an array of movements, such as trembling, surging, wilting, or creeping, along with odours and secretions, and sensory impressions of solidity or fragility, fixity or flow. Higher-order human activities also feature, often counterpointing anodyne social interaction with images of extreme violence or peril, such as tight-rope walking over a fatal drop, or using another person as a human shield against enemy fire.[12] Similar intensifications come from recourse to images from fantasy or fairy-tales: a privileged gathering is isolated in the artificial atmosphere of a spaceship, the narrator of *Martereau* picks his way through a conversation like Tom Thumb following a trail of pebbles through the forest.[13] Animal and plant images are the most plentiful of all, returning tropisms to their scientific origins and emphasizing the instinctive or automatic quality of the mental event: tentacles and gossamer threads drift out to ensnare others, conversation partners are figured as predators and prey, people withdraw into themselves like snails into shells. Again, metaphors are deliberately mixed into a collage of images which jointly express a more complex and nuanced sensation. In the course of a page-long encounter between the narrator of *Portrait d'un inconnu* (*Portrait of a Man Unknown*, 1948) and the man who obsesses and intimidates him, images are evoked of a small animal sniffed out by a predator, then a rock-pool crab poked with a metal rod, then a patch of nettle-stung skin; seven lines later the crab image reappears with the narrator having switched roles from the crab to its tormentor.[14]

Such accumulations are an integral part of Sarraute's style. Words are lined up, examined and discarded in the attempt to conjure a wordless feeling. In *Childhood*, the narrator considers 'happiness', 'felicity', 'exaltation', and 'ecstasy' as possible descriptions of the intense sensation she once experienced in the Jardin du Luxembourg, before settling on 'joy', with the proviso that the word 'cannot gather up what fills me, brims over in me, disperses, dissolves, melts into the pink bricks, the blossom-covered espaliers, the lawn, the pink and white petals, the air vibrating with barely perceptible tremors'.[15] The sequence serves a number of functions. It dramatizes the mental process in the present as the narrator and her double search for the language that will express the remembered sensation. Hesitancy and uncertainty are the chief traits of this process: the paragraph in question contains twelve negatives, three question marks, and fourteen ellipses in the space of two sentences, suggesting a mind groping its way towards a definition. The sensation itself is thereby characterized as something precise yet linguistically undefinable, and the string of discarded labels has the dual purpose of distinguishing the tropism from the emotions of conventional psychology and encircling it with a series of not-quite-apt descriptions which gesture towards the non-existent term lying beyond them, a process Stéphane Bikialo calls 'a compromise with the failure of words and sensations to coincide'.[16] The sequence is completed with the inadequate word 'joy' grudgingly accepted, and modified by the transcendent image of vibrations in the air, but it's clear that the sensation evoked lies not in this final word and image as the 'correct answer' to the narrator's search for expression but in the entire sequence, in the alternatives considered along the way, and in the struggle itself to render the sensation through language.

Sarraute's particular fascination with non-linguistic or pre-linguistic thought, and the conundrum of how to render it through words on the page, sets her in the lineage of the experimental writers of literary modernism (including Beckett), with Virginia Woolf as a notable and acknowledged forebear. Wordless mental activity is constantly emphasized in Woolf's fiction, as in this example from *To the Lighthouse* (1927), in which Lily Briscoe finds herself standing outside the drawing-room window through which she watched the now-dead Mrs Ramsay ten years previously, and silently feels her loss:

> For how could one express in words these emotions of the body? Express that emptiness there? (She was looking at the drawing-room steps; they looked extraordinarily empty.) It was one's body feeling, not one's mind. The physical sensations that went with the bare look of the steps had become suddenly extremely unpleasant. To want and not to have, sent all up her body a hardness, a hollowness, a strain.[17]

Lily's inchoate grief takes the form of a nondeclarative memory from ten years before, linking her present moment looking towards the drawing-room window with the previous occasion, but without conscious awareness of anything but an emptiness to her perception and an unpleasantness to her emotions. The *style indirect libre* leaves it ambiguous as to whether it is the impersonal narrator or Lily herself who then analyzes these feelings and expresses them in language, but either way, the original experience did not involve language, and indeed felt so far from such higher cognitive functions as to not be a mental event at all, but rather a purely corporeal one. This interconnection of mind and body, particularly where strong emotion is concerned, is clear link between Woolf's and Sarraute's work.

If tropisms exist at a level of the mind beneath that of language, do they also exist at a level beneath consciousness? Their uncertain status between thought, sensation, and reflex puts into question the whole concept of the divisibility of the mind into conscious and unconscious realms.

Like the depths and nuances of the Proustian mind, tropisms may become *perceptible* to consciousness with patience and effort, but they are certainly not conscious processes in their everyday occurrence:

> I am trying to piece together these dramas, which are not perceived by consciousness as they are happening, as they are extremely faint and quick, I am trying to recreate them as if they were seen through a microscope in slow-motion. Outside, in the clarity of our consciousness, they are covered by a word like 'malaise'. Or 'sympathy', etc. But this 'malaise' and this 'sympathy' are only the breach, the arrival at the surface—where they are caught and held in an established definition—of indefinable movements, which, in my eyes, exist in the way of the invisible movement of atomic particles.[18]

The texts present mental activity as a continuum, in which non-linguistic tropisms develop into the 'pre-dialogue' or 'sub-conversation' which is Sarraute's equivalent of internal monologue, and corresponds to what we would ordinarily consider thought: 'In my books, there is inner monologue but it is preceded by these movements, these tropisms which push the words and bring on the inner sentence'.[19] We see the smooth transition from wordless sensation to unspoken then spoken language in this impression of Pierre from *Le Planétarium* (*The Planetarium*, 1959):

> It's a sort of beam he emits, like a fluid, it flows towards you from his narrowed eyes, from his Buddha smile, from his silence . . . she doesn't know what it is . . . it's his charm . . . he is charming: 'Your father-in-law is charming, don't you think?'[20]

We begin with tropistic images of exuded light or liquid which express a non-verbalized impression of his character, gained from remembered perceptions of his presence. From here reflective consciousness extrapolates the conventional psychological label 'charm', which is expressed first silently in linguistic thought, then, finally, spoken out loud as a communicated idea. In this example, unspoken and spoken language are clearly distinguished, but this is not always the case in Sarraute: 'No separation between pre-dialogue and dialogue,' Sarraute declares. 'One ends in the other'.[21] In Fragment XIV of *Tropismes*, the line, 'pay no attention, I'm quite all right like this', is associated with the figure of a maiden aunt surrounded by her younger relatives, but its status is unspecified.[22] Do we infer that the words are spoken aloud to ward off inclusion in the conversation? Do they represent a conscious but unspoken attitude on her part? Or an inference on the part of those who are with her? We are left to draw our own conclusions. *Ouvrez* takes this idea to its limit with its premise of autonomous utterances moving between the private spaces of the mind and a social space in which they interact with the utterances of others.

Given the incompatibility of their visions, it is not hard to understand Sarraute's impatience with Freud, and with those who would apply his theories to her work. She considers psychoanalysis 'a faith [which] has nothing to do with science', and says of its founder: 'Freud shows a universe which has nothing in common with what I am trying to write. A universe which can only be discovered via Freudian categories which are always identical and simple. I find his theories highly reductive and simplistic'.[23] The texts themselves are sometimes explicitly anti-Freudian. The psychoanalyst of *Portrait d'un inconnu* pathologizes the narrator's perception of tropisms; subsequent characters who venture into psychoanalytic discourse in *Le Planétarium* and the play *Isma* (1970) are shouted down by others, hilariously and at length in the latter: 'No. Not the parents. Not the children . . . Oh, no . . . Spare us . . . Not the complexes. The repressions. The regressions. The infant fixations. Not that: ready-made. Off-the-peg. All-purpose. These terrible mass-produced things'.[24] Sarraute is no more respectful of Lacan, telling Arnaud Rykner that the child's punning on the word 'héros' in *Entre la vie et la mort* (*Between Life and Death*, 1968) was in part intended to demonstrate that Lacanian wordplay was no different from the language-play common to all children.[25] Although Sarraute has long made clear that she considers psychoanalytic interpretations of her work to be 'almost always entirely wrong', there is abundant psychoanalytic criticism of all her œuvre, with *Childhood* an inevitable focus.[26] John Phillips cites as justification Sarraute's admission that 'the irrational, unconscious aspect' in the writing process is too great for her to fully understand her own creativity, and goes on to suggest that the very fact Sarraute appears 'anxious to dismiss' psychoanalytic interpretation may be evidence for its relevance.[27]

Certain aspects of *Childhood* do indeed contain echoes of the Freudian understanding of the mind. The narrator claims that her feeling of rejection on hearing her mother complain about reading at her sickbed 'had soon vanished', to which the double responds: 'sunk, perhaps, but. . . .', suggesting repression.[28] The narrator remains dubious, however, and the fragment ends with the assertion that maternal affection would wipe out such traumas. More generally, the relationship between the two voices has been described as similar to that between analyst and analysand, including by Monique Gosselin-Noat, who suggests the double's role is the midwifery of deep-lying memories.[29] Emer O'Beirne takes a similar view, but suggests that the self-analysis is in fact an anti-Lacanian strategy to ward off any encounter with a genuine Other, such as the reader.[30] Marianne Schmutz is one critic to express scepticism towards such readings, pointing out that, with only one example in the book of the double imposing an interpretation against the narrator's resistance, the figure seems closer to sympathetic friend than therapist.[31]

It is in the essay, 'Ce que voient les oiseaux' ('What Birds See', 1964) that Sarraute compares and condemns her two *bêtes noires* of psychological theory: psychoanalysis for oversimplifying mental life, and behaviourism for doing away with it entirely:

> One must only remember what a revelation the internal monologue was for us; the distrust with which we had considered, and sometimes still consider the efforts of Henry James or Proust to disassemble the delicate clockwork of our internal mechanisms; how eagerly we accept that some framework—like psychoanalysis—imposed on this great moving mass which we call our 'inner self', where you can discover whatever you want, covers it completely and takes account of all its movements; how satisfied we were, what a feeling of deliverance we had to allow ourselves to be convinced, and remain convinced, in the case of most of us, that this 'inner self', so recently still fertile in discoveries, did not exist, was nothing: emptiness, wind.[32]

Out of the two, it is behaviourism, rather than psychoanalysis, that Sarraute perceives as her most formidable enemy. While she is content generally to dismiss or ignore the latter, behaviourism and its influence on mid-twentieth-century literature form the target of her active opposition, as she asserts to the *Times Literary Supplement*: 'All my articles strive to defend what these days is contemptuously referred to as "psychology" against so-called "behaviourist" tendencies'.[33] What Sarraute objects to is the 'radical behaviourism' of psychologists like Skinner, for whom consciousness is an epiphenomenon, a mental by-product, and feelings are the consequences of actions rather than the cause. In this view, our actions can be understood in terms of the successive reinforcements that determine our behaviour, without reference to the thoughts, intentions, and emotions of traditional psychology.[34] Sarraute sums up the behaviourist view of humanity as a 'soulless body buffeted by hostile forces, [which] was definitively nothing other than what it appeared to be from the outside': behind the received ideas and conditioned behaviour lies 'a deep void'.[35] Sarraute regarded such ideas as being both scientifically and culturally dominant at the time of writing (the essay was first published in 1947). She felt their cultural effect had been to render introspective fiction like Proust's, and by implication, her own, hopelessly old-fashioned, while the behaviourist novel ruled the roost, exemplified by Hemingway and other American writers of his generation, by Kafka and, most particularly, by Camus's *L'Étranger* (*The Outsider*, 1942). The behaviourist novel as defined by Sarraute is a novel of surfaces, viewing its characters from the outside and ignoring their inner lives as irrelevant or non-existent:

> Behaviourist novelists, who use dialogue abundantly set with brief indications or discreet comments, are pushing the novel dangerously towards the domain of theatre, where is can only find itself in a state of inferiority. By renouncing the means that are available to the novelist alone, they renounce everything that makes it a separate art form, not to say what makes it an art form at all.[36]

Kafka is perhaps unfairly included in this company: his characters may reveal little of their private thoughts and emotions, but the environment in which they find themselves resembles a dreamscape conjured from their secret shame and fear. With Hemingway and the other American writers (John Steinbeck and John Dos Passos are cited), Sarraute seems more justified in her characterization, as much of Hemingway's writing renounces focalization to give us an exclusively external perspective.[37] As she acknowledges, cinema may be as much an influence as behaviourism here. With *L'Étranger*, however, there can be no doubt:

> [Meursault] had the undeniable advantage over Dos Passos's or Steinbeck's heroes of being depicted, not externally and from a distance as theirs are, but from the inside, by the classic procedure of introspection dear to lovers of the psychological: it was from up close, and, one might say, seated in the front row, that we could see his inner void.[38]

Sarraute accuses Camus of not having the courage of his convictions. The dénouement of *L'Étranger*, she contends, restores the full psychological richness to Meursault as he rediscovers his passion in the condemned cell, and thereby reveals his former blankness to have been a ruse all along. It has been a deliberate concealment by both narrator and author, rather than an authentic absence, and the reader can't help but feel 'a certain resentment' at the misdirection.[39]

Regardless of whether we agree with Sarraute's interpretation of Camus, it provides a clear illustration of her notion of behaviourist literature, and demonstrates how her own creativity defines itself in opposition. Sarraute ranges herself on the side of those who believe in inner life, and attempt to represent its complexity. Dostoevsky is the precursor: his methods of representing the 'underlying movements' of conventional psychology may have been 'primitive procedures', but they paved the way for his modernist successors.[40] Proust, whom Sarraute first read in 1924, left her 'literally overwhelmed' and strongly affected her own creative development.[41] She shares with him an interest in the small details of consciousness, the methods of quiet introspection into the self combined with forensic observation of others which are needed to uncover them, and the widespread use of metaphor to evoke mental phenomena too subtle to be rendered in conventional psychological discourse. The hyper-sensitive narrators of Sarraute's first two novels are strongly reminiscent of Proust's Narrator, underlining the formative aspect of Proust's influence, from which Sarraute will subsequently move away. Where *Childhood* is concerned, we see a similarly vivid recapture of memory over the distance of a lifetime. Emer O'Beirne writes that Sarraute's text displays 'a Proustian faith in a sensory memory which preserves sensations intact over time and outside language'.[42] Schmutz concurs that memory in Sarraute has the power to revive events with the intensity of relived experience, but emphasizes the highly fragmentary nature of this recall: a single sensation or snatched perception is brought to life, but, unlike in Proust, it fails to resurrect a world of past experience in its wake.[43] In her own discussion of Proust, it is the difference from her work that is Sarraute's focus:

> In Proust, it remains as retrospective analysis, of a complex kind, because it is about rediscovering the various temporal threads from which the movement is woven: there are temporal layers, but in order to 'result' in that moment. It's no longer in progress.[44]

Rather than retrospective presentation, 'at rest and as if frozen in memory', Sarraute plunges the reader into their midst; rather than analysis, Sarraute aims for vivid evocation, urging her readers to feel viscerally rather than understand intellectually: 'Conversation et sous-conversation' calls for:

> a technique which would manage to plunge the reader into the flow of these subterranean dramas that Proust only had the time to fly over, and of which he only observed and reproduced the immobile outlines: a technique which might give the reader the illusion of carrying out these actions himself with a more lucid consciousness, with more order, clarity and strength than he can achieve in life, without the actions losing the aspect of indeterminacy, the opacity and mystery that one's actions always have for the person experiencing them.[45]

Sarraute charts a modernist development from Proustian fixity to a more fluid representation of consciousness in Joyce and Woolf, both of whom she discovered shortly after reading Proust. Comparing these writers to Proust, she comments: 'With *Ulysses* and *Mrs Dalloway*, it becomes mobile, but in Virginia Woolf it is interior monologue, thoughts, etc., formulated, but in the process of arrival'.[46] In Woolf and Joyce, then, Sarraute finds the immediacy of consciousness in flow, but considers its representation to be limited to the higher orders of consciousness in which thoughts are formulated linguistically. Combining this immediacy with the pre-linguistic realms of the most basic mental activity explored by Proust and Dostoevsky, Sarraute opens up new literary territory for her own work.

If Sarraute's understanding of her own work thus ranks her among the introspective modernists, in opposition to 'behaviourist' Hemingway and Camus, there remains to be explained her curious choice of the proto-behaviourist concept of the tropism as the central element of her writing. An early critic of the *nouveau roman*, Yvon Belaval, expresses scepticism at the perceived opposition between Alain Robbe-Grillet, her fellow 'New Novelist' whose work was labelled 'objective literature' by Roland Barthes, and the 'subjectivity' of Sarraute:

> A rather curious polemic, with Alain Robbe-Grillet taking his agronomist's subjectivity for objectivity, and Nathalie Sarraute her psychologist's objectivity for subjectivity. And anyway, if we're dealing with behaviourist objectivity, it is really not sufficient to talk of stripped-down language, it is necessary that what is seen should be of interest to nobody and that the facts should be linked up between themselves, rather than linked to the gaze of a Voyeur or a Jealous husband. Conversely, a psychologist's objectivity, especially in art, resides in the interest of what is seen—looking inwards? outwards? no matter!—that is, in the linking of the facts to a subject. We have this all wrong. Is it by chance that the behaviourist takes his titles from introspection—*The Voyeur, Jealousy*—while the poet of consciousness entitles her first publication *Tropismes?*[47]

Belavel is undoubtedly correct in his assessment of Robbe-Grillet, who would himself in later years repudiate 'objective' interpretations of his work to insist on the 'hidden monsters' of the observing psyche in the apparently clinical descriptions of what is observed.[48] Where Sarraute is concerned, though, the comparison pushes her into a stance she would not recognize: far from insisting on the 'subjectivity' of her writing, she voluntarily adopts the discourse of the scientific observer to describe her perspective on her material, as we have seen. Nevertheless, Belavel is right in characterizing Sarraute's view as a psychologist's objectivity, and one that is arguably more objective than Robbe-Grillet's focalizations through disturbed minds, and he is prescient to do so in 1958, before Sarraute abandoned first-person narrators for impersonal perspectives.

Sarraute's quarrel with the psychologists stems from behaviourism's dismissive attitude to conscious experience, such as Skinner's contention that 'mental life and the world in which it is lived are inventions. They have been invented on the analogy of external behaviour occurring under external contingencies. Thinking is behaving. The mistake is in allocating the behaviour to the mind'.[49] Her attitude is less clear towards the other major behaviourist tenet implied in the term 'tropism', the determinist conception of behaviour as innate or conditioned response to stimulus, without the intervention of free will. Sarraute's one mention of determinism, in the essay 'De Dostoïevsky à Kafka' ('From Dostoevsky to Kafka', 1947), quotes with scepticism Claude-Edmonde Magny's description of modern man as 'reduced [. . .] to the triple determinism of hunger, sexuality and social class: Freud, Marx and Pavlov', an attitude which Sarraute sees as conducive to Hemingway's and Camus's literary projects.[50] Yet in her own writing, the emphasis is often on the involuntary nature of the acts she describes. Words are blurted out thoughtlessly, as in *Ouvrez*, where a rogue 'au revoir' escapes prematurely from the private mental sphere to put a premature end to a telephone call mid-conversation.[51] Thoughts themselves can be equally beyond the control of the subject, as most dramatically illustrated in *Childhood* by Natacha's 'ideas'. As a young child, she is prey to thoughts she cannot control, such as the idea that her mother is less beautiful than a doll seen in a shop window:

> Now that this idea has entrenched itself in me, it is not just a matter of willpower for me to dislodge it. I can force myself to uproot it, to put another idea in its place, but only for a time . . . it's still there, crouching in a corner, ready to get up at any moment, to push everything else out of its way, to occupy the whole space. . . . It seems that trying to keep it down, to suppress it, only increases its growth.[52]

It's true that the older Natacha registers a victory of self-control over such thoughts, but similar representations of the self as the victim of uncontrolled thoughts are prevalent in many of Sarraute's adult characters, such as Tante Berthe's obsession with the handle of her new door in *Le Planétarium*, or the father's compulsive deciphering of his children's laughter in *Vous les entendez?* (*Can You Hear Them?*, 1972). (Roquentin's thoughts of the dead café owner in *Nausea* are a similar phenomenon.) Behaviour too is often compulsive: 'Once I have embarked on this business, I simply can't stop', writes Sarraute of her uncontrollable childhood urge to work through with her paper knife to the end of a book, once she has begun the process of cutting the pages.[53] Most often, the compulsion comes from an external source. The 'vomit-reflex' tropism we saw earlier for rebellion against authority lends to the mental process an air of automatism, of simple cause and effect that is very much in tune with a behaviourist understanding of the mind. Similarly, *L'Usage de la parole* (*The Use of Speech*, 1980) is based around a series of examples in which a spoken phrase has an impact on the receiving consciousness which can seem mechanistic, as when the force of a speaker's conversation seems to physically prevent his listener from objecting to the condescending use of the phrase 'my lad':

> What has happened to him? He can't move, it is as if he has been tied up. It's, who among us hasn't felt this way . . . it's that he is caught up in the thread of the conversation, or rather that this thread is wrapping itself around him, holding him trapped.[54]

Such examples have interesting parallels with contemporary research into the mental activity underlying decision-making in experimental psychology, which may undermine confidence in our free will by bringing to light the lower-order mental activity subtending our conscious decisions. Separate experiments by W. Grey Walter and Benjamin Libet measured cerebral activity with electrodes as the subject decided when to clench a fist or progress through a slide show. The discovery that the brain activity which led to the action preceded the subject's awareness of having taken a decision to act by around 400 milliseconds encouraged Libet to make the claim that 'cerebral initiation of a spontaneous voluntary act begins unconsciously'.[55] The experiment doesn't, of course, prove that conscious decision-making is an illusion, and Daniel C. Dennett is one philosopher to take a sceptical view of Libet's findings.[56] (Dennett argues that our intuition of consciousness unified at a single point in time is a fallacy, and that it is in fact the product of many nearly-but-not-quite simultaneous events occurring in different parts of the brain.) It does, though, present a view of the mind which has much in common with the automatic responses to external stimuli that Sarraute places 'at the origin of our gestures, our words, the feelings that we display, that we think we are feeling and that it is possible to define'.[57]

In the end, though, we must conclude that Sarraute's emphasis on the involuntary, on the instinctive, and on the mental activity occurring upstream of conscious thought are not sufficient to make her a determinist. There are demonstrations of free will in action in several of her texts. The most notable example from *Childhood* is the choice Natacha is required to make between continuing to live with her father or returning to her mother. The narration of the episode leaves no doubt that Natacha is in control of the decision: 'It will be painful for me to be the one to sever the bond that still attaches me to my mother', she says as she makes up her mind, and feels afterwards 'the certainty that I had made the right choice for myself'.[58] The mental processes of creativity demonstrate in microcosm Sarraute's ambivalence between passive and active conceptions of the subject. In *Childhood*, as Natacha discovers her love of writing in a school essay on 'My First Sorrow', the narration highlights her conscious mastery of the language she employs:

> I make them reverberate . . . should I change the place of that one? . . . I listen once again . . . really, the sentence they make unfolds and falls into place very nicely . . . still just a slight rearrangement perhaps . . . and then I must stop examining it, I might easily spoil it.[59]

In the earlier *Entre la vie et la mort*, however, the unnamed writer-protagonist seems under the control of the systems of language itself as he writes:

> Words reign over him. Their humble subject feels only too honoured to offer them his home. They are to make themselves at home, everything is theirs here, they are wholly in command. [. . .] They reflect each other, they mirror each other . . . And he is caught in the labyrinth of their mirrors, imprisoned by the interlacing of their reflections. . . . He turns, sent from one to another.[60]

While her representation of free will in consciousness must remain ambiguous, we can see clearly that mind for Sarraute is a very different entity from the absolute freedom and self-determination that we saw in Sartre's existentialist model. Where Sartre's subject has complete control over choices taken, and any abdication of responsibility for them is a moral failing, in Sarraute the reflective consciousness in which free will may plausibly operate is only the visible outcome of more humble mental processes in the shadows, processes which have little to do with choice or freedom. In memory, it is Proust's involuntary version she echoes, rather than voluntary memory, and even here, the method of recovery is far more passive than it is in *In Search of Lost Time*: the first three fragments of *Ici* (*Here*, 1995) all narrate the return of forgotten memories in a process for which conscious effort is either a hindrance or an irrelevance.[61] And, much as she would no doubt be displeased at the comparison, Sarraute is closer to Breton's mystical view of consciousness shaped and channelled by unknown forces emanating from within and without, or even to Bernanos's view of minds unwittingly guided by a higher power, than she is to the clear-sighted helmsman of existentialist consciousness found in Sartre's texts.

Where Sarraute finds more common ground with Sartre is in their shared focus on intersubjectivity, on the importance of other people in the formation of the self and the processes of thought. As Sarraute tells Simone Benmussa, 'I seek reactions between consciousnesses, and I don't care which ones. It could be an old woman or a young man, it doesn't matter. At that level, the effect on the other consciousness is the same'.[62] When *communicating vases* appear as a metaphor for minds in Sarraute, they don't refer to the conscious and unconscious mind of a single individual, as was the case in Breton, but to the interaction of a pair of minds, which, in the case of the aunt and uncle of *Martereau*, appear to have a fixed quantity of cheer that flows periodically from one to the other.[63] In isolation, consciousness in Sarraute does not conceive of itself as such, but instead is both everything and nothing, 'a world unto itself . . . the whole world'.[64] Minds in Sarraute are seen in terms of a subjective universe, an outward-looking, un-self-conscious, unique perspective on the world. Rykner argues that a Husserlian phenomenological view is essential to understand the merging of self and world which occurs in Sarraute's writing.[65] We're shown the subjective nature of perception in *Childhood*, as the narrators matter-of-factly describe Natacha's fever-hallucinations as if they were real (p. 1007; trans. 29), or more extensively in *Portrait d'un inconnu*, where the father's gaze seems to create its object as much as receive it:

> According to his whim or his mood, depending on which or other of them has his preference at the time, the spectacle changes. Everything changes. According to his whim. The world tamely expands to infinite proportions, or on the contrary, contracts. It becomes narrow and dark or immense and transparent. At his whim, colours change. Nothing is fixed. Nothing is imposed on him. Under his impulse, like the light web on which the spider sways, the world rocks and trembles.[66]

The idiosyncratic nature of our own subjective universe is invisible to us until contact with another makes us aware of our different outlooks, as indeed happens to the father in *Portrait d'un inconnu*, when he finds himself 'ripped from his malleable, cosy world' by a discussion with the maid about a bathroom leak, and 'brutally thrust into her world, which is hard, aggressive and implacable'.[67] *Le Planétarium* takes its title from such violent shifts in perspective, demonstrated most vividly in the closing pages when a sudden awareness that Germaine's value-judgments differ fundamentally from his own is experienced by Alain like the disorienting whirl of stars on a planetarium ceiling: 'Everything suddenly swings around, tips over . . . she herself recedes, she is disappearing over the other side'.[68]

It is in these meetings of minds that Sarraute's aesthetic project of exploding the fixed character-types of realist fiction merges with her narrative project, as this very process of constructing character out of the ever-shifting complexity of consciousness is seen, not only as the activity of the traditional novelist, but as the universal reflex of human interaction. The psychological categories out of which the traditional literary character is constructed are no different from the permanent attributes and crude approximations through which we conceive the personality of others. Sarraute differentiates between the 'psychique' and the 'psychologique', the former being the chaotic and undefinable movements that are found within our own minds, and the latter being the recognizable, stable elements we see in the minds of others. Speaking of the terms in relation to literary creativity, she says:

> Psychic life is not definable, it doesn't fit into ready-made categories. That's why I no longer say 'psychological'. [. . .] People say of a character, 'He's selfish', 'he's a miser': that's what psychology is. If we open that up and see what is behind it, we find a whole world, of tropisms, of all kinds of movements.[69]

In her writing, we see the process of imposed 'psychology' on many occasions. In *Childhood*, Natacha fights to tear off 'this yoke, this carapace' of victimhood imposed by the pity in the maid's exclamation, 'what a tragedy, though, to have no mother!' Later in the text, the narrators propose and reject psychological terms like 'resentment', 'reproach', and 'contempt' for the father's feelings towards the mother, and fret that their depiction of Véra risks solidifying her into the stock character of the 'wicked stepmother'.[70] *L'Usage de la parole* offers one of the most detailed examples. In the vignette entitled 'Aesthetics', two acquaintances run into each other by chance in the street. Sarraute contrasts the sense of self with the apprehension of the other:

> Let us dare to say it anyway, it has to be said, that this indefinable thing, this everything, this nothing, this void, this plenitude which is each of them suddenly encounters this: a crudely traced-out shape, a rough outline, an identikit portrait . . . a doll like the ones children cut out of cardboard . . . you just have to follow the dotted line.[71]

Conscious of the other's gaze upon it, the self is aware that it is being constituted into what is described as 'this character traced from an illustration in a novel from the last century', through a process that Sarraute narrates as follows:

> Something is emanating from her . . . like a fluid . . . like beams of light . . . he can feel that under their effect he is undergoing an operation through which he is being shaped, given a body, a sex, an age, having a sign attached to him like a mathematical formula that sums up a long development.[72]

In contrasting an indefinably complex and ever-changing consciousness with the blunt terminology of psychological analysis forced upon it, Sarraute echoes the views of Bergson, who similarly contrasts 'the word with well-defined contours [. . .] which crushes, or at least covers the delicate, fugitive impressions of our individual consciousness' in his *Essai sur les données immédiates de la conscience*.[73]

As in existentialism, for Sarraute it is the Other who constitutes the flux of being-for-itself into the facticity of being-in-itself. The example from *L'Être et le Néant* of the voyeur surprised at the keyhole demonstrates how the experience of Sartre's being-for-others links closely to Sarraute's view of human interaction: 'Thus for me the Other is first the being for whom I am an object, that is the being *through whom* I gain my objectness'.[74] Just as Sartre's voyeur's own sense of self is modified by his awareness of another's judgement, so, in Sarraute, people internalize others' view of them.[75] This internalization may be experienced as the hostile imposition of an alien definition, as with Natacha's 'yoke' of misfortune, or when Berthe sees the caricature of herself as an old fusspot in the workmen's eyes in *Le Planétarium*. Elsewhere, it may be welcomed and assimilated into a more permanent self-image. The multiple selves sharing a consciousness of *Tu ne t'aimes pas* (*You don't love yourself*, 1989) wonder why other people feel themselves to be a single, unified personality, and conclude that it's the result of a self-image calqued on the external perspective of others:

> 'How do they manage to feel so neat, so simple?'
>
> 'They must train themselves very early . . . they're given powerful help in that right from the start. . . . The most gifted, the most precocious among them already see themselves as everyone sees them: as babies . . . then as little boys, little girls, tomboys . . .'
>
> 'Once they've got into the habit of feeling the way people see them, they keep it forever . . . at every stage of their lives they feel that they are women, that they are men.'
>
> 'And nothing else. "Real" women, "real" men . . . conforming as closely as possible to the pattern'.[76]

In these multiple selves and social façades we also see, incidentally, the clearest heritage so far of Proust's 'little inner figures' of different dispositions for social and private spheres.

Images of dolls, statues and waxworks abound in the text as representatives of the social veneer constructed by or imposed upon the self: the Guimiers of *Le Planétarium* are reconstituted as effigies, the fakeness of which is underlined, in the polite conversation of others; the multiple selves of *Tu ne t'aimes pas* lament that the figure they constructed of themselves melts like a snowman the moment they are alone.[77] The deceptive nature of the social self is everywhere revealed as interactions between characters construct themselves out of mutual incomprehension, false inferences of the other's thoughts, and words taken at cross-purposes. In a typically complex layering of viewpoints, the narrator of *Le Planétarium* tells us what Pierre (mistakenly) thinks that Berthe (mistakenly) thinks that Pierre thinks of her: 'She must be thinking that he wanted to rub her nose in her little obsessions', he imagines. She is thinking nothing of the sort.[78] Just how awry such tangled inferences can be is demonstrated by the replay of a discussion between the two of them, focalized through the consciousness of each in turn: his impression that he appears amused and distant is belied by her perception of him as hostile and flustered; for her part, Berthe is unaware that her attempt to flatter Pierre with a request for financial advice she does not need has been shrewdly diagnosed for what it is.[79] The complex mixture of perceptiveness and blindness is here presented in terms of a keen eye for the inauthenticity of others combined with an over-confidence in our own power to project a manufactured façade. As Ann Jefferson notes, such concerns about knowing and being known by others amount to an 'anxiety about the boundaries of the self', as other minds penetrate our defences, or impose upon us a personality that is alien to our inner self.[80] Such anxieties extend even to the real mind of the reader, whose possible interpretations of the behaviour represented are discussed and challenged by the narrators of later works.[81]

Yet, despite all these differences in perspective, Sarraute's ultimate aim is the representation of commonality: specifically, the advancement of her thesis that *all* minds, viewed at sufficient depth, consist of the same tropistic movements. The first fragment of *L'Usage de la parole* invites readers to discover their own tropisms behind the words discussed, and assures them that 'they can be sure in any case that they are not mistaken, everything they may notice is indeed there, in all of us'.[82] All that makes us unique individuals is contained within the superficial and deceptive social façade which originates in others' external perception of us. Behind this façade, Sarraute claims, and beneath the reflective consciousness that draws on it to construct a sense of self, we're each a broadly similar mass of tropistic activity. She tells Simone Benmussa: 'I have no feeling of identity. I think that inside each of us, very deep down, we are the same'.[83] This similarity between minds at the level of tropisms not only levels out the idiosyncrasies of personality which separate us from others, but also, more controversially, removes the differences of gender. Look deep enough into consciousness, Sarraute claims, and you will reach a level where the male and female minds are indistinguishable. This is strikingly demonstrated in *Childhood* by the use of masculine grammatical forms with reference to the narrator's double, who is described in the opening pages as '*grandiloquent*' and '*outrecuidant*' ('presumptuous').[84] The lack of feminine adjectival endings is intended to imply an absence of gender, rather than the presence of masculinity, as Sarraute explains: 'My double is necessarily sexless. If I used a feminine adjective, that would mean that I feel myself to be a woman. Which I don't. I am not anything'.[85] Similarly, the representation of Natacha in the book avoids any gendered interpretation of her feelings or behaviour. Sarraute claims, 'I wanted to describe a child rather than a little girl'.[86]

Jefferson points out that Sarraute is of a generation with Simone de Beauvoir, and shares a similar scepticism towards innate, rather than culturally inculcated, differences between men and women.[87] Despite this common understanding of her thought, Beauvoir's own slate of innate female characteristics is not entirely blank. *Le Deuxième Sexe* accepts as physiologically determined several mental traits which now seem redolent of dated stereotypes of femininity:

> Neural and muscular control [in women] is imperfectly assured. This lack of stability and control brings about their emotivity, which is directly linked to vascular variations: heart palpitations, blushing, etc.; and they are thereby subject to convulsive symptoms: tears, hysterical laughter, attacks of nerves.[88]

However, Beauvoir accepts these characteristics—based on now superseded medical authority—the better to refute those who would turn biological data into moral precepts: 'What we refuse is the idea that [this biological data] constitutes a fixed destiny for her'.[89] For Beauvoir, the great majority of psychological characteristics considered 'feminine' are the contingent product of social conditioning, and a programme of consciousness-raising is required to make women aware of how their minds have been moulded into passive acceptance of oppression. Sarraute's politics may remain implicit in her texts, but she and Beauvoir share a common foundation for their thought in their view of gender.

Sarraute's stance is, however, at odds with dominant currents of feminist thought at the time of *Childhood's* publication, when the *écriture feminine* movement and related theories brought celebration of difference and focus on female embodiment to the fore. Annie Leclerc, for example, suggests that women's time-perception is less linear, more cyclical than men's, due to the influence of menstrual cycles on their experience of living in the world.[90] Hélene Cixous, who is a novelist and playwright as well as a theorist, puts into practice in her creative writing the contention that patriarchy cannot be effectively countered through a discourse that is itself shaped by a long history of male hegemony. Female experience and the female body can be the source of a new discourse, available for men as well as women to use, which will be free of the legacy of oppression. As she writes in *La Venue à l'écriture* (*Coming to Writing*, 1977):

> I do not 'begin' by 'writing': I do not write. Life makes text from my body. I am already text. History, love, violence, time, work, desire write it into my body, I take myself where the 'fundamental language' makes itself heard, the body language into which are translated all the languages of things, of acts and beings, in my own breast, the whole of reality worked upon in my flesh, captured by my nerves, by my senses, by the labour of all my cells, projected, analysed, recomposed into a book.[91]

Cixous and like-minded critics have looked for examples of creative writing that express their femininity in their very style and structure, as well as in their themes, and the names of Colette and, most particularly, Duras are frequently cited. Cixous's famous essay, 'Le Rire de la Méduse' names Duras, along with Colette, Jean Genet, and James Joyce, as practitioners of a kind of *écriture feminine* before the concept was invented. Adèle King notes that Duras's writing has many features that might suggest a female perspective on the world: she employs themes of all-powerful, never-fulfilled passion, and presents characters whose sense of self is uncertain and fragmentary; her texts blur genres and hold few events and little plot; her style is elliptical, paradoxical, and uncertain, with disjunctions between 'objective' events and narrative rendering.[92]

Écriture féminine remains highly controversial. Both the women writers in this study are strongly opposed, with Darrieussecq denouncing it as 'a ghettoizing, minoritizing idea', and declaring its implication that women's minds are significantly different from men's a fallacy. Sarraute's own pithy verdict is that the whole idea is 'just so stupid'.[93] Critics of Sarraute with a more sympathetic attitude to the claims of *écriture féminine* include Leah Hewitt, who describes Sarraute's stance as 'a stunning denial of gender', and John Phillips who psychoanalyzes *Childhood* as 'struggling to voice a feminine which it has repressed'.[94] For Phillips, Sarraute's texts refuse to accept gender difference because of the author's ambivalent feelings towards her mother, and thence towards her own femininity.[95] Others see an involuntary femininity in Sarraute's representation of the mind, regardless of her assertion that 'inside, where I am, sex does not exist'.[96] The (male) narrator of *Portrait d'un inconnu* is described in an early review of the novel as 'a nameless and somewhat hermaphroditic individual'.[97] King suggests that Sarraute's tropisms themselves often seem feminine, and that the view of the mind as composed of merging and dissociating selves within a permeable ego boundary seems more reminiscent of a female mind than a male one.[98] It's undeniable that the metaphors of tropisms, in their flowing, sticky, palpitating, enveloping, and recoiling biologism are often similar to the imagery employed by Cixous and others in their attempt to write an *écriture féminine*. Hewitt comments:

> [Sarraute's] images of oozing fluids, viscosity, secretions, rhythmic waves . . . are designed to suggest a hesitant, vacillating and unnameable experience that underlies and betrays 'objective' reality. These metaphorical dichotomies of solid versus fluid not only belong to our western cultural mythologies distinguishing masculine and feminine, they also continue to play a role for psychoanalytic theorists of the feminine such as Luce Irigaray, Julia Kristeva, and Nancy Chodorow. [. . .] Sarraute's tropisms have much in common with Irigaray's fluids and Kristeva's semiotic in the way they afford a stylistic breakdown in conventional forms of representation. Their vocabularies to describe all three phenomena are strikingly similar in many respects and all three writers devise strategies to suggest something that exceeds the boundaries of rational discourse.[99]

To accept this common ground with *écriture féminine* might seem to imply that Sarraute succeeds only in representing the female mind, which she falsely attributes in her novels to male and female characters alike. Such an implication is misguided on three counts. First, it ignores the presence of violent and militaristic metaphors in the imagery of tropisms applied to male and female minds, such as the woman who skins the writer alive with her praise and laughter in *Entre la vie et la mort*.[100] Second, it relies on a stereotype of maleness that downplays the role of anxiety, uncertainty, impressionability, and fluidity or multiplicity of identity in the masculine psyche, and we need only look back to Proust in order to see a male writer affirming the importance of all of these within his representation of a male mind. And lastly, it overlooks the presence of more conventionally masculine traits in Sarraute's male characters, such as the aggression in the old gentleman's conversational questioning of the girl in Fragment XIV of *Tropismes*, narrated in terms reminiscent of a sexual assault.[101] Indeed, the exploration and dissection of stereotypical masculinity is an important aspect of Sarraute's work. Several texts, including *Portrait d'un inconnu*, *Les Fruits d'or* (*The Golden Fruits*, 1963), *Vous les entendez?*, and *Tu ne t'aimes pas*, foreground a male character whose outward solidity and self-assurance are exposed as mere bluster, concealing the same shifting, anxious, shapeless self that many of the female characters, or 'feminine' male ones, acknowledge as their own. The narrator of *Portrait* describes the moment when the father's constructed masculinity is breached: 'I had managed to grasp something alive, protruding from the solid armour he had made himself, and in which he thought he was quite safe, his hand which reached furtively out to me'.[102] Sarraute is thus clearly not to be categorized as an exclusive specialist in female psychology, and the critical interest the issue provokes perhaps says less about her work than about the enduring novelty in the mid-twentieth century of a woman novelist offering a detailed portrait of male consciousness.

*

In encountering Sarraute's work, then, we meet at first the paradox of a writer who attempts to counter the influence of behaviourism on literature with her own representation of the human mind in terms of involuntary responses to external stimuli, along with the equally striking paradox of a writer whose insistence on genderless consciousness is expressed in a discourse which prefigures that of *écriture féminine*. On closer inspection, however, these apparent contradictions vanish away. Sarraute is reacting against the 'black box' of behaviourism that regards psychological processes as either non-existent or irrelevant to the understanding of human nature, and the literature that would follow its lead with a purely external representation of its characters. Where the 'conditioned responses' of Watson and Skinner are concerned, she is more ambivalent. While rejecting strongly determinist positions that would banish free will altogether, she nevertheless takes a particular interest in the involuntary, and is keen to delve down beneath apparently freely chosen words and actions to discover their origins in impulses and reflexes of which we're unaware. In the same way, the similarity between her 'universal' tropisms and the 'feminine' imagery of Irigaray, Cixous, and Kristeva is only a problem if we hold that such images are exclusively relevant to the processes of female consciousness, something that even the practitioners of *écriture féminine* themselves do not claim. Sarraute's representation is in line with her social constructivist view of gender, in which gendered psychological traits are the product of upbringing and environment rather than innate predispositions. In associating single-mindedness, sturdiness, and consistency with the social exterior, and fluidity, uncertainty, and vacillation with the inner self, Sarraute aims an implicit rebuke at any who might consider such attributes masculine and feminine traits respectively.

At the start of her career, Sarraute's representation of the mind was lauded by Sartre in the preface to *Portrait d'un inconnu* as venturing beyond psychology to reach 'human reality in its very existence'. Two decades later, Sartre's opinion soured somewhat: 'She believes that she is reaching interpersonal and elementary relationships through the protoplasmic exchanges she describes, but she is only showing the tiny, abstract effects of a very restricted social milieu'.[103] Predictably, it's on political grounds that the resolutely bourgeoise and apolitical Sarraute was found wanting by the increasingly radical Sartre. Valerie Minogue defends Sarraute by saying that exactly the same tropistic psychodramas might equally well have been set among working-class Welsh people as among the wealthy upper-middle-classes of Passy whom we find in Sarraute's texts. Sarraute never ventures beyond her own social circle in order to prove this, however, and we may be forgiven for finding something intrinsically bourgeois in, say, her merciless struggles for dominance fought with the subtlest nuances of language, or the violent emotions she shows boiling beneath exquisite politeness. Class aside, there is an undeniable narrowness to Sarraute's focus. While her metaphors for tropistic activity may include images of violence and terror, violent or terrifying situations from real life and their associated mental activity are not explored. There are none of the extreme life events that allow the other writers of our corpus to explore extraordinary states of consciousness. It is telling that, when deep grief appears in *Ici*, an extreme state if ever there was one, the focalization of the episode is not through the consciousness of the person in mourning, but rather through the minds of his conversation partners who anxiously struggle to maintain the exchange on a level of polite commonplaces.[104] Most notably, sexual desire, and associated mental states such as passionate love or consuming jealousy, are entirely absent from the minds Sarraute depicts, making them very different in character from all but those of the celibate priests in Bernanos. Asked about the absence, Sarraute replies:

> What interests me is discovering tropisms in things that appear insignificant, uninteresting, in a banal conversation, in anodyne words, in situations where you might think nothing is happening. It's when nothing is happening that I'm interested to see what is really happening . . . Sexual issues are huge things, ground that has already been covered. A real public place.[105]

We may speculate that the expressed desire to avoid replicating others' work may be compounded by a distaste for the vulgar or sensational, or a concern for her own privacy, but whatever the reason, Sarraute has voluntarily restricted her representation of the mind to a limited range of mental states within a limited range of situations. But in doing so, she has made her own a sphere of mental life that literature had hitherto neglected: the subterranean dramas beneath everyday social interactions. The choice of topic is, of course, not arrived at by chance. The microscope of Sarraute's style magnifies half-perceived sensations and trivial emotions into shattering blows and life-or-death struggles. Her texts have no need of thoughts and feelings which are already significant or well-developed enough to be visible to the naked eye. Unusually, then, it is Sarraute's autobiographical text which explores a greater range of human experience than her fiction: the author's eventful and sometimes traumatic childhood takes her memoirs into psychological regions that her fiction prefers to avoid. Her fictional characters spar over the literary merits of a recent novel, while her autobiographical self decides between life with the mother who abandoned her and the stepmother who resents her presence. But in fiction and autobiography alike, Sarraute's tropisms and pre-dialogue go further than Proust, Bernanos, Breton, Sartre, or even Beckett in transcending the limits of a linguistic medium to represent the non-linguistic aspects of the mind. Her work is all the more important as a counterbalance to widespread literary tendencies to exaggerate the importance of language in consciousness, or even to reduce conscious thought to linguistic activity, as in the stream-of-consciousness monologue. Such fixation on language in the mind may be a natural hazard of the writer's priorities, or it may be a more general misconception caused by the dominant role of language in the forefront of our reflective consciousness masking other forms of thought from our awareness. Nathalie Sarraute is an important figure in the realignment of literary representation of consciousness away from exclusively language-based thought, and her work will have far-reaching influence. One among many to acknowledge her debt to Sarraute's view of consciousness is the final author of this study, Marie Darrieussecq.

Notes

1. 'Mouvements intérieurs ténus, qui glissent très rapidement au seuil de notre conscience', Nathalie Sarraute, 'Le Gant retourné', in *Œuvres complètes*, ed. by Jean-Yves Tadié, pp. 1707–17 (p. 1707).
2. Valerie Minogue, 'Fragments of a Childhood: Nathalie Sarraute's *Enfance*', *French Autobiography: Texts, Contexts, Poetics, Romance Studies*, 9 (Winter 1986), pp. 71–83 (p. 72); Philippe Lejeune, 'Paroles d'Enfance', *Revue des sciences humaines*, 93 (1990), pp. 23–38 (p. 32).
3. 'Un côté plus raisonnable, un côté qui relit et demande: pourquoi tu dis cela', Interview with Pierre Boncenne in *Lire*, 94 (June 1983), pp. 87–92 (p. 92).
4. 'En attendant de s'attaquer à l'homme, Anthime Armand-Dubois prétendait simplement réduire en "tropismes" toute l'activité des animaux qu'il observait. Tropismes! Le mot n'était plus tôt inventé que déjà l'on ne comprenait plus rien d'autre; toute une catégorie de psychologues ne consentit plus qu'aux *tropismes*. Tropismes! Quelle lumière soudaine émanait de ces syllabes! Évidemment l'organisme cédait

aux mêmes incitations que l'héliotrope lorsque la plante involontaire tourne sa face au soleil (ce qui est aisément réductible à quelques simples lois de physique et de thermo-chimie). Le cosmos enfin se douait d'une bénignité rassurante. Dans les plus surprenants mouvements de l'être on pouvait uniment reconnaître une parfaite obéissance à l'agent', André Gide, *Les Caves du Vatican*, in *Romans et récits*, ed. by Pierre Masson (Paris: Gallimard, Pléiade edition, 2009), p. 683. For a discussion of Gide's tropisms, see Harlan R. Patton, 'Tropismes and the Satire of Scientism in *Les Caves du Vatican*', *South Atlantic Review*, 48.1 (January 1983), pp. 35–42.

5. 'Roman et réalité', *OC*, pp. 1643–56 (p. 1651).
6. 'Ce terme "tropisme" était un pis-aller. Je cherchais pour mon premier livre un titre qui puisse évoquer tant bien que mal toutes ces sensations indéfinissables et, à l'époque, "tropisme" était dans l'air. Je pensais qu'il pourrait s'appliquer à ces sortes de mouvements instinctifs qui sont indépendants de notre volonté, qui sont provoqués par des excitations venant de l'extérieur', 'Conversation avec Nathalie Sarraute', interview with Serge Fauchereau and Jean Ristat, *Digraphe*, 32 (March 1984), pp. 9–18 (p. 9).
7. 'Des coups de sonde par lesquels je suis arrivée à un certain niveau de la conscience où je me suis installée', Simone Benmussa, *Entretiens avec Nathalie Sarraute* (Tournai: La Renaissance du Livre, 1999), p. 136.
8. 'Mon lieu d'investigation se situe juste au bord du subconscient, n'importe qui peut le retrouver s'il prend le temps de s'y arrêter, d'y consacrer des efforts, mais en général il a autre chose à faire [. . .]. Moi je m'arrête là précisément. J'installe mon microscope, je fais un film au ralenti et je regarde ce qui se passe', 'Rencontre avec Nathalie Sarraute', interview between Nathalie Sarraute and Isabelle Huppert, ed. by M.-A. Guérin and T. Jousse, *Cahiers du cinéma*, 477 (March 1994), pp. 8–14 (p. 11).
9. 'La source secrète de notre existence', Nathalie Sarraute, 'Préface', *L'Ère du soupçon*, *OC*, pp. 1553–6 (p. 1554).
10. '"Non, tu ne feras pas ça . . ." dans ces mots un flot épais, lourd coule, ce qu'il charrie s'enfonce en moi pour écraser ce qui en moi remue, veut se dresser . . . et sous cette pression ça se redresse, se dresse plus fort, plus haut, ça pousse, projette violemment hors de moi les mots . . . "Si, je le ferai"', Nathalie Sarraute, *Enfance, in Œuvres complètes* (Paris: Gallimard, Pléiade edition, 1996), pp. 987–1145 (p. 993). The translation is taken from Nathalie Sarraute, *Childhood*, trans. by Barbara Wright (New York: Braziller, 1984), pp. 5–6. Translations of all other texts by Sarraute are my own.
11. 'Il n'était possible de les communiquer au lecteur que par des images qui en donnent des équivalents et lui fassent éprouver des sensations analogues', Nathalie Sarraute, *Préface* to *L'Ère du soupçon*, *OC*, pp. 1553–6 (p. 1554).
12. The latter two examples can be found in *Portrait d'un inconnu*, *OC*, pp. 33–175 (p. 120) and *Le Planétarium*, *OC*, (p. 431).
13. *Ici*, *OC*, pp. 1293–1373 (p. 1321); *Martereau*, *OC*, pp. 177–337 (p. 309).
14. *Portrait d'un inconnu*, *OC*, pp. 55–6.
15. 'Bonheur', félicité', 'exaltation', 'extase', 'joie'; 'n'est pas capable de recueillir ce qui m'emplit, me déborde, s'épand, va se perdre, se fondre dans les briques roses, les espaliers en fleurs, la pelouse, les pétales roses et blancs, l'air qui vibre parcouru de tremblements à peine perceptibles', *OC*, pp. 1024–5; trans. 57.
16. 'Un compromis à la non-coïncidence des mots et de la sensation.' Stéphane Bikialo, 'La Nomination multiple: un compromis à la non-coïncidence des mots et la sensation', in *Nathalie Sarraute: du tropisme à la phrase*, ed. by Agnès Fontvieille and Philippe Wahl (Lyon: Presses Universitaires de Lyon, 2003), pp. 85–98.
17. Virginia Woolf, *To the Lighthouse* (Oxford: Oxford University Press, 1992), p. 241.
18. 'Ces actions dramatiques, qui ne sont pas perçues par la conscience tandis qu'elles se produisent, car elles sont extrêmement ténues et rapides, je cherche à les reconstituer, à les recréer comme si elles étaient vues au microscope, au ralenti. Au-dehors, c'est-à-dire dans notre conscience claire, elles se recouvrent d'un mot comme "malaise". Ou "sympathie", etc. Mais ce "malaise" et cette "sympathie" ne sont que le surgissement, l'aboutissement à la surface—où ils sont pris et enfermés dans une définition connue—de mouvements indéfinissables qui, à mes yeux, existent comme le mouvement invisible des particules atomiques', Letter from Nathalie Sarraute, published in Frida S. Weissman, *Du monologue intérieur à la sous-conversation* (Paris: Nizet, 1978), p. 10.
19. 'Dans mes livres, il y a du monologue intérieur mais précédé par ces mouvements, ces tropismes qui poussent les mots et amènent la phrase intérieure', Benmussa, p. 89.
20. 'C'est une sorte de rayonnement qu'il dégage, comme un fluide, cela coule vers vous de ses yeux étroits, de son sourire de Bouddha, de son silence . . . elle ne sait pas ce que c'est . . . c'est son charme . . . il est charmant: "Ton beau-père a du charme, tu ne trouves pas?"', *Le Planétarium*, *OC*, p. 418.
21. 'Pas de séparation entre le prédialogue et le dialogue. L'un aboutit à l'autre', Benmussa, p. 81.
22. 'Me faites pas attention, je suis très bien ainsi', *Tropismes*, *OC*, p. 20.
23. 'Une croyance [qui] n'a rien d'une science'; 'Freud montre un univers qui n'a rien de commun avec ce que je cherche à écrire. Un univers qu'on ne peut découvrir qu'à travers les catégories freudiennes

toujours identiques et simples. Je trouve ses théories extrêmement réductrices et simples', Interview with François-Marie Banier, *Le Monde des livres*, 15 April 1983, p. 16; Interview with Michèle Pardina, *Le Monde*, 26 February 1993, p. 29; reprinted in *OC*, p. 1738.

24. *Portrait d'un inconnu*, *OC*, pp. 76–8; *Le Planétarium*, *OC*, p. 478; 'Non. Pas les parents. Pas les enfants . . . Oh non . . . Pitié . . . Pas les complexes. Les refoulements. Les régressions. Les fixations infantiles . . . Pas ça: le préfabriqué. La confection. Les passe-partout. Les affreux objets de série', *Isma, ou ce qui s'appelle rien*, *OC*, pp. 1421–49 (p. 1433).
25. Rykner, p. 161.
26. 'Presque toujours entièrement faux', Rykner, p. 168.
27. 'La part de l'irrationnel, de l'inconscient', John Phillips, *Nathalie Sarraute: Metaphor, Fairy-Tale and the Feminine of the Text* (Bern: Peter Lang, 1994), p. 2.
28. 'S'est vite effacé'; 's'est enfoncé, plutôt', *OC*, p. 1009; trans. 31.
29. Monique Gosselin-Noat, *Enfance* (Paris: Gallimard, 1996), p. 32.
30. Emer O'Beirne, *Reading Nathalie Sarraute: Dialogue and Distance* (Oxford: Clarendon Press, 1999), p. 70.
31. Marianne Schmutz, *Enfance de Nathalie Sarraute comme autobiographie* (Lyon: Aldrui, 1999), p. 127.
32. 'Il suffit de se rappeler quelle révélation a été pour nous le monologue intérieur; la méfiance avec laquelle nous avons considéré et considérons parfois encore les efforts de Henry James ou de Proust pour démonter les rouages délicats de nos mécanismes intérieurs; avec quel empressement nous acceptons de croire que telle grille—comme la psychanalyse—posée sur cette immense masse mouvante qu'on nomme notre "for intérieur", où l'on peut trouver tout ce qu'on veut, la recouvre tout entière et rend compte de tous ses mouvements; et avec quelle satisfaction, quel sentiment de délivrance nous nous sommes laissés convaincre, et sommes restés, pour la plupart d'entre nous, convaincus, que ce "for intérieur", tout récemment encore si fertile en découvertes, n'existait pas, n'était rien: du vide, du vent', 'Ce que voient les oiseaux', *OC*, pp. 1607–20 (pp. 1611–2).
33. 'Tous mes articles s'efforcent de défendre ce que l'on désigne avec mépris aujourd'hui sous le nom de "psychologie" contre les tendances dites "behavioristes"', The line appears in a letter from Sarraute to the *Times Literary Supplement*, published 13 March 1959 (p. 145), in which she corrects critical misconceptions about her views. Reprinted in *OC*, p. 2079.
34. Introductions to Skinner's ideas, and behaviourism more generally, can be found in *The Oxford Companion to the Mind*, ed. by Richard L. Gregory, 2nd edn (Oxford: Oxford University Press, 2004), pp. 89–91, or Tony Malim and Ann Birch, *Introductory Psychology* (Basingstoke: Palgrave, 1998), pp. 8–9.
35. 'Corps sans âme ballotté par des forces hostiles, [qui] n'était rien d'autre en définitive que ce qu'il apparaissait au-dehors'; 'un néant profond', 'De Dostoïesvsky à Kafka', *OC*, pp. 1557–77 (p. 1558).
36. 'Les romanciers behavioristes, qui se servent abondamment de dialogues sertis de brèves indications ou de discrets commentaires, poussent dangereusement le roman sur le domaine du théâtre, où il ne peut que se trouver en état d'infériorité. Et renonçant aux moyens dont seul le romancier dispose, ils renoncent à ce qui fait de lui un art à part, pour ne pas dire un art tout court', 'Conversation et sous-conversation', *OC*, p. 1602.
37. 'De Dostoïevsky à Kafka', p. 1560; Hemingway is discussed in 'Conversation et sous-conversation', p. 1589.
38. 'Meursault avait sur les héros de Dos Passos ou de Steinbeck eux-mêmes cet incontestable avantage d'être dépeint non, comme eux, à distance et du dehors, mais du dedans, par le procédé classique d'introspection cher aux amateurs du psychologique: c'était de tout près, et, pour ainsi dire, installés aux premières loges, que nous pouvions constater son néant intérieur', 'De Dostoïevsky à Kafka', p. 1560.
39. 'Un certain ressentiment', 'De Dostoïevsky à Kafka', p. 1563.
40. 'Mouvements sous-jacents'; 'des procédés de primitif', 'De Dostoïevsky à Kafka', p. 1566.
41. 'Littéralement bouleversée', Arnaud Rykner, *Nathalie Sarraute* (Paris: Seuil, 1991), p. 163.
42. O'Beirne, p. 81.
43. Schmutz, p. 181.
44. 'Chez Proust, ça reste de l'analyse rétrospective, complexe, parce qu'il s'agit de retrouver les divers fils temporels dont le mouvement est ficelé: il y a des couches temporelles, mais pour "aboutir" à ce moment-là. Ce n'est plus en progrès', In conversation with Valerie Minogue. *OC*, p. 1717.
45. 'Au repos et comme figés dans le souvenir'; 'une technique qui parviendrait à plonger le lecteur dans le flot de ces drames souterrains que Proust n'a eu le temps que de survoler et dont il n'a observé et reproduit que les grandes lignes immobiles: une technique qui donnerait au lecteur l'illusion de refaire lui-même ces actions avec une conscience plus lucide, avec plus d'ordre, de netteté et de force qu'il ne peut le faire dans la vie, sans qu'elles perdent cette part d'indétermination, cette opacité et ce mystère qu'ont toujours ses actions pour celui qui les vit', 'Conversation et sous-conversation', *OC*, pp. 1595, 1604.
46. 'Avec *Ulysse* et *Mrs Dalloway*, cela devient mobile, mais chez Virginia Woolf, c'est du monologue intérieur, des pensées, etc., formulées, mais en train d'arriver', In conversation with Valerie Minogue, *OC*, p. 1717.

47. 'Assez curieuse polémique, Alain Robbe-Grillet prenant pour objectivité sa subjectivité d'ingénieur, et Nathalie Sarraute pour subjectivité son objectivité de psychologue. Et enfin, s'il s'agit d'une objectivité behavioriste, il ne suffit point de parler d'un langage d'épure, il faut que le spectacle n'intéresse personne et que les faits soient rapportés les uns aux autres et non au regard d'un Voyeur ou d'un Jaloux. Inversement, l'objectivité du psychologue, surtout en art, réside dans l'intérêt du spectacle—interne? externe? qu'importe!—c'est-à-dire dans le rapport des faits à un sujet. On s'y trompe. Est-ce par hasard que le behavioriste demande des titres à l'introspection—*Le Voyeur, La Jalousie*—tandis que le poète de la conscience intitule *Tropismes* sa première publication?', Yvon Belaval, *La Nouvelle Nouvelle Revue Française*, February 1958, reprinted in *OC*, p. 1730.
48. 'Monstres cachés', Alain Robbe-Grillet, *Le Miroir qui revient* (Paris: Minuit, 1984), p. 69.
49. B. F. Skinner, *About Behaviourism* (London: Vintage, 1976), p. 115.
50. 'Réduit [. . .] au triple déterminisme de la faim, de la sexualité, de la classe sociale: Freud, Marx et Pavlov', 'De Dostoïevsky à Kafka', p. 1557.
51. *Ouvrez* (Paris: Gallimard, 1997), pp. 23–32.
52. 'Maintenant cette idée s'est installée en moi, il ne dépend pas de ma volonté de la déloger. Je peux m'obliger à la repousser au second plan, à la remplacer par une autre idée, mais pour un temps seulement . . . elle est toujours là, blottie dans un coin, prête à tout moment à s'avancer, à tout écarter devant elle, à occuper toute la place . . . On dirait que de la repousser, de trop la comprimer augmente encore sa poussée', *OC*, p. 1043; trans. 86.
53. 'Une fois que je me suis embarquée sur cette galère, il ne m'est plus possible de la quitter', *OC*, p. 1033; trans. 71.
54. 'Que lui est-il arrivé? Il ne peut pas bouger, il est comme ligoté . . . c'est, qui de nous ne l'a éprouvé . . . c'est qu'il est pris dans le fil de la conversation ou plutôt que ce fil autour de lui s'enroule, le tient enfermé', *L'Usage de la parole*, *OC*, pp. 921–86 (p. 963).
55. Benjamin Libet, 'Unconscious Cerebral Initiative and the Role of Conscious Will in Voluntary Action', *Behavioral and Brain Sciences*, 8 (1985), 529–66 (p. 529).
56. Dennett, *Consciousness Explained*, pp. 139–70.
57. 'À l'origine de nos gestes, de nos paroles, des sentiments que nous manifestons, que nous croyons éprouver et qu'il est possible de définir', 'Préface' to *L'Ère du soupçon*, *OC*, pp. 1553–6 (p. 1553).
58. 'Ce sera douloureux pour moi de trancher moi-même le lien qui m'attache encore à ma mère'; 'la certitude que j'avais fait pour moi d'abord le bon choix', *OC*, p. 1086; trans. 155–6.
59. 'Je les fais résonner . . . faut-il changer celui-ci de place? . . . j'écoute de nouveau . . . vraiment la phrase qu'ils forment se déroule et se retombe très joliment . . . encore peut-être un léger arrangement . . . et puis ne plus l'examiner, je risquerais de l'abîmer . . .', *OC*, p. 1107; trans. 188.
60. 'Les mots sont ses souverains. Leur humble sujet se sent trop honoré de leur céder sa maison. Qu'ils soient chez eux, tout est à eux ici, ils sont les seuls maîtres. [. . .] Ils se reflètent, ils miroitent . . . Et il est pris dans le dédale de leurs miroirs, emprisonné dans les entrelacs de leurs reflets . . . Il tourne, renvoyé des uns aux autres', *Entre la vie et la mort*, *OC*, pp. 621–734 (p. 663).
61. *Ici*, pp. 1295–301.
62. 'Je cherche des réactions entre des consciences, peu importe lesquelles. Que ce soit une vieille femme ou un jeune homme, cela n'a pas d'importance. A ce niveau-là, l'effet sur l'autre conscience est le même', Benmussa, p. 159.
63. *Martereau*, *OC*, p. 256.
64. 'À soi seul un monde . . . le monde entier', *L'Usage de la parole*, p. 957.
65. Rykner, p. 64. Monique Gosselin-Noat reports that Sarraute took courses involving phenomenology as a student, but when questioned, the writer disclaims interest or knowledge of the field (Gosselin-Noat, pp. 19, 186).
66. 'Au gré de son caprice, de son humeur, suivant que va à tel ou tel d'entre eux sa préférence du moment, le spectacle se modifie. Tout change. Au gré de son caprice. Le monde, docile, s'élargit à l'infini ou au contraire se contracte; devient étroit et sombre, ou immense et transparent. A son gré, les couleurs changent. Rien n'est fixe. Rien ne s'impose à lui. Sous son impulsion, comme la toile légère où se balance l'araignée, le monde oscille et tremble', *Portrait d'un inconnu*, p. 103.
67. 'Arraché à son monde malléable et douillet'; 'projeté brutalement dans son monde à elle, dur, agressif, implacable', *Portrait d'un inconnu*, p. 131.
68. 'Tout bascule d'un coup, se renverse. . . elle-même s'éloigne, elle disparaît de l'autre côté. . .', *Le Planétarium*, p. 518.
69. 'La vie psychique n'est pas définissable, n'entre pas dans des catégories toutes faites. C'est pourquoi je ne dis plus "psychologique". [. . .] On dit du personnage "C'est un égoïste", "C'est un avare": voilà la psychologie. Si l'on ouvre cela et que l'on regarde ce qu'il y a derrière, on découvre tout un monde, de tropismes, de mouvements de toutes sortes', *OC*, p. 1749.

70. 'Ce carcan, cette carapace'; 'Quel malheur quand même de ne pas avoir de mère!', *OC*, pp. 1055–6; trans. 105–7; 'rancune', réprobation', 'mépris'; 'méchante marâtre', pp. 1059–60; trans. 113–15.
71. 'Osons dire quand même, il le faut bien, que cet indéfinissable, ce tout, ce rien, ce vide, ce plein qu'est chacun d'eux soudain rencontre ceci: une forme tracée à grands traits, un schéma grossier, un portrait-robot . . . une poupée pareille à celles que les enfants découpent dans du carton . . . il suffit de suivre le pointillé', *L'Usage de la parole*, p. 956.
72. 'Ce personnage calqué sur une page illustrée d'un roman du siècle dernier'; 'D'elle quelque chose se dégage . . . comme un fluide . . . comme des rayons . . . il sent que sous leur effet il subit une opération par laquelle il est mis en forme, qui lui donne un corps, un sexe, un âge, l'affuble d'un signe comme une formule mathématique résumant un long développement', *L'Usage de la parole*, pp. 956, 957.
73. 'Le mot aux contours bien arrêtés [. . .] qui écrase ou tout au moins recouvre les impressions délicates et fugitives de notre conscience individuelle', Bergson, *Essai sur les données immédiates de la conscience*, p. 98.
74. 'Ainsi autrui est d'abord pour moi l'être pour qui je suis objet, c'est-à-dire l'être *par qui* je gagne mon objectité', Sartre, *L'Être et le Néant*, p. 309.
75. Sarraute denies direct influence of existentialist ideas on her writing, responding to suggestions of Sartrean influence on her first novel with the words, 'si j'ai fait de l'existentialisme dans *Portrait d'un inconnu*, c'est comme M. Jourdain écrivait en prose, sans le savoir', Interview with Gabriel d'Aubarède, *Les Nouvelles littéraires*, 30 July 1953, quoted in *OC*, p. 1745.
76. '—Comment font-ils pour sentir si nets, si simples? /—Ils doivent s'y entraîner très tôt. . . ils y sont dès leur plus jeune âge puissamment aidés . . . Les mieux doués, les plus précoces se voient déjà eux-mêmes tels que tout le monde les voit: en bébés . . . puis en petits garçons, en fillettes, en garçons manqués . . . —Une fois qu'ils ont pris ce pli de se sentir tels qu'on les voit, ils le gardent toujours . . . à chaque étape de leur vie, ils se sentent être des femmes, des hommes . . . /—Et rien que cela. De "vraies" femmes, de "vrais" hommes . . . le plus conformes possible aux modèles', *Tu ne t'aimes pas*, *OC*, pp. 1147–291 (p. 1164).
77. *Le Planétarium*, *OC*, p. 480; *Tu ne t'aimes pas*, *OC*, p. 1170.
78. 'Elle doit penser qu'il a voulu lui mettre le nez dans ses petites manies', *Le Planétarium*, *OC*, p. 439.
79. *Le Planétarium*, *OC*, pp. 481–503.
80. Ann Jefferson, *Nathalie Sarraute: Fiction and Theory* (Cambridge: Cambridge University Press, 2000), p. 42.
81. Most particularly in *L'Usage de la parole*, where, for instance, in the fragment 'Ton père, ta sœur', the reader is imagined as having a wholly different interpretation of the words under discussion from that of the narrator, *OC*, pp. 939–46.
82. 'Ils pourront en tout cas être sûrs de ne pas se tromper, tout ce qu'ils apercevront est bien là, en chacun de nous', *L'Usage de la parole*, *OC*, p. 927.
83. 'Je n'ai pas de sentiment d'identité. Je pense qu'à l'intérieur de chacun de nous, très profondément, nous sommes pareils', Benmussa, p. 109.
84. *OC*, p. 990; trans. 2.
85. 'Mon double est forcément asexué. Si je mettais un féminin, cela voudrait dire que je me sens être une femme. Ce que je ne me sens pas. Je ne suis rien', Interview with Michèle Gazier, *Télérama*, no. 1800 (July 1984), p. 38; reprinted in *OC*, p. 1948.
86. 'J'ai voulu décrire un enfant plutôt qu'une petite fille', Gosselin-Noat, p. 21.
87. Jefferson, p. 92.
88. 'Le contrôle nerveux et musculaire [chez les femmes] est imparfaitement assuré. Ce manque de stabilité et de contrôle entraîne leur émotivité, directement liée aux variations vasculaires: battements de cœur, rougeur, etc.; et elles sont par là sujettes aux manifestations convulsives: larmes, fou rire, crises de nerfs', Beauvoir, *Le Deuxième Sexe*, I, p. 70.
89. 'Ce que nous refusons, c'est l'idée que [ces données biologiques] constituent pour elle un destin figé', Beauvoir, *Le Deuxième Sexe*, I, p. 71.
90. 'Mon corps revient à lui-même par un cycle de métamorphoses. Son appréhension du temps est circulaire, encore que jamais close ou répétitive', ('My body returns to itself through a cycle of metamorphoses. Its apprehension of time is circular, although never closed or repetitive'), Annie Leclerc, *Parole de femme* (Paris: Grasset, 1974), p. 72.
91. 'Je ne "commence" pas par "écrire": je n'écris pas. La vie fait texte à partir de mon corps. Je suis déjà du texte. L'Histoire, l'amour, la violence, le temps, le travail, le désir l'inscrivent dans mon corps, je me rends où se donne à entendre "la langue fondamentale", la langue corps en laquelle se traduisent toutes les langues des choses, des actes et des êtres, dans mon propre sein, l'ensemble du réel travaillé dans ma chair, capté par mes nerfs, par mes sens, par le labeur de toutes mes cellules, projeté, analysé, recomposé en un livre', Hélène Cixous, 'La Venue à l'écriture', in *Entre l'écriture* (Paris: Des femmes, 1986), p. 63.
92. Hélène Cixous, 'Le Rire de la Méduse', *L'Arc*, 61 (1975), pp. 39–54 (p. 42); King, p. 134.

93. 'Une idée ghettoïsante, minorisante', Marie Darrieussecq, 'Deux femmes la mort dans l'âme: Laure Adler et Marie Darrieussecq', interview with François Busnel and Thierry Gandillot, *L'Express*, 23 (August 2001), p. 12; 'tellement stupide', Rykner, p. 168.
94. Leah Hewitt, *Autobiographical Tightropes: Simone de Beauvoir, Nathalie Sarraute, Marguerite Duras, Monique Wittig and Maryse Condé* (Lincoln, NE: University of Nebraska Press, 1990), p. 63; Phillips, p. 258.
95. Phillips, p. 139.
96. 'À l'intérieur où je suis, le sexe n'existe pas', Benmussa, p. 184.
97. 'Un individu innommable et quelque peu hermaphrodite', Jean Cathelin, *Demain*, 7 February 1957, reprinted in *OC*, p. 1748.
98. Adèle King, *French Women Novelists: Defining a Female Style* (Basingstoke: MacMillan, 1989), p. 86.
99. Hewitt, pp. 65–7.
100. *Entre la vie et la mort*, *OC*, p. 691.
101. *Tropismes*, *OC*, pp. 13–14.
102. 'J'avais réussi à saisir, dépassant de l'armure solide qu'il s'était fabriquée et où il se croyait bien en sûreté, quelque chose de vivant—sa main qui se tendait vers moi furtivement', *Portrait d'un inconnu*, *OC*, p. 106.
103. 'La réalité humaine, dans son existence même', Jean-Paul Sartre, Preface to *Portrait d'un inconnu*, *OC*, pp. 35–9 (p. 39); 'Elle croit atteindre par les échanges protoplasmiques qu'elle décrit, des relations inter-individuelles et élémentaires alors qu'elle ne fait que montrer les effets abstraits et infinitésimaux d'un milieu social très défini', *Les Écrivains en personne*, ed. by M. Chapsal (Paris: Julliard, 1960), pp. 213–14.
104. *Ici*, *OC*, pp. 1336–43.
105. 'Ce qui m'intéresse, c'est de découvrir des tropismes dans ce qui apparaît comme insignifiant, inintéressant, dans une conversation banale, dans des mots anodins, dans des situations où l'on peut croire qu'il ne se passe rien. C'est quand il ne se passe rien que cela m'intéresse de voir ce qui se passe en réalité . . . Les questions sexuelles sont des choses énormes, un terrain très défriché. Vraiment un lieu public', Gretchen R. Besser, 'Colloque Avec Nathalie Sarraute 22 Avril 1976', *The French Review*, 50 (1976), pp. 284–9 (p. 287).

7

BRAIN

Marie Darrieussecq

Marie Darrieussecq (b. 1969) is the only living writer considered here, and the only writer to engage with the new models of the mind emerging from cognitive science and evolutionary psychology. A trained psychoanalyst, Darrieussecq is equally at home with more traditional understandings of the mind, and maintains an irreverent and often sceptical stance towards all the ideas on which her fiction draws. She may not yet have achieved the canonical status of the other authors in this study, but her two-decade writing career has already made a major impact on French literary culture, and it is not purely for her neuroscientific leanings that she is included here.

After her controversial and best-selling debut, *Truismes* (*Pig Tales*, 1996), a searing satire in which a woman metamorphoses into a pig, while society around her collapses into brutal totalitarianism, Darrieussecq has gone on to produce eight further critically acclaimed novels, along with novellas, translations and children's tales, a memoir of motherhood (*Le Bébé*, 2002), a collection of short stories (*Zoo*, 2006), a play (*Le Musée de la mer*, *'The Sea Museum'*, 2009), and an essay (*Rapport de police*, *Police Report*, 2010). The later novels are all psychological studies centred on female protagonists, filled with detail of the characters' thoughts and perceptions, with little emphasis on plot. Unlike *Truismes*, they are set in recognizable environments in which characters live through familiar and routine activities, although the familiarity is tempered by subtle elements of science fiction or the fantastic, and the routine is liable to be disrupted by sudden, shocking intervention. *Naissance des fantômes* (*My Phantom Husband*, 1998) explores the psychological disintegration of a housewife following her husband's disappearance. It is followed by *Le Mal de mer* (*Breathing Underwater*, 1999), which shifts focalization between consciousnesses to recount the story of a woman who has fled the family home with her daughter in tow. After *A Brief Stay with the Living* (2001), Darrieussecq's longest novel to date, and the one with the most sustained focus on the mind, comes *White* (2003), a love story in a near-future polar research station, and *Le Pays* (2005), the semi-autobiographical story of a Parisian writer's return to her newly independent homeland, which strongly resembles Darrieussecq's own native Basque country. Most recently, *Tom est mort* (*Tom is Dead*, 2007) is a therapeutic diary written by a mother in mourning for her child, and *Clèves* (2011) recounts the sexual initiation of a teenage girl in the 1980s, whose story is continued in the Médicis-prize-winning *Il faut beaucoup aimer les hommes* (*Men*, 2013), in which the protagonist is a successful film actress in an interracial relationship. The workings of the mind are a central theme in all of Darrieussecq's work. Mental life is rendered subjectively through stream-of-consciousness and related techniques to express interior monologue, while a variety of often experimental methods is used to evoke non-linguistic thought. The nature of mind is also considered in the abstract, using discourses from folk psychology to Freudian psychoanalysis to Darwinian theory and neuroscience. As with Proust, there is a particular interest in memory, and the involuntary return of the past, as well as a concern to evoke the particularities of different states of consciousness, such as somnolence, concentration, or blind panic. As with Beckett and Sarraute, there is a suspicion of language, with both writers challenging both the primacy of the linguistic in our conscious thoughts, and the efficacy of conventional psychological language in describing mental activity. With Sartre and phenomenological thought, Darrieussecq shares an interest in the mind as an embodied entity, and as an active engagement with the world it perceives. And with both Breton and Bernanos is shared an interest in the uncanny aspects of consciousness, including the possibility of telepathic communication or the survival of consciousness beyond death, although in Darrieussecq's case it is the symbolic potential of such themes, rather than the advocacy of their real existence, which is foregrounded. In this chapter we shall end our investigation by exploring in turn Darrieussecq's conception of consciousness; her depiction of the images and words of mental life; her interest in the irrational mind of dreams, madness, and the unconscious; and her treatment of the body and brain upon which the mind supervenes. As a writer with a keen sense of her own literary ancestry, a stake in traditional psychoanalytic conceptions of mind, yet also an enthusiasm for science and for science fiction, Darrieussecq's work stands as a twenty-first century milestone to mark how far we have travelled since Proust, and the continuity of the route which has led us here.

Darrieussecq's eclecticism in her influences means she is not to be co-opted into the 'neuro-novel', which, with its cousin the 'neuro-film', has become a major phenomenon in Western culture. These fictions, in which the psychological depiction of characters is laced with liberal reference to cognitive science and neurophysiology, are nevertheless an important element of the cultural context to Darrieussecq's work. Ian McEwan's *Saturday* (2005), with its neurologist hero, is a notable example:

> Even as he turns towards Baxter in surprise, and even as he sees, or senses, what's coming towards him at such speed, there remains in a portion of his thoughts a droning, pedestrian diagnostician who notes poor self-control, emotional lability, explosive temper, suggestive of reduced levels of GABA among the appropriate binding sites on striatal neurons. This in turn is bound to imply the diminished presence of two enzymes in the striatum and lateral pallidum-glutamic acid decarboxylase and choline acetyltransferase. There is much in human affairs that can be accounted for at the level of the complex molecule. Who could ever reckon up the damage done to love and friendship and all hopes of happiness by a surfeit or depletion of this or that neurotransmitter? And who will ever find a morality, an ethics down among the enzymes and amino acids when the general taste is for looking in the other direction?[1]

Elsewhere, Jonathan Franzen's *The Corrections* (2001) explores how psychoactive pharmaceuticals affect our understanding of the self, in an era where brain chemistry can be 'corrected' to free us of anxiety or depression, and contemporary fiction and film overflow with evocations of neurological disorders, from Capgras syndrome to de Clérambault's syndrome, anteretrograde amnesia to autism.[2] Darwinian views of human nature are also much in evidence in contemporary literature. In French fiction, Michel Houellebecq's cynical outlook on social and sexual behaviour presents the human race as still in thrall to genetic imperatives. Houellebecq's Goncourt-winning *La Carte et le territoire* (*The Map and the Territory*, 2010), describes the family as an institution designed for the reproduction of the species, and fashion trends as an oscillation around Darwinian norms. The view of human sexuality held by the novel's protagonist is one often repeated through Houellebecq's work:

> Probably marked by the trendy ideas of his generation, he had up to that point considered sexuality to be a force for good, a source of union which could increase harmony between humans via the innocent pathways of shared pleasure. Now, though, he saw more and more often the struggle, brutal fighting for dominance, elimination of rivals and the risky proliferation of acts of coitus for no other reason than to ensure the maximum propagation of genes.[3]

Texts like these contribute to the cultural environment in which Darrieussecq published her most significant novel on mind and brain. *A Brief Stay with the Living* recounts twenty-four hours in the lives of the Johnson family, the unnamed mother and her three daughters, Jeanne, Anne, and Nore, plus, for a brief interlude, the English-speaking father and ex-husband. Through a mixture of stream-of-consciousness and free indirect style, the novel narrates the thoughts, emotions, and perceptions that pass through each character's mind, switching abruptly from one to the other in a manner that can leave readers struggling to orient themselves each time they are plunged into the middle of a new train of thought.[4] The characters are geographically separated, with Jeanne in Argentina, Anne in Paris, the father in Gibraltar and the mother and youngest daughter together in the Basque country, and the novel juxtaposes the dreams of Jeanne asleep in Buenos Aires with the simultaneous morning routine of her sisters awake in France. Despite their isolation—even the mother and daughter who share a house don't meet in the course of the day—the characters are connected through their shared memories, common familial traits, and concern for each other. One memory in particular links the characters: twenty-seven years previously, a moment of distraction on the beach allowed their three-year-old brother, Pierre, to be washed out to sea and drowned. The anniversary of the recovery of his body falls in the month of October, in which the story is set. None of the characters marks this anniversary, or discusses the incident in any way, but the traumatic event lurks in all their minds, including, to some extent, that of the teenage Nore, who has been kept ignorant of the tragedy in her family's past. The novel encourages the reader to piece together the story from the associative flashes and veiled allusions which appear unbidden in the characters' thoughts. Also linking the characters are more uncanny psychic connections: two sleeping sisters, Nore and Jeanne, share the same dream, while the third, Anne, has schizophrenic delusions of telepathic powers, yet seems genuinely to perceive her distant sisters, and perhaps her brother's ghost, at the novel's close. The professional scientific knowledge of the mind and brain of psycholinguist Anne, and the amateur interest in the same displayed by the other characters, all of whom spend much of the novel thinking about consciousness, is counterbalanced by this strain of the fantastic which links Darrieussecq's novel into the tradition of psychological ghost stories.

The 'hard problem' of the relationship between neuronal activity and conscious experience is a fascination for Darrieussecq, and her fiction shifts perspective constantly between mind and brain. 'What is it that thinks, inside our cranium?' she asks in the essay *Rapport de police*:

> Neurons and biochemistry, how can we leave it at that? How can we understand that this is what is thinking, these two whitish lobes shaped like a cauliflower, like a fœtus, like intestines, like a labyrinth? The same and not the same for every human being, and nobody knows what happens in there, what is thought in there, not why nor how. [. . .] Yes, what is it that thinks, in that hard casing traversed by air, saliva and blood—my head, balancing

> on my neck? What thinks, the next floor up from my mouth, perched between my ears, between my pulsing temples, what thinks when I think that I am thinking? It would be easier to believe in thinking with your guts, writing with your heart, all those myths of our own offal, than writing with these intangible *nothings* that are our thoughts.[5]

In *A Brief Stay*, the narrator and characters frequently imagine the physiological substrate on which their conscious thoughts supervene. Jeanne imagines her own small epiphany of recognizing an animal as a platypus in terms of 'two neurons linked up', or sleepily confuses the 'bang in your head' of orgasm with the bang of a literal bullet through the brain; Nore wonders if her lack of childhood memories stems from neurons lost while sniffing ether.[6] The mind's dependence on the physical brain is heavily underlined by Anne's anxious thoughts about the effect on the self of damage to or experiment on the brain: her knowledge of neurology skips from Wilder Penfield stirring memories with electrical stimulation of the temporal lobe to Edgar Moniz's Nobel Prize for lobotomizing the mentally ill, and thence to the horror of Shiro Ishii's vivisection of the conscious brains of Chinese prisoners of war: 'Imagine being in that head at that moment. . . . A stretch of the world goes blind, a colour vanishes, half my body, the bit of my brain that says "I" is snipped off'.[7] This last example stands as a vivid refutation of the immaterial Cartesian mind. Descartes's *Méditations* proffer as evidence for dualism the claim that 'there is a great difference between mind and body, in that the body is by its nature always divisible, while the mind is wholly indivisible'. For Descartes, the divisibility of the material body (in the very literal sense that parts of it can be lopped off) proves that the mind can't be of the same substance, since 'I cannot distinguish any parts to it, but conceive myself as something sole and entire'.[8] The parallel Darrieussecq imagines between the scalpel carving out the victim's grey matter and the corresponding loss of a specific sector of mental function takes on Descartes's postulate to the letter, and makes divisibility itself the evidence for a materialist understanding of consciousness.

The self conjured by this materialist mind is fragile and subject to drastic transformation. Anne's sleepwalking, for instance, presents her unconscious behaviour as another persona, perhaps even a more authentic one: 'The person she was in her sleep liked Coca-Cola, didn't bother to close doors and went for walks in the moonlight, and these three trivial characteristics seemed more real to her, more *Anne*, than everything her waking self pretended to be'.[9] Minds without self-consciousness, 'absent from yourself' (p. 40; trans. 22) are figured even in the typography of the text as 'j/e', a first person that has been struck through or split apart.[10] Where the self is present, it is sometimes doubled through reflexive thinking. Nore crashes her car as her consciousness is filled with self-awareness, to the extent that the mental processes involved in driving a car are crowded out: '*I'm driving*, she's gripped, brutally assaulted by the idea. Amazed, not because she's driving, but because she's here. I was observing myself observing myself'.[11] There is a Sartrean flavour to Darrieussecq's representation in this regard, as the essential reflexivity of consciousness is linked to its intentionality: 'When I was little, with Jeanne, we played at not thinking, at thinking of nothing, in our woolly way'. Anne remembers at one point. 'But you still think about thinking nothing, you reproduce yourself, that's the snag in exercises like this, you see yourself thinking and so no longer think'.[12] The impossibility of an empty consciousness occupies the thoughts of several characters in the novel, and, in a move typical of Darrieussecq, serves to connect a philosophical question to an emotional drama: for these women, a clear consciousness is not an abstract notion but an unreachable ideal for minds haunted by guilt and pain. Elsewhere the changing self through different states of consciousness is evoked through the style and rhythm of Darrieussecq's prose. Anne's thoughts and perceptions are an incoherent, disjointed rush during her panic attack as she flees the Bibliothèque Nationale after a failed morning rendez-vous; at the other end of the day, the narrative of her thoughts luxuriates in slow associations, clumsy wordplay, and emphatic capital letters as she dances, drunk and alone, in a night-club.[13] Most strikingly, the novel's climactic scene takes Jeanne through a range of disparate mental states as she is trapped in her slowly sinking car after driving off the road into a canal in a moment of distraction. The episode begins with complex syntax and logical connections as Jeanne marvels at her own calm and attempts to reason her way out of the situation. We then follow her increasing panic through shorter, choppier phrases reflecting half-formed thoughts and snatched perceptions, interrupted by angry expletives and futile imperatives ('stop calm down'). With resignation comes wandering attention, as perceptions and practical thoughts are interspersed with fragments of memory, songs, regrets, and morbid imagination. Imperceptibly the episode moves into its final phase as Jeanne's oxygen-starved brain enters a dream-like state of perceptual hallucinations ('green and black, sparkling flies') and cognitive misfires, before breaking down into single words and silence.[14]

This emphasis on differing mental states builds an image of a self which is less permanent and less coherent than we may find comfortable. Such an impression is reinforced both by the impersonal content of many of the characters' thoughts, and the frequent lack of volition in their manner of development. Helena Chadderton comments on the patchwork of song lyrics, nursery rhymes, advertising slogans, and clichéd expressions that make up much of the mental flow of all the characters: 'Paradoxically, the reproduction of social discourses is essential to the authentic capturing of individual consciousness'.[15] The characters are immersed in a shared cultural soup, as, presumably, is the novel's implied reader, and are recognizable as contemporary Europeans through the extent to which these cultural artefacts infuse their mental life. What is more, these artefacts are not simply a passive mental stock to be called on and manipulated by the mind at will. Rather, they actively divert and control the stream of thought, as the characters' structures of mental association are hijacked by ear-worms and viral memes. Anne's contemplation of the courtyard 'forest' at the National Library conjures a whimsical image of wildlife leaping to safety as a rectangle of woodland is uprooted wholesale to be airlifted to Paris; unbidden, an image of James Bond leaping from a telephone box in similar circumstances appears in her mind (p. 9; trans. 2). Such lack of control of your own thoughts can be distressing: 'Get it out of your head, those gunshots in your head, bang, bang, coming back like a song, a tune that sticks in your head', Jeanne tells herself as she is tormented by a memory of the Stephen King novel, *It*, with its children lured to death by drowning, which leads in turn to association with the memory of her own brother's death.[16]

Mental association of this kind acts as one of the guiding principles of *A Brief Stay's* narrative structure. Intrigue is generated as the largely trivial daily activities of the protagonists spark associations, through which the network of an emotional history between the four women is gradually sketched in, and, most particularly, the mysterious event in their shared past that they each try *not* to think about. Darrieussecq's narrative records the flow of thought, slipping into first-person stream-of-consciousness to capture inner monologue, then sliding out to free indirect style when an impersonal narrator is required for purposes of elucidation or to evoke non-linguistic thoughts and perceptions (to which we will return shortly). As we saw in the Introduction, the subject-matter may be closely related to Proust's, but the effect is different. This is mental activity as it is experienced, flowing as if in real time, with no attempt to pause, delve and analyze retrospectively the nature of the processes which have taken place. Darrieussecq's decision to eschew introspection would be endorsed by William James, who laments in his *Principles of Psychology* the inefficacy of the introspective method to comprehend the flux of conscious experience:

> Let anyone try to cut a thought across in the middle and get a look at its section, and he will see how difficult the introspective observation of the transitive tracts is. The rush of the thought is so headlong that it almost brings us up at the conclusion before we can

> arrest it. Or if our purpose is nimble enough and we do arrest it, it ceases forthwith to be itself. As a snowflake crystal caught in the warm hand is no longer a crystal but a drop, so, instead of catching the feeling of a relation moving to its term, we find we have caught some substantive thing, usually the last word we were pronouncing, statically taken, and with its function, tendency, and particular meaning in the sentence quite evaporated. The attempt at introspective analysis in these cases is in fact like seizing a spinning top to catch its motion, or trying to turn up the gas quickly enough to see how the darkness looks.[17]

A Brief Stay with the Living is a novel of the transitive tracts—the flights between the perchings of thought in James's metaphorical terms. Darrieussecq strives to reproduce, insofar as it's possible to do so in a linguistic medium, the bazaar of competing thoughts and impressions that make up a consciousness constantly in motion.[18] As she freely admits in discussing the novel, psychological analysis must give way in order to evoke subjective immediacy, and in this it is Joyce, rather than Proust, who is the novel's more closely related antecedent:

> I write psychological books in opposition to psychology. I don't settle for sentences like 'I felt very anxious' or 'She was very happy'. Those sentences were expanded upon, stretched to their fullest extent, at the turn of the nineteenth century to the twentieth, with Proust. Then there came the break that was Joyce: how it happens in the mind itself. *Ulysses*, among other books, gave sustenance to *A Brief Stay with the Living*. I want to know what anxiety is, what happiness is, what the sea or a baby is, what it is from the inside, as if it were the first time I'd entered these regions. I want to say to the reader: 'See, feel, hear: this is a wave, this is a woman who's losing herself, this is a mind thinking.'[19]

The lineage is not a direct one, however. Darrieussecq, perhaps surprisingly, rejects the label 'stream-of-consciousness' to categorize her novel's style, and indeed, the relationship between the discourse of her novel and that of her modernist precursors is sufficiently intriguing and complex to be worth a quick detour.[20]

Interior monologue of the kind pioneered by Édouard Dujardin in *Les Lauriers sont coupés* (1888) and made famous by *Ulysses* (1922) is generally more coherent and controlled in its flow than Darrieussecq's, as well, of course, as being exclusively linguistic in its content. Dujardin's claim to have invented the form from scratch may be exaggerated, but his story is the first attempt to narrate an entire novel through what purports to be a fragmented running commentary of thoughts and perceptions passing through the protagonist's mind. As we can see, the realism of the monologue is hampered by the need to introduce characters, describe settings and narrate action within the idiom:

> The waiter. The table. My hat on the hat-stand, take off my gloves. They should be thrown carelessly on the table, next to the plate; or in my coat pocket, rather; no, on the table. Little things like this are a matter of manners. My overcoat on the hat-stand; I sit down; ah, I was weary.[21]

Nevertheless, his work is acknowledged by Joyce as the inspiration for the famous 'Penelope' episode at the end of *Ulysses*, in which we eavesdrop on the thoughts running through the head of Leopold Bloom's wife as she lies in bed, rendered in conversational idiom, associative structure, and without punctuation or division of any kind. Here is an extract, in which Molly Bloom recalls her tryst with Boylan earlier that day:

> no thats no way for him has he no manners nor no refinement nor no nothing in his nature slapping us behind like that on my bottom because I didnt call him Hugh the ignoramus that doesnt know poetry from a cabbage thats what you get for not keeping them in their proper place pulling off his shoes and trousers there on the chair before me so barefaced without even asking permission and standing out that vulgar way in the half of a shirt they wear to be admired like a priest or a butcher or those old hypocrites in the time of Julius Caesar[22]

Joyce evades Dujardin's problem of communicating meaning to the reader via a discourse which is essentially non-communicative by placing his own stream-of-consciousness writing at the very end of his novel. (The interior monologues of Stephen Dedalus and Leopold Bloom feature prominently in earlier parts of the novel, but are intercut with impersonal narration to orient the reader.) There is thus little burden of imparting information to the reader, since the characters and their relationships, the setting and actions of the day have all been laid out already in the preceding chapters, and 'Penelope' simply offers a meditation on the established story from a new perspective. In this extract, for instance, we know that 'Hugh' refers to Boylan, and we know already, or at least share Leopold Bloom's strong suspicions, of the sexual encounter referred to. Molly Bloom is not required to tell herself stories inside her head: she performs no actions in the present, and doesn't so much recount past events as pass judgement upon them, allowing Joyce to obliquely sketch in the memories which arouse her feelings.

Stream-of-consciousness style has had a huge impact on the representation of the mind in western literature in the century since Joyce's novel. Notable examples of it in subsequent French fiction include Simone de Beauvoir's 'Monologue' (1967), Philippe Sollers's *Paradis* (*Paradise*, 1981), and Nina Bouraoui's *Mes mauvaises pensées* (*My Bad Thoughts*, 2005), although the latter two texts blur the boundary between internal monologue and written or spoken language, while closely adhering to the Joycean form. Stream-of-consciousness also has affinities with the products of the 'automatic writing' experiments of Breton and the Surrealists, and even makes a somewhat incongruous appearance in Roquentin's diary in *Nausea*. Joyce and his successors restored a sense of chaos and spontaneity to the representation of thought, and foregrounded the immediacy of consciousness as never before. We might query with Beckett and Sarraute whether a continuous verbal commentary really exists in mental life, and whether language is the dominant mode of thought and thereby deserving the focus of our attention. Proust, who died the year *Ulysses* was published, offers a pre-emptive critique of the interior monologue in the final volume of his novel:

> But while, in cases where the imprecise language of, say, vanity is involved, realigning interior indirect speech (which as it goes on moves further and further away from the original, central impression) until it coincides with the straight line which ought to have run directly from the impression, while this realignment is a difficult matter and something which our idle nature is reluctant to take on, there are other instances, where love is involved for example, where the same realignment becomes painful.[23]

Like Sarraute after him, Proust's concern isn't so much with the presence of running monologue in consciousness as with its authenticity. For Proust, inner monologue is a poor guide to the truth of mental life, since it may often be mendacious and self-serving. Extended consciousness, acting in something very like Sartrean bad faith, employs inner monologue to distract itself from psychic realities which are very much present at a more primal level of the mind. Literary representation which restricts itself to the monologue thus risks offering a distorted view of what the subject is 'really thinking', and would do better to look at what lies behind the linguistic thoughts. This, as we have seen, was precisely the project to which Sarraute devoted herself, and one which she explicitly formulated in opposition to stream-of-consciousness style. In *L'Ère du soupçon*, she declares her own principal interest to lie in:

> what is hiding behind the interior monologue: an immeasurable abundance of sensations, images, feelings, memories, urges, latent little acts that no inner language expresses, which jostle at the gates of consciousness, gather in compact groups and suddenly burst forth, disintegrate immediately, combine in different ways and reappear in a new form, while within us, like the ribbon which patters out of the slot on a Teletype, the uninterrupted flow of words continues to unfurl.[24]

Sarraute befriended Darrieussecq after the publication of *Truismes*, becoming what the younger writer refers to as a 'spiritual grandmother'. Darrieussecq notes in interview both the similarities and differences between their literary projects:

> Nathalie Sarraute gave me the strength not to write 'she felt very anxious'. I tried to find something else. Her own thing was subconversations, what was going on at the margins, and mine is not exactly that, it's, how can I define it, an absence from oneself. [. . .] I try to describe this void that we are, which is filled by all these other things that aren't us, but become us. [. . .] As for her, she was much more interested in dialogue, conversation, what's going on beneath the words. I'm more interested in what goes on beneath the skin, I'd say, I'm almost more physical than her, I deal with a form of desire.[25]

Sarrautean aspects to Darrieussecq's representation are not hard to find in the text. The relatively few lines of direct speech in the text are inevitably accompanied by *sub-conversation* at variance with the spoken meaning, as when Nore attempts to make small-talk with a good-looking stranger walking his dog on the beach:

> *Nice dog you've got there*, the little bugger's sniffing at my, which only makes him laugh, *Charlie! What a clown . . .* Say something, speak when you're spoken to, they're calling to you from the back of the house, *I've seen you here a few times*, brilliant.[26]

Nore's inner monologue encompasses the dialogue, which is inserted seamlessly within it without attribution to tell us which words Nore speaks and which she hears. As is often the case with Sarraute, the thoughts are comically at odds with the social façade presented by the spoken language, although there is nothing reminiscent of Sarraute's extreme or violent imagery here, simply an honest inner discourse flowing in counterpoint to the spoken presentation of the social self. Even when she draws a distinction between herself and Sarraute, Darrieussecq's description of the self as a void filled with the stuff that permeates into us from outside is interestingly reminiscent of Sartre's (mis)interpretation of Sarraute in his preface to *Portrait d'un inconnu*. Sartre suggests in the preface that Sarraute's minds are under the 'reign of the commonplace', in that the characters' thoughts are banal, and that they are communally, rather than individually, produced. He goes on to compare her writing to conventional novelists who 'attempt [. . .] to persuade us that the world is composed of irreplaceable individuals, all exquisite, even the bad ones, all passionate, all unique. Nathalie Sarraute shows us the wall of inauthenticity; she shows it everywhere. And behind this wall? What is there? Precisely nothing'.[27] The image of empty minds bombarded by the commonplace thoughts of a common culture doesn't precisely match Darrieussecq, who presents markedly different characters despite shared culture and upbringing, but it is a closer likeness than the writer Sartre is actually describing.

One feature of non-linguistic thought that is very much more prominent in Darrieussecq than Sarraute is the visual. Like Breton's *Mad Love*, Darrieussecq's text brings the reader into direct contact with the perceptions of its characters. Line drawings reproduce imagined images, while typeface mimicry serves to reproduce the magazine horoscopes read by the characters as if they have been literally cut and pasted into the book. Less directly, perceived sounds and remembered tunes are rendered through inventive onomatopoeia and quoted lyrics, to give the text as near as possible its own soundtrack. The procedures foreground the raw material of perception in order to offer the reader a taste of the immediacy of the characters' subjectivity, and to allow the author to break down the processes of interaction between the perceived world and the interpreting self. Perception in Darrieussecq is not a precise and neutral recording of reality. 'Since the phone rang, you can hear the garden. A contrast', notes Nore, as a previously subliminal noise accedes to her awareness.[28] Rather, perception is an active mental reconstruction, reminiscent of what Ramachandran memorably dubs the 'best-fit hallucination for data'.[29] Darrieussecq's characters speculate on how other minds might hallucinate their perceptual data differently. Looking at the sea, Nore thinks of those who are unable to combine and interpret their raw sense-impressions to produce a coherent object:

> There are sick, sad people for whom the sea is just a stack of parallel blue, white and grey lines, but having sound, smell and motion. But they can't make the connection, unfortunately their illness makes them incompatible with this idea, not so much as far as the sea is concerned, but with vision, the coherency of the world.[30]

Anne offers the philosophical formulation of the same issue when she refers to the 'Molyneux problem', the question posed to John Locke by his friend William Molyneux as to whether a man born blind would, on regaining his sight, be immediately able to distinguish a cube from a sphere.[31] Locke thought not, and Anne confirms his intuition with evidence from neurology:

> A person born blind will never really see anything. He will see colours, lines, a varied muddle of optical stimuli, but no relief, no way of organizing them. His brain will be incapable of decoding what his eyes are capturing and his nerves transmitting. To see, you must have already seen. Of the two case studies: 1) committed suicide; 2) committed suicide. Because the promised light was incomprehensible.[32]

Much later, Nore considers idly how her seascape might impress itself on the mind of a cat: 'What would he see? A shadowless, hostile world. The soft sand beneath his feet. The seaweed smelling of fish'.[33] Thus, not only is perception a construct from data, it is a contingent construct, ordered differently according to who or what is doing the perceiving. This is also suggestive of phenomenological attitudes to perception: the world is perceived, not as it *is*, but according to the projects of the perceiver and the 'readiness-to hand' (to borrow Heidegger's term) of what is present.[34] Feline priorities are different from human priorities, and so the shore is a different world in the cat's eyes from how it appears in ours. The best-fit hallucination is a common model of perception across Darrieussecq's work, from the literal aural and visual hallucinations caused by the low-stimulus environment of the South Pole in *White*, to the poignant metaphor which concludes *Naissance des fantômes*, when the question of whether other animals (including 'cats, birds, fish and flies with compound eyes') perceive the world as humans do becomes an acknowledgement that the narrator has never really known how her husband saw her, or how he viewed the state of their marriage.[35]

Darrieussecq's interest in visual consciousness extends beyond issues of perception. *A Brief Stay with the Living* is filled with mental images from dreams, memory and imagination, and their centrality to mental life is emphasized. Nore comments: 'There are images with different densities, night dreams and daydreams, memories and flashbacks, and sometimes I see places and people from way back, even from before I was born, but Arnold doesn't believe me. Showers of barely glimpsed, wordless images. They must mean something'.[36] Darrieussecq explains this element of her work as a deliberate reaction against models of the mind which would seek to assimilate thought and language:

> I'm chasing after something impossible in that zone where there are no words, but that's what drives me onwards. I remember my philosophy teacher in the sixth form, quite excellent and always very convincing: she opened up a whole universe for me, the conceptual universe, but in doing so she also explained to us that there is no such thing as a wordless thought. That really bothered me, because it really did seem to me that in my own head thoughts could exist without words. And note that she wasn't talking about the unconscious mind, about which I had no idea at the time, incidentally, and which also is constituted without words, even though it is a complex entity. My philosophy teacher represented that French tradition of 'anything that can be well conceived can be clearly expressed'. Well, it seemed to me that you could also conceive of things 'poorly': you could think, not 'well' according to the great French tradition, but think all the same, without clearly expressing things in your head, without necessarily using words.[37]

The idea that thought requires language is discussed and explicitly rejected in *Le Bébé* with regard to the writer's own infant son ('that you need to speak in order to think, that concepts only come with words, seems a poor theory'), and in *A Brief Stay with the Living* too it is early childhood that is the focus of much of the discussion of linguistic determinism.[38] Nore's tutor offers the determinist thesis: 'Arnold says that infants don't speak and so have no memories. That nothing exists apart from what is thought, in other words what is spoken'.[39] Arnold's ideas recall the hypothesis of linguistic relativism, expounded by Benjamin Lee Whorf and Edward Sapir, according to which our thoughts are determined by the language in which we (necessarily) express them, and thus different language-groups will share within the group distinct conceptions of self and world.[40] Such ideas found favour in several quarters of French poststructuralist thought, including in Michel Foucault's 'epistemes' of successive historical conceptions of truth and knowledge, or in the emphasis of Lacanian psychoanalysis on the linguistic structure of the mind. While there is evidence that, say, people distinguish two colours more easily if their language has a separate word for each, the stronger implications of Whorf's hypothesis now have little credit among linguists and psychologists.[41] In *A Brief Stay with the Living*, the suggestion that different languages build different minds is touched on facetiously when Jeanne's Argentinian husband wonders if she is the same person when she speaks Spanish as she is when she speaks French. Her response is double edged. On the one hand, the most significant difference between Spanish-speaking Jeanne and French-speaking Jeanne is the position of her tongue: 'If I am different, then all I can say is that French is pronounced at the front of the palate'; on the other hand: 'I don't even know if I'm the same from one sentence to the next'.[42] Her self may not divide along a linguistic faultline, but it is no less fragmented for that. It is the psycholinguistic research carried out by Anne, though, that allows the novel to make its case clearly against linguistic determinism. In experiments modelled on genuine research carried out by the psychologist Peter Eimas and colleagues, Anne plays nonsense syllables to one- and two-month-old infants, sometimes made up of the phonemes of French, sometimes from foreign languages, and observes the results:

> When their dark blue eyes (a common colour at that age) suddenly stop for a second, stare fixedly, when their fingers stop fiddling with their rattles, and their mouths stop sucking for a second, then you can see a wordless idea forming, a wide-open idea, which seizes them, shakes them to the bone, unfolding at once, *I RECOGNIZE THIS, I'VE ALREADY HEARD IT SOMEWHERE, BUT WHERE?* when they hear, taratara, their mother tongue.[43]

The extract asserts unequivocally that (in Anne's view at least) the infants are capable of conscious thought, and of quite complex conceptual thought, without the use of language. Furthermore, it demonstrates to the reader of *A Brief Stay with the Living* that the language of the text itself can be employed not only to record the language of inner monologue, but to transpose into words thoughts that were not themselves linguistic—in this case the capitalized infant epiphanies, which are obviously not intended to be understood literally as words expressed in the babies' minds. Elsewhere in the novel, the same point is made with regard to adult cognition as Nore considers the case of an unnamed man who wakes up in the hospital with his mind wiped clean of both memory and language, and imagines his first thought on opening his eyes: 'He sees the whiteness of the hospital, his first unspoken idea is that everything's white'.[44]

The relationship of thought to language has been of interest to psychologists and philosophers of mind throughout the period we are discussing. On Darrieussecq's side of the argument we find both Bergson (as touched on in the previous chapter) and William James: the former refers to the 'unhoped-for good fortune' with which the creative writer discovers the word that encapsulates his wordless concept, while the latter's stream of consciousness is not a flow of language, but a flow of 'mind-stuff' that may include words, images, and much else besides.[45] Sartre too is concerned to include the non-linguistic in his representation of consciousness. 'I am struggling against words', declares Roquentin in *Nausea* as he fights to explain his Bouville park revelation.[46] In *Qu'est-ce que la littérature?*, Sartre directly considers the validity of the novelist's stream of words in representing the mind's flow of thought:

> In the end, it is not without a certain amount of doctoring that the flow of consciousness can be reduced to a succession of words, even malformed ones. If the word is given as an intermediary *signifying* a reality which, in its essence, transcends language, then so much the better: the word makes itself forgotten, offloading our attention onto the object. But if it presents itself as *mental reality*, if the author, in writing, claims to be giving us an ambiguous reality which is a sign in its objective essence, i.e. to the extent that it relates to something outside us, and a thing in its formal essence, i.e. as immediate mental datum in that case we can reproach him for not having taken a side, and for ignoring the rule of rhetoric which might be formulated thus: in literature, where you use signs, you must use *only* signs; and if the *reality* you wish to signify is *a word*, you must render it to the reader by means of different words. We might also reproach him for having forgotten that the greatest riches of mental life are *silent*.[47]

Sartre's aesthetic objection to stream-of-consciousness is dubious: if it's acceptable to quote the words of spoken language directly in dialogue, there seems no good reason why the unspoken language of inner monologue shouldn't be treated the same way, since in both cases the word is at the same time an existent in itself and a signifier of something beyond itself. However, his suggestion that consciousness is better represented by words on the page standing as intermediaries to signify thoughts which are not those same words connects closely to Darrieussecq's literary project, at least where thoughts concerned are more than, or other than, words. As for the mental silence Sartre mentions in the final line, Howells has commented on the phenomenon in Sartre's own fiction, examining the silent inner shame of Daniel in *L'Âge de raison* as he returns from his failed attempt to drown his cats, and noting that, when the character's inner monologue returns, it comes as a (Proustian) distraction from his mental state rather than an expression of it.[48] Mental silence is not something readers would readily associate with Darrieussecq's representation, however: mental cacophony would seem nearer the mark. Even here, though, there is a connection between the writers. Sartre reproaches literary stream-of-consciousness for neglecting the times in which the mind is filled with silent attention, emotion or sensation. Darrieussecq rejects stream-of-consciousness for drowning out the hubbub of competing mental events with a smooth flow of joined-up monologue. Both seek to disrupt the stream of inner words in order to make room for the rest.

Current scientific thinking on consciousness and language also generally sides with Darrieussecq in uncoupling the two phenomena. Steven Pinker argues against linguistic determinism in *The Stuff of Thought*, and proposes instead his own model of 'conceptual semantics', in which a proto-linguistic level of thought, which Pinker dubs 'mentalese', maps simple 'digital' concepts of space, time, substance, and causality onto the 'analogue' flow of reality, combining them into propositions about the world, and, through metaphor, into complex and abstract ideas at the higher level at which language operates.[49] Damasio also downgrades language, as we saw earlier in this study, claiming that core consciousness is a 'non-languaged map of logically related events'.[50] Interestingly from the perspective of literary analysis, he suggests that, while language is not central to consciousness, narrative *is*. Telling stories is, for Damasio, a 'brain obsession', but with a process that has closer parallels to the image-flow of film narrative than the language-based storytelling. Damasio speculates that the phenomenon of creating a second-order mental narrative to reflect what is happening to the organism and its environment is widespread in the animal kingdom, and that what sets humanity apart is our creation of a third-order verbal translation of this narrative. Language is thus a transposition of non-linguistic concepts which exist prior to it in the core self. In this regard, Damasio finds himself at odds with some contemporary theorists, including Daniel Dennett and Julian Jaynes, who emphasize the linguistic aspects of consciousness.[51] The disagreement is perhaps not ultimately over the role of language in the mind, but simply, as with so many other arguments in this area, over the definition of 'consciousness' itself. The most sophisticated activity of the mind is often linguistic or language-related; the most basic functions operate on an instinctive level in which language plays no role. Once we exchange the psychoanalytic model of a sharply divided mind for a continuum of activity from unconscious, through core consciousness, to extended consciousness, the limits become blurred. As we saw with Beckett, the more you restrict the definition of consciousness to the highest and most complex mental activity, the more central language appears to be. Darrieussecq, we can be sure, favours no such restriction in her own view of the mind.

Away from the question of language, we find Darrieussecq has more in common with psychoanalytic models when it comes to another of her obsessions: the irrational mind. Dreams, madness and the uncanny feature strongly in *A Brief Stay with the Living*, often linked to a traditional Freudian conception of the Unconscious as product and repository of repressed trauma. The characters' psyches have many conventionally Freudian traits: Anne's earliest memory is a 'primal scene' of listening through a door to her parents having sex; the scarred face of the mother's second husband leads to 'inevitable slips of the tongue' from his conversation partners; Nore is 'excited' by the idea of going back in time to kill her mother and have sex with her father, and is given pause for thought by the reminder that no time machine is required for either activity.[52] Darrieussecq's treatment of mental illness in the novel offers the most sustained example of psychoanalytic influence on the writer's understanding of the mind. Anne, the middle daughter, exhibits symptoms of what appears to be a form of paranoid schizophrenia, a distressing condition to herself and her family, with none of the associations of creativity or liberation celebrated by Breton. She believes herself to have been 'recruited' into a network of global telepathic surveillance, the agents of which are selected for their 'extraordinarily open mind' in order to watch over the global consciousness of humanity.[53] She believes that people she sees in the street may be recruiters, that such people are able to read her thoughts, and that she too has the power to read minds. The novel explicitly connects Anne's mental health to the childhood trauma of her brother's death. The mother refers to her as 'the only one who really went mad' in the aftermath of the drowning.[54] This is not necessarily at odds with current medical knowledge: the causes of schizophrenia remain in debate, but the 'stress-vulnerability' model, in which a combination of neurological vulnerability and life events trigger the onset of the condition, is now widely accepted.[55] Where the representation of Anne's mental illness takes on a distinctly Freudian tone, though, is in the linking of the symptoms manifested with the traumatic event in the character's past. Darrieussecq explains in interview:

> In the network of this family, there was a momentary lapse of guard, by the whole family's lack of attention a child drowned. They all feel guilty, and Anne has developed paranoia because she needs to control the world and to think that an infallible network exists to watch over us, in which she imagines she plays a role.[56]

Thus, the common schizophrenic delusion that others may be able to read your thoughts becomes in *A Brief Stay with the Living* an idiosyncratic reaction which reflects the particular trauma that gave rise to it. Anne blames herself for a failure of surveillance at the beach on the day her brother drowned, and this unmastered guilt has been repressed into her Unconscious, from where it makes its presence felt through coded symptoms: Anne becomes part of a universal supernatural surveillance network, through which she and all humanity will be forever under a watchful eye, and no such tragedy can ever recur. The amenability of Anne's delusions to being traced back to an original cause, and interpreted in the light of this cause, clearly sets Darrieussecq on the side of psychoanalysis, against clinical psychology and psychotherapies based on cognitive models of the mind. For these latter, the particular symptoms exhibited by a mentally ill person are unlikely to have such a direct link to events which triggered the onset of the illness, and there would be little profit in exploring the details of the delusion in the hope of understanding its origin. Cognitive Behavioural Therapy, in fact, would be inclined to dissuade a paranoid patient from dwelling on her delusion, believing that to do so would more likely exacerbate the symptoms than elucidate the condition.

There is a further twist to Anne's illness which complicates the situation, and that is the fact that her telepathic powers may not be delusional at all. Towards the end of the novel, Anne has a vision of her sister Nore having sex in their childhood home precisely as it occurs. Anne also perceives a third, ghostly presence in the house, which the reader presumes to be that of Pierre. The lovers themselves feel haunted: Nore is spooked by a face at the window, and Nicolas finds the atmosphere of the house 'hostile'. A little later, Anne wakes screaming at the moment her elder sister drowns on the other side of the world. Other incidents corroborate the existence of the supernatural in the diegesis: the mother may also glimpse Pierre's ghost, and Nore and Jeanne appear to share a dream.[57] The supernatural is boldly presented within the materialist framework of the novel: Anne considers herself to be 'tied hook line and sinker to the flow of my neurons into everyone's thoughts' and says of the surveillance network, 'they can film the inside of my mind' ('l'intérieur de mon cerveau' in the original French, which can mean both 'inside my mind' and 'inside my brain').[58] The contradiction between the immaterial mind implied in the existence of ghosts and telepaths and the resolutely material brain activity emphasized throughout Darrieussecq's text isn't directly addressed within her work, but it is one of several elements pointing to a metaphorical reading, and indeed a psychoanalytic reading, of the supernatural themes in her work, as we shall see.

Darrieussecq has made clear that she doesn't believe in the real existence of the supernatural phenomena described in her novels: 'I've often found myself making clear once again that ghosts, in my opinion, exist only in fiction', she writes in *Rapport de police*, but also declares elsewhere: 'The fantastic comes naturally to me. It offers a description of the way we can experience reality within ourselves. There's nothing rational about reality'.[59] Across her œuvre, apparently supernatural events disturb otherwise rationally explicable narratives, from the animal transformations of *Truismes* to the abundant ghosts, who also make their presence felt in one way or another in *Naissance des fantômes*, *White*, *Le Pays*, and *Tom est mort*. With the exception of *Truismes*, where magical metamorphoses are accepted at face value as part of its surreal dystopian world, all Darrieussecq's texts present psychologically plausible characters in largely realist settings. The supernatural forms an uncanny irruption into these worlds, and the narratives leave open the question of whether the protagonists' experiences are a matter of coincidence, hallucination, or genuine encounters. With reference to the supernatural experiences of the protagonist of *Naissance des fantômes*, Darrieussecq explains: 'I want to take my character at face value. That means that, what she is saying and experiencing, she really is saying and experiencing it and you have to believe her'.[60] If we're wondering whether Anne is 'really' telepathic, or if Pierre's ghost is 'really' there, we are probably asking the wrong question. The intent is not ontological but phenomenological: Darrieussecq is interested in the subjectivity of her protagonists' minds, not the objective truth of reality, and the reader's uncertainty allows us to share in the characters' uncertainty, the better to experience the disorienting effect of the unexplained.

The psychoanalytic reading of Darrieussecq's supernatural is encouraged by several comments within her novels and outside of them. In an interview, Darrieussecq defines her ghosts as 'everything that is kept silent, everything that is unspoken, everything that is left unsaid'.[61] In *Le Pays*, the protagonist connects seeing the ghost of her dead brother with her recent visit to her psychoanalyst, 'whose work raises spectres like dust under a broom', and the narrator ends the novel with the assertion, 'ghosts are born from our haunted minds, which spark and extinguish them, guttering, feeble candles. They are for us alone'.[62] All Darrieussecq's ghostly visitations are the return of lost loved ones to grieving parents and siblings, who are often burdened by guilt over the death, as is the case in *A Brief Stay with the Living*. Freud's definition of the uncanny is built around such situations, playing on etymological connections between the German word, *unheimlich*, and related terms *heimisch* ('homely') and *heimlich* ('secret'). The uncanny is thus 'something which is secretly familiar [*heimlich-heimisch*], which has undergone repression and then returned from it'.[63] This has clear validity for Darrieussecq's ghosts: in *A Brief Stay with the Living*, when the memory of Pierre's death appears in the characters' consciousness, it generally comes as an involuntary association, and is quickly displaced by less painful thoughts. In fact, while the traumatic memories may have been 'repressed' in the commonly used sense that characters avoid thinking of them, they are not repressed in the strict psychoanalytic sense, which would imply they have been sealed in an area of the mind beyond the voluntary reach of consciousness. Darrieussecq's characters, in line with current psychological theories on the consequences of trauma, are only too aware of their painful memories, as this description of the mother makes clear: 'the inside of her brain colonized by hermit crabs, thoughts snapping their tiny pincers . . . her maddening tune in the hollow of her ear, in the depths of the lobes of her brain—that tweeting never stops'.[64]

Darrieussecq's experience with psychoanalysis as analysand and later analyst demonstrates the discipline's importance to her view of the mind, and her comments on the subject attest to the deliberate inclusion of its theories in her work:

> I've read Freud a little and practised him a lot, which is to say I've undergone psychoanalysis myself, for eight years, which allowed me among other things to separate (as far as it was possible to do so) my neurosis from my writing. Before, my manuscripts were all about me, my family, my navel. I couldn't have written *Pig Tales* without psychoanalysis. I wouldn't have managed to invent a character, to separate my voice from the character's voice. Thanks to the analysis, my neurosis feeds into my books without overwhelming them, and in doing so makes them readable, orients them outwards. I also have to thank it for giving me a career which is an adventure in itself, since, besides the writing, I have now become a psychoanalyst myself. It's a whole other story, which includes a long training period and infinite readings of Freud. And Lacan. But it has to be said that Freud is a writer as well as being a great researcher. [. . .] The guy is a great western sage, like there are great eastern sages.[65]

Psychoanalysis is one of the few points in which Darrieussecq finds herself in serious disagreement with Sarraute, and comments on the older writer's critique of Freud as follows:

> I did like it when Nathalie Sarraute would get worked up about that charlatan, Freud. I think that if she put so much vehemence into denying the validity of his theses, it must be because she saw him as her double. She valued 'her own' invention, sub-conversation, what she had unveiled with that. And the room that Freud left her, broad as it was, must have seemed to her to be dangerously narrow.[66]

Darrieussecq here employs a familiar psychoanalyst's response to criticism of the discipline, which is to recast the critique from a reasoned objection to an emotional response, allowing resistance to psychoanalysis to be itself psychoanalyzed. As we've seen, Sarraute's view of the mind is in several respects incompatible with Freud's, and it seems unlikely either that she secretly regarded him as her double, or that she thought he left her little to say on the nature of consciousness.

Where her own work is concerned, Darrieussecq's attitude to psychoanalysis offers an implied endorsement to critics' efforts to interpret her fiction through its framework, and many have taken up the invitation. These range from the implausible, such as the critic who would read the narrator's transformation in *Truismes* as a female fantasy of penis-envy, on the grounds that the nipples of her new breasts might be seen as resembling atrophied male genitals, to more subtle application of psychoanalytic theory, which, regardless of its validity in the real world, convincingly mirrors the mentality of the fictional characters. Kathryn Robson's discussion of melancholia is an example of the latter: taking Freud's conception of melancholia as a lingering state of unresolved grief due to a failure to work through the process of mourning, Robson profitably interprets Darrieussecq's literal hauntings as metaphors for grief and loss.[67]

Stories which blur the supernatural with the psychological are, of course, legion, and many of them pre-date Freud's theory of the uncanny, which was itself inspired by Hoffmann's *Sand Man*, as we saw earlier. Darrieussecq's uncanny owes at least as much to this literary heritage, which includes such notable French texts as Maupassant's *Le Horla* (*The Horla*, 1887), as it does to her psychoanalytic grounding. On this reading, Darrieussecq's supernatural becomes a further means to write the mind without using the hackneyed discourse of the psychological novel: the ghosts are an externalized symbol of inner grief and guilt, and their manifestations to the characters allow emotions to be played out as if an interaction with something outside of the self. We might incidentally read a similar literary-psychological metaphor into *A Brief Stay with the Living*'s telepathy. There are two ways in which a human mind can slip inside another person's consciousness to experience their thoughts vicariously: telepathy is one, and fiction is the other. The novel lists its protagonists to the reader on its back cover, before announcing: 'We are inside their minds'.[68] If Anne is really dipping in and out of the minds of her sisters in the latter pages of the story, then her actions mirror what we as readers have been doing since the first page, and what might be seen as the quintessential literary experience.

French psychotherapy may be riven by the 'guerre des psys' between psychoanalysts and cognitive therapists, while the 'Freud Wars' rage in the humanities with bitter exchanges between the proponents and detractors of the psychoanalytic view of the mind.[69] In Darrieussecq, however, psychoanalytic elements coexist harmoniously with scientific ideas drawn from various areas of cognitive science, neurology and evolutionary theory. As we have seen, Darrieussecq is fascinated by the brain as well as the mind. Her characters are equally interested: Anne recites to herself the organ's vital statistics: 'The human brain weighs in at 1.4 kilos, it is made up of 20,000 to 30,000 million neurones and about 10,000 times more synapses linking them together'.[70] They also consider themselves in some sense to *be* their brains, or at least to be the product of its activity. Nore remembers where she left her car 'after she'd quite simply plugged her brains in' (the French original uses the more anatomically specific 'méninges').[71] Anne fantasizes about reshaping her self with a re-modeled brain via a pre-frontal lobotomy administered with a sharp pencil: 'No more anxiety, no more mood swings, no more crises or blues, no more projects, no more concentration: a complete, pleasant, carefree distraction'.[72] A focus on the physiological underpinning of the mind inevitably raises the question of how different physiologies might give rise to different kinds of minds. Three such differences are particularly at issue in Darrieussecq: the difference between simple and complex brains in human development from infant to adult, the difference in both complexity and configuration between human brains and those of other animals, and the differences, or lack thereof, between male and female brains. Let's take them in turn.

Darrieussecq's characters have no time for the Cartesian idea of a divinely implanted soul at conception. 'You're not going to tell me eggs can think', scoffs Nore.[73] Rather, for Darrieussecq, consciousness is a phenomenon that dawns gradually with increasing neural complexity in the foetus. Jeanne considers in detail how the mind might develop *in utero* in tandem with the development of the brain:

> How to know at what age it starts thinking? Bang, conception, contact between two conducting bodies, a time bomb . . . First connection, it was black and then . . . Even if it's just the sensation of being here, of being here rather than nowhere, warmth, presence, and the din of a train, a beating heart, no ears yet, just the vibrations of the mother's heart, and skin not yet skin, something growing and beating in turn.[74]

This might be seen as another version of Beckett's spiral: an adult mind thinking its way back to the simplest, blankest state of conscious awareness, which in this case is represented by the beginnings of cognition in the womb. As the human develops from a bundle of cells to embryo, infant, child, and adult, the increasing sophistication of its mental activity rapidly matches and outstrips that of other forms of animal life. This reflection of evolutionary development (phylogeny) in the development of the individual (ontogeny) interests Darrieussecq's Darwinian side, and forms the basis of her exploration of the human mind within the wider sphere of living things. Anne as a baby had 'the wet fur of a little creature'; Nore as a toddler might well have been mentally bested by a chimpanzee at the zoo, as her sister speculates:

> Who was looking at who, we wondered, with its emotively human eyes, its human hands, and it could sit up better than Nore, take objects between thumb and index finger better

> than Nore, you might even wonder if Nore would be better off, brainpower-wise, at the triangle-in-the triangle game.[75]

We have seen earlier how Darrieussecq uses animal cognition to reflect on different ways of perceiving the world. Just as frequently, however, it is the similarity between human and non-human minds which draws her attention. Nore notes that pigs and octopuses have the most human-like eyes of the animal kingdom, and speculates that they see the world as we do (p. 36; trans. 19); later she finds 'troubling' the quivering eyelids of a cat in REM sleep, evidence that dreaming is not an exclusively human phenomenon (p. 205; trans. 125). Nore herself is playfully demoted down the cognitive scale in the scene on the beach, where her sexual interest in the dog-owner is referred to in terms of her 'snout snuffling inquisitively'.[76]

Darrieussecq's most famous exercise in blurring boundaries between human and animal minds is not in *A Brief Stay with the Living* at all, but in the metamorphosis into a pig of the narrator of *Truismes*. The pig-woman of this novel, and to a lesser extent her werewolf lover, offer the reader a fictional account of the subjective experience of being a human, being an animal, and, for much of the novel, being an undecidable hybrid somewhere between the two. Naama Harel's study of metamorphosis literature notes a conventional 'psycho-physical split' in such tales, which is to say that the stories generally recount a metamorphosis from human to animal where the character's body is concerned, but no corresponding transformation of their mind.[77] Aside from minor preferences, like Gregor Samsa's developing taste for rotten food in *Die Verwandlung* (*Metamorphosis*, 1915), metamorphosis literature presents us with the story of a human mind trapped in an animal body, and Harel includes Darrieussecq's tale as uncontroversially inhabiting this genre. Certainly, the character retains human-like mental traits while in pig form: other pigs are wary of her, as 'they are well aware that the thinking in there continues to be like human thinking'.[78] The author goes so far as to say: 'For me, at the end she is much more human than at the beginning. Whatever she may look like'.[79] As a monster and outcast the narrator does indeed learn to re-evaluate her life and her treatment by society, and to escape the received ideas she originally lived by, and according to which she was abused and exploited. She also gains the power of self-expression, both in the episode in which she talks the werewolf down from murderous bloodlust with a calming evocation of the natural world, and in the act of narrating the novel itself. However, Harel is surely wrong to claim that the novel deals purely with corporeal rather than psychological transformation. The human mentality sensed by the other pigs in the pig-sty is maintained only tenuously and with great struggle, as is made clear by the narrator's attempt to escape:

> My body didn't understand why it had to wrestle with the piece of steel, my body's movements lacked conviction while all my neurons were exhausting themselves to keep this one idea in mind, *the bolt, the bolt*, it was exhausting to struggle against yourself like that.[80]

Elsewhere, she forgets human things when in pig form, like the fact that church services happen on Sundays (she is becoming 'un peu bête', she explains in an untranslatable pun).[81] Memory of her human life fades, and she can no longer recall her boyfriend's face, and no longer read. Rather than feeling frustration at this latter phenomenon, she attempts to eat the books; she also eats corpses and sleeps in her own excrement in the same period. Most disturbingly, the narrator in pig form comes across a baby strapped into a car-seat, the mother of whom is loading up the car in haste as if to escape an abusive husband. The truth of the woman's situation occurs to the narrator 'like a flash of understanding' in retrospect, after the woman has fled.[82] During the encounter itself, however, there is little of the human in the narrator's cognition as she roots through the scattered belongings, fails to distinguish whether the sounds made by the baby as she pokes at it with her snout are laughing or crying (we presume the latter), and appears to be at real risk of killing and eating the infant: 'It seems, how can I put it, that it would have been easy to eat it, to sink my teeth into that nice pink flesh'.[83]

What is particularly striking about Darrieussecq's representation of the narrator's mind is its ever-shifting position on a continuum between human and animal. Just as the narrator's body is in constant flux between the two states, making it often impossible to visualize her, so her mentality moves between the two, while never completely reaching one or other condition. Crucially, the early stages of the transformation are already underway at the novel's opening, so there is no 'purely human' yardstick against which to measure the narrator's change. We infer that the narrator's character has always been one of naïve, trusting stupidity and uninhibited appetites, and that her social status has always been that of someone exploited for others' pleasure, profit, and contempt, all of which characteristics are exaggerated by the metamorphosis, until the exploitation at last turns her naivety to self-assertion and revolt. The novel is of course primarily a satire on society's attitudes to women, not a study of non-human cognition, and as a referent for what the narrator becomes, the 'grosse truie' ('fat sow') of misogynistic insults is at least as important as the actual farmyard animal, *sus domesticus*. Nevertheless, the novel does offer a striking portrait of the non-human, as in this example of animal fear:

> She shut the door, it went click clack, and that put a kind of restlessness in the air. I couldn't sleep because of these fearful waves, everything was quivering and getting off balance. All my fellow pigs were stirring, their good, honest smell was going sour, full of bad hormones, of stress, of fear. The smell split into separate blocks, each smell around each pig, their snouts seeking out the corners of the room, underneath the doors, a gap through which to flee, each wanting to leave the other to his own victim smell.[84]

In these few lines, sense-impressions, quasi-scientific physiological analysis, and physical metaphors to externalize emotion all combine to present a recognizable depiction of anxiety, but one that excludes higher cognitive functions specific to human fear.

Darrieussecq's experiments in focalizing narrative through animal minds—a pig in this novel, and brief forays in other novels into the mental perspective of a basking shark or a sealion—exploit the representation of non-human consciousness in order to comment on the human.[85] '[Animals] force us into on-the-spot metaphysics: what is it that separates us from them? What is it that makes us human?', the writer asks in an interview.[86] First of all, Darrieussecq is asserting that there *is* such a thing as non-human consciousness, in contradiction of the Cartesian concept of animals as unconscious automata, and the philosophical tradition that would make language a prerequisite for true consciousness. Second, in placing human and animal minds on a cognitive continuum, she figures the human as no more than a 'thinking mammal', as the narrator of *Le Pays* describes herself.[87] This sets her at odds with religious ideas of ensoulment, as reflected in Bernanos, as well as the exceptionalism of Sartre's being-for-itself. In other strands of philosophy, Darrieussecq's approach has elements in common with philosophers like Thomas Nagel, whose famous essay, 'What is it like to be a bat?' grounds its definition of consciousness on the presence of subjective experiences which cannot be described in neurophysiological or other scientific discourse.[88] Among recent French thinkers, Deleuze and Guattari stand out for their concept of 'le devenir-animal', for which Darreussecq expresses enthusiasm, although she was not aware of it at the time of writing her first novel. *Truismes* is not in fact particularly close to Deleuze and Guattari's idea: their conception of a loss of human individuality in the undifferentiated multitude of animal existence is quite different from Darrieussecq's own example of a human becoming animal, in which the process leads to an escape from cultural conditioning into self-assertion.[89]

Closer in modern thought is Darrieussecq's affinity with evolutionary psychology, with its search for parallels between human and animal behaviour to demonstrate adaptive origins to our psychological traits.

In the end, though, Darrieussecq's contextualization of the human mind among other kinds of mind stops short of the 'Darwinitis' diagnosed by Tallis among humanities scholars eager to emphasize the *bête humaine* at the expense of the uniquely human. If we return to Nore on the beach, we see Nore initially conceive Nicolas's dog in anthropomorphic terms—'the dog, looking playful, delighted'—only for this view to be queried. 'Even supposing the dog's eyesight is centred on itself', thinks Nore checking her train of thought: 'even supposing it can see the difference between itself and the world (its master, smells, this great stretch of water)—or else it may have a pleasant tendency to confuse itself with the world, who knows?'. Moments later, she goes on to wonder: 'Dogs recognize their dead, and why is it that they always blink when you stare at them? How do they know where your eyes are? They could look at our noses, for instance, our chins or our feet'.[90] The idea that true consciousness requires a differentiation of self from world—a negation which constitutes the perceiver by subtracting it from the objects of perception—is the keystone of Sartre's philosophy, as we saw in *Nausea*, and countered by Beckett through the awareness without self-awareness attributed to Worm. Nore's speculation (as ever in the novel, left undeveloped in the constant flow of new impressions and ideas) at first considers the possibility that the dog's mind lacks this implicit sense of self which would distinguish extended consciousness from basic sentience. Her next thought, though, implicitly rejects this idea, and instead attributes a theory of mind to the dog: the dog looks at its master's eyes, rather than his nose, because it knows that this is from where the master is looking out. It is not just looking at eyes, it is meeting a gaze. Of course, none of this tells us what it's like to be a dog, or if it is 'like' anything at all. The ability to detect and respond appropriately to a (possibly predatory) gaze is a useful adaptation for any species, and possessed by many which we would be unlikely to consider conscious in any meaningful sense. But Nore's tentative speculations on the creature in front of her, speculations made up more of questions than of answers, move from ideas of automatism to intimations of inner life, and end distinctly in the latter camp, while respecting the gulf that separates human mentality from that of other animals.

Animal consciousness, finally, brings Darrieussecq back into contact with the opening sequence of *In Search of Lost Time*, and to the comparison with which we began this study, many pages ago. A few lines further on from the passage examined in the Introduction, Proust narrates the transition from sleep to waking through reference to non-human and early-human consciousness:

> When I woke in the middle of the night, since I did not know where I was, I did not even understand in the first moment who I was; all I had, in its original simplicity, was the sense of existence as it may quiver in the depths of an animal; I was more bereft than a caveman; but then the memory—not yet of the place where I was, but in several of those where I had lived and where I might have been—would come to me like help from on high to pull me out of the void from which I could not have got out on my own; I passed over centuries of civilization in one second, and the image confusedly glimpsed of oil lamps, then of wing-collar shirts, gradually recomposed my self's original features.[91]

The passage offers a further example of Proust's off-hand Darwinism, demonstrating the cultural status of evolutionary theory at the time of writing as 'a popularized scientific reference that has entered everyday language', as Céline Surprenant puts it.[92] The 'void' from which the Narrator emerges ('néant' in the French original, the same term as the 'nothingness' of Sartrean existentialism) is not sleep, but rather the core consciousness of the just-awoken mind, which Proust likens to animal awareness, here again figured as little more than bare sentience. As with Beckett's Worm and Darrieussecq's dog, the relationship between consciousness and self-consciousness is in question. Proust's imagery is equivocal here: a sense of existence that 'quivers in the depths' of the animal mind is a dim but not entirely absent awareness of self as distinct from the world around. We are a fraction further along the path towards full human complexity than the place where Worm is said to dwell. From this starting point, the journey to extended consciousness is playfully viewed as a race through human evolution and history from animal minds to those of the earliest humans, presumably without language or culture, and then dashing through the centuries to the present day. Parallel to this, a journey through the Narrator's own history, in terms of his past bedrooms leading towards his present situation, reconstitutes an autobiographical self around the core self as past experience returns through memory.[93] These personal and evolutionary histories in Proust mirror the spiral of increasing sophistication that links Worm to Molloy in Beckett, and Proust's first moment of waking offers a similar view of starkly denuded mentality as do the animal speculations and the evocation of the first moment of foetal awareness in Darrieussecq.

After adult and child and human and animal, the last of the three differences explored by Darrieussecq is that of the male and female mind. Darrieussecq sets herself firmly with Sarraute on the side of social constructivism where gender difference is concerned. She asserts that 'writing is sexless, as is the brain', and explicitly links this belief with feminism: 'What I love about feminism is that for me the human brain has no sex. For me, we all have the same brain'.[94] While both cognitive and physiological differences between male and female brains have now been convincingly demonstrated, Darrieussecq isn't necessarily wrong on this point: it remains an open question how far such differences might be counterbalanced by natural variation among the population, as well as by cultural and developmental factors in the individual.[95] There are wide psychological variations within each sex, and countless psychological similarities between the sexes, such that sex difference is in no way the most 'natural' or self-evident line of division between the mentality of any two individuals. And, of course, we can't refute Darrieussecq's assertion with regard to the male and female minds in her novels, who are the fictional inhabitants of her fictional universe. From the premise of the ungendered brain follows the Beauvoirean argument that psychological and behavioural differences between men and women are a result of familial and social conditioning. Unlike with Sarraute, however, there is little in Darrieussecq's fiction with which to test the validity of the assertion, since the later writer specializes in psychological studies of female characters. In *A Brief Stay with the Living*, only the six-page English-language episode in which John, the father, talks to Jeanne on the telephone, ventures into a male consciousness. We might note a tendency towards the practical and goal-oriented in his case, and a lesser emphasis on the emotional and interpersonal than can be seen in the female characters. John is chided by Jeanne for failing to keep in contact with his daughters, his interest in her life seems dominated by geographical details of Argentina, and he is intermittently distracted from the conversation by thoughts about wind-turbine engineering (p. 253–59; trans. 156–62). In other novels, the minor character of the detective in *Le Mal de mer* and the more substantial figure of Peter in *White* are the only other male characters for whom the reader is granted access to their consciousness. (Her most substantial male character, Kouhouesso of *Il faut beaucoup aimer les hommes*, is seen exclusively from the outside.) Peter is another engineer—this time of heating systems—and similarly phlegmatic in his emotional life and prosaic in his imagination. He does, however, have the most in common with Darrieussecq's female protagonists. He too is haunted by the loss of a sibling; he too has a mental life filled with associative leaps, half-formed thoughts and chaotic interruptions from memory and perception. In this respect, at least, his mind is not different from those of Darrieussecq's female characters. As for the practical bent, social awkwardness, and emotional restraint shared by Peter Tomson and John Johnson, it may be that Darrieussecq considers these to be typical male psychological traits, or it may be that she considers them typical traits of engineers, or of northern Europeans, or not to be typical of any group at all. While men remain at the margins of her psychological studies, questions of the gendered mind are difficult to fathom. There is perhaps a warning not to delve too deeply to be seen in Darrieussecq's satirical play with the hackneyed tropes of gender difference: Nore's attraction to Nicolas is expressed in terms of the 'mystery' of the inscrutable masculine thought-process (p. 105; trans. 63), while in *Truismes*, the narrator must cope with irrational and aggressive mental states on a regular twenty-eight-day cycle as a consequence of having a werewolf for a boyfriend.

Darrieussecq's minds are very much embodied, probably more so than with any of the previous writers examined here, and while the sex of the mind may be irrelevant to the author, the sex of the body is often to the fore in characters' thinking. 'It's the brain that comes', asserts Jeanne in *A Brief Stay with the Living*. 'When the vaginal surface and brain surface precisely coincide, then it's orgasm time, no doubt about it. . . . Membrane to membrane, fibre to fibre, nerve to nerve, two adjusted organs, brain/vagina'.[96] For Anne, this inextricability is perceived as a burden. She rails against her status as 'this body linked to this consciousness', and indulges in a dualist fantasy of the body as a separate instrument of the mind: 'Put my body someplace, be in charge of myself, as though of the mothership. Technical control. Autonomy'.[97] (The image recalls Descartes's image of his mind 'housed within my body like a sailor on his ship', which he raises only to dismiss: even the Cartesian mind is 'confused and intertwined to such an extent' with its body as to form an apparently unified whole.)[98] Solange in *Clèves* feels alienated from her body as a self-conscious teenage wedding guest: 'She doesn't know what to do with her arms. They've burst out of her body and she's lugging them around hanging from her shoulders'.[99] However, this latter kind of Sartrean *être-pour-autrui* is rare in Darrieussecq. More usually, mental life is lived out through the body with hardly a distinction between psychological and physiological. The mental breakdown of the narrator in *Naissance des fantômes* is a 'physical implosion' to mirror the 'physical explosion' of *Truismes*.[100] Indeed, throughout this novel, the narrator's distress at her husband's unexplained disappearance is described in resolutely corporeal terms, as the following typical example shows:

> I stood up. The void in my chest seemed to dissipate a little with the movement, the void's strange heaviness vanished, and then it returned, it installed itself again, centred right between my bones, boring into the hollow of my chest, enough to make you spit blood.[101]

Darrieussecq's embodied consciousness is reminiscent of Merleau-Ponty's notion of the body-subject, which rejects the notion of the body as an assemblage of parts, or the instrument of the mind, and conceives it rather as a global unity which includes and is wholly permeated by the mind:

> The psycho-physical event can no longer be conceived after the model of Cartesian physiology and as the juxtaposition of a process in itself and a cogitatio. The union of soul and body is not an amalgamation between two mutually external terms, subject and object, brought about by arbitrary decree. It is enacted at every instant in the movement of existence.[102]

Merleau-Ponty takes up Descartes's account of the phenomenon of the 'phantom limb' experienced by some amputees to support his own, anti-Cartesian view. For Merleau-Ponty, the stubborn presence of the missing appendage in the subject's sense of self demonstrates how consciousness conceives of itself, not as a free-floating bubble of intellect, but as a corporeal presence in the world, a thinking being down to the fingertips.[103]

Contemporary science may quibble with the details of Merleau-Ponty's understanding of phantom limbs, which are now known to be caused more by the physiology of nerve impulses from the remaining stump than by the psychology of loss, regret, and wish-fulfilment, as the philosopher's rather Freudian interpretation would have it. In his reintegrated conception of mind and body, however, Merleau-Ponty is very much in tune with current thinking on consciousness (and rather more so than his fellow phenomenologist, Sartre, on this score). The 'error' committed by Descartes, which Damasio famously sets out to correct in his book of that name, is 'the separation of the most refined operations of mind from the structure and operation of a biological organism'.[104] Damasio's thesis is that the ancient sub-cortical processes of basic regulation of the body continue to underpin the complex neo-cortical mental activity that our species has evolved, and thereby remain the basis of our sense of self. Perception is not an unmediated meeting of mind and world, but an active modification of the whole organism in order to interface with the environment; emotions are somatic feedback which colours our decision-making with neural and hormonal responses born in the flesh. This kind of 'thinking with the body' is precisely in harmony with Darrieussecq's own representation of consciousness, made tangible in the corporeal despair of *Naissance des fantômes*, and equally so in *A Brief Stay with the Living*, the aim of which, according to its author, was above all to represent 'something cerebral, in the sense that the brain is an organ of the body'.[105]

*

For Shirley Jordan, *A Brief Stay with the Living* 'may be regarded as a novel approaching the question of what, in this new century, it will mean to be human'.[106] We have seen how Darrieussecq's representation in this novel and others is strongly influenced by recent advances in our understanding of the mind and brain. The stamp of neuroscience, along with those of contemporary clinical psychology and evolutionary theory, is much in evidence throughout the writer's work. In it, we are shown minds which are brought into being by the electro-chemical activity of the physical organ, but which are neither reducible to nor explicable by this biological substrate. While uniquely human, these minds are also part of a wider sphere of cognition encompassing animal life more generally, and the contrasts and connections between human and non-human mentality are explored in Darrieussecq's comparisons and metamorphoses. These new conceptions of mind afford new possibilities for the literary representation of consciousness, but they also affect the minds represented. Darrieussecq's protagonists are aware of their Darwinian status as naked apes, and reflect on the echoes in their own mentality of their evolutionary cousins and ancestral past. They are equally aware of their ontological status as material beings, composed of brains and bodies within which neural and hormonal systems connect up every part, and whose thoughts are a consequence of electrical activity between the synapses of their neurons. While accepting intellectually the fact that they are part of the animal kingdom, the characters wonder at the gulf between their human nature and their fellow mammals, whose mental life can only be guessed at. Accepting the fact that they are the product of their brains, the characters struggle in vain to bridge the conceptual gap between their subjective experience and what they know of its biological basis. In Darrieussecq's world, scientific advances in our understanding of the human mind have not demystified the once-miraculous phenomenon of consciousness. Rather, they have opened up whole new mysteries and miracles, leaving us confounded by the blossoming of our immensely rich and complex inner lives from cellular activity, and marvelling at the aeons of blind mutation and incremental change which have built our brains from the constituent parts we still share with the humblest forms of life.

Yet alongside this forward-looking, science-inspired novelist is another Darrieussecq. This writer declares herself 'deeply haunted by Freud, quite simply', combines her creative work with psychoanalytic practice, and conceives her characters' haunted psyches very much in the manner of Freudian neurosis.[107] The narrator of *Tom est mort* writes down her story as an explicitly therapeutic act, and, as in the psychoanalytic talking cure, it's at the very end of the process that she is able to face her traumatic memory and recount it in words. Elsewhere, as we have seen, Darrieussecq's own storytelling echoes the structure of the Freudian case-study, allowing the reader to piece together the story of a past trauma from oblique mental references and involuntary glimpses. Mourning processes stall, leaving characters trapped in melancholia; mental illness encodes its cause within its symptoms. Darrieussecq's minds have much in common with the Freudian psyches explored by André Breton, and exhibit none of the hostility towards the psychoanalytic model that is often found in enthusiasts of neuroscientific, cognitive, and evolutionary paradigms of mind.

In the final reckoning, though, the impression held by the reader is not of two Darrieussecqs, one scientific, the other psychoanalytic, clashing through the course of her novels. There is only one vision in these texts. Darrieussecq's representation of the mind is eclectic, but it is not incoherent: ideas from science, philosophy, and psychoanalysis jostle together, with no attempt to build a unified system of interpretation of mental phenomena. Rather, the subjective experience of consciousness is her central concern, and she invites us to share the subjectivities of her protagonists, minutely described, riotous with thoughts, feelings, memories, and perceptions, and ever-changing in quality as the mental and emotional state of the character varies with situation. The characters, and the texts, strive to understand the nature of the mental activity displayed, and to connect it to a broader realm of mind and brain, but more questions are offered than answers, and the psychoanalytic or scientific analyses proposed are tentative and partial.

Darrieussecq's writing on the mind is situated at a cultural and historical crossroads, and none more so than *A Brief Stay with the Living*, written at the very end of the twentieth century and published at the very start of the twenty-first. We see in the novel the legacy of a century in which public discourse on the mind was dominated by the theories of Freud and his successors, where childhood traumas and dark desires are locked in the Unconscious mind, to be liberated by a winding path of narrative. Equally we see one of the earliest attempts in French literature, or indeed literature of any language, to put into fiction the new concepts of the mind coming from advances in neuroscience, along with renewed interest in consciousness from clinical psychology, psycholinguistics and evolutionary theorists. The last century was most certainly the century of Freud where the understanding of the mind was concerned. It's still too early to tell if the present century will be the century of cognitive science, although its extraordinary rise to prominence and eclipse of much earlier thought on the topic certainly holds promise. If so, Darrieussecq's work stands as a marker of the point of change, a time when old and new models of the conscious and unconscious mind coexist, and each offers a possible understanding of what lies behind our subjective experience.

Notes

1. Ian McEwan, *Saturday* (London: Cape, 2005), pp. 91–2.
2. Capgras syndrome appears in *The Echomaker* (2006) by Richard Powers and *Atmospheric Disturbances* (2008) by Rivka Galchen; de Clérambault's syndrome appears in McEwan's *Enduring Love* (1997) and its 2004 film adaptation, as well as the French thriller, *À la folie . . . pas du tout* (2002); anteretrograde amnesia is the subject of *Memento* (2000), and autism of Mark Haddon's novel, *The Curious Incident of the Dog in the Night-Time* (2003) and its acclaimed stage adaptation.
3. 'Marqué sans doute par les idées en vogue de sa génération, il avait jusque-là considéré la sexualité comme une puissance positive, une source d'union qui augmentait la concorde entre les humains par les voies innocentes du plaisir partagé. Il y voyait au contraire maintenant de plus en plus souvent la lutte, le combat brutal pour la domination, l'élimination du rival et la multiplication hasardeuse des coïts sans aucun raison d'être que d'assurer une propagation maximale aux gènes', Michel Houellebecq, *La Carte et le territoire* (Paris: Gallimard, 2010), p. 303. The views on fashion and the family in can be found on pp. 73, 105.

4. The English translation includes the name of the character at the head of each section. Darrieussecq comments: 'Dans la traduction anglaise, j'ai accepté que l'on mette le nom du personnage en entrée de paragraphe parce qu'il semble que les Anglais sont plus bêtes que les Français. C'était l'avis en tout cas de mon éditeur' ('In the English translation, I allowed the name of the character to be included as a header, because the English are apparently stupider than the French. That was my publisher's opinion in any case'), '"Comment j'écris", entretien avec Marie Darrieusecq', with Jean-Marc Terrasse, *La Création en acte*, ed. by Paul Gifford and Marion Schmid (Amsterdam: Rodopi, 2003), pp. 253–68 (p. 263).
5. 'Qu'est-ce qui pense, dans nos boîtes crâniennes? Neurones et biochimie, comment s'arrêter là? Comment comprendre que ça pense, ces deux lobes blanchâtres en forme de chou-fleur, de fœtus, de boyaux, de labyrinthe? Les mêmes et pas les mêmes pour chaque être humain, et personne ne sait ce qui s'y passe, ce qui s'y pense, ni pourquoi ni comment. [. . .] Oui, qu'est-ce qui pense, dans cette boîte dure traversée d'air, de salive et de sang—ma tête, en équilibre sur mon cou? Qu'est-ce qui pense, à l'étage de ma bouche, perché entre mes deux oreilles, entre mes tempes battantes, qu'est-ce qui pense quand je pense que je pense? Penser avec ses tripes, écrire avec son cœur, on y croirait plus facilement, à cette mythologie des abats, qu'écrire avec cet intangible *rien* qu'est notre pensée', *Rapport de police* (Paris: POL, 2010), pp. 197–8.
6. 'Deux neurones se connectant', Marie Darrieussecq, *Bref Séjour chez les vivants* (Paris: POL, 2001), p. 176; trans. 108; 'Bang dans la tête', p. 86; trans. 51; p. 119; trans. 71. Translations from this novel are taken from *A Brief Stay with the Living*, trans. by Ian Monk (London: Faber, 2003). All other translations are my own.
7. 'Imaginer être dans cette tête à ce moment-là. Un pan du monde devient aveugle, une couleur disparaît, une moitié de mon corps; la part de mon cerveau qui dit *je* s'enraye', p. 112; trans. 67.
8. 'Il y a une grande différence entre l'esprit et le corps, en ce que le corps, dans sa nature, est toujours divisible, et que l'esprit est entièrement indivisible'; 'je n'y puis distinguer aucunes parties, mais je me conçois comme une chose seule et entière', Descartes, pp. 203–204.
9. 'Celle qu'elle était dans son sommeil aimait le Coca-Cola, se fichait de fermer les portes, et se promenait sous la Lune: ces trois maigres traits de caractère lui semblaient plus vrais, plus *Anne*, que tout ce qui prétendait, à l'état de veille, être elle', p. 220; trans. 135.
10. 'L'absence à soi-même'; 'J/e' appears in *A Brief Stay* in the narration of Jeanne's dream: 'j/e suis très grande, agrandie de haut en bas m/e dirigeant vers ce point', p. 16, and more extensively in *Le Pays*, which opens with a sequence evoking the absent state of mind of the protagonist while running.
11. '*I'm driving*, un saissisement, une brutale attaque opérée par cette idée. Stupéfaite, non de conduire, mais d'être là; je me constatais, je me regardais', p. 268; trans. 165 (translation modified), italics Darrieussecq's.
12. 'Petites, avec Jeanne, on s'amusait à ne pas penser, à penser à rien, cotonneusement . . . Mais on pense à ne rien penser, on se dédouble c'est le problème de ces exercices, on se voit penser et on n'y pense plus', p. 30; trans. 15.
13. Thoughts on an empty consciousness occur on pp, 40, 62; trans. 22, 35; the panic attack is on pp. 18–20; trans. 8–9; night-club thoughts are on pp. 269–73; trans. 166–8.
14. 'Arrête calme-toi', p. 299; trans. 184; 'Vert et noir mouches paillettes', p. 306; trans. 189.
15. Helena Chadderton, *Marie Darrieussecq's Textual Worlds: Self, Society, Language* (Bern: Peter Lang, 2012), p. 129.
16. 'Arrête avec ça mes coups de revolver dans la tête bang bang qui reviennent comme des chansons, des scies', p. 166; trans. 102, translation modified.
17. William James, *The Principles of Psychology* (1890), 3 vols (Cambridge, MA: Harvard University Press, 1981), I, p. 244.
18. Gerald M. Edelman, whose 'internal Darwinism' of a plethora of different neural impulses competing for access to consciousness made a poor fit for the Sartrean mind in Chapter 4, seems very much more in tune with Darrieussecq's view: 'When we think, it's very rare for a full sentence to occur to us; it's more like a fleeting memory or a fantasy, a smell or a song heard on the radio coming back to us. . . . That's what the mind is, a great bazaar structured differently for each of us', Busnel and Gandillot.
19. 'J'écris des livres psychologiques contre la psychologie. Je ne me satisfais pas de phrases type "Je me sentais très angoissée" ou "Elle était très heureuse". Ces phrases ont été élaborées, tendues à leur point maximum, à la charnière du 19ème et du 20ème siècle, avec Proust. Ensuite, il y a la cassure Joyce: comment ça se passe à même le cerveau. *Ulysse*, entre autres livres, a nourri *Bref Séjour chez les vivants*. Je veux savoir ce que c'est, l'angoisse, le bonheur, la mer, un bébé, ce que c'est de l'intérieur, comme si c'était la première fois que j'abordais ces parages. Je veux dire au lecteur: "Voyez, sentez, entendez: ceci est une vague, ceci est une femme qui se perd, ceci est un cerveau qui pense"', Becky Miller and Martha Holmes, 'Interview with Marie Darrieussecq', Marie Darrieussecq website, University of Arizona (December 2001) http://darrieussecq.arizona.edu/fr/entetien2001.html.
20. Gaudet, p. 117.

21. 'Le garçon. La table. Mon chapeau au porte-manteau, retirons nos gants. Il faut les jeter négligemment sur la table, à côté de l'assiette; plutôt dans la poche du par-dessus; non, sur la table; ces petites choses sont de la tenue générale. Mon par-dessus au porte-manteau; je m'assieds; ouf; j'étais las', Édouard Dujardin, *Les Lauriers sont coupés, suivi de Le Monologue intérieur*, ed. by Carmen Licari (Rome: Bulzoni, 1977), p. 103.
22. James Joyce, *Ulysses* (1922) (London: Penguin, 1992), pp. 923–4.
23. 'Or si, quand il s'agit du langage inexact de l'amour-propre par exemple, le redressement de l'oblique discours intérieur (qui va s'éloignant de plus en plus de l'impression première et centrale), jusqu'à ce qu'il se confonde avec la droite qui aurait dû partir de cette impression, si ce redressement est chose malaisée contre quoi boude notre paresse, il est d'autres cas, celui où il s'agit de l'amour, par exemple, où ce même redressement devient douloureux', Proust, *RTP*, *iv*, 469; trans. 199.
24. 'Ce qui se dissimule derrière le monologue intérieur: un foisonnement innombrable de sensations, d'images, de sentiments, de souvenirs, d'impulsions, de petits actes larvés qu'aucun langage intérieur n'exprime, qui se bousculent aux portes de la conscience, s'assemblent en groupes compacts et surgissent tout à coup, se défont aussitôt, se combinent autrement et réapparaissent sous une nouvelle forme, tandis que continue à se dérouler en nous, pareil au ruban qui s'échappe en crépitant de la fente d'un téléscripteur, le flot ininterrompu des mots', Nathalie Sarraute, 'Conversation et sous-conversation', *L'Ère du soupçon*, *OC*, pp. 1587–607 (p. 1594).
25. 'Nathalie Sarraute m'a donné la force de ne pas écrire "Elle se sentait très angoissée". J'ai essayé de trouver autre chose. Elle, son truc c'était les sous-conversations, ce qui se passait autour, et moi, ce n'est pas exactement cela, ça serait, comment définir ça, ça serait l'absence à soi-même [. . .] J'essaie de décrire ce vide qu'on est et qui est rempli par des tas d'autres choses qui ne sont pas nous mais qui le deviennent [. . .] Elle, elle s'intéressait beaucoup plus au dialogue, à la conversation, à ce qui se passe sous les mots. Moi, c'est plutôt à ce qui se passe presque sous la peau, je dirais, je suis presque plus physique qu'elle, je suis dans une forme de désir', Nelly Kaprièlian, *Écrire, écrire, pourquoi? Entretien avec Marie Darrieussecq* (Paris: Éditions de la Bibliothèque publique d'information/Centre Pompidou, 2010), p. 7.
26. '*Beau chien que vous avez là*, saloperie de chien qui me flaire la, ça le fait rire, *Charlie! il est joueur. . .* dis quelque chose, on te parle répond, on t'appelle du fond de la maison, *je vous vois depuis quelque temps*, bravo', pp. 81–2; trans. 48, italics Darrieussecq's.
27. 'Règne du lieu commun'; 's'efforcent [. . .] de nous persuader que le monde est fait d'individus irremplaçables, tous exquis, même les méchants, tous passionnés, tous particuliers. Nathalie Sarraute nous fait voir le mur de l'inauthentique; elle nous le fait voir partout. Et derrière ce mur? Qu'y a-t-il? Eh bien justement *rien*', Sartre, Preface to Nathalie Sarraute's, *Portrait d'un inconnu*, *OC*, pp. 36–7.
28. 'On entend le jardin depuis que le téléphone a sonné, contraste', p. 22; trans. 10.
29. Ramachandran, p. 229.
30. 'Il y a des gens très malheureux, malades, pour qui la mer se résout à une série de lignes superposées bleu blanc gris parallèles, et à du son, une odeur, un mouvement: ils ne font pas le lien, ils sont incompatibles par malheur par maladie avec l'idée, non de mer, mais de vision, de cohérence du monde', p. 42; trans. 23.
31. p. 140; trans. 85. The Molyneux problem is discussed in Locke's, *Essay Concerning Human Understanding*, Book Two, Chapter Nine.
32. 'Un aveugle-né ne verra rien. Il verra des couleurs, des lignes, tout un bazar de stimuli optiques, mais sans relief, ni principe organisateur. Son cerveau ne saura pas décoder ce que l'œil capte et que le nerf transmet. Pour voir il faut avoir déjà vu. Les deux cas étudiés se sont 1) suicidé 2) suicidé. Car la lumière promise était indéchiffrable', p. 140; trans. 85.
33. 'Il verrait quoi, une étendue hostile et pas d'ombre. Le sable, mou sous les pattes. Les algues à odeur de poisson', p. 206; trans.126 (translation modified).
34. For Heidegger, the objects of our perception are usually seen, not as inertly present-at-hand ('vorhanden'), but are rather conceived within a framework of our own desires and intentions in terms of their possible role in our projects: they are ready-to-hand ('zuhanden') in the manner of a tool. See Martin Heidegger, *Being and Time*, trans. by John Macquarrie and Edward Robinson (Oxford: Blackwell, 1962), pp. 101–8.
35. *White*, p. 99 and elsewhere; 'les chats, les oiseaux, les poissons et les mouches aux yeux à facettes', *Naissance des fantômes*, p. 158. Darrieussecq notes of the former: 'It's an extremely cold place where the air is saturated with ice crystals and all the explorers and scientists who have been there and are there now claim to be victims of various optical illusions because the sunlight is refracted in the crystals and produces images. There are also auditory illusions, to the extent that the most rational and scientific people think they hear creatures calling to them, or see processions, herds, things like that', Terrasse, p. 267.
36. 'Il existe des densités différentes d'images, le rêve et la rêverie et le souvenir et le flash-back, et parfois je vois des lieux et des gens d'il y a très longtemps; d'avant même que je sois née; mais Arnold ne me croirait pas. Des cascades d'images entrevues, sans mots, elles veulent bien dire quelque chose', p. 178; trans. 108.

37. 'Je cours après quelque chose d'impossible dans cette zone où il n'y a pas de mots, mais c'est ce qui me fait avancer. Je me rappelle ma prof de philo en terminale, absolument excellente et toujours très convaincante: elle m'a ouverte à tout un univers, celui des concepts, mais ce faisant elle nous a aussi expliqué qu'il n'y a pas de pensée sans mot. Cela m'a beaucoup troublée, parce qu'il me semblait bien que dans ma tête la pensée pouvait exister sans mots. Et notez bien qu'elle ne parlait pas de l'inconscient, dont je n'avais d'ailleurs pas idée à l'époque, et qui se fait aussi sans mots, même si c'est complexe. Ma prof de philo était une représentante de cette tradition française du "ce qui se conçoit bien s'énonce clairement". Or, il me semblait qu'on pouvait aussi concevoir les choses "pas bien": penser non pas selon la grande tradition française, " bien", mais penser tout de même, sans énoncer clairement dans sa tête, sans nécessairement les mots', Kaprièlian, p. 5.
38. 'Qu'il faille parler pour penser, que les notions ne viennent qu'avec les mots, la théorie me paraît pauvre', *Le Bébé*, p. 112.
39. 'Arnold dit, les enfants ne parlent pas, donc ils n'ont pas de mémoire. Que rien n'existe hors ce qui est pensé c'est-à-dire parlé', pp. 150–51; trans. 91.
40. On the Sapir-Whorf hypothesis, see Benjamin Lee Whorf, *Language, Thought and Reality: Selected Writings* (Cambridge, MA: The MIT Press, 1967).
41. The theory of linguistic determinism is countered by Stephen Pinker, *The Language Instinct* (London: Allen Lane, 1994), pp. 55–82.
42. 'Si je suis différente, tout ce que je peux dire, c'est que le français se prononce à l'avant du palais'; 'Je ne sais même pas si je suis la même d'une phrase à l'autre', pp. 96, 95; trans. 58, 57.
43. 'Quand les yeux bleu foncé une seconde s'immobilisent, s'ouvrent en grand, quand les doigts cessent de tripoter le hochet, et que la bouche, une seconde, cesse de chuquer, on la voit, là, l'idée, sans mots, l'idée grande ouverte, qui les atteint, les occupe à fond, déferle une seconde, *JE CONNAIS ÇA, J'AI DÉJÀ ENTENDU ÇA, ÇA ME DIT QUOI*, au son de la langue maternelle', p. 226; trans. 139. For the original research, see P. D. Eimas, E. R. Siqueland P. Jusczyk and J. Vigorito, 'Speech Perception in Infants', *Science*, 171 (1971), pp. 303–6.
44. 'Il voit le blanc de l'hôpital, c'est sa première idée, sans mots, que tout est blanc', p. 175; trans. 107.
45. 'Bonne fortune inespérée'; Henri Bergson, *Les Deux Sources de la morale et de la religion* (Paris: Alcan, 1932), p. 43; James, *The Principles of Psychology*, I, p. 233.
46. 'Je me débats contre les mots', *La Nausée*, *OR*, p. 153; trans. 185.
47. 'Enfin, ce n'est pas sans quelque truquage qu'on peut réduire le fleuve de la conscience à une succession de mots, même déformés. Si le mot est donné comme intermédiaire *signifiant* une réalité transcendante, par essence, au langage rien de mieux: il se fait oublier, il décharge la conscience sur l'objet. Mais s'il se donne comme *la réalité psychique*, si l'auteur, en écrivant, prétend nous donner une réalité ambiguë qui soit signe, en son essence objective, c'est-à-dire en tant qu'elle se rapporte au dehors, et chose en son essence formelle, c'est-à-dire comme donnée psychique immédiate, alors on peut lui reprocher de n'avoir pas pris parti et de méconnaître cette loi rhétorique qui pourrait se formuler ainsi: en littérature, où l'on use de signes, il ne faut user *que* de signes; et si la *réalité* que l'on veut signifier est *un mot*, il faut la livrer au lecteur par d'autres mots. On peut lui reprocher en outre d'avoir oublié que les plus grandes richesses de la vie psychique sont *silencieuses*', Sartre, *Qu'est-ce que la littérature?*, pp. 200–1, italics Sartre's.
48. Howells, *Sartre: The Necessity of Freedom*, p. 63. The episode in *L'Âge de raison* is to be found in Sartre, *OR*, p. 490.
49. Pinker, *The Stuff of Thought*, pp. 153–233.
50. Damasio, *The Feeling of What Happens*, p. 185.
51. See Dennett, *Consciousness Explained*, pp. 227–52, and Julian Jaynes, *The Origin of Consciousness in the Breakdown of the Bicameral Mind* (Boston: Houghton Mifflin, 1976).
52. p. 49; trans. 27; 'lapsus inévitables', p. 194; trans. 118; p. 267; trans. 164.
53. 'Disponibilité mentale', p. 30; trans. 15.
54. 'La seule qui ait viré folle', p. 274; trans. 169.
55. See J. Zubin and B. Spring, 'Vulnerability—a New View of Schizophrenia', *Journal of Abnormal Psychology* 86 (1977), pp. 103–26.
56. 'Dans le réseau de cette famille, il y a eu à un moment un défaut de surveillance, par inattention de toute la famille un enfant s'est noyé. Ils se sentent tous coupables, et Anne a développé une paranoïa parce qu'elle a besoin de contrôler le monde et de penser qu'existe un réseau de surveillance infaillible auquel elle imagine participer', Nicholas p. 2.
57. Anne's vision is on p. 272; trans.167; Nore sees the face on p. 283; trans. 174; Nicolas finds the house 'hostile' on p. 308; trans. 190; Anne screams on p. 307; trans. 189; the mother sees Pierre on p. 273; trans. 168; the shared dream is on pp. 12, 16; trans. 4, 6.
58. 'Reliée fil à fil par l'influx de mes neurones aux pensées de tous', p. 113; trans. 68; 'on filme l'intérieur de mon cerveau', p. 49; trans. 27.

59. 'Je me suis souvent retrouvée à préciser que les fantômes, à mon avis, n'ont d'existence que fictive'. *Rapport de police*, p. 18; 'Le fantastique m'est naturel. Il offre une description de la façon dont nous pouvons vivre intérieurement le réel. Le réel n'a rien de rationnel', 'Marie Darrieussecq, *Truismes*', with Alain-Philippe Durand, online discussion, 20 September 2011, http://nonlieux2011.blogspot.co.uk/2011/09/marie-darrieussecq-truismes-1996.html.
60. 'J'ai envie de prendre au pied de la lettre mon personnage. C'est-à-dire que ce qu'elle est en train de dire et de vivre, elle le dit et le vit vraiment et il faut la croire', Gaudet, pp. 113–14.
61. 'Tout ce qui est passé sous silence, tout ce qui est tu, tout ce qui est non-dit', Gaudet, p. 111.
62. 'Dont le travail soulevait les spectres comme la poussière sous un balai'; 'les fantômes [. . .] naissent de notre hantise, qui les allume et les éteint, oscillants, pauvres chandelles. Ils ne sont que pour nous', *Le Pays*, p. 236.
63. Freud, *The Uncanny*, in *The Standard Edition*, XVII, pp. 219–52.
64. David S. Holmes's study, quoted in the opening chapter, is an example of current thinking on trauma. 'L'intérieur de son cerveau colonisé par les Bernard-l'hermite, la pensée qui claquette de ses petites pinces [. . .] sa scie musicale dans le creux de l'oreille au fond des lobes du cerveau—ça n'arrête pas', pp. 73–4; trans. 43 (translation modified).
65. 'Freud, j'ai lu un peu et pratiqué beaucoup, c'est-à-dire que j'ai fait une analyse, huit ans, qui m'a permis entre autres de séparer (autant que faire se peut) ma névrose de mon écriture. Avant, mes manuscrits ne concernaient que moi, mes proches, mon nombril. Je n'aurais pas pu écrire *Truismes* sans analyse. Je n'aurais pas réussi à inventer un personnage, à séparer ma voix de la voix du personnage. Grâce à l'analyse ma névrose vient nourrir mes livres sans les étouffer, et donc les rend lisibles, les tourne vers les autres. J'y ai aussi gagné un métier qui est une aventure en soi, puisque, en plus de l'écriture, je suis maintenant devenue psychanalyste. C'est une autre histoire, qui passe par une longue formation et la lecture infinie de Freud. Et de Lacan. Mais il faut dire que Freud est un écrivain en plus d'être un grand chercheur. [. . .] Ce type est un grand sage occidental, comme il y a les grands sages orientaux', 'Je suis devenue psychanalyste', interview with Baptiste Liger, *Lire*, 1 November 2006, retrived from www.lexpress.fr/culture/livre/je-suis-devenue-psychanalyste-par-marie-darrieussecq_811700.html. Other comments demonstrate that Darrieussecq subscribes to the existence of such psychoanalytic phenomena as the Œdipus Complex and the Death Drive (see *Rapport de police*, p. 42), which mainstream psychiatry now views with scepticism.
66. 'J'aimais beaucoup quand Nathalie Sarraute s'énervait contre ce charlatan de Freud. Je pense que si elle mettait tant de véhémence à nier la validité de ses thèses, c'est parce qu'elle le percevait comme un double. Elle tenait à son invention "à elle", la sous-conversation, ce dévoilement-là. Et l'espace que lui laissait Freud, pour large qu'il fût, devait lui sembler, à elle, dangereusement étroit', *Rapport de police*, p. 182.
67. Kathryn Robson, 'Virtual Reality: The Subject of Loss in Marie Darrieussecq's *Naissance de fantômes* and Regine Detambel's *La Chambre d'echo*', *Australian Journal of French Studies*, 61 (2004), pp. 3–15.
68. 'Nous sommes dans leur cerveau'.
69. On Darrieussecq and the tensions between scientific and psychoanalytic concepts of the mind, see my earlier article, 'Darrieussecq's Mind', *French Studies*, 62 (2008), pp. 429–41.
70. 'Le cerveau humain pèse un kilo quatre il est constitué de vingt à trente milliards de neurones et d'à peu près dix mille fois plus de synapses les connectant', p. 140; trans. 85.
71. 'En faisant marcher tout bêtement ses méninges', p. 50; trans. 28.
72. 'Plus d'anxiété, plus de sautes d'humeur, plus de crises ni d'idées noires, plus de projets, plus de concentration: une totale, agréable et insouciante distraction', pp. 183–4; trans. 112.
73. 'On ne va pas me faire croire qu'un œuf, ça pense', p. 117; trans. 70–71.
74. 'À partir de quand ça se met à penser, comment savoir . . . clic, la conception, mise en contact des corps conducteurs, petite bombe . . . première connexion, tout était noir, opaque, ça commence par quoi, par rien, et puis . . . ne serait-ce que le sentiment d'être ici, d'être ici plutôt que rien, chaleur, présence . . . et le fracas de locomotive, battement, pas encore d'oreille, juste les vibrations du cœur de la mère et la peau pas encore peau, ce qui pousse là battant à son tour', p. 231; trans. 142.
75. 'Le poil mouillé d'un petit animal', p. 22; trans. 10; 'qui regardait qui on se demandait, ça a des yeux humains pathétiques, et des mains humaines, et ça s'assoit ça s'asseyait mieux que Nore, ça saisissait entre pouce et index mieux que Nore, à se demander si au jeu du triangle dans le triangle elle aurait été, question méninges, la mieux lotie', p. 202; trans. 124 (translation modified).
76. 'Truffe inquisitrice', (p. 82; the phrase is omitted from Monk's translation).
77. Naama Harel, 'Challenging the Species Barrier in Metamorphosis Literature: The Case of Marie Darrieussecq's Pig Tales', *Comparative Critical Studies*, 2 (2005), pp. 397–409.
78. 'Ils sentent bien que ça continue à penser comme les hommes là-dedans', *Truismes*, p. 141.
79. 'Pour moi, à la fin elle est beaucoup plus humaine qu'au début. Quelle que soit son apparence', Gaudet, p. 111.

80. 'Mon corps ne comprenait pas pourquoi il devait s'acharner sur cette pièce d'acier, mon corps se mouvait sans conviction alors que tous mes neurones s'épuisaient à garder cette idée en tête, *le verrou, le verrou*, c'était épuisant de lutter ainsi contre soi-même', *Truismes*, p. 145.
81. *Truismes*, p. 74. 'Bête' means 'stupid' as an adjective and 'animal' as a noun.
82. 'Comme un éclair de compréhension', *Truismes*, p. 84.
83. 'Il me semble, comment dire, que ça m'aurait été facile de le manger, de planter mes dents dans cette chair bien rose', *Truismes*, p. 84.
84. 'Elle a fermé la porte, ça a fait *clic clac*, et ça a mis comme une agitation dans l'air. Je n'ai pas pu dormir à cause de ces ondes angoissantes, ça vibrait et ça déséquilibrait tout. Tous mes congénères remuaient, leur bonne odeur bien franche devenait aigre, pleine d'hormones mauvaises, de stress, de peur. L'odeur se scindait en blocs isolés, chaque odeur autour de chaque cochon, les groins cherchant les angles des murs, le bas des portes, l'interstice par où fuir, chacun voulait laisser l'autre à sa propre odeur de victime', *Truismes*, p. 144.
85. The basking shark appears in *Le Mal de mer*, p. 128, the sealion in *Naissance des fantômes*, p. 65.
86. '[Les animaux] nous obligent à une métaphysique instantanée: qu'est-ce qui nous sépare d'eux? Qu'est-ce qui nous fait humain?' (with Becky Miller and Martha Holmes), 'Interview with Marie Darrieussecq', Marie Darrieussecq website, University of Arizona (December 2001) http://darrieussecq.arizona.edu/fr/entetien2001.html.
87. 'Mammifère pensant', *Le Pays*, p. 170.
88. Thomas Nagel, 'What Is It Like to Be a Bat?', *Philosophical Review*, 83 (1974), pp. 435–50.
89. Gilles Deleuze and Félix Guattari, *Capitalisme et Schizophrénie 2: Mille Plateaux* (Paris: Minuit, 1980), pp. 284–380. Darrieussecq writes of Deleuze in *Rapport de police*: 'ni Derrida ni Foucault ni Barthes n'avaient théorisé si bien et si à l'avance ce qu'allait être mon imaginaire' ('Neither Derrida, nor Foucault, nor Barthes theorized so well and so much in advance what my imagination would hold'), p. 152. She cites the Deleuzian concepts of 'le devenir-animal, la déterritorialisation, le corps sans organes, les plis et les rhizomes' as having parallels in her own thinking (p. 152).
90. 'Le chien, œil farceur, ravi'; 'Même à supposer que la vision du chien soit centrée sur lui-même, même à supposer qu'il fasse une différence entre lui et le monde (son maître, les odeurs, cette grande plaine d'eau)—ou au contraire, aimable tendance à se confondre avec le monde'; 'est-ce qu'un chien reconnaît un chien mort, et comment se fait-il, là, que les chiens clignent des yeux quand on les fixe, comment savent-ils que ce sont là nos yeux? Ils pourraient regarder, je ne sais pas, le nez, le menton, les pieds', pp. 79–80; trans. 46–7 (translation modified).
91. 'Quand je m'éveillais au milieu de la nuit, comme j'ignorais où je me trouvais, je ne savais même pas au premier instant qui j'étais; j'avais seulement dans sa simplicité première le sentiment de l'existence comme il peut frémir au fond d'un animal; j'étais plus dénué que l'homme des cavernes; mais alors le souvenir—non encore du lieu où j'étais, mais de quelques-uns de ceux que j'avais habités et où j'aurais pu être—venait à moi comme un secours d'en haut pour me tirer du néant d'où je n'aurais pu sortir tout seul; je passais en une seconde par-dessus des siècles de civilisation, et l'image confusément entrevue de lampes à pétrole, puis de chemises à col rabattu, recomposaient peu à peu les traits originaux de mon moi', *RTP*, I, pp. 5–6; trans., I, 9.
92. Céline Surprenant, 'Darwin and Proust', in *The Literary and Critical Reception of Charles Darwin in Europe*, ed. by Thomas F. Glick and Elinor Shaffer, 4 vols (London: Bloomsbury, 2014), IV, pp. 431–57 (p. 432).
93. Erika Fülöp examines this passage in detail as part of an exploration of liminal states of consciousness in Proust, arguing that the transition from sleep to waking echoes F.W.J. von Schelling's theory of the development of self-consciousness. Erika Fülöp, *Proust, the One and the Many: Identity and Difference in A la recherche du temps perdu* (Oxford: Legenda, 2012), p. 56. The Schelling parallels are examined more generally in Anne Henry, *Marcel Proust: theories pour une esthétique* (Paris: Klincksieck, 1983).
94. 'L'écriture est sans sexe, de même que le cerveau', Interview with Amy Concannon and Kerry Sweeney in March 2004, www.uri.edu/artsci/ml/durand/darrieussecq/fr/entretien2004.html; 'ce que j'aime dans le féminisme, c'est pour moi que le cerveau humain n'est pas sexué. Pour moi, on a tous le même cerveau', Lambeth p. 815.
95. The chapter on 'Gender' in Pinker's, *The Blank Slate*, pp. 337–71, includes an overview of evidence of neurological difference between male and female brains, and of psychological and behavioural difference between men and women. Cordelia Fine's *Delusions of Gender* and Angela Saini's *Inferior* contest some of these findings.
96. 'C'est le cerveau qui jouit [. . .] Quand se superposent très exactement sans plus la moindre incertitude la zone vaginale et la zone cérébrale alors jouissance. Membrane à membrane fibre à fibre nerf à nerf, deux organes ajustés cerveau/vagin', pp. 97–8; trans. 58–59.
97. 'Ce corps cette conscience accouplés'; 'Être à la tête de soi comme à la tête d'un *spaceship:* maîtrise technique, autonomie', pp. 19, 76; trans. 8, 44.

98. 'Logé dans mon corps, ainsi qu'un pilote en son navire'; 'tellement confondu et mêlé', Descartes, p. 195.
99. 'Elle ne sait pas quoi faire de ses bras. Ils ont jailli de son corps et elle les trimballe accrochés à ses épaules', *Clèves* (Paris: POL, 2011), p. 223.
100. Lambeth, p. 810.
101. 'Je me suis levée. Le vide dans ma poitrine se dissipait peut-être un peu avec le mouvement, la pesanteur bizarre de ce vide s'annulait, et puis il revenait, il se remettait en place, bien centré pile entre mes os, foré au creux de mon thorax, à en cracher le sang', *Naissance des fantômes*, p. 24.
102. 'L'événement psychophysique ne peut plus être conçu à la manière de la physiologie cartésienne et comme la contiguïté d'un processus en soi et d'une cogitatio. L'union de l'âme et du corps n'est pas scellée par un décret arbitraire entre deux termes extérieurs, l'un objet, l'autre sujet. Elle s'accomplit à chaque instant dans le mouvement de l'existence', Merleau-Ponty, *Phénoménologie de la perception*, p. 105.
103. Merleau-Ponty, *Phénoménologie de la perception*, pp. 87–105.
104. Damasio, *Descartes' Error*, p. 250.
105. 'Quelque chose de cérébral au sens où le cerveau est un organe qui appartient au corps', Kaprièlian, p. 7.
106. Jordan, ' "Un grand coup de pied"', p. 66.
107. Très hantée par Freud, tout bêtement', Kaprièlian, p. 17.

CONCLUSION

Our minds are literary. Metaphor and narrative, the essential features of literary prose, are also, it now appears, essential features of human cognition. In the mind, image schemas are taken from concrete instances of movement in space and agents manipulating objects, and put into service in abstract thought, where they underlie our conceptual reasoning. Almost any utterance suffices to demonstrate, including the previous sentence, where the use of one kind of mental representation to stand in for another is figured in terms of *taking from*, *putting into*, and *lying under*. Such figurative constructions betray the presence of unnoticed spatial metaphors framing our thinking about a non-spatial subject, metaphors such as 'the mind is a place', or 'thoughts are objects to be moved and exchanged'. Moreover, we instinctively conceptualize the reality before us into discrete objects and events, and combine these through intuited causality into the micro-stories through which we make sense of the world. Here too, the concrete narratives of physical interaction are readily transposed into the abstract realm: from 'she forced the key out of the lock' to 'she forced the idea out of her mind'. These metaphorical narratives are everywhere we look, including, of course, in literature, where a half-asleep narrator may find his confused recollections of his book 'weighing on his eyes', until such time as the subject-matter of the book 'detaches itself' from his thoughts. For Mark Turner, the evidence may not yet be strong enough for us prove that narrative and metaphor based on space and the body underpin all our abstract reasoning, but we can venture something close to it:

> We may say comfortably that our understanding of spatial and bodily stories is so rich, and our powers of parable so developed, that imagination can project spatial and bodily stories at will to any point of the conceptual compass. We may also say comfortably that for many abstract concepts, the spatial and bodily instances are the archetypes.[1]

More literal storytelling also seems to be an integral part of what makes us human. Stories are universal across all human cultures, and fictional invention develops spontaneously in children in pretend play.[2] The cognitive play of creating and interpreting stories enables individuals in a cultural community to order and corroborate their experience, consolidate a shared value-system, evaluate risks and problems through hypothetical scenarios, explore the social interactions of virtual agents, and vicariously perceive reality through another human consciousness. Whether or not such characteristics suffice to make an interest in stories evolutionarily adaptive—and there are certainly theorists who make that claim—or whether our taste for stories is a by-product of other, more directly beneficent traits in our nature, it seems probable that there is more than cultural coincidence to our species's love of fiction throughout history and across the globe.[3] While literary fiction in the twentieth century may pride itself on how far it has travelled from the archetypes of storytelling, we still hear echoes of the oldest and most fundamental structures of narrative, as when a long quest across unknown country, beset with peril and lively incident, brings its hero at last to the safety and rest of his mother's house, or when a noble-hearted priest struggles against antagonistic locals and his own weakness to reach a conclusion in which he has resolved his troubles, using the wisdom gained from the experiences he has traversed.

In early-modern Western culture, the rise of the novel as a privileged form of storytelling brought with it an increased focus on fictional minds. Where drama offered an external view of its characters, and had to externalize inner life through soliloquy if it was to allow the audience access, and where folk-tales, *chansons de geste*, and other precursors to the novel often placed incident above psychology, and might populate the story with stock characters fulfilling set roles, the true territory of the novel quickly proved itself to lie inside the protagonist's head. Impersonal narrators could exploit their omniscience to delve into characters' thoughts and explore their motivations. First-person narrators could confess their feelings and evoke their memories. All novels could focalize their story from the perspective of a character, and offer the reader a phenomenal world, in which the objective truth of what *is* becomes displaced by the subjectivity of what *seems to me*. The novel became a consciousness simulator, taking us inside the mind of another human where we could explore an inner life and an outlook that were different from our own, and identify or contrast its traits with our own mentality.

The exploration of the human mind has always been an important part of the novel's repertoire, and the 'psychological novel' of the kind we have been examining here is not a genre apart, but simply an expansion of the mental life that all fiction explores to at least a cursory extent. Novels of the mind can slow down what is too rapid to grasp, expand the infinitesimal or capture the evanescent. The text can fix a momentary sensation for our contemplation, or stretch out a train of thought for our perusal, allowing us to possess or inhabit a virtual consciousness in a way we are never able to manage with our own minds. The dramatic incidents on which conventional fiction thrives may thereby be downsized, as when the mental repercussions of a single line of conversation become the narrator's exclusive preoccupation, or they may be reconfigured, as when the drama of being trapped in a sinking car becomes a study in the changing mentality of an oxygen-starved brain.

As well as mirroring back to the reader an individual conscious experience, the psychological novel can also take us into less familiar mental realms. It can show us what it might be like for consciousness to encounter reality in the raw, divested of the intellectual categories through which we order and mediate our experience to keep the world at bay. Or a text can speculate about the unconscious forces which may lie beneath the conscious mind, and imagine how our actions and feelings might be dictated by hidden urges deep within us, or by subliminal influences infiltrating from outside us, without the self being granted any awareness of the decisive mental processes involved. The psychological novel can depict mental states that we have never experienced, perhaps, in Sartre's case, states that have never *been* experienced; it can posit the existence of mental activity outside consciousness, either in a Freudian Unconscious or otherwise conceived; and, at a further level of abstraction, it can assert ontological characteristics of the mind it depicts, figuring it as immaterial in substance, as having semi-autonomous ego and id, or a transcendent self that ceases to exist when not conjured up by an intentional consciousness. There is a sense in which the kind of writing we have seen in the work of these seven writers brings literary discourse around in a circle. Our cognitive architecture which processes thoughts through metaphor and narrative, and our evolutionary adaptations which may incline us to multiply our experience through the virtual lives of fiction, have helped to build the culture of storytelling from which the Western novel emerged. Proust, Bernanos, Breton, Sartre, Beckett, Sarraute, and Darrieussecq turn the novel inwards to explore the mystery of the phenomenon at its source.

I began with the contention that from each of these writers' work could be inferred a particular theory of the mind, which might be more or less consistent through the course of text and œuvre, and more or less explicit in its formulation within the fiction. My methodology sprang from the belief that conventional critical approaches to the psychological novel risk obscuring what they set out to uncover, as the imposition of a framework of theory selects and homogenizes the material it analyzes. Psychoanalytic studies look to dreams and slips for evidence of a character's Unconscious, and look to childhood relationships with parents to interpret what they find there. Phenomenological studies ignore such matters to investigate the self-world of perception coloured by the traits of the perceiving mind, which has itself been moulded by the perceived environment. And cognitive studies sift the universals of human nature and speculate about the neural substrates of experience from the thoughts and behaviour of the character. We have even seen the phenomenon in this study as we glanced at other critical appraisals of our texts. To some readers, Proust's *In Search of Lost Time* is the story of an adult psyche shaped by a son's Œdipal possessiveness of his mother during childhood. To others, it is the evocation of a phenomenological *Umwelt* as it impinges on an individual, and idiosyncratic, subjectivity.

Reading *out* the text's own theory of mind doesn't necessarily contradict such readings in. However, as we have seen, the process does bring to the fore the author's own singular conception of mental life, and his or her priorities in choosing the fundamental attributes of a mind. It is in this way that we gain an understanding of the true diversity of literary models of consciousness across the century. Of course, the minds we have seen in the work of these writers have much in common. Not only are the fundamentals of human nature and the broad outlines of mental life present and correct across the corpus, there is also often agreement on more obscure or contested areas of psychology. The importance of non-linguistic thought in human cognition, for instance, is highlighted by Proust at the start of the century, and continues to be foregrounded in novelists of succeeding generations, perhaps anxious that their exclusively linguistic medium of representation should not inadvertently imply the same about the minds they are representing. But in our corpus of writers we have seen major differences in the understanding of the mind. The Sartrean mind has no unconscious processes to it, only a lucid awareness that may strive to shield itself from unwelcome truths. In Breton, on the other hand, consciousness is dwarfed by the unconscious realm, which is vast in scope, mystically connected to supernatural forces in the world outside, and a stronger determinant of identity than the waking self. Between these two conceptions is the Sarrautean mind, for which the activity beneath the threshold of awareness is equally important to making us who we are, but is construed as a quasi-physiological continuum of reactions, instincts, and reflexes. A similar spread of positions can be seen over the substance of mind. Consciousness in Bernanos is a phenomenon of the immaterial soul, which can commune with God and survive the death of the body. In Proust it is a phenomenon based in the physical, altering in quality with altered bodily states and exquisitely vulnerable to physiological damage. Beckett and Darrieussecq hesitate between these two positions. Minds in Beckett are firmly and debilitatingly shackled to the declining physical body, yet appear to persist when the body is no more than a memory. Darrieussecq's minds are the clear product of the material brain, and the neuronal activity on which they supervene is referenced several times in the text. Yet in the phenomenal worlds of the characters, scientific rationalism fails to hold sway, and their desperate loss summons up the disembodied spirits of their loved ones.

Such outright contradictions between the novelists are comparatively rare, however, and are arguably not the most interesting element to emerge from the comparison. What is more striking is the difference in emphasis that each author places on various aspects of human mentality. In Proust, we saw the focus on memory, perception, and desire as the major elements of the psyche, and multiplicity, discontinuity, and temporality as the modes in which they were conceived. In Bernanos and Breton, the mystical aspects of consciousness are in the forefront, with uncanny coincidences leading the one to an intimation of the divine and the other to a narcissistic sense of communion between self and world. In Sartre it is the conscious mind which once again draws our attention. Like Proust, Sartre dwells on perception, particularly visual perception, but unlike Proust, it's not the subjective encounter of an individual sensibility with the external world that is of interest, but rather the universal faculties by which the human mind processes what its senses receive, and what might happen should these faculties cease to mediate our experience for us. For Beckett, sentience itself is the mystery at the core of conscious existence, towards which his characters grope without ever managing to grasp its essence. In Sarraute, it is the intersubjective that is most at stake: minds in her fiction reach out and recoil, oppress or revolt, and all at a level which is neither conscious in the sense of full, lucid awareness, nor unconscious in a sense that Breton or the psychoanalysts would recognize. Finally, Darrieussecq puts her own stress on rendering the chaotic stream of thoughts and impressions that flows constantly over the mind's surface, combined with an intermittent meditation on the brain that produces such profusion.

Some of these changing emphases stem from the changing cultural influences as the century progressed. We have seen in literature how the era of modernism gave way to a period of postmodern experimental fiction, which was in turn displaced by a return to more representational forms of writing, while scientific progress and changing fortunes in philosophy and psychoanalysis altered the broader cultural environment. Freud made his entrance into French culture in the 1920s, and his discipline grew to dominate understanding of the mind by the mid-century, taking a linguistic turn with the advent of poststructuralist psychoanalysis in later decades, before growing criticism and scientific encroachment precipitated its decline. The science itself moved from a discipline very much in harmony with philosophical theorizing on the mind at the start of the period, to a radical rejection of consciousness and the subjective as a suitable field of research in the mid-century, and thence to a spectacular return to consciousness studies at the century's end, capturing the public's imagination with startling new hypotheses about the nature of perception, free will, and the development of the self. Philosophy, as we saw, was present at this rendez-vous, having previously moved away from empiricism in France to explore intuition, phenomenology, and existentialism through the twentieth century, only to form a new alliance with the scientists through the neurophenomenology of the twenty-first century. All these theories of mind are themselves part of culture, of course, not only as influences on cultural production but through being, to varying extents, cultural products in themselves. We have seen evidence of this in the literary inspirations of psychoanalysis or the symbiosis of existentialist fiction and philosophy. This means that the relationship between theories of mind and its cultural representations has not always been a one-way street. Theoretical understanding of the mind has also been affected by cultural changes through the course of the century, even by literary ones, as when Surrealism and its successors popularized and disseminated psychoanalytic theories among the reading public, or when feminist critiques of Freud's androcentric views brought about their modification and decline.

At the present moment, several older theories of mind find themselves undermined by twenty-first century developments in the understanding of human nature. Existentialism retains a wisp of dualism in ascribing a qualitatively different mode of being to consciousness from that of material things. In this, and its refusal to countenance the existence of the unconscious, it sits uncomfortably with a neuroscientific rapprochement of thought and brain activity, and with our developing understanding of high-level unconscious phenomena.[4] Freudian psychoanalysis is challenged by modern psychology for its sealed and censor-guarded Unconscious formed by repression, and contradicted by Darwinian theory in its claims of a death drive and an Œdipus complex inherent to human nature. Evolutionary theory similarly confronts the social constructivist conception of the gendered mind, casting doubt on the plausibility of gender norms being wholly acquired characteristics, and the circumstantial evidence against the 'blank slate' at birth continues to accumulate. The immense diversity held within the bounds of human nature, coupled with the continuing difficulty for science to establish objective truths about the private and nebulous phenomenon of consciousness, mean that none of these ideas is 'disproved' scientifically, nor is likely to be in the foreseeable future. Where beliefs about the nature of the mind are bound up with religious faith, there is naturally even less prospect of evolutionary or neuroscientific perspectives displacing traditional views. In the worlds of our seven authors, however, the validity or otherwise of these conceptions is often perfectly clear: male and female natures in Breton, for instance, are constituted quite differently from those in Sarraute, with essential differences between the sexes in the former and no distinction beyond cultural impositions in the latter.

Some aspects of our authors' work reflect the cultural moment in which they were writing. Proust's mind is clearly pre-Freudian; Darrieussecq's is perceptibly on the cusp between psychoanalytic and neuroscientific dominants in the understanding of consciousness. In others we see inspiration drawn from the zeitgeist as a starting point for the writer's own idiosyncratic view. Breton's unconscious is a good example: while clearly inspired by psychoanalysis, it is far from an orthodox Freudian Unconscious, being a well-spring of creative and revolutionary potential rather than a dangerous breeding-ground of harmful neuroses. And in others still we see outright reaction against prevailing wisdom, most notably in Sarraute, who comes to define her art in opposition to behaviourist approaches to the mind and their harmful effect on psychological literature. Beckett may have absorbed some prevailing ideas of phenomenology and existentialism, but his preferred debating partners on the nature of the self are early-modern philosophers such as Descartes, Leibniz, and Geulincx. These texts are not simple reflections of the moments in cultural history in which they were produced. Each contains echoes of the principal non-literary influences on their author's milieu, but each remains a unique expression of a personal conception of mental life.

It would be an exaggeration to claim that the very concept of mind is rendered unstable by these various literary representations. But it is nonetheless true to say that these fictional minds are sufficiently distinct from each other to inhabit slightly different universes, where human nature, conscious experience, unconscious mental activity, and the relationship of self to world are perceptibly dissimilar. As we have seen, this is every bit as much the case for the autobiographical texts of Breton and Sarraute as it is in the fictional worlds of the other five, even if the minds depicted in the memoirs claim to share their world with each other and with the reader. While we as readers may not always be aware of it, we pass through a different gateway for our rendez-vous with each of them, and each time we emerge on the other side we find the world and all the people in it subtly changed. Despite the enormous advances in our understanding of the mind since the dawn of the twentieth century, it remains a largely open question as to which of these seven universes most nearly resembles ours. We are free to use our own conscious experience, and our intuitions of the structures which may lie behind it, as our primary guide in choosing for ourselves which of these writers best reflects our own mentality.

At the start of this exploration, I suggested that novels, and psychological novels more than most, are meeting places for minds. What we see at its close is that these meeting places don't quite meet each other. As the reader's mind engages with each of these fictional consciousnesses, we see not only that they conceive of themselves differently from the inside, but that their intuitions are confirmed from the outside by a fictional reality to which they are permeable or impermeable, with which they are harmonious or discordant, and which does or does not allow the presence of the immaterial. Implicit in each text is a claim by its author: 'I have looked into myself', they are telling us, 'into the consciousness I can access directly and into what I might infer beneath it, and I have looked outwards to examine the relationship of this mind with the world and with the other minds I encounter, and this is what I have found'. In dialogue with or reaction to their literary predecessors, they offer us their findings, sometimes directly in the form of a memoir of the author's own experience, sometimes transposed into a fiction (sometimes barely transposed, as is often the case with Proust), in which situations, environment, and interactions may be arranged in demonstration of a particular thesis. Sometimes the knowledge found is the fruit of rational analysis, laid out as an argument from evidence, sometimes it more closely resembles love's knowledge, an emotional understanding on the part of the character that may be echoed in the readers' feelings as we dwell as a guest in another consciousness. Sometimes the knowledge draws on the author's religious, scientific, philosophical, or psychoanalytic beliefs, sometimes on pure introspection, but mostly on a subtle mutual inflection of both. In this way, the literary texts are able to include knowledge of mind as it is expressed in other disciplines, but also to exceed these other modes of expression. In their content, they can go beyond what is permitted in other discourses through their freedom to include the intuitive, the imaginary, and the subjective. And in their form, they are free not only to explain, but to reconstruct lived mental experience in the text, which the reader is then able to participate in vicariously, and to appreciate in a mode that is not only intellectual, but also emotional, and perhaps even partly unconscious. We may reject this knowledge as incompatible with our own experience or beliefs. Few readers would be able to embrace both Sartre and Bernanos on the relation of self to world, both Breton and Sarraute on the nature of the male and female mind. Or we may, critically and partially, or warmly and wholeheartedly, see a truth of our own nature in an insight on the page in front of us. A neuron sparks in our brain, a glow of recognition pervades our consciousness, and a connection is established. We find ourselves to be like-minded.

Notes

1. Mark Turner, *The Literary Mind: The Origins of Thought and Language* (Oxford: Oxford University Press, 1996), p. 51.
2. Brian Boyd, *On the Origin of Stories: Evolution, Cognition and Fiction* (Cambridge, MA: Belknap Harvard, 2009), p. 189.
3. For an adaptational theory of fiction, see John Tooby and Leda Cosmides, 'Does Beauty Build Adapted Minds? Toward an Evolutionary Theory of Aesthetics, Fiction and the Arts', *SubStance* 94/95 (2001), pp. 6–27.
4. One such phenomenon would be blindsight, in which people with damage to their visual cortex have no sight that they are aware of in an area of their visual field, and yet are able to 'guess' with high levels of accuracy which of a series of simple shapes a researcher is displaying to that area. It is discussed in many studies of consciousness, including Dennett's, *Consciousness Explained*, pp. 322–33.

BIBLIOGRAPHY

Marcel Proust

A la recherche du temps perdu, ed. by Jean-Yves Tadié (Paris: Gallimard, Pléiade edition, 1987–89), 4 vols.
In Search of Lost Time, ed. by Christopher Prendergast (London: Penguin, 2002), 6 vols.

1. *Du côté de chez Swann/The Way by Swann's*, trans. by Lydia Davis
2. *A l'ombre des jeunes filles en fleurs/In the Shadow of Young Girls in Flower*, trans. by James Grieve
3. *Le Côté de Guermantes/The Guermantes Way*, trans. by Mark Treharne
4. *Sodome et Gomorrhe/Sodom and Gomorrah*, trans. by John Sturrock
5. *La Prisonnière/The Prisoner*, trans. by Carol Clark
   Albertine disparue/The Fugitive, trans. by Peter Collier (included in Volume Five)
6. *Le Temps retrouvé/Finding Time Again*, trans. by Ian Patterson.

Correspondance, ed. by Philip Kolb, 21 vols (Paris: Plon, 1970–1993).

Cahiers 1 à 75 de la Bibliothèque Nationale de France, ed. by B. Brun and others, 75 vols (Turnhout: Brepols, 2008)

with Élie-Joseph Bois, 'Variétés littéraires: *A la recherche du temps perdu*', in *Le Temps*, 13 November 1913, p. 4, reprinted in Marcel Proust, *Choix de lettres*, ed. by Philip Kolb (Paris: Plon, 1965), p. 287.

Alden, Douglas W., 'Origins of the Unconscious and Subconscious in Proust', *Modern Language Quarterly*, 4 (1943), 343–57.

Baldwin, Thomas, 'Philosophy', in *Marcel Proust in Context*, ed. by Adam Watt (Cambridge: Cambridge University Press, 2013), pp. 75–82.

Baudry, Jean-Louis, *Proust, Freud et l'autre* (Paris: Minuit, 1984).

Bersani, Leo, *Marcel Proust: The Fictions of Life and Art* (Oxford: Oxford University Press, 1965).

———, *The Culture of Redemption* (Cambridge, MA: Harvard University Press, 1990).

Bizub, Edward, *Proust et le moi divisé: La Recherche: creuset de la psychologie expérimentale (1874–1914)* (Paris: Droz, 2006).

Bowie, Malcolm, *Freud, Proust and Lacan: Theory as Fiction* (Cambridge: Cambridge University Press, 1987).

———, *Proust among the Stars* (London: Fontana, 1998).

Casey, E., 'Literary Description and the Phenomenological Method', *Yale French Studies*, 61 (1981), 176–201.

Compagnon, Antoine, *Proust entre deux siècles* (Paris: Seuil, 1989).

Deleuze, Gilles, *Proust et les signes* (Paris: Presses Universitaires de France, 1964).

Descombes, Vincent, *Proust: Philosophie du roman* (Paris: Minuit, 1987).

Doubrovsky, Serge, *La Place de la Madeleine: écriture et fantasme chez Proust* (Paris: Mercure, 1974).

Dow, Suzanne, 'How to Begin a Novel: Proust's *A la recherche du temps perdu* and the Author-Reader Relation', *French Studies*, 63 (2009), 283–94.

Dubois, Jacques, *Pour Albertine: Proust et le sens du social* (Paris: Seuil, 1997).

Ellison, David, 'Proust and Posterity', in *The Cambridge Companion to Proust*, ed. by Richard Bales (Cambridge: Cambridge University Press, 2001), pp. 200–15.

Flieger, Jerry Aline, 'Proust, Freud and the Art of Forgetting', *SubStance*, 29 (1981), 66–82.

Fülöp, Erika, *Proust, the One and the Many: Identity and Difference in À la recherche du temps perdu* (Oxford: Legenda, 2012).

Henry, Anne, *Marcel Proust: Theories pour une esthétique* (Paris: Klincksieck, 1983).

———, 'Habit in *À la recherche du temps perdu*', *French Studies*, 68 (2014), 344–58.

Hillenaar, Henk, 'Proust et la psychanalyse', in *Proust contemporain*, ed. by Sophie Bertho (Amsterdam: Rodopi, 1994).

Hughes, Edward J., *Marcel Proust: A Study in the Quality of Awareness* (Cambridge: Cambridge University Press, 1983).

Jordan, Jack, 'The Unconscious', in *The Cambridge Companion to Proust*, ed. by Richard Bales (Cambridge: Cambridge University Press, 2001), pp. 100–16.

Kristeva, Julia, *Le Temps sensible: Proust et l'expérience littéraire* (Paris: Gallimard, 1994).

Ladenson, Elisabeth, *Proust's Lesbianism* (Ithaca: Cornell University Press, 1999).

Landy, Joshua, *Philosophy as Fiction: Self, Deception, and Knowledge in Proust* (Oxford: Oxford University Press, 2004).

———, 'Proust among the Psychologists', *Philosophy and Literature*, 35 (2011), 375–87.

Lehrer, Jonah, *Proust Was a Neuroscientist* (Edinburgh: Canongate, 2011).

Lennon, Thomas M., 'Proust and the Phenomenology of Memory', *Philosophy and Literature*, 31 (2007), 52–66.

Lucey, Michael, *Never Say I: Sexuality and the First Person in Colette, Gide and Proust* (Durham, NC: Duke University Press, 2006).

Luckhurst, Nicola, *Science and Structure in Proust's A la recherche du temps perdu* (Oxford: Clarendon Press, 2000).

McCall, Ian, 'Swann dans les bras de Morphée: A Freudian Influence on Proust', *Neophilologus*, 78 (1994), 529–36.

Megay, Joyce, *Bergson et Proust: essai de la mise au point de la question de l'influence de Bergson sur Proust* (Paris: Vrin, 1976).

———, 'Elie Rabier, an Unknown Source of Proust's Psychology', *Modern Language Quarterly*, 39 (1978), 39–49.

Nussbaum, Martha, *Love's Knowledge: Essays on Philosophy and Literature* (Oxford: Oxford University Press, 1990).

Poulet, Georges, *L'Espace proustien* (Paris: Gallimard, 1982).

Prendergast, Christopher, *Mirages and Mad Beliefs: Proust the Skeptic* (Princeton, NJ: Princeton University Press, 2013).

Richard, Jean-Pierre, *Proust et le monde sensible* (Paris: Seuil, 1974).

Sedgwick, Eve Kosofsky, *Epistemology of the Closet* (London: Penguin, 1994).

———, *The Weather in Proust* (Durham, NC: Duke University Press, 2011).

Silverman, Kaja, *Male Subjectivity at the Margins* (London: Routledge, 1992).

Simon, Anne, 'Portrait de l'artiste en hibou: de l'usage anthropologique de la zoologie chez Proust', *Contemporary French and Francophone Studies*, 9 (2005), 139–50.

Slater, Maya, 'Proust, Psychoanalysis and Involuntary Memory', *Literature and Psychology* 37.1–2 (1991), 1–10.

Surprenant, Céline, 'Freud and Psychoanalysis', in *Marcel Proust in Context*, ed. by Adam Watt (Cambridge: Cambridge University Press, 2013), pp. 107–14.

———, 'Darwin and Proust', in *The Literary and Critical Reception of Charles Darwin in Europe*, ed. by Thomas F. Glick and Elinor Shaffer, 4 vols. (London: Bloomsbury, 2014), 4, pp. 431–57.

Tadié, Jean-Yves, *Proust et le roman: essai sur les formes et techniques du roman dans A la recherche du temps perdu* (Paris: Gallimard, 1971).

———, *Le Lac inconnu: entre Proust et Freud* (Paris: Gallimard, 2012).

Watt, Adam, *Reading in Proust's* A la Recherche*: 'le délire de la lecture'* (Oxford: Oxford University Press, 2009).

Georges Bernanos

Œuvres romanesques, ed. by Albert Béguin and others (Paris: Gallimard, Pléiade edition, 1961).
The Diary of a Country Priest, trans. by Pamela Morris (Cambridge, MA: Da Capo, 2002).

Essais et écrits de combat, ed. by Yves Bridel and others, 2 vols. (Paris: Gallimard, Pléiade edition, 1946).

Alston, William P., *Perceiving God: The Epistemology of Religious Experience* (Ithaca: Cornell University Press, 1991).
Bergson, Henri, *Les Deux Sources de la morale et de la religion* (1932) (Paris: Presses Universitaires de France, édition Quadrige, 2008).
Boyer, Pascal, *Religion Explained: The Evolutionary Origins of Religious Thought* (New York: Basic Books, 2001).
Bulbulia, Joseph A., 'The Evolution of Religion', in *The Oxford Handbook of Evolutionary Psychology*, ed. by R.I.M. Dunbar and Louise Barrett (Oxford: Oxford University Press, 2007), pp. 621–36.
Canérot, Marie-Françoise, '*Monsieur Ouine*, une seconde *Nausée?*', in *Bernanos et le monde moderne*, ed. by Monique Gosselin-Noat (Lille: Presse Universitaire de Lille, 1989), pp. 141–50.
Cor, Laurence W., 'Mystical Perception in *Journal d'un curé de campagne*', *Romance Notes*, 12 (1970–71), 244–50.
Daudin, Claire, *Dieu a-t-il besoin de l'écrivain? Péguy, Bernanos, Mauriac* (Paris: Cerf, 2006).
Dawkins, Richard, *The God Delusion* (London: Bantam, 2006).
Dennett, Daniel C., *Breaking the Spell: Religion as a Natural Phenomenon* (London: Penguin, 2006).
Flower, J. E., 'The Comtesse Episode in the *Journal d'un curé de campagne*', *The French Review*, 42 (1969a), 673–82.
———, *Intention and Achievement: The Novels of François Mauriac* (Oxford: Clarendon Press, 1969b).
Goetz, Stewart and Charles Taliaferro, *A Brief History of the Soul* (Oxford: Wiley-Blackwell, 2011).
Green, Julien, *Œuvres complètes*, ed. by Jacques Petit, 8 vols. (Paris: Gallimard, Pléiade edition, 1972).
Griffiths, Richard, *Le Singe de Dieu: François Mauriac entre le 'roman catholique' et la littérature contemporaine, 1913–1930* (Le Bouscat: L'Esprit du temps, 1996).
Herbermann, Charles G. and others (eds.), *The Catholic Encyclopedia*, 15 vols. (New York: Robert Appleton, 1907–14).
James, William, *Varieties of Religious Experience: A Study in Human Nature* (Marston Gate: Renaissance Classics, 2012).
Kemp, Simon, 'Representing the Mind in the French Catholic Novel', *MLR*, 107 (2012), 408–21.
Larkin, Maurice, 'Religion, Anticlericalism and Secularization', in *Modern France 1880–2002*, ed. by James McMillan (Oxford: Oxford University Press, 2003), pp. 203–227.
Léonard, Augustin, *François Mauriac ou la psychologie du pécheur* (Liège: La Pensée Catholique, 1951).
Mauriac, François, *Œuvres complètes*, 12 vols. (Paris: Fayard, 1950).
O'Donnell, Donat, 'François Mauriac: Catholic and Novelist', *Kenyon Review*, 10 (1948), 454–71.
Penn, Dorothy, 'Three French Writers of Contemporary Catholic Realism: The Inner Consciousness Studied by Georges Bernanos, Henri Ghéon and François Mauriac', *The French Review*, 12 (1938), 128–37.
Price, Matthew, 'Catholic Church "struggles" to win over young people', BBC report, 11 March 2013, <www.bbc.co.uk/news/world-europe-21738755>.
Renard, Pierrette, *Bernanos ou l'ombre lumineuse* (Grenoble: Publications de l'université Stendhal de Grenoble, 1990).
Sartre, Jean-Paul, 'M. François Mauriac et la liberté', in *Critiques littéraires* (Paris: Gallimard, 1947), pp. 33–52.
Scott, Malcolm, *The Struggle for the Soul of the French Novel* (Basingstoke: MacMillan, 1989).
Taliaferro, Charles, *Consciousness and the Mind of God* (Cambridge: Cambridge University Press, 1994).
Tertullian, 'De Anima', in *The Writings of Tertullian*, trans. by Peter Holmes, 3 vols. (Edinburgh: Clark, 1884), 2, pp. 410–541.
Thomson, Robert Stuart, 'Mauriac and Psychoanalysis', *Literature and Psychology*, 34.2 (1988), 41–51.
Tobin, Michael R., 'François Mauriac and Georges Bernanos: Two Theologies of the Body', *Christianity and Literature*, 44 (1995), 313–26.
———, *Georges Bernanos: The Theological Source of His Art* (Montreal: McGill-Queen's University Press, 2007).

André Breton

Œuvres complètes, ed. by Marguerite Bonnet, 4 vols. (Paris: Gallimard, Pléiade edition, 1988–2008).
Mad Love, trans. by Mary Ann Caws (Lincoln, NE: Bison, 1987).

Balakian, Anna, 'André Breton as Philosopher', *Yale French Studies*, 31 (1964), 37–44.
Ballabriga, Michel, *Sémiotique du surréalisme: André Breton ou la cohérence* (Toulouse: Presses universitaires du Mirail, 1995).
Béhar, Henri and Michel Carassou, *Le Surréalisme*, 2nd edn. (Paris: Livre de poche, 1992).
Carrouges, Michel, *André Breton et les données fondamentales du surréalisme* (Paris: Gallimard, 1967).
Caws, Mary Ann, *André Breton*, 2nd edn. (London: Prentice Hall, 1996).
Chesneau, Albert, 'André Breton et l'expérimentation poétique', *French Review*, 42 (1969), 371–79.
Cohen, Margaret, 'Mysteries of Paris: The Collective Uncanny in André Breton's *L'Amour fou*', in *André Breton Today*, ed. by Anna Balakian and Rudolf Kuenzli (New York: Locker & Owens, 1989), pp. 101–10.
Esman, Aaron H., 'Psychoanalysis and Surrealism: André Breton and Sigmund Freud', *Journal of the American Psychoanalytic Association*, 59.1 (2011), 173–81.
Grivel, Charles, 'André Breton, l'âme du voir', *Littérature*, 83 (1991), 3–11.
Laing, R. D., *The Politics of Experience, and, the Bird of Paradise* (London: Penguin, 1967).
———, *Wisdom, Madness and Folly: The Making of a Psychiatrist 1927–1957* (London: MacMillan, 1985).
Lejeune, Denis, *The Radical Use of Chance in Twentieth-Century Art* (Amsterdam: Rodopi, 2012).
Ligot, Marie-Thérèse, *L'Amour fou d'André Breton* (Paris: Gallimard, 1996).
Nadeau, Maurice, *Histoire du surréalisme* (Paris: Seuil, 1964).
Née, Patrick, 'Le "Hasard objectif": une allégorèse problématique (André Breton, *L'Amour fou*)', *Revue d'histoire littéraire de la France*, 108.1 (2008), 133–57.
Pierre, José, *Le Surréalisme* (Paris: Rencontre Lausanne, 1966).
Polizzotti, Mark, *Revolution of the Mind: The Life of André Breton* (London: Bloomsbury, 1995).
Plouvier, Paule, *Poétique de l'amour chez André Breton* (Paris: Corti, 1983).
Rosemont, Franklin, *André Breton and the First Principles of Surrealism* (London: Pluto, 1978).
Roudinesco, Elisabeth, *Jacques Lacan: Esquisse d'une vie, histoire d'un système de pensée* (Paris: Fayard, 1993).
Steinmetz, Jean-Luc, *André Breton et les surprises de L'Amour fou* (Paris: Presses Universitaires de France, 1994).
Wylie, Harold, 'Breton, schizophrenia and *Nadja*', *The French Review*, 43 (1970), 100–06.

Jean-Paul Sartre

Œuvres romanesques, ed. by Michel Contat and Micel Rybalka (Paris: Gallimard, Pléiade edition, 1981).
Nausea, trans. by Robert Baldick (London: Penguin, 1965).

L'Imagination (1936) (Paris: Presses universitaires de France, 1948).
La Transcendance de l'Ego et autres textes phénoménologiques (1936 for the title essay), ed. by Vincent de Coorebyter (Paris: Vrin, 2003).
Esquisse d'une théorie des émotions (1939) (Paris: Hermann, 1965).
L'Imaginaire (Paris: Gallimard, 1940).
L'Être et le Néant: essai d'ontologie phénoménologique (Paris: Gallimard, 1943).
L'Existentialisme est un humanisme (1946) (Paris: Gallimard, 1996).
Critiques littéraires (Situations I) (Paris: Gallimard, 1947).
'Preface to *Portrait d'un inconnu* (1948)', in Nathalie Sarraute, *Œuvres complètes*, ed. by Jean-Yves Tadié (Paris: Gallimard, Pléiade edition, 1996), pp. 35–9.
Qu'est-ce que la littérature? (Paris: Gallimard, 1948).
Critique de la raison dialectique, précédé de *Question de méthode*, I: *théorie des ensembles pratiques* (Paris: Gallimard, 1960).
'Foreword', in *Reason and Violence: A Decade of Sartre's Philosophy 1950–1960*, ed. by R. D. Laing and David Cooper (New York: Random House, 1964), pp. 7–8.
L'Idiot de la famille, 3 vols. (Paris: Gallimard, 1971).
'Sartre par Sartre', interview in *Le Nouvel Observateur*, 26 January 1970, reprinted in *Situations IX* (Paris: Gallimard, 1972), pp. 99–134.
'Autoportrait à soixante-dix ans (1975)', in *Situations X* (Paris: Gallimard, 1976), pp. 133–226.
'Sur *L'Idiot de la famille*', in *Situations X* (Paris: Gallimard, 1976), pp. 91–115.
(with M. Chapsal), 'Sartre', in *Les Écrivains en personne*, ed. by M. Chapsal (Paris: Julliard, 1960), pp. 213–14.

Barnes, Hazel E., 'Sartre as Materialist', in *The Philosophy of Jean-Paul Sartre*, ed. by Paul Arthur Schilpp (La Salle: Open Court, 1981), pp. 661–84.

———, 'Sartre's Ontology', in *The Cambridge Companion to Sartre*, ed. by Christina Howells (Cambridge: Cambridge University Press, 1992), pp. 13–38.
———, 'Sartre's Concept of the Self', in *Sartre and Psychology*, ed. by Keith Hoeller, (Atlantic Highlands, NJ: Humanities Press International, 1993), pp. 41–65 (p. 44).
———, 'Consciousness and Digestion: Sartre and Neuroscience', in *Sartre Today: A Centenary Celebration*, ed. by Adrian van den Hoven and Andrew Leak (Oxford: Berghahn, 2005), pp. 117–32.
Beaujour, Michel, 'Sartre and Surrealism', *Yale French Studies*, 30 (1963), 86–95.
Beauvoir, Simone de, *La Force de l'âge*, 2 vols. (Paris: Gallimard, 1960).
———, *La Cérémonie des adieux* (Paris: Gallimard, 1971).
Boulé, Jean-Pierre, *Sartre, Self-Formation and Masculinities* (Oxford: Berghahn, 2005).
Cabestan, Philippe, 'Rêve, obsession, hallucination: qu'est-ce qu'une conscience captive?' in *Sartre et la phénoménologie*, ed. by Jean-Marc Mouillie (Fontenay-aux-roses: Éditions ENS, 2000), pp. 21–76.
———, *L'Être et la conscience: recherches sur la psychologie et l'ontophénoménologie sartriennes* (Brussels: Ousia, 2004).
Charlesworth, Max, 'Sartre, Laing and Freud', in, *Sartre and Psychology*, ed. by Keith Hoeller (Atlantic Highlands, NJ: Humanities Press International, 1993), pp. 23–39.
Contat, Michel, *Pour Sartre* (Paris: Presses Universitaires de France, 2008).
Daigle, Christine, 'The Ethics of Authenticity', in *Reading Sartre: On Phenomenology and Existentialism*, ed. by Jonathan Webber (London: Routledge, 2011), pp. 1–14.
Deguy, Jacques, *La Nausée de Jean-Paul Sartre* (Paris: Gallimard, 1993).
Doubrovsky, Serge, '*La Nausée*: Fragment of an Analytic Reading', in *Sartre*, ed. by Christina Howells (London: Longman, 1995), pp. 49–57.
Due, Reidar, 'Freedom, Nothingness, Consciousness: Some Remarks on the Structure of *Being and Nothingness*', in *Sartre Today: A Centenary Celebration*, ed. by Adrian van den Hoven and Andrew Leak (New York: Berghahn, 2005), pp. 31–42.
Eshleman, Matthew C., 'What Is It Like to Be Free?', in *Reading Sartre: On Phenomenology and Existentialism*, ed. by Jonathan Webber (London: Routledge, 2011), pp. 31–47.
George, François, *Deux Études sur Sartre* (Paris: Bourgois, 1976).
Goldthorpe, Rhiannon, *La Nausée* (London: HarperCollins, 1991).
Gorman, Shawn, 'Sartre on Proust: Involuntary Memoirs', *Journal of Romance Studies*, 6 (2006), 56–68.
Hatzimoysis, Anthony, 'A Sartrean Critique of Introspection', in *Reading Sartre: On Phenomenology and Existentialism*, ed. by Jonathan Webber (London: Routledge, 2011), pp. 90–9.
Howells, Christina, *Sartre: The Necessity of Freedom* (Cambridge: Cambridge University Press, 1988).
Idt, Geneviève, La Nausée, *Sartre: Analyse Critique* (Paris: Hatier, 1971).
———, *Le Mur de Jean-Paul Sartre: techniques et contexte d'une provocation* (Paris: Larousse, 1972).
Ji, Young-Rae, 'Sartre, Admirateur Secret de Proust', *L'Esprit créateur* 46.4 (Winter 2006), 44–55.
Laing, R. D. and David Cooper, *Reason and Violence: A Decade of Sartre's Philosophy 1950–1960* (New York: Random House, 1964).
Leak, Andrew, 'Nausea and Desire in Sartre's *La Nausée*', *French Studies*, 43 (1989), 61–72.
McDonald, Christie, 'Sartre Rereading Proust', *Journal of Romance Studies*, 6 (2006), 197–207.
Morf, Martin E., 'Sartre, Skinner and the Compatibilist Freedom to be Authentically', *Behavior and Philosophy*, 26 (1998), 29–43.
Mouillie, Jean-Marc, *Sartre: Conscience, ego et psychè* (Paris: Presses universitaires de France, 2000).
Pacaly, Josette, *Sartre au miroir: une lecture psychanalytique de ses écrits biographiques* (Paris: Klincksieck, 1980).
Pilkington, A. E., 'Valéry and Sartre: The Nature of Consciousness', *French Studies*, 43 (1989), 182–94.
Prince, Gerald, '*La Nausée* and the Question of Closure', in *Sartre*, ed. by Christina Howells (London: Longman, 1995), pp. 58–65.
Webber, Jonathan, 'Bad Faith and the Other', in *Reading Sartre: On Phenomenology and Existentialism*, ed. by Jonathan Webber (London: Routledge, 2011), pp. 180–94.
Williford, Kenneth, 'Pre-Reflective Self-Consciousness and the Autobiographical Ego', in *Reading Sartre*, ed. by Jonathan Webber (London: Routledge, 2011), pp. 195–210.

Samuel Beckett

Molloy (Paris: Minuit, collection 'double', 1951/1982).
Malone meurt (Paris: Minuit, collection 'double', 1951/2004).

L'Innommable (Paris: Minuit, collection 'double', 1953/2004).
Three Novels: Molloy, Malone Dies, the Unnamable (New York: Grove Press, 1958).

Proust, and Three Dialogues with Georges Duthuit (1931, 1949) (London: Calder, 1965).
Murphy (Paris: Minuit, 1947)/*Murphy* (English version) (London: Routledge, 1938).
En Attendant Godot (Paris: Minuit, 1952)/*Waiting for Godot* (London: Faber, 2010).
Nouvelles et Textes pour rien (Paris: Minuit, 1958)/*Texts for Nothing and Other Shorter Prose, 1950–1976* (London: Faber, 2010).
Comment c'est (Paris: Minuit, 1961)/*How It Is* (London: Faber, 2009).
Watt (Paris: Minuit, 1968)/*Watt* (Paris: Olympia, 1953).
Oh les beaux jours, suivi de Pas moi (Paris: Minuit, 1975)/*Happy Days* (London: Faber, 2006); *Not I* (London: Faber, 1973).
Compagnie (Paris: Minuit, 1980)/Samuel Beckett, *Company, Ill Seen Ill Said, Worstward Ho, Stirrings Still* (London: Faber, 2009).
The Letters of Samuel Beckett, ed. by Martha Dow Fehsenfeld and Lois More Overbeck, 3 vols. (Cambridge: Cambridge University Press, 2009).
(with Tom F. Driver), 'Beckett by the Madeleine (Interview)', *Columbia University Forum*, 4 (1961), 21–5.

Ackerley, Chris, '"I, of Whom I Know Nothing": Biblical Echoes in Samuel Beckett's *L'Innommable* and *The Unnamable*', in *Samuel Beckett Today/Aujourd'hui: Revisiting* Molloy, Malone Meurt/Malone Dies *and* L'Innommable/The Unnamable, ed. by David Tucker, Mark Nixon and Dirk Van Hulle (Amsterdam: Rodopi, 2014), pp. 151–63.
Bailey, Iain, *Samuel Beckett and the Bible* (London: Bloomsbury, 2014).
Bernini, Marco, 'Gression, Regression and Beyond: A Cognitive Reading of *The Unnamable*', in *Samuel Beckett Today/Aujourd'hui: Revisiting* Molloy, Malone Meurt/Malone Dies *and* L'Innommable/The Unnamable, ed. by David Tucker, Mark Nixon and Dirk Van Hulle (Amsterdam: Rodopi, 2014), pp. 193–209.
Bloom, Harold, *Samuel Beckett's Molloy, Malone Dies, The Unnamable* (New York: Chelsea House, 1988).
Bryden, Mary, *Beckett and the Idea of God* (London: MacMillan, 1998).
Calder, John, *The Philosophy of Samuel Beckett* (London: Calder, 2001).
———, *The Theology of Samuel Beckett* (London: Calder, 2012).
Connor, Steven, *Samuel Beckett: Repetition Theory and Text* (Oxford: Blackwell, 1988).
———, 'Beckett and Bion', *Journal of Beckett Studies*, 17.1–2 (2008) (Special Issue: *Beckett, Language and the Mind*, ed. by Elizabeth Barry), pp. 9–34.
———, 'Beckett and Sartre: The Nauseous Character of All Flesh', in *Beckett and Phenomenology*, ed. by Matthew Feldman and Ulrika Maude (London: Continuum, 2009), pp. 61–4.
Dobrez, L.A.C., *The Existential and Its Exits: Literary and Philosophical Perspectives on the Works of Beckett, Ionesco, Genet & Pinter* (London: Athlone, 1986).
Dowd, Garin, *Abstract Machines: Samuel Beckett and Philosophy after Deleuze and Guattari* (Amsterdam: Rodopi, 2007).
Fanizza, Franco, 'The Word and Silence in Samuel Beckett's *The Unnamable*', in *Twentieth-Century Interpretations of* Molloy, Malone Dies *and* The Unnamable, ed. by J. D. O'Hara (Englewood Cliffs, NJ: Prentice Hall, 1970), pp. 71–81.
Fletcher, John, *The Novels of Samuel Beckett*, 2nd edn. (London: Chatto & Windus, 1970).
Frye, Northrop, 'The Nightmare Life in Death', in *Northrop Frye, Northrop Frye on Twentieth-Century Literature*, ed. by Glen Robert Gill (Toronto: University of Toronto Press, 2010), pp. 159–67.
Hesla, David H., *The Shape of Chaos: An Interpretation of the Art of Samuel Beckett* (Minneapolis: University of Minnesota Press, 1971).
Leslie Hill, *Beckett's Fiction: In Different Words* (Cambridge: Cambridge University Press, 1990).
Mélèse, Pierre, *Samuel Beckett* (Paris: Seghers, 1986).
Mercier, Vivan, 'The Mathematical Limit', *Nation*, 14 February 1959, 144–5.
O'Hara, J. D., 'Where There's a Will There's a Way Out: Beckett and Schopenhauer', *College Literature*, 8.3 (1981), 249–70.
Scruton, Roger, *The Aesthetic Understanding* (London: Methuen, 1983).
Stewart, Paul, 'Living the Unnamable: Towards a Phenomenology of Reading', in *Beckett and Phenomenology*, ed. by Matthew Feldman and Ulrika Maude (London: Continuum, 2009), pp. 177–93.

Trezise, Thomas, *Into the Breach: Samuel Beckett and the Ends of Literature* (Princeton, NJ: Princeton University Press, 1990).
Weller, Shane, 'Adorno's Notes on *The Unnamable*', *Journal of Beckett Studies*, 19.2 (2010), 179–95.
Zurbrugg, Nicholas, *Beckett and Proust* (Smythe: Gerrard's Cross, 1988).

Nathalie Sarraute

Œuvres complètes, ed. by Jean-Yves Tadié (Paris: Gallimard, Pléiade edition, 1996).
Childhood, trans. by Barbara Wright (New York: Braziller, 1984).

Ouvrez (Paris: Gallimard, 1997).
(with Gabriel d'Aubarède), 'Instantané: Nathalie Sarraute', *Les Nouvelles littéraires*, 30 July 1953, 4.
(with Gretchen R. Besser) 'Colloque avec Nathalie Sarraute, 22 april 1976', *The French Review*, 50 (1976), 284–9.
(with Isabelle Huppert), 'Rencontre avec Nathalie Sarraute', ed. by M. A. Guérin and T. Jousse, *Cahiers du cinema*, 477 (March 1994), 8–14.
(with Marc Saporta), 'Portrait d'une inconnue: conversation biographique', *L'Arc*, 95 (1984), 5–23.
(with Pierre Boncenne) 'Nathalie Sarraute Interview' *Lire*, 94 (June 1983), 87–92.
(with Serge Fauchereau and Jean Ristat),'Conversation avec Nathalie Sarraute', *Digraphe*, 32 (March 1984), 9–18.
(with Simone Benmussa) *Entretiens avec Nathalie Sarraute* (Tournai: La Renaissance du Livre, 1999).

Asso, Françoise, *Nathalie Sarraute: une écriture d'effraction* (Paris: Presses universitaires de France, 1995).
Barbour, Sarah, *Nathalie Sarraute and the Feminist Reader: Identities in Process* (London: Associated University Presses, 1993).
Bernal, Olga, 'Des Fiches et des fluides dans le roman de Nathalie Sarraute', *MLN*, 88 (1973), 775–88.
Bikialo, Stéphane, 'La Nomination multiple: un compromis à la non-coïncidence des mots et la sensation', in *Nathalie Sarraute: du tropisme à la phrase*, ed. by Agnès Fontvieille and Philippe Wahl (Lyon: Presses Universitaires de Lyon, 2003), pp. 85–98.
Britton, Celia, 'The Self and Language in the Novels of Nathalie Sarraute', *MLR*, 77 (1982), 577–84.
Cohn, Ruby, 'Nathalie Sarraute's Sub-Consciousversations', *MLN*, 78 (1963), 261–70.
Gosselin-Noat, Monique, *Enfance* (Paris: Gallimard, 1996).
Greene, Robert W., 'Nathalie Sarraute's *L'Usage de la parole*, or Re(en)trop(iz)ing *Tropismes*', *Novel: A Forum on Fiction*, 16 (1983), 197–214.
Hewitt, Leah, *Autobiographical Tightropes: Simone de Beauvoir, Nathalie Sarraute, Marguerite Duras, Monique Wittig and Maryse Condé* (Lincoln, NE: University of Nebraska Press, 1990).
Jefferson, Ann, *Nathalie Sarraute: Fiction and Theory* (Cambridge: Cambridge University Press, 2000).
Lejeune, Philippe, 'Paroles d'Enfance', *Revue des sciences humaines*, 93 (1990), 23–38 (p. 32).
Minogue, Valerie, *Nathalie Sarraute and the War of the Words: A Study of Five Novels* (Edinburgh: Edinburgh University Press, 1981).
———, 'Fragments of a Childhood: Nathalie Sarraute's *Enfance*', *French Autobiography: Texts, Contexts, Poetics, Romance Studies*, 9 (Winter 1986), 71–83 (p. 72).
O'Beirne, Emer, *Reading Nathalie Sarraute: Dialogue and Distance* (Oxford: Clarendon Press, 1999).
Patton, Harlan R., 'Tropismes and the Satire of Scientism in *Les Caves du Vatican*', *South Atlantic Review*, 48 (1983), 35–42.
Phillips, John, *Nathalie Sarraute: Metaphor, Fairy-Tale and the Feminine of the Text* (Bern: Peter Lang, 1994).
Pierrot, Jean, *Nathalie Sarraute* (Paris: Corti, 1990).
Rykner, Arnaud, *Nathalie Sarraute* (Paris: Seuil, 1991).
Schmutz, Marianne, Enfance *de Nathalie Sarraute comme autobiographie* (Lyon: Aldrui, 1999).
Sheringham, Michael, *French Autobiography: Devices and Desires: Rousseau to Perec* (Oxford: Clarendon Press, 1993).
Vineberg, Elsa, 'Marcel Proust, Nathalie Sarraute and the Psychological Novel', *MLN*, 90 (1975), 575–83.
Weissman, Frida S., *Du monologue intérieur à la sous-conversation* (Paris: Nizet, 1978).
Whiting, Charles G., 'Nathalie Sarraute: Moraliste', *The French Review, Special Issue*, 1 (1970), 168–74.

Marie Darrieussecq

Bref Séjour chez les vivants (Paris: POL, 2001).
A Brief Stay with the Living, trans. by Ian Monk (London: Faber, 2003).

Truismes (Paris: POL, 1996).
Naissance des fantômes (Paris: POL, 1998).
Le Mal de mer (Paris: POL, 1999).
Précisions sur les vagues (Paris: POL, 1999).
Le Bébé (Paris: POL, 2002).
White (Paris: POL, 2003).
Claire dans la forêt, suivi de *Penthésilée, premier combat* (Paris: Editions des femmes, 2004).
Le Pays (Paris: POL, 2005).
Zoo (Paris: POL, 2006).
Tom est mort (Paris: POL, 2007).
'Être libéré de soi', *Le Magazine littéraire* (March 2008), 58.
Le Musée de la mer (play) (Paris: POL, 2009).
'Fiction in the First Person, or Immoral Writing', *L'Esprit créateur*, 50 (2010), 70–82.
Rapport de police: accusations de plagiat et autres modes de surveillance de la fiction (Paris: POL, 2010).
Clèves (Paris: POL, 2011).
Être ici est une splendeur : vie de Paula M. Becker (Paris: POL, 2016)
(with Alain Nicolas), 'Marie et les cerveaux', *L'Humanité*, 13 September 2001, 8.
(with Alain-Philippe Durand), 'Marie Darrieussecq, *Truismes*', online discussion, 20 September 2011, <http://nonlieux2011.blogspot.co.uk/2011/09/marie-darrieussecq-truismes-1996.html>.
(with Amy Concannon and Kerry Sweeney), 'Interview', March 2004, <www.uri.edu/artsci/ml/durand/darrieussecq/fr/entretien2004.html>.
(with Baptiste Liger), 'Je suis devenue psychanalyste', *Lire*, 1 November 2006. Retrieved from www.lexpress.fr/culture/livre/je-suis-devenue-psychanalyste-par-marie-darrieussecq_811700.html
(with Becky Miller and Martha Holmes), 'Interview with Marie Darrieussecq', Marie Darrieussecq website, University of Arizona, December 2001, <http://darrieussecq.arizona.edu/fr/entetien2001.html>.
(with François Busnel and Thierry Gandillot), 'Deux femmes la mort dans l'âme: Laure Adler et Marie Darrieussecq', *L'Express*, 23 August 2001, 12.
(with Jeannette Gaudet), '"Des livres sur la liberté": conversation avec Marie Darrieussecq', *Dalhousie French Studies*, 59 (2002), 108–18.
(with Jean-Marc Terrasse), '"Comment j'écris", entretien avec Marie Darrieusecq', in *La Création en acte*, ed. by Paul Gifford and Marion Schmid (Amsterdam: Rodopi, 2003), pp. 253–68.
(with John Lambeth), 'Entretien avec Marie Darrieussecq', *The French Review*, 79 (2006), 806–18.
(with Nelly Kaprièlian), *Écrire, écrire, pourquoi?: Entretien avec Marie Darrieussecq* (Paris: Éditions de la Bibliothèque publique d'information/Centre Pompidou, 2010).

Amette, Jacques-Pierre, 'Un chantier de sensations', *Le Point*, 31 August 2001, 114.
Chadderton, Helena, *Marie Darrieussecq's Textual Worlds: Self, Society, Language* (Bern: Peter Lang, 2012).
Duffy, Jean, 'Liminality and Fantasy in Marie Darrieussecq, Marie NDiaye and Marie Redonnet', *MLN*, 124 (2009), 901–28.
Ferrer-Medina, Patricia, 'Wild Humans: The Culture/Nature Duality in Marie Darrieussecq's *Pig Tales* and Robert Louis Stevenson's *Dr Jekyll and Mr Hyde*', *The Comparatist*, 31 (2007), 67–87.
Harel, Naama, 'Challenging the Species Barrier in Metamorphosis Literature: The Case of Marie Darrieussecq's Pig Tales', *Comparative Critical Studies* 2 (2005), 397–409.
Jordan, Shirley Ann, *Contemporary French Women's Writing: Women's Visions, Women's Voices, Women's Lives* (Bern: Peter Lang, 2004).
———, '"Un grand coup de pied dans le château de cubes": Formal Experimentation in Marie Darrieussecq's *Bref Séjour chez les vivants*', *MLR*, 100 (2005), 51–67.
Kemp, Simon, 'Darrieussecq's Mind', *French Studies*, 62 (2008a), 429–41.

———, 'Homeland: Voyageurs et patrie dans les romans de Marie Darrieussecq', in *Nomadismes des romancières contemporaines de langue française*, ed. by Audrey Lasserre and Anne Simon (Paris: Presses Sorbonne Nouvelle, 2008b), pp. 159–66.

Robson, Kathryn, 'Virtual Reality: The Subject of Loss in Marie Darrieussecq's *Naissance de fantômes* and Regine Detambel's *La Chambre d'echo*', *Australian Journal of French Studies*, 61 (2004), 3–15.

Rodgers, Catherine, '"Entrevoir l'absence des bords du monde" dans les romans de Marie Darrieussecq', in *Nouvelles écrivaines: nouvelles voix?*, ed. by Nathalie Morello and Catherine Rodgers (Amsterdam: Rodopi, 2002), pp. 82–103.

Rolls, Alistair, '"Je suis comme une truie qui broute": une lecture pomologique de *Truismes* de Marie Darrieussecq', *Romanic Review*, 92 (2001), 479–90.

——— and Marie-Laure Vuaille-Barcan, 'Une seule ou plusieurs femmes-truies? Une lecture virtualisante de *Truismes* de Marie Darrieussecq', *Australian Journal of French Studies*, 46 (2009), 31–44.

Sarrey-Strack, Colette, *Fictions contemporaines au féminin: Marie Darrieussecq, Marie NDiaye, Marie Nimier, Marie Redonnet* (Paris: L'Harmattan, 2002).

Swarbrick, Katharine, 'Truismes and Truths', *Forum for Modern Language Studies*, 46 (2010), 58–70.

Young, Morag, 'Shifting Perspectives: Innovative Narrative Tense usage in Marguerite Duras's *Moderato Cantabile*, Patrick Modiano's *Rue des Boutiques Obscures* and Marie Darrieussecq's *Naissance des fantômes*', *Journal of Romance Studies*, 8.2 (2008), 59–72.

General Literature, Criticism and Theory

Alexander, Ian W., *French Literature and the Philosophy of Consciousness: Phenomenological Essays* (Cardiff: University of Wales Press, 1984).

Ansell-Pearson, Keith, *Philosophy and the Adventure of the Virtual: Bergson and the Time of Life* (London: Routledge, 2002).

Armstrong, D. M., 'What Is Consciousness?', in *Philosophy of Mind*, ed. by John Heil (London: Routledge, 1998), pp. 607–16.

Atack, Margaret, *May 68 in French Fiction and Film* (Oxford: Oxford University Press, 1999).

Beauvoir, Simone de, *Le Deuxième Sexe*, 2 vols. (Paris: Gallimard, 1949).

Beer, Gillian, *Darwin's Plots: Evolutionary Narrative in Darwin, George Eliot and Nineteenth-Century Fiction*, 3rd edn. (Cambridge: Cambridge University Press, 2009).

Berthold-Bond, Daniel, 'Hegel, Nietzsche, and Freud on Madness and the Unconscious', *The Journal of Speculative Philosophy*, 5 (1991), 193–213.

———, *Hegel's Theory of Madness* (Albany, NY: SUNY Press, 1995).

Bergson, Henri, *Essai sur les données immédiates de la conscience* (1927) (Paris: Presses Universitaires de la France, 2003).

Block, Ned, 'On a Confusion about a Function of Consciousness', *Behavioural and Brain Sciences*, 18 (1995), 227–87.

———, 'Qualia', in *The Oxford Companion to the Mind*, ed. by Richard L. Gregory, 2nd edn. (Oxford: Oxford University Press, 2004), pp. 785–80.

Borch-Jakobsen, Mikkel, 'La Vérité sur le cas de Mlle Anna O.', in *Le Livre noir de la psychanalyse*, ed. by Catherine Meyer (Paris: Les Arènes, 2005), pp. 25–32.

Bouraoui, Nina, *Mes mauvaises pensées* (Paris: Stock, 2005).

Boyd, Brian, *On the Origin of Stories: Evolution, Cognition and Fiction* (Cambridge, MA: Belknap Harvard, 2009).

———, 'Getting It All Wrong: Bioculture Critiques Cultural Critique (2006)', in *Evolution, Literature and Film*, ed. by Brian Boyd, Joseph Carroll and Jonathan Gottschall (New York: Columbia University Press, 2010), pp. 197–210.

Brentano, Franz von, *Psychology from an Empirical Standpoint*, trans. by A. C. Rancurello, D. B. Terrell and L. L. McAlister (London: Routlege, 1995).

Butler, Judith, *Gender Trouble: Feminism and the Subversion of Identity* (New York: Routledge, 1990).

———, 'Sex and Gender in Simone de Beauvoir's *The Second Sex*', *Yale French Studies*, 72 (1986), 35–49, reprinted in *Simone de Beauvoir: A Critical Reader*, ed. by Elizabeth Fallaize (London: Routledge, 1998), pp. 29–42.

Camus, Albert, *Œuvres completes*, ed. by Jacqueline Lévi-Valensi (Paris: Gallimard, Pléiade edition, 2006).

Caracciolo, Marco, 'Blind Reading: Towards an Enactivist Theory of the Reader's Imagination', in *Stories and Minds: Cognitive Approaches to Literary Narrative*, ed. by Lars Bernaerts, Dirk de Geest, Luc Herman and Bart Vervaek (Lincoln, NE: University of Nebraska Press, 2013), pp. 81–106.

———, *The Experientiality of Narrative: An Enactivist Approach* (Berlin: de Gruyter, 2014).

Cardinal, Marie, *Les Mots pour le dire* (Paris: Grasset, 1975).

Carroll, Joseph, *Literary Darwinism: Evolution, Human Nature, and Literature* (London: Routledge, 2004).

———, Jonathan Gottschall, John Johnson and Daniel Kruger, 'Imagining Human Nature', in *Evolution, Literature and Film*, ed. by Brian Boyd, Joseph Carroll and Jonathan Gottschall (New York: Columbia University Press, 2010), pp. 211–18.

Cave, Terence, *Thinking with Literature: Towards a Cognitive Criticism* (Oxford: Oxford University Press, 2016).

Chalmers, David J., 'Facing Up to the Problem of Consciousness', *Journal of Consciousness Studies*, 2 (1995), 200–19.

———, *The Conscious Mind* (Oxford: Oxford University Press, 1996).

———, *The Character of Consciousness* (Oxford: Oxford University Press, 2010).

Chrétien, Jean-Louis, *Conscience et roman, I: la conscience au grand jour* (Paris: Minuit, 2009).

———, *Conscience et roman,* II*: la conscience à mi-voix* (Paris: Minuit, 2011).

Churchland, Paul, *Matter and Consciousness* (Cambridge, MA: The MIT Press, 1984).

Cixous, Hélène, 'Le Rire de la Méduse', *L'Arc*, 61 (1975), 39–54.

———, 'La Venue à l'écriture', in *Entre l'écriture* (Paris: Des femmes, 1986), pp. 7–69.

Cohn, Dorrit, *Transparent Minds: Narrative Modes for Presenting Consciousness in Fiction* (Princeton, NJ: Princeton University Press, 1978).

Colombetti, Giovanna, *The Feeling Body: Affective Science Meets the Enactive Mind*, (Cambridge, MA: The MIT Press, 2014).

Cooper, John W., *Body, Soul and Life Everlasting: Biblical Anthropology and the Monism-Dualism Debate*, 2nd edn. (Michigan and Cambridge: Eerdmans, 2000).

Cottraux, Jean, 'Chronique d'une génération: comment la psychanalyse a pris le pouvoir en France', in *Le Livre noir de la psychanalyse*, ed. by Catherine Meyer (Paris: Les Arènes, 2005), pp. 243–63.

Crick, Francis, *The Astonishing Hypothesis: The Scientific Search for the Soul* (New York: Simon and Schuster, 1995).

Daly, Martin and Margo Wilson, *Homicide: Foundations of Human Behaviour* (Hawthorne, NY: Aldine, 1988).

Damasio, Antonio, *The Feeling of What Happens: Body, Emotion and the Making of Consciousness* (London: Vintage, 2000).

———, *Descartes' Error: Emotion, Reason and the Human Brain* (London: Vintage, 2006).

———, *Self Comes to Mind: Constructing the Conscious Brain* (London: Heinemann, 2010).

Deleuze, Gilles and Félix Guattari, *Capitalisme et Schizophrénie 1: L'Anti-Œdipe* (Paris: Minuit, 1972).

———, *Capitalisme et Schizophrénie 2: Mille Plateaux* (Paris: Minuit, 1980).

Dennett, Daniel C., *Consciousness Explained* (London: Penguin, 1993).

———, *Darwin's Dangerous Idea: Evolution and the Meanings of Life* (London: Penguin, 1995).

———, *Freedom Evolves* (London: Penguin, 2004).

Derrida, Jacques, *La Voix et le phénomène: introduction au problème du signe dans la phénoménologie de Husserl* (Paris: Presses Universitaires de France, 1967).

Descartes, René, *Méditations métaphysiques*, ed. by Marie-Frédérique Pellegrin (Paris: Flammarion, 2009).

Doubrovsky, Serge, *Le Livre brisé* (Paris: Grasset, 1989).

Duras, Marguerite, *Le Ravissement de Lol V. Stein* (Paris: Gallimard, 1964).

Dutton, Denis, *The Art Instinct: Beauty, Pleasure and Human Evolution* (New York: Bloomsbury, 2009).

Eccles, John C., *Evolution of the Brain: Creation of the Self* (London: Routledge, 1989).

Edelman, Gerald M., *Bright Air, Brilliant Fire: On the Matter of the Mind* (London: Penguin, 1994).

———, *Wider Than the Sky: A Revolutionary View of Consciousness* (London: Penguin, 2004).

Eimas, P. D., E. R. Siqueland, P. Jusczyk and J. Vigorito, 'Speech Perception in Infants', *Science*, 171 (1971), 303–6.

Evans, Dylan, 'From Lacan to Darwin', in *The Literary Animal: Evolution and the Nature of Narrative*, ed. by Jonathan Gottschall and David Sloan Wilson (Evanston, IL: Northwestern University Press, 2005), pp. 38–55.

Fallaize, Elizabeth, *French Women's Writing: Recent Fiction* (Basingstoke: MacMillan, 1993).

Fedrigo, Gabriele, *Valéry et le cerveau: dans les Cahiers* (Paris: Harmattan, 2000).

Fine, Cordelia, *Delusions of Gender: The Real Science Behind Sex Differences* (London: Icon, 2010).
Foucault, Michel, *Histoire de la folie à l'âge classique* (Paris: Gallimard, 1972).
Franzen, Jonathan, *The Corrections* (London: Fourth Estate, 2002).
Freud, Sigmund, *The Standard Edition of the Complete Psychological Works of Sigmund Freud*, trans. by James Strachey, 24 vols. (London: Hogarth Press, 1953–74).
Gallagher, Shaun, *How the Body Shapes the Mind* (Oxford: Clarendon Press, 2005).
———, *Phenomenology* (Basingstoke: Palgrave, 2012).
——— and Dan Zahavi, *The Phenomenological Mind: An Introduction to Philosophy of Mind and Cognitive Science* (London: Routledge, 2008).
Genette, Gérard, *Figures III* (Paris: Seuil, 1972).
———, *Nouveau Discours du récit* (Paris: Seuil, 1983).
Gide, André, *Romans et récits*, ed. by Pierre Masson (Paris: Gallimard, Pléiade edition, 2009).
Goncourt, Edmond and Jules de, *Journal des Goncourt: Mémoires de la vie littéraire*, 9 vols. (Paris: Charpentier, 1891).
Gottschall, Jonathan, *Literature, Science, and a New Humanities* (New York: Palgrave Macmillan, 2008).
Gregory, Richard L. (ed.), *The Oxford Companion to the Mind*, 2nd edn. (Oxford: Oxford University Press, 2004).
Guerlac, Suzanne, *Thinking in Time: An Introduction to Henri Bergson* (Ithaca: Cornell University Press, 2006).
Hegel, G.W.F., *Phenomenology of Spirit*, trans. by A. V. Miller (Oxford: Oxford University Press, 1977).
———, *Philosophy of Mind*, trans. by W. Wallace and A. V. Miller (Oxford: Clarendon Press, 2006).
Heidegger, Martin, *Being and Time*, trans. by John Macquarrie and Edward Robinson (Oxford: Blackwell, 1962).
Henrich, Joseph and Richard McElreath, 'Dual-Inheritance Theory: The Evolution of Human Cultural Capacities and Cultural Evolution', in *The Oxford Handbook of Evolutionary Psychology*, ed. by R.I.M. Dunbar and Louise Barrett (Oxford: Oxford University Press, 2007), pp. 555–70.
Herman, David, '1880–1945: Reminding Modernism', in *The Emergence of Mind: Representations of Consciousness in Narrative Discourse in English*, ed. by David Herman (Lincoln, NE: University of Nebraska Press, 2014), pp. 243–72.
Hogan, Patrick Colm, *Philosophical Approaches to the Study of Literature* (Gainesville: University Press of Florida, 2000).
———, *Cognitive Science, Literature and the Arts: A Guide for Humanists* (London: Routledge, 2003).
Holmes, Diana, *French Women's Writing 1848–1994* (London: Athlone, 1996).
Holmes, David S., 'The Evidence for Repression: An Examination of Sixty Years of Research', in *Repression and Dissociation: Implications for Personality Theory, Psychopathology and Health*, ed. by Jerome L. Singer (Chicago: University of Chicago Press, 1990), pp. 85–102.
Houellebecq, Michel, *La Carte et le territoire* (Paris: Gallimard, 2010).
Hurlbert, Anya C. and Yazhu Ling, 'Biological Components of Sex Differences in Color Preference', *Current Biology*, 17 (2001), R623–5.
Husserl, Edmund, *The Phenomenology of Internal Time Consciousness*, trans. by James Churchill (Bloomington, IN: Indiana University Press, 1964).
———, *Logical Investigations* (1900–01), trans. by J. N. Findlay, 2 vols. (London and New York: Routledge and Kegan Paul/Humanities Press, 1970).
Jackendoff, R., *Consciousness and the Computational Mind* (Cambridge: MIT Press, 1987).
Jackson, Tony, 'Questioning Interdisciplinarity: Cognitive Science, Evolutionary Psychology, and Literary Criticism', *Poetics Today*, 21 (2000), 319–47.
Jaén, Isabel and Julien J. Simon, 'An Overview of Recent Developments in Cognitive Literary Studies', in *Cognitive Literary Studies: Current Themes and New Directions*, ed. by Isabel Jaén and Julien J. Simon (Austin: University of Texas Press, 2012), pp. 13–32.
James, William, *The Principles of Psychology* (1890), 3 vols. (Cambridge, MA: Harvard University Press, 1981).
———, *Varieties of Religious Experience: A Study in Human Nature* (1902) (Marston Gate: Renaissance Classics, 2012).
Janet, Pierre, *La Psychanalyse de Freud* (1913) (Paris: L'Harmattan, 2004).
———, *La Médecine psychologique* (Paris: L'Harmattan, 2005).
Jaynes, Julian, *The Origin of Consciousness in the Breakdown of the Bicameral Mind* (Boston: Houghton Mifflin, 1976).
Joyce, James, *Ulysses* (1922) (London: Penguin, 1992).
Kafka, Franz, *The Complete Stories*, ed. by Nahum N. Glatzer (New York: Schocken, 1976).

Kemp, Simon, *French Fiction into the Twenty-First Century: The Return to the Story* (Cardiff: University of Wales Press, 2010).

———, 'Bergson, Bauby and the Neuroscience of Emotion', *French Studies Bulletin*, 121 (2011), 73–5.

Kim, Jaegwon, *Philosophy of Mind*, 2nd edn. (Cambridge, MA: Westview, 2006).

King, Adèle, *French Women Novelists: Defining a Female Style* (Basingstoke: MacMillan, 1989).

Kristeva, Julia, *Soleil noir: dépression et mélancholie* (Paris: Gallimard, 1987).

Kruks, Sonia, *Retrieving Experience: Subjectivity and Recognition in Feminist Politics* (Ithaca: Cornell University Press, 2001).

Lacan, Jacques, *Écrits* (Paris: Seuil, 1966).

———, 'Hommage fait à Marguerite Duras, du ravissement de Lol V. Stein', in *Marguerite Duras*, ed. by François Barat and Joël Farges (Paris: Albatros, 1975), pp. 7–15.

Larkin, Maurice, *France Since the Popular Front: Government and People 1936–1986* (Oxford: Clarendon Press, 1988).

Lauer, Gerhard, 'Going Empirical: Why We Need Cognitive Literary Studies', *JLT*, 3 (2009), 145–54.

Locke, John, *Essay Concerning Human Understanding*, ed. by Gary Fuller, Robert Stecker and John P. Wright (London: Routledge, 2000).

Leclerc, Annie, *Parole de femme* (Paris: Grasset, 1974).

Levine, Joseph, 'Materialism and Qualia: The Explanatory Gap', *Pacific Philosophical Quarterly*, 64 (1983), 354–61, reprinted in *Philosophy of Mind*, ed. by John Heil (London: Routledge, 1998), pp. 772–80.

Libet, Benjamin, 'Unconscious Cerebral Initiative and the Role of Conscious Will in Voluntary Action', *Behavioral and Brain Sciences*, 8 (1985), 529–66.

———, E. W. Wright, B. Feinstein and D. K. Pearl, 'Subjective Referral of the Timing for a Conscious Sensory Experience', *Brain*, 194 (1979), 191–221.

Lodge, David, *Consciousness and the Novel* (London: Penguin, 2003).

Lowe, E. J., 'Non-Cartesian Dualism', in *Philosophy of Mind*, ed. by John Heil (London: Routledge, 1998), pp. 851–65.

Mäkelä, Maria, 'Cycles of Narrative Necessity: Suspect Tellers and the Textuality of Fictional Minds', in *Stories and Minds: Cognitive Approaches to Literary Narrative*, ed. by Lars Bernaerts, Dirk de Geest, Luc Herman and Bart Vervaek (Lincoln, NE: University of Nebraska Press, 2013), pp. 129–51.

Malabou, Catherine, *Que faire de notre cerveau?*, 2nd edn. (Paris: Bayard, 2011).

Malim, Tony and Ann Birch, *Introductory Psychology* (Basingstoke: Palgrave, 1998).

Mameli, Matteo, 'Evolution and Psychology in Philosophical Perspective', in *The Oxford Handbook of Evolutionary Psychology*, ed. by R.I.M. Dunbar and Louise Barrett (Oxford: Oxford University Press, 2007), pp. 21–34.

McEwan, Ian, 'Literature, Science and Human Nature (2001)', in *The Literary Animal: Evolution and the Nature of Narrative*, ed. by Jonathan Gottschall and David Sloan Wilson (Evanston, IL: Northwestern University Press, 2005a), pp. 5–19.

———, *Saturday* (London: Cape, 2005b).

McGinn, Colin, 'Can We Solve the Mind-Body Problem?', *Mind*, 98 (1989), 349–66, reprinted in *Philosophy of Mind*, ed. by John Heil (London: Routledge, 1998), pp. 781–97.

Merleau-Ponty, Maurice, *Phénoménologie de la perception* (Paris: Gallimard, 1945).

———, *Signes* (Paris: Gallimard, 1960).

———, *Le Visible et l'invisible* (Paris: Gallimard, 1964).

Metzinger, Thomas, *Being No One: The Self-Model Theory of Subjectivity* (Cambridge, MA: The MIT Press, 2003).

Monfrans, Manet von, *Georges Perec: la contrainte du réel* (Amsterdam: Rodopi, 1999).

Murphy, Carol J., *Alienation and Absence in the Novels of Marguerite Duras* (Lexington: French Forum, 1982).

Nagel, Thomas, 'What Is It Like to be a Bat?', *Philosophical Review*, 83 (1974), 435–50.

Nalbantian, Suzanne, *Memory in Literature: From Rousseau to Neuroscience* (Basingstoke: Palgrave, 2003).

Nietzsche, Friedrich, *The Birth of Tragedy*, trans. by Francis Golffing (New York: Doubleday, 1956).

Noë, Alva, *Strange Tools: Art and Human Nature* (New York: Hill and Wang, 2015).

Nordlund, Marcus, 'Consilient Literary Interpretation', in *Evolution, Literature and Film*, ed. by Brian Boyd, Joseph Carroll and Jonathan Gottschall (New York: Columbia University Press, 2010), pp. 224–30.

Onfray, Michel, *Crépuscule d'un idole: l'affabulation freudienne* (Paris: Grasset, 2010).

Palmer, Alan, *Fictional Minds* (Lincoln, NE: University of Nebraska Press, 2004).

———, '1945: Ontologies of Consciousness', in *The Emergence of Mind: Representations of Consciousness in Narrative Discourse in English*, ed. by David Herman (Lincoln, NE: University of Nebraska Press, 2014), pp. 273–97.

Pascal, Blaise, *Pensées*, ed. by Michel Le Guern (Paris: Gallimard, 1977).

Perec, Georges, *W ou le souvenir d'enfance* (Paris: Denoël, 1975).

Pilkington, A. E., *Bergson and His Influence: A Reassessment* (Cambridge: Cambridge University Press, 1976).

Pinker, Steven, *The Language Instinct* (London: Allen Lane, 1994).

———, *How the Mind Works* (New York: Norton, 1997).

———, *The Blank Slate: The Modern Denial of Human Nature* (London: Allen Lane, 2002).

———, *The Stuff of Thought: Language as a Window into Human Nature* (London: Allen Lane, 2008).

Plato, *Phaedo*, trans. by David Gallop (Oxford: Clarendon Press, 1975).

Powrie, Phil, 'Reading for Pleasure: Marie Cardinal's *Les Mots pour le dire* and the Text as (Re)Play of Œdipal Configurations', in *Contemporary French Fiction by Women: Feminist Perspectives*, ed. by Margaret Atack and Phil Powrie (Manchester: Manchester University Press, 1990), pp. 163–76.

Proust, Joëlle, 'La Psychanalyse au risque des neurosciences', in *Le Livre noir de la psychanalyse*, ed. by Catherine Meyer (Paris: Les Arènes, 2005), pp. 650–59.

Ramachandran, V. S., *The Tell-Tale Brain: Unlocking the Mystery of Human Nature* (London: Heinemann, 2011).

Robbe-Grillet, Alain, *La Jalousie* (Paris: Minuit, 1957).

———, *Le Miroir qui revient* (Paris: Minuit, 1984).

Rorty, Richard, 'Contemporary Philosophy of Mind', *Synthese*, 53 (1982), 323–48.

Roudinesco, Elisabeth, *Jacques Lacan & Co.: A History of Psychoanalysis in France 1925–1985* (London: Free Association, 1990).

———, (ed.), *Pourquoi tant de haine?: anatomie du Livre noir de la psychanalyse* (Paris: Navarin, 2005).

Rye, Gill, *Reading for Change: Interactions between Text and Identity in Contemporary French Women's Writing (Baroche, Cixous, Constant)* (Bern: Peter Lang, 2001).

Saini, Angela, *Inferior: How Science Got Women Wrong and the New Research that's Rewriting the Story* (London: Fourth Estate, 2017).

Savigneau, Josyane, 'Écrivains et choix sentimentaux', *Le Monde*, 15 October 1999. Retrieved from www.lemonde.fr/cgi-bin/ACHATS/acheter.cgi?offre=ARCHIVES&type_item=ART_ARCH_30J&objet_id=46796

Schopenhauer, Arthur, *The World as Will and Representation*, trans. by E.F.J. Payne, 2 vols (New York: Dover, 1966).

Searle, John R., *The Rediscovery of the Mind* (Cambridge, MA: The MIT Press, 1992).

———, 'Minds, Brains and Programs', in *Behavioural Brain Sciences*, 3 (1980), 417–57, reprinted in *Philosophy of Mind*, ed. by John Heil (London: Routledge, 1998), pp. 234–52.

Sellers, Susan, *Hélène Cixous: Authorship, Autobiography and Love* (Cambridge: Polity, 1996).

Selous, Trista, 'Marguerite and the Mountain', in *Contemporary French Fiction by Women: Feminist Perspectives*, ed. by Margaret Atack and Phil Powrie (Manchester: Manchester University Press, 1990), pp. 84–95.

Shorter, Edward, 'Splendeur et décadence de la psychanalyse', in *Le Livre noir de la psychanalyse*, ed. by Catherine Meyer (Paris: Les Arènes, 2005), pp. 147–61.

Skinner, B. F., *About Behaviourism* (London: Vintage, 1976).

Sloan Wilson, David, 'Evolutionary Social Constructivism', in *The Literary Animal: Evolution and the Nature of Narrative*, ed. by Jonathan Gottschall and David Sloan Wilson (Evanston, IL: Northwestern University Press, 2005), pp. 20–37.

Squire, Larry R. and Eric R. Kandel, *Memory: Form Mind to Molecules*, 2nd edn. (Greenwood Village, CO: Roberts and Company, 2009).

Starobinski, Jean, *La Relation Critique* (Paris: Gallimard, 1970).

Stockwell, Peter, *Cognitive Poetics* (Routledge: London, 2002).

Sugiyama, Michelle Scalise, 'Reverse-Engineering Narrative: Evidence of Special Design', in *The Literary Animal: Evolution and the Nature of Narrative*, ed. by Jonathan Gottschall and David Sloan Wilson (Evanston, IL: Northwestern University Press, 2005), pp. 177–96.

———, 'New Science, Old Myth: An Evolutionary Critique of the Œdipal Paradigm', in *Evolution, Literature and Film*, ed. by Brian Boyd, Joseph Carroll and Jonathan Gottschall (New York: Columbia University Press, 2010), pp. 306–15.

Taine, Hippolyte, *Histoire de la littérature anglaise*, 5 vols. (Paris: Hachette, 1863).
Tallis, Raymond, 'The Neuroscience Delusion', *Times Literary Supplement*, 15 April 2008. Retrieved from www.the-tls.co.uk/articles/private/the-neuroscience-delusion/
———, *Aping Mankind: Neuromania, Darwinitis and the Misrepresentation of Humanity* (Durham: Acumen, 2011).
Tooby, John and Leda Cosmides, 'Does Beauty Build Adapted Minds? Toward an Evolutionary Theory of Aesthetics, Fiction and the Arts', *SubStance*, 94/95 (2001), 6–27.
Turner, Mark, *The Literary Mind: The Origins of Thought and Language* (Oxford: Oxford University Press, 1996).
Valéry, Paul, *Œuvres*, ed. by J. Hytier, 2 vols. (Paris: Gallimard, Pléiade edition, 1957).
Van Rillaer, Jacques, 'Les Méchanismes de défense des freudiens', in *Le Livre noir de la psychanalyse*, ed. by Catherine Meyer (Paris: Les Arènes, 2005), pp. 413–441.
Vermeule, Blakey, 'The New Unconscious: A Literary Guided Tour', in *The Oxford Handbook of Cognitive Literary Studies*, ed. by Lisa Zunshine (Oxford: Oxford University Press, 2015), pp. 463–82.
Webster, Richard, *Why Freud Was Wrong: Science, Sin and Psychoanalysis*, 3rd edn. (Oxford: Orwell Press, 2005).
Whorf, Benjamin Lee, *Language, Thought and Reality: Selected Writings* (Cambridge, MA: The MIT Press, 1967).
Widmer, C. H., *Gabriel Marcel et le théisme existentiel* (Paris: Cerf, 1971).
Wittig, Monique, *La Pensée Straight* (Paris: Balland, 2001).
Woolf, Virginia, *Mrs Dalloway* (1925) (Oxford: Oxford University Press, 2000).
———, *To the Lighthouse* (1927) (Oxford: Oxford University Press, 1992).
Wright, Elizabeth, *Psychoanalytic Criticism: A Reappraisal*, 2nd edn. (Cambridge: Polity, 2006).
Young, Kay, *Imagining Minds: The Neuro-Aesthetics of Austen, Eliot and Hardy* (Columbus, OH: Ohio State University Press, 2010).
Zahavi, Dan, *Subjectivity and Selfhood: Investigating the First-Person Perspective* (Cambridge, MA: The MIT Press, 2005).
Zubin, J. and B. Spring, 'Vulnerability: A New View of Schizophrenia', *Journal of Abnormal Psychology* 86 (1977), 103–26.

INDEX